# The Protected Landscape Approach

## Linking Nature, Culture and Community

# The Protected Landscape Approach

## Linking Nature, Culture and Community

Edited by
Jessica Brown, Nora Mitchell and Michael Beresford

IUCN – The World Conservation Union
2005

This publication has been made possible in part by funding from The Countryside Agency, the IUCN inter-commission Theme on Indigenous and Local Communities, Equity, and Protected Areas (TILCEPA) and QLF/Atlantic Center for the Environment, with additional support from the Conservation Study Institute of the U.S. National Park Service and the International Centre for Protected Landscapes.

Published by:  IUCN, Gland, Switzerland and Cambridge, UK

# IUCN
The World Conservation Union

Citation:  Brown, Jessica, Mitchell, Nora and Beresford, Michael (Eds.) (2005). *The Protected Landscape Approach: Linking Nature, Culture and Community.* IUCN, Gland, Switzerland and Cambridge, UK. xv + 268pp. plus 12 colour plates.

ISBN:  2-8317-0797-8

Cover design by:  IUCN Publications Services Unit

Cover photos:  Front cover: *El Parque de la Papa* in the Sacred Valley of the Incas, southern Peruvian Andes, *Alejandro Argumedo;* Shepherd in Central Slovakia, *Jessica Brown;* Arvari River Parliament, Rajasthan, India, *Ashish Kothari*; White Carpathian Protected Landscape Area, Czech and Slovak Republics, *Brent Mitchell*; Fishermen, Mata Atlantica region, Brazil, *Clayton F. Lino* and The Rice Terraces of the Philippine Cordilleras World Heritage Site, *Adrian Phillips* Back cover: Alinya Mountain Reserve, Catalonia, Spain, *Fundació Territori i Paisatge*

Photo editor:  Stephanie Tuxill

Layout by:  IUCN Publications Services Unit

Produced by:  IUCN Publications Services Unit

Printed by:  Page Bros (Norwich) Ltd.

Available from:  IUCN Publications Services Unit
219c Huntingdon Road, Cambridge CB3 0DL
United Kingdom
Tel: +44 1223 277894, Fax: +44 1223 277175
E-mail: books@iucn.org
www.iucn.org/bookstore
A catalogue of IUCN publications is also available

*The text of this book is printed on Fineblade Extra 90gsm made from low chlorine pulp*

## Dedication

This publication is dedicated to the memory of PHC (Bing) Lucas who died in December 2000.

Bing was a great advocate of the Protected Landscape approach. He was the author of the first published guidance on Protected Landscapes in 1992 and took a leading role in the early organisation and drafting of ideas for this book.

Bing was an extraordinary man. His infectious enthusiasm, integrity and great kindness to all made him friends wherever he travelled around the world. He is greatly missed, but his memory is undimmed.

# Table of contents

# Preface

In every corner of the world can be found landscapes that have been shaped by the interactions of people and nature over time. These landscapes have been created by traditional patterns of land use that have contributed to biodiversity and other natural values, have proven sustainable over centuries, and are living examples of cultural heritage. They are rich in natural and cultural values not in spite of but *because of the presence of people*. Protecting these landscapes requires a conservation approach that recognises natural as well as cultural values, sustains traditional connections to the land, and engages people in stewardship of the places where they live and work.

As countries worldwide move to expand and strengthen their national protected area systems, greater attention must be paid to protecting landscapes. By no means an alternative to strictly protected areas, protected landscapes are a complementary element and an essential part of any protected area system. They are particularly appropriate in areas where biodiversity and cultural practices are linked, and where management practices must accommodate traditional uses, land ownership patterns, and the need to sustain local livelihoods. Protected landscapes can contribute to the viability of more strictly protected areas by reinforcing connectivity among areas and linkages within the broader landscape, especially in situations where conservation objectives are being met over a large area of land.

Our intention in this book is to introduce the protected landscape approach and demonstrate its relevance to the conservation challenges facing protected areas. While it draws especially from experience with IUCN Category V protected areas and the World Heritage Cultural Landscape designation, the protected landscape approach is broader than single protected area category or designation. We have chosen examples from around the world that illustrate how the protected landscape approach works in diverse settings. The authors who have contributed to this volume argue the importance of this approach and through their case-studies show how it is being adapted to different contexts. The experience presented here demonstrates the values and benefits of the protected landscape approach, and points the way toward meeting future challenges.

This book is a project of the Protected Landscapes Task Force of IUCN's World Commission on Protected Areas, and is part of a collection of publications produced by the Task Force over the last few years. An important companion volume is the *Management Guidelines for IUCN Category V Protected Areas: Protected Landscapes/Seascapes* (Phillips, 2002) in the IUCN/Cardiff University series, which provides guidance in planning and managing protected landscapes. In addition, Task Force members have contributed to a recent issue of the journal *PARKS* on Category V Protected Areas (Beresford, 2003), as well as an issue of *George Wright Forum* (Brown, Mitchell and Sarmiento, 2000), both of which brought out case-studies of current practice with Protected Landscapes and Seascapes.

Many of the case-studies in this collection were presented at a workshop on Protected Landscapes and Seascapes at the V[th] World Parks Congress (Durban, South Africa, 2003), and at an earlier meeting of the Protected Landscapes Task Force (Stow-on-Wold, UK, 2001). The workshop at the World Parks Congress spanned three sessions within the Linkages in the Landscape and Seascape stream, and the cross-cutting theme on Communities and Equity, and was preceded by a panel focusing on the role of communities in sustaining landscapes. These sessions at the World Parks Congress are discussed in more detail in the introductory chapter of this book.

We are grateful to the Countryside Agency, UK, which has supported the production of this book as a publication of IUCN and its World Commission on Protected Areas. We thank also the organizations and working groups which have co-sponsored this publication: IUCN's inter-commission Theme on Indigenous and Local Communities, Equity and Protected Areas (TILCEPA); the Quebec-Labrador Foundation/Atlantic Center for the Environment (QLF); the Conservation Study Institute of the National Park Service; and the International Centre for Protected Landscapes.

As noted earlier, many of the chapters in this book grew out of presentations at a recent workshop and panel at the World Parks Congress. We thank Peter Bridgewater, who coordinated the stream on Linkages in the Landscape and Seascape, and Ashish Kothari and Grazia Borrini-Feyerabend, who coordinated the cross-cutting theme on Communities and Equity, for their support of these sessions.

We thank the chapter authors who have contributed to this book. It has been a privilege to work with each of them. Special thanks are due to Adrian Phillips for his helpful guidance and review during development of the book, and Richard Partington for his support throughout this project. We are greatly indebted to Stephanie Tuxill for her work as Photo Editor, and for her many contributions to the production of this publication.

We are pleased to have the opportunity to bring out the rich and diverse experience with the protected landscape approach that is presented in this collection.

*Jessica Brown*
*Nora Mitchell*
*Michael Beresford*

# About the authors

**Alejandro Argumedo** is coordinator of the Sustaining Local Food Systems, Agricultural Biodiversity and Livelihoods Programme for Asociacion ANDES-IIED. ANDES (the Quechua-Aymara Association for Sustainable Livelihoods) is a Cusco-based indigenous peoples' NGO working to protect and develop Andean biological diversity and the rights of indigenous peoples of Peru. Alejandro is also the international coordinator of the Indigenous Peoples' Biodiversity Network (IPBN), a global coalition. He is member of IUCN's World Commission on Protected Areas (WCPA), Commission on Environmental, Economic and Social Policy (CEESP) and Indigenous Peoples Ad Hoc Committee on Protected Areas.

**Edmund G.C. Barrow**, Ireland, has been working with community-based approaches to natural resource management in Africa for nearly thirty years, with particular emphasis on social and equity issues, and on how natural resource management contributes to improved livelihood security, particularly in the drylands. Since 1997 he has coordinated the IUCN Eastern Africa Regional Office's work in forest and dryland conservation, and on social policy and livelihood issues. He is a member of the core group of the IUCN inter-commission (WCPA/CEESP) Theme on Indigenous and Local Communities, Equity and Protected Areas (TILCEPA).

**Michael Beresford** has been involved in Protected Landscape management for more than thirty years. Formerly Head of the Brecon Beacons National Park in Wales – a Category V Protected Landscape – he is the co-founder and director of the International Centre for Protected Landscapes, Wales, UK. He is past co-chair of the Protected Landscapes Task Force of IUCN's World Commission on Protected Areas (WCPA)

**Marilia Britto de Moraes** is an architect, Master in Landscape Planning, and has worked in coastal management and zoning since 1989 at the Secretariat for the Environment of São Paulo State, Brazil. She has coordinated participatory planning for the northern and southern coasts, as well as for coastal Environmental Protection Areas (APAs), and currently works as Director of Ilhabela State Park, São Paulo, Brazil. As a member of IUCN's WCPA-Brazil, she has coordinated the APAs working group since 1999 and serves on the WCPA Protected Landscapes Task Force.

**Jessica Brown** is Vice President for International Programs at the Quebec-Labrador Foundation/Atlantic Center for the Environment (QLF), a bi-national NGO working in rural areas of New England (USA) and eastern Canada. She is responsible for training, technical assistance, policy research and peer exchange programmes in regions including the Caribbean, Latin America, Central and Eastern Europe, and the Middle East, and conducts joint projects with the Conservation Study Institute of the US National Park Service. Her work focuses on landscape stewardship, private land conservation, and fostering community involvement in protected areas. She is co-chair of the WCPA Protected Landscapes Task Force, and a member of the core group of TILCEPA.

**Prabhu Budhathoki** is currently doing PhD research on conservation governance at the International Centre for Protected Landscapes (ICPL), Wales, UK. He has twenty years of active experience in the field of forestry and integrated conservation and development in Nepal, including six years as National Programme Manager of the Park People Programme (under the UNDP), Department of National Parks and Wildlife Conservation.

**Susan Buggey** is former Director of Historical Services, Parks Canada and now Adjunct Professor, School of Landscape Architecture, Université de Montréal, Canada. She has been active in research, evaluation, and writing on cultural landscapes for 25 years. Her research interests focus on the associative values of cultural landscapes and the meanings of landscapes in diverse cultures.

**Elizabeth Hughes** is Executive Director of the International Centre for Protected Landscapes, Wales, UK. The Centre offers international academic and professional training programmes in protected landscape management and related topics; it also undertakes capacity-building, consultancy and advisory work on behalf of protected area agencies, governments, and NGOs around the world. Dr Hughes' particular interests are in the fields of partnership-building, participatory approaches, and the role of civil society in protected area management.

**Blažena Hušková** works as a private consultant and trainer and as a project manager for the Jizerske hory Public Benefit Organization, Czech Republic. Previously she was a landscape ecologist with the Jizerske hory Mountains Protected Landscape Area and was the founding director of the Foundation for the Rescue and Restoration of the Jizera Mountains. Past projects have focused on the revitalization of forest ecosystems affected by air pollution; more recently she has specialized in public participation in planning and decision-making processes, cross-sectoral communication and cooperation, and the role of NGOs in the process of formulating and implementing sustainable development strategies.

**Brian T. B. Jones** is the Senior Community-based Natural Resource Management (CBNRM) Technical Adviser to USAID in Namibia. Formerly he was an independent consultant in the environment and development sector. For several years he was a Namibian government official, coordinating the CBNRM programme of the Namibian Ministry of Environment and Tourism. (The views expressed by him in this book do not necessarily represent the official position of USAID or the US Government).

**Miroslav Kundrata** is the Director of Nadace Partnerství (the Czech Environmental Partnership Foundation), the Czech Republic's most significant grant-making foundation active in the area of environment and sustainable development. As chairman of the Czech Donors Forum board, and a member of the Czech Governmental Council for NGOs (chair of the EU Committee), he is active in institution-building within the NGO sector, and in development and fundraising for various national and international programmes. He is chairman of the board of the Veronica Ecological Foundation, and founding member of the Traditions of the White Carpathians Association and of the Union for the Morava River.

**Jane L. Lennon** is currently an adjunct professor at the Cultural Heritage Centre for Asia and the Pacific, Deakin University, Melbourne (Australia) specializing in cultural landscapes. She has over thirty years of experience in planning and management of national park and heritage places, including assessments for the Australian Heritage Commission and preparing cultural landscape management guidelines for UNESCO's World Heritage Centre. She is a member of the Australian Heritage Council, and is a past president of Australia ICOMOS (International Council on Monuments and Sites).

**Clayton F. Lino**, Brazil, is an architect who specializes in Urban Environmental Patrimony and the Management of Protected Areas. He is also a photographer and speleologist, and has authored several books and technical-scientific texts about caves, the Mata Atlantica rainforest, and protected areas in Brazil. At present, he is president of the National Council of the Mata Atlantica Biosphere Reserve, coordinator of the Brazilian Network of Biosphere Reserves (linked to the UNESCO Man in the Biosphere programme), and a member of IUCN's WCPA-Brazil.

**Claudio Maretti** has more than twenty years experience working with environmental, regional and land-use planning, protected area management, and sustainable development including projects in natural resource use, and participatory approaches to working with local communities. He is currently in charge of the Amazon Protected Areas Programme for WWF-Brasil. He has been a member of the IUCN WCPA for almost a decade, mostly as Vice Chair for the Brazil Region, and is also a member of the CEESP Collaborative Management Working Group and the core group of the WCPA/CEESP TILCEPA.

**Nora Mitchell** is adjunct faculty at the University of Vermont, USA, and the founding director of the Conservation Study Institute, established to enhance leadership in the field of conservation. In her 23-year career with the U.S. National Park Service (NPS), she has worked on both natural and cultural resource management of many national parks and has actively sought partnerships for accomplishing this work within the NPS and with academic and non-governmental organizations. Since 1988 she has been actively involved with the IUCN WCPA (and is a member of its Protected Landscapes Task Force), ICOMOS (International Commission on Monuments and Sites), and UNESCO's World Heritage Centre.

**Moses Makonjio Okello** is Associate Professor of Wildlife Management at the School for Field Studies (SFS), Center for Wildlife Management Studies in Kenya. He taught at Moi University Department of Wildlife Management before joining the School for Field Studies as a resident faculty in 1999. Dr Okello teaches Wildlife Management and Conservation, and topics in biostatistics.

**Richard Partington** is a landscape and rural affairs professional experienced in policy development and operational management, specializing in protected landscapes, sustainable tourism and recreation. He is a member of the Countryside Management Association, the IUCN WCPA and the EUROPARC Atlantic Isles executive committee. He has worked in national parks in New Zealand and England, been a consultant for many European countries, and has served for the past five years as senior advisor for the Countryside Agency, a government body providing a leading source of rural expertise in England, UK.

**Neema Pathak Broome** has been a member of Kalpavriksh Environment Action Group, India, for the last ten years. During this time she has helped prepare a Status Report on the Protected Areas of Maharashtra, worked on the issues of community involvement in wildlife management in South Asia, and studied the efforts of a tribal community in Mendha-Lekha village towards forest conservation. Neema is currently working on a national report on local rural communities' efforts at biodiversity conservation. She is a member of the core group of the IUCN inter-commission (WCPA/CEESP) TILCEPA.

**Adrian Phillips** is the Vice Chair for World Heritage of IUCN's WCPA. Between 1994 and 2000, he was chair of WCPA, and has been the Series editor of the IUCN Best Practice Protected Area Guidelines series. He is a member of the WCPA Protected Landscapes Task

Force. Formerly he was Professor in the Department of City and Regional Planning at Cardiff University, Wales; for 11 years the Director General of the Countryside Commission (UK); and before that an employee of IUCN and UNEP. He now serves in a voluntary capacity in support of several conservation NGOs in the UK.

**Guillermo E. Rodríguez-Navarro** is a founding member of Fundación Pro-Sierra Nevada de Santa Marta, Colombia, now serving as its coordinator for fundraising and international relations. Together with his colleagues at the Foundation he has developed a complex management plan for the Sierra Nevada region, geared towards the creation of a participatory process involving all the groups that co-exist in that environment, and helping them define a shared interest in the region's well-being. Current appointments include lecturer at the Jorge Tadeo Lozano University, president of the Fundacion Jardin Etnobotanico Villa Ludovica, and work with the Archaeological Museum Casa del Marques de San Jorge.

**Giles Romulus** is the former Executive Director of the Saint Lucia National Trust and currently represents the island of Saint Lucia on UNESCO's World Heritage Committee. He is a member of the IUCN WCPA and its Protected Landscapes Task Force, and the Caribbean Conservation Association. Currently he is the Programme Coordinator for the Global Environment Facility Small Grants Programme/United Nations Development Programme for Barbados and the Organisation of Eastern Caribbean States.

**Mechtild Rössler** obtained her PhD in Geography from the University of Hamburg, Germany, in 1988 and joined UNESCO's Division of Ecological Sciences in 1991 after a year at the Science Museum in La Villette, Paris, France, and as Visiting Professor at the geography department of University of California-Berkeley, USA. She has been working for the UNESCO World Heritage Centre since its creation in 1992, mainly on natural heritage and cultural landscapes and is currently the Chief of Europe and North America (in charge of fifty countries and 385 World Heritage sites).

**Fausto O. Sarmiento**, PhD, is director of the Office of International Education and Assistant Professor of Environmental Design at the University of Georgia, USA. His research focuses on restoration of neotropical montane landscapes. He is Regional Editor for Latin America for the journal *Mountain Research and Development* and is on the board of global organizations in favor of mountains. He has served as UNESCO/IUCN regional expert for topics related to cultural landscapes, biodiversity conservation and sustainable development, including the recent II Cultural Encounter of the Americas, where he spoke on Cultural Landscapes, Identity and Common Cultural Spaces in Latin America. He is a member of the IUCN WCPA Protected Landscapes Task Force.

**Guy S. Swinnerton** is Professor Emeritus, Parks and Protected Areas, in the Faculty of Physical Education and Recreation, University of Alberta, Canada. His nearly forty years of both academic and professional experience with parks and protected areas has focused on policy and management issues in both the UK and Canada. He is particularly interested in land-use planning and management issues associated with lived-in landscapes. Currently, he is a member of the IUCN WCPA Protected Landscapes Task Force, and is a member of the Science Advisory Committee for Elk Island National Park and the Coordinating Committee for the Beaver Hills Initiative in Alberta.

**Jacquelyn L. Tuxill** has 25 years experience in conservation, most recently focused on building partnerships between the public and private sectors that encourage community-based conservation and landscape stewardship. Based in Vermont, USA, she works with QLF/ Atlantic Center for the Environment and the National Park Service Conservation Study Institute, where she serves as its director for partnership programmes.

**Augusto Villalón** has been involved in architecture and cultural heritage for over twenty years, with work completed in the Philippines, Asia and Latin America. His firm, A. Villalón Architects, won a UNESCO Asia-Pacific Heritage Award in 2003. He represented the Philippines on the UNESCO World Heritage Committee and is a Member of the Executive Committee of ICOMOS.

**Bobby E. L. Wishitemi**, PhD, is Professor and Head of the Department of Tourism Management at Moi University, Kenya. He is co-chair of the IUCN WCPA Protected Landscapes Task Force and a member of the European Union Project Advisory Board for the College of Africa Wildlife, Mweka, Moshi, Tanzania.

# Part I
## Introduction and global overviews

# 1. Protected landscapes: a conservation approach that links nature, culture and community

*Jessica Brown, Nora Mitchell and Michael Beresford*

## Introduction

This book is about an approach to protected areas that is gaining growing recognition and that offers the potential to meet many conservation challenges. The *protected landscape approach* links conservation of nature and culture, and fosters stewardship by people living in the landscape. While grounded in experience with Category V Protected Landscapes/ Seascapes,[1] this approach is broader than a single protected area category or designation. Rather, it relies on different tools and designations to achieve protection, and on an array of processes and traditional systems to sustain people's relationship to the land.

Landscapes, the places where people and nature meet, are shaped by the inter-relationships between humans and their environment. In turn, the natural setting has shaped how people live, their settlement patterns, livelihoods, cultural practices and beliefs – indeed their very way of life. Landscapes encompass history and the present, the physical as well as the intangible. As Adrian Phillips writes in this volume, landscape can be seen as a meeting ground, between nature and people, between the past and the present, and between tangible and intangible values.

Protected landscapes are cultural landscapes that have co-evolved with the human societies inhabiting them. They are protected areas based on the interactions of people and nature over time. Living examples of cultural heritage, these landscapes are rich in biological diversity and other natural values not in spite of but rather *because of the presence of people*. It follows that their future relies on sustaining people's relationship to the land and its resources.

The traditional patterns of land use that have created many of the world's cultural landscapes contribute to biodiversity, support ecological processes, provide important environmental services, and have proven sustainable over centuries. Protected landscapes serve as living models of sustainable use of land and resources, and offer important lessons for sustainable development.

Shaped by cultural forces, landscapes are central to the cultures of the world and, indeed, to our identity as people. In addition to their tangible physical qualities, they possess intangible or "associative" values – among them spiritual, cultural, and aesthetic values. As Mechtild Rössler writes in this volume, cultural landscapes "represent a tightly woven net of relationships that are the essence of culture and people's identity."

The cultural and natural values of these landscapes are bound together. Cultural landscapes are at the interface between biological and cultural diversity, as Rössler observes. It is this complex mix of cultural and natural values, of tangible and intangible heritage, that makes

---

[1] Category V in *Guidelines for Protected Area Management Categories* (IUCN, 1994).

protection of landscapes so vital, and at the same time so challenging. It requires an approach that is interdisciplinary, inclusive, and that engages people and communities.

## The protected landscape approach

The concept of a *protected landscape approach* emerged in a workshop held at the V[th] World Parks Congress in Durban, South Africa (September 2003) and in discussions among members of the IUCN World Commission on Protected Areas (WCPA) Protected Landscapes Task Force. Participants found that, while Category V Protected Landscapes and Seascapes are the primary tool for creating these areas, strategies to protect landscapes are often broader than a single designation, typically drawing on a combination of protected area designations and tools. Importantly, these strategies must respond to the local context and its cultural, natural and social features.

As places that have been shaped by the interactions between people and the land, protected landscapes rely on processes that sustain this relationship. With that in mind, the term *protected landscape approach* is used in this volume, encompassing the diverse strategies needed to achieve this challenging goal, examples of which are presented in this book.

The protected landscape approach recognises that the cultural and natural values of landscapes are inextricably linked, and that the communities living in or near these landscapes are central to sustaining them. It embraces the central role of indigenous and local communities as stewards of the landscape, and puts them at the heart of management of these protected areas, sharing in the benefits and responsibilities of conservation. It is an inclusive approach, relying on participatory

The Sacred Valley of the Incas (Peru), whose agricultural landscape was shaped by pre-Colombian Inca cultures, today is managed by Quechua communities who have created *El Parque de la Papa*, or Potato Park. The traditional patterns of land use that have created this cultural landscape contribute to biodiversity, support ecological processes, and have proven sustainable over centuries.
*Alejandro Argumedo*

processes and partnerships that link a diverse array of stakeholders in stewardship and sustainability.

The protected landscape approach takes a holistic and inter-disciplinary view of the environment. It emphasises the integration of humans and nature, not the attempted isolation of one from the other. It presents an opportunity to understand better the relationship between people and nature, and to learn from these places where harmonious relationships can occur, and sustainable use can be modelled. It accommodates different concepts of nature conservation and strategies for protection. It recognises that to conserve biodiversity in many parts of the world, we must pay attention also to cultural diversity.

The protected landscape approach can provide valuable models of how to integrate biodiversity conservation, cultural heritage protection and sustainable use of resources. It is an approach that brings conservation "home" to the places where people live and work.

An approach that emphasises lived-in landscapes should in no way be seen to diminish the importance of strictly protected areas, nor should it be viewed as a rejection of other conservation models. Rather it is a complementary model, part of a range of strategies for achieving conservation objectives – and one that is particularly appropriate in settings where biodiversity and cultural practices are linked, and where management must accommodate traditional uses, land ownership patterns and the need to sustain local livelihoods.

Protected landscapes can contribute to the viability of more strictly protected areas (such as Category Ia Strict Nature Reserves and Category II National Parks), by strengthening linkages within the broader landscape and connectivity among protected areas. Particularly when conservation objectives are to be met over a large area of land (often referred to as "landscape-scale" conservation), strategies are needed that can accommodate different land uses, ownership patterns and management objectives. Typically this involves a variety of conservation tools and designations. In such a mosaic, protected area designations, such as Category V Protected Landscapes and Category VI Managed Resource Protected Areas, complement more strictly protected areas, and can enhance their impact.

Several of the contributors to this book offer their perspectives on a protected landscape approach. Writing of pastoralist communities in Africa, Brian Jones, Moses Okello and Bobby Wishetimi call for conservation thinking that puts people back into the landscape. In a coda to their paper, Fausto Sarmiento, Guillermo Rodríguez and Alejandro Argumedo call for a "new approach of sustaining living landscapes for conservation in cooperation with the communities that have created and inhabit them". In his chapter, Claudio Maretti proposes several elements for this approach.

# Stewardship

Central to the protected landscape approach is the idea of stewardship, which is based on individual and community responsibility. Landscapes typically encompass a mosaic of land ownership: private, public and, in many countries, customary or communal ownership. It follows that protection of these landscapes inevitably must rely on fostering stewardship by those who own and/or live on the land.

*Stewardship* means, simply, people taking care of the earth. In its broadest sense, it refers to the essential role individuals and communities play in the careful management of our common

A shepherd tends his flock in a mountainous region of Central Slovakia.
*Jessica Brown*

natural and cultural wealth for now and future generations. More specifically, it can be defined as "efforts to create, nurture and enable responsibility in landowners and resource users to manage and protect land and its natural and cultural heritage" (Brown and Mitchell, 1999).

Stewardship taps our basic human impulse to care for our home and its surroundings – be it a parcel of land, a neighbourhood, or an historic monument, or the larger area of a watershed, mountain range or stretch of coastline. It builds on our sense of obligation to other people: our family, our community, and future generations. By fostering individual and community responsibility, stewardship puts conservation in the hands of the people most affected by it.

The protected landscape approach engages local communities in stewardship of landscapes by reinforcing individual and community responsibility for resource management. It builds on existing institutional responsibilities; and encourages flexible arrangements for management of resources, including collaborative management agreements and the range of private land stewardship tools.

## New directions in protected areas

Protected areas are the cornerstone of conservation policy, an inter-generational legacy of the planet's most valuable assets and special places. Covering over 10% of the earth's surface, the global estate includes over 100,000 formally protected areas. As eloquently expressed in the Durban Accord, a statement from the 3,000 participants in the V[th] World Parks Congress, protected areas are:

> *Those places most inspirational and spiritual, most critical to the survival of species and ecosystems, most crucial in safeguarding food, air and water, most essential in stabilizing climate, most unique in cultural and natural heritage and therefore most deserving of humankind's special care.*

The roots of the protected area idea go back thousands of years – long before governments created national parks – to the conservation regimes that human societies have been devising for millennia, among which are community-conserved areas (Borrini-Feyerabend, 2002). However, the modern foundation for protected areas was established in the late nineteenth century, with the designation of Yellowstone National Park in the United States.

A major milestone in the history of environmental conservation, Yellowstone National Park shaped the perception of protected areas as uninhabited wilderness. Its creation marked the start of one of the greatest conservation achievements of the twentieth century, laying the foundation for the creation of a world-wide protected area network of national parks, nature reserves and other kinds of strictly protected areas. The "Yellowstone model" is seen as representing the preservation of large and wild areas by governments, where people are allowed as visitors, but not as residents. While in many places the public image of protected areas is still rooted in this national park model, in reality the protected area idea has evolved, moving beyond a single model to include many different kinds of protected areas.

Today the world's protected areas vary in almost every respect, including the purposes for which they are managed, their size, the kind of places and resources they protect, and the management body responsible (Phillips, 2002). For this reason, IUCN – The World Conservation Union has created a category system, which identifies six categories of protected areas according to management objectives (IUCN, 1994; see Appendix 1). It defines protected areas as follows:

*An area of land and/or sea especially dedicated to the protection and maintenance of biological diversity and of natural and associated cultural resources and managed through legal or other effective means.*

The Alinya Mountain Reserve, the largest private reserve in Catalonia, Spain, is owned by the Fundació Territori i Paisatge - Caixa Catalunya. The rich agri-forestal mosaic of this mountainous landscape is characteristic of the region. *Fundació Territori i Paisatge*

Within this system are Category V Protected Landscapes/Seascapes – protected areas based on the interaction of people and nature, and the principal designation for lived-in landscapes. This category of protected areas, along with Category VI Managed Resource Protected Areas, is introduced briefly in the next section, and explored in more detail in this book's chapters.

Emerging trends in conservation and protected area management set the stage for a greater emphasis on protecting landscapes, and for a new approach that engages people in stewardship and embraces the interactions of people and nature.

Conservation strategies are becoming increasingly bio-regional. The field of conservation biology has highlighted the pressing need to work on the scale of ecosystems and the wider landscape to conserve biological diversity. Worldwide, there is growing recognition that protected areas can no longer be treated as islands, but must be seen in a larger context. The phenomenon of "paper parks"– protected areas in name only – has demonstrated forcefully that approaches that rely solely on regulation and enforcement are costly and too often meet with failure. Recognising that protected areas cannot be viewed in isolation from the communities within and near them, protected area managers are adopting inclusive models, in which collaborative management, partnerships and community-based approaches play a growing role (Brown and Mitchell, 2000a).

An important trend, basic to the protected landscape approach articulated here, is a new understanding of the linkages between nature and culture: that healthy landscapes are shaped by human culture as well as the forces of nature, that rich biological diversity often coincides with cultural diversity, and that conservation cannot be undertaken without the involvement of those people closest to the resources.

In the chapter that follows this one, Adrian Phillips presents the elements of a new paradigm for protected areas.

## What are protected landscapes and seascapes?

Landscapes may be protected by a variety of designations and tools, including some that are not formally recognised within national or international protected area systems, and yet play an important role in sustaining landscapes. Often protected landscapes are located adjacent to, or within, other categories of protected areas, as part of a mosaic of protection.

As noted earlier, a primary tool is through formal designation as a Protected Landscape/ Seascape – Category V in the IUCN category system (see Appendix 2). According to the 1994 IUCN *Guidelines for Protected Area Management Categories*, the definition of a Category V Protected Landscape/Seascape is:

> *... an area of land, with coast and sea as appropriate, where the interaction of people and nature over time has produced an area of distinct character with significant aesthetic, ecological and/or cultural value, and often with high biological diversity.*[2]

---

[2] For a comprehensive introduction to Category V protected areas, and guidance for managing these areas, refer to *Management Guidelines for IUCN Category V Protected Areas: Protected Landscapes/ Seascapes* (Phillips, 2002).

The Category V designation explicitly recognises that "safeguarding the integrity of this traditional interaction is vital to the protection, maintenance and evolution of such an area", making Category V Protected Landscapes both a designation and a process aimed at sustaining people's relationship to the landscape.

In this book Adrian Phillips reviews experience with the Category V designation globally, and explores the relationship between Category V protected areas and those recognised as World Heritage Cultural Landscapes – another important designation in protecting landscapes globally. Since 1992 the UNESCO World Heritage Committee has recognised and protected Cultural Landscapes selected based on the outstanding value of the interaction between people and their environment. The Operational Guidelines for the Implementation of the World Heritage Convention, an international treaty, define Cultural Landscapes as:

> *...illustrative of the evolution of human society and settlement over time, under the influence of the physical constraints and/or opportunities presented by their natural environment and of successive social, economic and cultural forces, both external and internal and as a diversity of manifestations of the interaction between humankind and its natural environment* (UNESCO, 1996). (See Appendix 4).

In her chapter Mechtild Rössler discusses global experience with World Heritage Cultural Landscapes in the context of broader landscape linkages. She observes that *cultural landscapes are a symbol of the growing recognition of the intrinsic links between communities and their past heritage, and between humankind and its natural environment*. She notes the important role of these exceptional sites as a centrepiece of many protected area systems, and their ability to complement Category V sites, as well as those protected through other designations discussed in this book.

Category V Protected Landscapes and World Heritage Cultural Landscapes share much common ground – especially their focus on landscapes where human relationships with the natural environment over time define their essential character. However, there are important distinctions between the two designations, in particular related to how they are selected. In

---

**Box 1.  The protected landscape approach – appropriate to diverse settings**

The protected landscape approach can be appropriate to diverse settings, including those in developing countries, because it:

- links people's needs and biodiversity conservation;
- typically comprises a mosaic of land ownership patterns, including private and communally owned property;
- can accommodate diverse management regimes, including customary laws governing resource management and traditional practices;
- has important specific objectives related to conservation of cultural heritage;
- seeks to bring benefits to local communities and contribute to their well-being, through the provision of environmental goods and services; and
- has proven to work well in certain indigenous territories where strict protected areas have failed.

*Sources*: Brown and Mitchell, 2000a; Oviedo and Brown, 1999.

---

designation of Category V Protected Landscapes, the natural environment, biodiversity con-servation, and ecosystem integrity have been the primary emphases. In contrast, the emphasis in World Heritage Cultural Landscape designation has been on human history, continuity of cultural traditions, and social values and aspirations (Mitchell and Buggey, 2001). As Adrian Phillips further notes in his chapter, "outstanding universal value" is a fundamental criterion in recognising a World Heritage Cultural Landscape, while the emphasis in Category V Protected Landscapes is on sites of national, or sub-national significance.

Other protected area designations can play an important role in protecting landscapes, although their management objectives differ. One example is Category VI Managed Resource Protected Areas (see Appendix 3), which shares with Category V an emphasis on sustainable use of natural resources. However, they differ in that Category V protected areas involve landscapes that typically have been modified extensively by people over time, Category VI protected areas emphasise areas with predominantly unmodified natural systems, to be man-aged so that at least two-thirds remain that way (Phillips, 2002).

Drawing on Brazil's experience with extractive reserves, Claudio Maretti argues that landscape protection must be viewed in the local context – social, cultural and natural – and that for certain lived-in landscapes the Category VI designation may be more appropriate. In the Brazilian Amazon, for example, communities established Category VI extractive reserves in order to protect their lived-in, working landscapes.

Another important example considered here is the Biosphere Reserve designation, an instrument of UNESCO's Man in the Biosphere (MaB) programme, dedicated to sustainable development and the conservation of biodiversity, as well as the support of environmental education, research, and the monitoring of the most important natural areas of the world. The chapter by Clayton F. Lino and Marilia Britto de Moraes considers experience from the Mata Atlantica Biosphere Reserve to explore how this designation supports large-scale conservation and, at the same time, helps to sustain traditional landscapes and seascapes in Brazil's coastal zone.

Central to the protected landscape approach, though not expressed in any formal designa-tion, are the array of strategies that indigenous and local communities have been using for millennia to protect land and natural and cultural resources important to them. Long ignored by governments, and not included in the accounting of official protected areas, community-conserved areas are now receiving growing attention in the protected areas field. In their chapter Edmund Barrow and Neema Pathak introduce community-conserved areas, which they define as

*...modified and natural ecosystems, whether human-influenced or not, and which contain significant biodiversity values, ecological services, and cultural values, that are vol-untarily conserved by communities, through customary laws and institutions.*

Community-conserved areas have long played a role in how communities all over the world care for the landscapes they inhabit (Borrini-Feyerabend, Kothari and Oviedo, 2004).

Finally, private land conservation tools (such as conservation easements and management agreements) and public-private partnerships play an important role in protecting landscapes, as discussed in several of the chapters in this volume.

# Some milestones in advancing protected landscapes and seascapes

While Protected Landscapes have come relatively late to the protected area scene, they play a growing role in national systems of protected areas, and in regional and global conservation strategies. Significant progress has been made over the last 25 years, running parallel to broader trends in conservation and in new approaches to protected areas generally. Selected milestones in advancing this approach, with particular reference to Category V protected areas, are presented in Box 2.

---

**Box 2.  Milestones in recognising and developing the protected landscape approach**

- In 1978 IUCN, through its then Commission on National Parks and Protected Areas, published a report on "Categories, Objectives and Criteria for Protected Areas," which established ten categories, including protected landscapes, formally recognising the value of lived-in, working landscapes as protected areas.

- In 1987 IUCN and the UK Countryside Commission co-hosted a symposium on Protected Landscapes (Lake District, UK), which adopted the "Lake District Declaration," a statement of principles underpinning the value of the protected landscape approach.

- In 1988 an IUCN General Assembly resolution recognised protected landscapes as "living models of sustainable use" and urged governments and others to give more attention to Category V protected areas.

- In 1990 the International Centre for Protected Landscapes was established in Aberystwyth, Wales, UK.

- In 1992 the first publication providing guidance on the protected landscapes approach was published. Written by the late P.H.C. (Bing) Lucas, and published by IUCN, the *Guide on Protected Landscapes for Policy-makers and Planners* was prepared as a contribution to the IVth World Congress on National Parks and Protected Areas, (Caracas, Venezuela).

- At the IVth World Congress on National Parks and Protected Areas (1992), following critical review of the IUCN protected area management categories, IUCN acknowledged the need to give more attention to protected area models based upon people living alongside nature.

- Also in 1992 the World Heritage Committee, after nearly a decade of debate, agreed that cultural landscapes could meet the criteria of "outstanding universal value" and revised the World Heritage Guidelines to include a Cultural Landscapes category, an important development in linking conservation of natural and cultural heritage.

- In 1994 IUCN published its *Guidelines for Protected Area Management Categories,* which put Category V areas – now formally known as Protected Landscapes and Seascapes – on an equal footing with other categories of protected areas.

- In 1996 the first IUCN World Conservation Congress (Montreal, Canada), adopted a resolution regarding conservation on privately owned land, with special reference to Category V protected areas.

- In 1999 the Conservation Study Institute (US National Park Service and QLF/Atlantic Center for the Environment), in cooperation with IUCN's World Commission on Protected Areas, convened an international workshop on Stewardship of Protected Landscapes (Woodstock, Vermont, USA). As a result, the WCPA Steering Committee created a Commission Task Force on Protected Landscapes to draw together global expertise and promote the approach.

Cont.

---

---

**Box 2. Milestones in recognising and developing the protected landscape approach (cont.)**

■ The WCPA Protected Landscapes Task Force, working with partner organizations, has produced several publications (see examples below), convened international meetings (e.g., working session and seminar, Stow-on-the-Wold, England, UK, 2001) and regional workshops (e.g., Andean landscapes – Baeza, Ecuador, 2001), and led a workshop at the V[th] World Parks Congress.

■ In 2002 IUCN published *Management Guidelines for IUCN Category V Protected Areas: Protected Landscapes/Seascapes* (Phillips, 2002), as part of the IUCN/Cardiff University series on best practice in protected area management. Other recent publications coming out of the work of the Protected Landscapes Task Force include an issue of the journal *PARKS* on Category V Protected Areas (Beresford, Ed. 2003) and an issue of *George Wright Forum* on Stewardship of Protected Landscapes (Brown, Mitchell and Sarmiento, Eds. 2000).

■ Recent international symposia have highlighted the importance of cultural landscapes, including a 2002 session on "Cultural Landscapes – the Challenges of Conservation," convened by UNESCO on the occasion of the 30th anniversary of the World Heritage Convention (Ferrara, Italy, 2002); and "Learning from World Heritage" a US/ICOMOS symposium on cultural and ecological landscapes of global significance (Natchitoches, Louisiana, USA, 2004).

■ At the V[th] World Parks Congress (Durban, South Africa, 2003), the WCPA Protected Landscapes Task Force convened a workshop on Protected Landscapes and Seascapes. A Congress workshop stream on Linkages in the Landscape/Seascape and cross-cutting themes on Local Communities and Equity and World Heritage, respectively, highlighted the importance of landscape-scale conservation, community involvement in protected areas, and cultural landscapes, points formalized in recommendations and in the Durban Accord.

*Sources*: Phillips, 2002; Mitchell and Buggey, 2001.

---

# Protected landscapes at the V[th] World Parks Congress

The topic of Protected Landscapes and Seascapes featured prominently at the V[th] World Parks Congress (WPC) in 2003, in venues that included workshops, panels, and debate.

The World Parks Congress recognised the important role of indigenous and local communities in creating and managing protected areas. Far from being a side topic, the role of communities was a central part of the debate in Durban on protected areas and their future. Communities and Equity was a cross-cutting theme of the Congress, and was on the agenda as never before, integrated into each of the seven workshop streams, and addressed in plenary discussions and in Congress products such as the Durban Accord. This integration came about thanks to the vision of the WPC steering committee and the work of members of the Theme on Indigenous and Local Communities, Equity and Protected Areas (TILCEPA), an inter- commission group of WCPA and the IUCN Commission on Environmental, Economic and Social Policy (CEESP). The participation of community and tribal leaders from around the world greatly enriched discussions at the Congress.

Several sessions in WPC Stream 1 (Linkages in the Landscape and Seascape) focused on Protected Landscapes and Seascapes. The Linkages in the Landscape and Seascape stream focused on the challenge of designing new ecological networks for a better integration of protected areas in the global landscape and seascape, investigating the application of the ecosystem approach to protected areas and the new governance mechanisms necessary to achieve this. It recognised that protected areas need to be connected or reconnected to the surrounding landscape in order to meet conservation goals, and to ensure effective land, water and marine ecosystem planning, and noted that good ecological science must be coupled with an understanding that cultural and biological diversity are inextricably linked. The Stream on Linkages in the Landscape and Seascape looked at five key elements of linkages to and from protected areas – ecological, economic, institutional, cultural, as well as the effectiveness of these linkages in benefiting protected areas.[3]

A panel on the *The Role of Communities in Sustaining Linkages in the Landscape and Seascape* highlighted the experience of traditional communities in managing landscapes, with special emphasis on that of mobile peoples. At a joint session of Stream 1 and the Stream on Governance (New Ways of Working Together), the panel explored the various institutional and management arrangements for environmental management at the community level in pastoralist societies, as well as some of the problems that face mobile communities in terms of lost power, lost access and lost mobility. One conclusion of the session was the need for a more holistic approach that integrates wider landscape requirements with those at the community level and which, in turn, requires a much greater understanding of the social aspects of conservation issues.

Spanning three sessions, the workshop on *Protecting Landscapes and Seascapes: IUCN Category V, World Heritage Cultural Landscapes and Other Designations* sought to demonstrate how the Protected Landscape/Seascape concept can work effectively in different settings, using a variety of designations and other tools. Overview presentations set the context for how designations such as Category V, Category VI, World Heritage Cultural Landscapes and Biosphere Reserves protect landscapes globally. Through case-study presentations and small group discussions, workshop participants explored the central role of communities in protected areas and in managing linkages in the landscape and seascape. Small group discussions explored experience and new opportunities in regions including Africa, Asia, Europe, Latin America and North America. The workshop included a debate on Protected Landscapes and the IUCN Category System, which considered the role of Category V and VI designations with respect to other categories of Protected Areas.

Key points emerging from discussions in the workshop on Protecting Landscapes and Seascapes included:

■ The important role of Categories V and VI within the IUCN system of protected areas management categories, noting their ability to complement other protected area categories and maintain and restore biological diversity, while accommodating the relationship between people and nature.

■ The role played by communities in conserving important ecological linkages in the broader landscape, such as watersheds and the terrestrial-marine interface, as well as biodiversity.

---

[3] From report on the Linkages in the Landscape and Seascape Stream, posted at www.iucn.org/themes/wcpa/wpc2003/english/programme/workshops/linkages.htm

- The value of an integrated approach drawing on all the protected area categories and using a mosaic of these designations in order to sustain linkages in the landscape and seascape.

- Workshop participants, who came from many different regions, noted that many of the world's biodiversity hotspots are linked to places where the activities of humans over time have contributed to the biodiversity in the landscape. They argued the need for a greater understanding of the link between cultural diversity and biodiversity. Finally, they found that Categories V and VI, and international designations such as World Heritage Cultural Landscapes and Biosphere Reserves, are particularly well suited to accommodate the particular conditions of landscapes shaped by people over time (see also Box 1).

Most importantly, as discussed earlier in this chapter, workshop participants advocated a "landscape approach" and began to articulate the elements of such an approach.

The World Parks Congress produced recommendations on a broad array of issues and challenges facing protected areas in the coming decade. A number of these focused on themes relevant to the protected landscapes approach, including recommendations on integrated landscape management, governance, indigenous and mobile peoples, World Heritage, and community-conserved areas.

## Experience from diverse regions of the world

Drawing on experience from many countries and regions, the chapters in this book illustrate how the protected landscape approach can work in very different settings, addressing a variety of conservation objectives and challenges.

Adrian Phillips and Mechtild Rössler, in their respective chapters, present case-studies of World Heritage Cultural Landscapes in the Philippines, Austria, Hungary, Portugal, Iceland, Italy, Lebanon, Nigeria, Russia and Lithuania. Rössler observes that the inclusion of Cultural Landscapes within the World Heritage Convention has contributed to the recognition of intangible values and the heritage of local and indigenous communities, and to the value of traditional land systems that represent the continuity of people working the land over centuries and millennia.

Also in this volume, Augusto Villalón and Jane Lennon further explore experience with the World Heritage Cultural Landscape designation. In her discussion of two Australian cases – Uluru-Kata Tjuta National Park and Kosciuszko National Park – Lennon finds that World Heritage Cultural Landscape designation has brought public attention to Australian landscapes deemed of global importance. By enhancing the value placed on cultural heritage, including intangible values, and recognising the importance of management by indigenous people, Lennon observes that the Cultural Landscape designation has contributed to the evolution of heritage protection in Australia toward increasing integration of natural and cultural values.

Writing about two continuing cultural landscapes in the Philippines, Villalón explores the challenges of balancing progress and tradition. For the Rice Terraces of the Philippines Cordilleras, the first continuing cultural landscape to be inscribed on the World Heritage list, the future depends on continuing the culture-based traditional practices that have created and maintain the landscape. He describes a rich array of culture-nature connections, including intricate terracing and irrigation systems, the planting of forest parcels ringing each terrace group, and the spiritual practices of the Ifugao culture. The challenge, Villalón argues, is for local communities to move forward into the 21st century, while maintaining their culture and traditions.

In Nepal, half of the country's protected areas include settlements and farmlands, and all national parks are adjacent to areas with high populations. Prabhu Budhathoki writes that since the inception of its protected area system, Nepal has had to adopt a broad landscape approach, linking local people with resource conservation and directing the benefits of resource conservation to them. He discusses the case of the Terai Arc Landscape Conservation Initiative, an effort to link 11 protected areas to protect critical habitat for many species, including tigers, rhino and elephants. Given the area's mosaic of land use practices and the livelihood needs of mountain communities, Budhathoki observes that efforts to scale up conservation initiatives to a larger landscape level are relying on the principles of partnerships, inclusion and linkages.

The challenges of protecting landscapes and seascapes in Brazil's coastal zone are discussed in the chapter by Clayton Lino and Marilia Britto de Moraes. They present the cases of the Mata Atlantica Biosphere Reserve, an international designation under the MaB programme, and the federally designated Cananéia-Iguape-Peruíbe Area de Proteção Ambiental (APA). A uniquely Brazilian model, the APA, or Environmental Protection Area, is well suited to management of working landscapes, the authors argue, given its emphasis on participatory and democratic approaches to management, reliance on stewardship by local communities, and ability to be flexible and adapt to different contexts. Comparing the APA and Biosphere Reserve models,

Fernando de Noronha, in the Mata Atlantica Biosphere Reserve (Brazil). In Brazil's coastal zone, complementary designations such as Biosphere Reserves and Areas de Proteção Ambiental (Environmental Protected Areas) work together to protect landscapes and seascapes. *Clayton F. Lino*

Lino and Britto de Moraes write that these designations are complementary, working in harmony with each other and with other kinds of protected areas, such as Category II National Parks, to manage natural resources in the coastal zone while involving local communities.

Also drawing on the Brazilian experience, Claudio Maretti writes about the role of Category VI extractive reserves in protecting landscapes. The Chico Mendes extractive reserve (Brazilian Amazon) and the coastal Mandira extractive reserve (south-eastern Brazil) are examples of landscapes created by and belonging to local communities, he argues. Reflecting on the courage of these communities when in response to threats to these places they created extractive reserves, Maretti stresses that local communities and their activities related to natural resources present an opportunity, rather than a problem, in developing an overall nature conservation strategy.

Giles Romulus explores the applicability of the various protected area management categories to the situation of Small Island Developing States in the Caribbean. This chapter presents two cases from Saint Lucia: the Praslin Protected Landscape and the Soufriere Marine Management Area. Romulus argues that Categories V and VI are most appropriate to the needs of Small Island Developing States, and that effective management of natural and cultural resources should be based on the principles of equity, participation and sustainability. Also in that chapter, a box by Wil Maheia on the Maya Mountain Marine Corridor/Port Honduras Marine Reserve illustrates the role of an NGO working with local communities to create a protected area.

North American experience with protected landscapes is described in the chapter by Nora Mitchell, Jacquelyn Tuxill, Guy Swinnerton, Susan Buggey and Jessica Brown. The authors observe a growing appreciation of the conservation values of lived-in landscapes in the United States and Canada, and a broadening of protected area systems in both countries to include a greater diversity of sites, and an array of management partnerships. Their chapter presents examples from diverse settings in the United States and Canada, and documents a growing appreciation of the importance of partnerships, community engagement and participatory governance models. They observe that the term "protected landscapes" refers not only to particular sites, but to a process that guides and accommodates change, and this represents a fundamental shift in thought and practice in the two countries.

In the United Kingdom, with its long history of human settlement and dense population, and with almost all land and water in some form of multiple use, conservation effort has always focused on lived-in landscapes. In this book Adrian Phillips and Richard Partington review the UK's half-century of experience with Category V protected areas, which include National Parks, Areas of Outstanding Natural Beauty (AONBs), Regional Parks and National Scenic Areas. England, Wales, Scotland and Northern Ireland are adopting different strategies, illustrating a varied approach to pursuing social, economic and environmental aims within their protected landscapes. Phillips and Partington write that in the UK it is recognised that protected areas will not survive, nor achieve their aims, without local support – all the more necessary given that many people live in these Category V protected areas and play an active role in their management and protection.

Case studies from Central Europe of two Czech Protected Landscapes – the Bílé Karpaty (southern Moravia) and the Jizersky hory (northern Bohemia) – demonstrate the contributions of the stewardship approach to rural economic development, community revitalization and fostering civil society in the post-Communist societies of the region. In their discussion of innovative projects in the protected landscapes of these two mountainous regions, Miroslav Kundrata and Blažena Hušková observe that an approach that reinforces local people's relationship to nature, supports their resources and traditions, and encourages sensitive management of the landscape can contribute to economic strengthening of rural areas. They also note the important role played by NGOs in bringing new vision and innovation to traditionally conservative rural areas, and the value of international exchange in further advancing these community-based initiatives.

In their chapter on community-conserved areas (CCAs) Edmund Barrow and Neema Pathak discuss the efforts of rural people to conserve areas of land and biodiversity through management systems that have evolved over centuries. While the history of this kind of conservation is much older than government-managed protected areas, Barrow and Pathak note that an emphasis on "official" protected areas has tended to overlook the contribution of CCAs. They present examples of community-conserved areas from Asia, South America and Africa that illustrate the importance of cultural, utilitarian and sacred associations in protecting landscapes and biodiversity. Their chapter highlights the importance of communities' spiritual association with nature, and the contribution of sacred sites, such as sacred groves, to protecting landscapes.

These themes of spiritual associations with nature and sacred sites are explored in the chapter on Andean South America, a region rich in landscapes shaped by traditional land uses that have proven sustainable over centuries. Fausto Sarmiento, Guillermo Rodríguez and Alejandro Argumedo write of Andean landscapes that culture and nature are interlocked in a closely knit fabric where the resulting mosaics of land uses have provided diversity and stability to the ecology of mountain landscapes. Their case-studies from Peru, Ecuador and Colombia illustrate the role of indigenous communities and *colono* communities in sustaining landscapes. They argue the need for conservation based on traditional knowledge practices and innovation systems, in order to protect local landscapes while providing for livelihoods.

In their chapter on experience from Kenya and Namibia, Brian Jones, Moses Okello and Bobby Wishitemi describe how pastoralist communities have for centuries been presiding over landscapes now recognised as important for biodiversity. The land-uses of these communities and the sustainable nature of their grazing management regimes have helped to preserve landscapes that still provide important habitat for wildlife. They argue that the protected landscape model can offer a new vision for conservation and rural development in the region that does not displace people from their lands, nor cause them to lose access to resources important to their livelihoods.

Because protected landscapes represent an integrated and holistic approach to conservation, they require special management styles and skills, according to Elizabeth Hughes. In her chapter on building leadership and professionalism, Hughes discusses a broad array of training needs to build the leadership qualities and skills required for management of protected landscapes. She presents case studies of programmes that include academic and professional training, international exchange, and partnerships between protected areas, and argues that building a high level of professionalism is critical if we are to achieve conservation of natural and cultural resources within a framework of sustainable development.

# A final note on landscape

As Phillips writes here, "[l]andscape is universal. It is found everywhere that people and nature have interacted". At the same time, our cultural perspective shapes how we understand the idea of *landscape*, just as it shapes our view of the idea of *wilderness*. Writing from very different parts of the world, many of the authors here challenge us to broaden our view of landscape, and to consider that many seemingly "untouched" lands are, in fact, cultural landscapes.

For example, the complex landscape heritage of Australia has been shaped over millennia by the Aboriginal and Torres Strait Islander peoples and over recent centuries by European occupation. Observing that the first Australians modified the environment through the use of fire and hunting, gave the landscape its creation stories, and left behind evidence of their culture in rock art and sacred sites, Lennon argues that the whole of Australia can be considered a cultural landscape.

Jones *et al.* write about the "mind maps" of pastoralists in Africa, which shape their view of the landscapes they inhabit. Their mind maps do not have fixed boundaries or specific land use designations, but rather reflect the pastoralists' mobile way of life and flexible resource management regimes.

Writing about Andean South America, Sarmiento *et al.* describe a view of the landscape in which "identity and ethnicity go hand-in-hand with mythical concepts of sacred hills," and in which the mountain deities are seen as offering protection to the communities living below them.

In his discussion of remote areas in the Amazon and coastal wetlands of Brazil, Maretti argues that even these places are living cultural landscapes. He writes:

> ... *[they] may not be 'classical' examples of cultural landscapes (or 'European types' of landscape) – for the marks are less visible to the 'non-local' and 'untrained' eye, which may not be prepared in these settings to see the long interactions between humans and nature over time ..... But what then are lands that are divided by paths, shaped by use, with their limits defined by customs and respected by local communities, (as, for example, with the significance of trees) if not landscapes – cultural landscapes – and therefore ideally managed through a landscape approach?*

While the cultural features of a landscape may be hard for the outsider to discern, they are kept alive and understood well by those living closest to the place and its resources. As stewards, local communities bring their wealth of knowledge, traditional management systems, innovation and love of place to managing these landscapes. Maretti's question prompts us to consider that the protected landscape approach may be an appropriate option in places where the assumption might have been otherwise. The rich array of experience presented in the coming chapters confirms the value of this approach in very different settings, offers guidance on how it can be tailored to new contexts, and highlights its potential to meet future conservation challenges.

# 2. Landscape as a meeting ground: Category V Protected Landscapes/Seascapes and World Heritage Cultural Landscapes

*Adrian Phillips*

## Introduction

This chapter explores the relationship between the topic of this book – Category V Protected Landscapes/Seascapes – and the category of Cultural Landscapes under the World Heritage Convention. It does this by:

- Identifying the shared context in which both ideas are attracting increasing attention: a growing interest in landscape, and the emergence of a new paradigm for protected areas;

- Analysing the relationship between Category V Protected Landscapes/Seascapes (as well other categories of protected area) and the 36 World Heritage Cultural Landscapes inscribed by 2003; and

- Examining four case studies of World Heritage Cultural Landscapes in order to explore aspects of this relationship in greater detail.

## An introduction to the idea of "landscape" [1]

The word comes from the Dutch – *landschap*[2] – and that tells us much that we need to know. Dutch artists painted scenes of broad skies, long, low horizons, water and trees, in which are set fishermen, cattle drovers and so forth: ordinary people in a countryside they had helped to make. Contrast this with the Italian renaissance landscape painting tradition in which the rural scene provides "the auxiliary setting for the familiar motifs of classical myth and sacred scripture" (Schama, 1995).

Even though landscape painting may be thought of as a two-dimensional representation of the view, it is in fact much more than that since it embodies the artist's interpretation. Similarly, landscape itself is much more than scenery, a passive object, which is just seen. This claim is made for several reasons.

First, the impact of landscape is felt through *all* the senses: it is heard, smelt and felt too. Think of a cliff top walk on a windy day: the landscape presents itself as a combination of sights, sounds and the tang of the salt spray – with the feel of springy turf underfoot.

Secondly, landscape has a two-way relationship with us. It has a power to shape and reinforce our values, to inspire us, to reflect and reinforce our sense of identity.

---

[1] These introductory thoughts were developed in the course of preparing a presentation for an unpublished keynote paper on landscape given at the ICOMOS/IUCN Conference on Future Landscapes (Oxford, May, 2004).

[2] *Landschap* became *landskip* in seventeenth century England, and then – quite soon – *landscape*.

And it is more than scenery in another sense too. Because the landscape embodies the past record of human use of the land, it is what generations of people have made of the places in which we now live. Thus it both absorbs layers of history and embodies layers of meaning.

Therefore we can see landscape as a meeting ground[3] between:

- Nature and people – and how these have interacted to create a distinct *place*;

- Past and present – and how therefore landscape provides a *record* of our natural and cultural history;

- Tangible and intangible values – and how these come together in the landscape to give us a sense of *identity*.

Herein lie both the strength and the weakness of the idea of landscape. The strength of landscape is that it embodies many facets and appeals to us in all sorts of ways. Its weakness is that – just because it is a meeting ground – no single profession owns it or can champion it unaided: the proper understanding of landscape calls for contributions from many disciplines. Furthermore landscape is a cultural construct and often culturally contested: different groups will see it differently, and ideas about it are not constant but change over time. Thus an Australian aboriginal will read quite different things into the outback landscape than a farmer of European origin; and rugged Alpine scenery that eighteenth century travellers thought of as repugnant became the spiritual heartland of the Romantic movement. Finally, because many of the values of landscape cannot be quantified, they are open to challenge in a world where what cannot be measured is at risk.

## Landscape and policy[4]

These various characteristics of landscape make it an elusive concept, and a difficult topic to embed in policy. Of course, love of landscape has driven public policy in many countries for many years. It has also motivated millions of people to support powerful voluntary sector organisations like the National Trust in the UK or many of the Land Trusts of the US. But landscape has usually been seen as a second class member of the environmental club. "Lacking a coherent philosophy, thin on quantification and without a strong, unified disciplinary core, it has often been viewed as a 'soft' topic, to be swept aside in the rush to develop and exploit the environment, a trend that is justified by that trite commentary: 'jobs before beauty'" (Phillips and Clarke, 2004). Compared to the wilderness movement in North America, and its equivalents in Australia and other countries, the idea of taking an interest in lived-in, working landscapes was slow to emerge, and confined to relatively few countries for many years. In this it contrasts with the demands of wildlife conservation or pollution control. The protection, management and planning of landscape has generally been a less powerful movement, and has taken longer to emerge as a political force.

The contrast is particularly evident at the international level. Some regional nature conservation agreements (e.g., that for the Western Hemisphere) and two global biodiversity-related

---

[3] The European Landscape Convention captures this in its definition of a landscape: "an area, as perceived by people, whose character is the result of the action and interaction of natural and/or human factors".

[4] These thoughts derive from Adrian Phillips and Roger Clarke: Our Landscape from a Wider Perspective in Bishop, K. and Phillips, A. 2004.

agreements, the Convention on Wetlands of International Importance (Ramsar) and the World Heritage Convention, were signed more than 30 years ago. In 1992, the Convention on Biological Diversity (CBD) was adopted at the Earth Summit. But until very recently, there were no international landscape agreements.

## Landscape comes in from the cold

Things are changing now. This is because several of the characteristics of landscape are particularly relevant to the search for more sustainable ways of living. These are:

- Landscape is *universal*. It is found everywhere that people and nature have interacted, in remote places, in farmed countryside, even in villages, towns and cities. It needs to be stressed that a concern for landscape should not be confined to what is conventionally considered as the most beautiful or "least spoilt" landscapes.

- It is *dynamic*. Landscapes inevitably change and evolve over time, in response to natural processes and to the changing needs and activities of people. Landscape cannot be 'frozen'.

- It is *hierarchical*. Like a Russian doll, a large landscape area contains smaller landscape units within it; they in turn contain still smaller ones; and so on.

- It is *holistic* – or it is nothing: any attempt to understand it as a wholly natural, wholly historic or entirely physical phenomenon is doomed. It cannot be understood or managed except through an integrated, multi-disciplinary approach, which embraces all its eco-logical, economic, cultural and social components.

These qualities are all very relevant to sustainable development, which can only be achieved by connecting (or reconnecting) people and nature, and which demands multi-disciplinary approaches. In this sense, landscape is not only an environmental *resource* in its own right but also a *medium* through which to pursue sustainable development.

Such thinking is well expressed in the preamble to the world's first landscape treaty, the European Landscape Convention (ELC), which came into force in March 2004.[5] It is also a driver behind the themes of this chapter, the growing importance given by IUCN to Category V protected areas – or Protected Landscapes/Seascapes – and the emergence of the 'Cultural Landscapes' category under the World Heritage Convention.

The connection is very clear when we look at the types of landscape action that are at the core of the ELC. Indeed, the three-fold classification provided by Article 1 of the convention offers an excellent general typology that is relevant in all parts of the world:

- 'Landscape protection', defined by the ELC as "actions to conserve and maintain the significant or characteristic features of a landscape justified by its heritage value derived from its natural configuration and/or human activity;"

- 'Landscape management', meaning "from a perspective of sustainable development, to ensure the regular upkeep of all landscape, so as to guide and harmonise changes which are brought about by social, economic and environmental processes;"

---

[5] See Council of Europe web site: http://conventions.coe.int/Treaty/EN/cadreprincipal.htm

- 'Landscape planning', meaning "strong forward-looking action to enhance, restore or create landscape" (COE, 2002).

Both Category V protected areas and World Heritage Cultural Landscapes are focused on the first task that the ELC seeks to promote: landscape protection.

## Category V Protected Landscapes/Seascapes – protecting biodiversity and other values

Protected areas of all kinds are essential for biodiversity conservation, landscape protection and for many other aspects of conservation and sustainable development. IUCN has defined a protected area as "an area of land and/or sea especially dedicated to the protection and maintenance of biological diversity, and of natural and associated cultural resources, and managed through legal or other effective means" (IUCN, 1994).

Within this broad definition, protected areas are managed for many different purposes in addition to biodiversity protection. To help improve understanding of protected areas, and to promote awareness of the range of protected area purposes, IUCN has developed a system for categorizing protected areas by their primary management objective. It identifies six distinct categories (IUCN, 1994), which are set out in Appendix 1; the fifth of these is Protected Landscapes/Seascapes. The categories system is being increasingly accepted by national governments as a framework to guide the establishment and management of protected areas. A growing number of countries have used it in domestic legislation or policy.[6] Its importance was confirmed at the V[th] World Parks Congress in Durban, South Africa in 2003.[7] In February 2004, the Seventh Conference of the Parties to the CBD (Kuala Lumpur, Malaysia) gave this IUCN system intergovernmental support.[8]

Looking at the history of IUCN's involvement in protected areas, led by its World Commission on Protected Areas (WCPA),[9] it is possible to detect a progressive broadening of thinking among those working in protected area policy and practice. Thus, for many years the preoccupation at the international level was with pristine or near-pristine areas, that is national parks (in the Yellowstone model), and the categories of relatively strict protection (i.e. I–IV). However in the past 10–15 years or so, the importance of protected areas that focus on lived-in working landscapes has been increasingly recognised. This process can be dated to the 1987 international symposium on protected landscapes which led to the Lake District Declaration (Foster, 1988), soon to be followed by the adoption of a resolution about the importance of Category V areas at the 1988 IUCN General Assembly. It continued with the publication of the late Bing Lucas's guide to protected landscapes (Lucas, 1992). It was confirmed with the publication of the *Guidelines for Protected Area Management Categories* (IUCN, 1994). Further important steps were the publication of the *Management Guidelines for IUCN*

---

[6] For a fuller account, see the research project into the category system, "Speaking a Common Language" accessible at www.cf.ac.uk/cplan/sacl/

[7] See Workshop Recommendation 5.19, on the IUCN web site: www.iucn.org/themes/wcpa/wpc2003/english/outputs/recommendations.htm

[8] See CBD web site www.biodiv.org/

[9] Formerly the IUCN Commission on National Parks and Protected Areas (CNPPA).

*Category V Protected Areas: Protected Landscapes/Seascapes* (Phillips, 2002), and of a special issue of *PARKS* magazine on the topic (Beresford, 2003).

Every few years, the United Nations Environment Programme's World Conservation Monitoring Centre (UNEP/WCMC) in Cambridge, UK and IUCN WCPA produce the so-called 'UN List of Protected Areas'. First called for by the United Nations, this is a global assessment of the extent and distribution of protected areas as defined above. The most recent published version of the UN list (Chape *et al.,* 2003) was presented to the World Parks Congress held in Durban, South Africa in September 2003. This records no less than 102,102 individual protected areas of all categories, totalling 18.8 million km$^2$, the equivalent of 11.5% of the world's total land area but less than 1% of the marine environment.

Category V protected areas comprise quite a small proportion of all these protected areas, (6,555 or 6.4% of all protected areas). However, their significance lies as much in the great potential to establish new protected areas of this kind as in the coverage of those areas that has already been achieved. In the words of the IUCN President, Yolanda Kakabadse, who wrote a Preface to the Category V guidelines mentioned above:

*Protected areas should ... include those lived-in, humanised landscapes where people and nature live in some kind of balance. These places, and the communities that live in them, are important in themselves and for the lessons they can teach all of us about*

Volunteers mow a protected wet orchid meadow in the White Carpathian Protected Landscape Area (Czech Republic). Category V protected areas must be managed in close cooperation with local people. *Radim Machu*

*sustainable living. This is the idea behind Protected Landscapes and Seascapes, or Category V in the IUCN system of protected area categorisation.*

*The Category V approach is not a soft option: managing the interface between people and nature is just about the toughest challenge facing society, and Category V management is all about that. Nor are such places second class protected areas: rather they are an essential complement to more strictly protected ones. Indeed, Protected Landscapes are an idea whose time has come, and IUCN is pleased to promote their wider use and higher management standards* (Phillips, 2002).

## Category V and the new paradigm

As Yolanda Kakabadse observed, Category V protected areas can teach us about sustainable living, a theme that was touched on in the general discussion on landscape above. Indeed, the growing interest in Category V protected areas reflects a wider process that has led to the emergence of a new paradigm for protected areas.

Though the coverage of protected areas has grown impressively over the years, serious gaps remain. Moreover, many existing protected areas face serious threats. Indeed the crude total number and extent of protected areas tell us nothing about how well they are managed. Thus, even when these areas exist in law, they often suffer from encroachment, poaching, unregulated tourism, deforestation, desertification, pollution and so forth. Most protected areas lack management plans, yet such plans are essential if a national park or a nature reserve is to achieve its stated aims. Many protected area managers lack the necessary skills – business skills for example (see Hughes in this volume). Often these places are ignored in national and

Participatory approaches and partnerships with diverse groups are part of a new paradigm for protected areas management. *Clayton F. Lino*

regional development planning, and in sectoral planning. Most important, everywhere local communities tend to be alienated from protected areas nearby or in which they live – yet without winning the "hearts and minds" of the people directly affected, conservation is at best a means of buying time.

Moreover, threats will increase in future: rising numbers of people, increased demands for resources of all kinds, pollution of many sorts (often novel and insidious), accelerating climate change, the effects of globalization – all these represent a new order of challenge to protected areas around the world.

## Table 1.
## Contrasting paradigms (from Phillips, 2003a)

| Topic | As it was: protected areas were ... | As it is becoming: protected areas are ... |
|---|---|---|
| **Objectives** | ■ Set aside for conservation<br>■ Established mainly for spectacular wildlife and scenic protection<br>■ Managed mainly for visitors and tourists<br>■ Valued as wilderness<br>■ About protection | ■ Run also with social and economic objectives<br>■ Often set up for scientific, economic and cultural reasons<br>■ Managed with local people more in mind<br>■ Valued for the cultural importance of so-called "wilderness"<br>■ Also about restoration and rehabilitation |
| **Governance** | ■ Run by central government | ■ Run by many partners |
| **Local people** | ■ Planned and managed against people<br>■ Managed without regard to local opinions | ■ Run with, for and, in some cases by local people<br>■ Managed to meet the needs of local people |
| **Wider context** | ■ Developed separately<br>■ Managed as 'islands' | ■ Planned as part of national, regional and international systems<br>■ Developed as 'networks' (strictly protected areas, buffered and linked by green corridors) |
| **Perceptions** | ■ Viewed primarily as a national asset<br>■ Viewed only as a national concern | ■ Viewed also as a community asset<br>■ Viewed also as an international concern |
| **Management techniques** | ■ Managed reactively within short timescale<br>■ Managed in a technocratic way | ■ Managed adaptively in long term perspective<br>■ Managed with political considerations |
| **Finance** | ■ Paid for by taxpayers | ■ Paid for from many sources |
| **Management skills** | ■ Managed by scientists and natural resource experts<br>■ Expert-led | ■ Managed by multi-skilled individuals<br>■ Drawing on local knowledge |

Protected areas face ever-greater threats to their continued existence just when their values are growing in importance to humankind. If protected areas are indeed of growing value to society, but are nonetheless increasingly at risk, it would appear that there is something badly wrong in the way in which we plan and manage them. Only some of the answers, of course, are available to protected area managers themselves. Issues like the global patterns of trade, war and conflict, demographic pressures and climate change are matters to be addressed by national govern-ments or the international community. But it is also widely recognised that a new approach is needed to the planning and management of protected areas themselves. The main elements of this have been captured in a "new paradigm" (see Table 1).

The new paradigm provides support for Category V protected areas. In most respects, they match well the profile in the far right column of Table 1. For example, Category V protected areas must, by their nature, be run with a range of environmental, social and economic objectives in mind, and managed in close co-operation with local people.

## World Heritage Cultural Landscapes

The World Heritage Convention was adopted in 1972 and is now one of the most widely supported international agreements on the environment. It provides for the identification and protection of the world's heritage of outstanding universal value. The convention combines two ideas: cultural heritage and natural heritage, and in operating the convention two separate streams of activity have developed. The cultural one is served by ICOMOS (and ICCROM) and the natural one by IUCN. The result has been two sets of World Heritage sites: cultural ones and natural ones (there are also "mixed" sites, being those that were inscribed under both natural and cultural criteria).

Over the years, the sharp separation and differentiation of these two approaches has been found less and less helpful in understanding the world's heritage and its needs for protection and management. As the foregoing discussions on landscape and the development of the new paradigm of protected areas have made clear, the separation of the cultural and natural world – of people from nature – makes little sense. Indeed it makes it more difficult to achieve sustainable solutions to complex problems in the real world in which people and their environment interact in many ways. It ignores the well documented evidence that many so-called wilderness areas have in fact been modified by people over long periods of time. It ignores evidence that in many areas disturbance of natural systems can be good for nature; and that many rural communities have shown great respect for nature. It overlooks the rich genetic heritage of crops and livestock associated with farming in many parts of the world. Moreover, excluding people from the land (or water) on grounds of nature conservation often meets with resistance from local communities; collaborative approaches are needed instead. Finally, nature conservation has to be concerned with the lived-in landscape because it cannot be achieved sustainably within 'islands' of strict protection surrounded by areas of environmental neglect.

As a result, IUCN, and the nature conservation movement generally, now recognise far more than they did only 10 or 20 years ago the importance of 1) the humanized, lived-in landscapes as well as 'natural' environments, and 2) the cultural dimension to the conservation of nature. It is thus easy to see in general terms why IUCN has taken an interest in the development and implementation of the World Heritage Cultural Landscapes, and in bringing the cultural and natural worlds closer together (see Rössler in this volume). Through a former Chair of its then Commission on National Parks and Protected Areas, the late Bing Lucas, IUCN helped to draw up the recommendations on Cultural Landscapes from La Petite Pierre which were adopted by the World Heritage Committee at Santa Fe in 1992 (see Appendix 4).

Since 1992, IUCN has worked with colleagues in ICOMOS to help implement the Operational Guidelines relating to Cultural Landscapes in several ways:

- by carrying out joint evaluations with ICOMOS of nominated Cultural Landscape properties where there is an important nature conservation interest;

- by undertaking State of Conservation reporting and evaluation missions for inscribed World Heritage Cultural Landscape sites that are similarly important for nature conservation;

- by providing technical input to a number of global and regional meetings concerning the intellectual development of World Heritage Cultural Landscapes;

- by promoting the concept of Cultural Landscapes, and its interest in them, in its publications, advice etc.;

- by demonstrating in particular the degree of shared experience between IUCN protected area management Category V (Protected Landscapes/Seascapes) and World Heritage Cultural Landscapes;

- by joining with ICCROM to advise the World Heritage Committee and World Heritage Centre on the revision of the Operational Guidelines, which incorporate a more integrated view of World Heritage values; and

- by developing guidance on how to identify the natural values of World Heritage Cultural properties.

The guidance referred to in the last item above is set out in Appendix 5. It shows the various ways in which natural values of concern to IUCN may be a feature of Cultural Landscapes (and will be returned to in the last part of this chapter).

## World Heritage Cultural Landscapes and protected areas

It is evident that the concept of World Heritage Cultural Landscapes (as spelt out in Appendix 4) has a number of similarities with the thinking behind Category V protected areas. This is especially so in the common emphasis placed on human/nature interaction. As will become clear later, the overlap is greatest in respect of the continuing form of organically evolved cultural landscape (type 2(b)), which acknowledges the value of landscape-related cultural traditions that continue to this day.

However, there are also important differences. In protected landscapes, "the natural environment, biodiversity conservation and ecosystem integrity have been the primary emphases. In contrast, the emphasis in Cultural Landscapes has been on human history, continuity of cultural traditions, and social values and aspirations" (Mitchell and Buggey, 2001). Moreover, World Heritage Cultural Landscapes include a designed type of landscape (type (1)) that is not reflected in the IUCN notion of a Category V protected area (though a protected landscape may include important designed features). Finally, the fundamental criterion for recognition of a World Heritage Cultural Landscape is that of "outstanding universal value". There is less stress placed on outstanding qualities in the case of Category V protected areas, although the areas should certainly be *nationally* significant to merit protection[10] – see Table 2 below.

**Table 2. World Heritage Cultural Landscapes and Category V Protected Landscapes/Seascapes**

| Initiative | Character of landscape affected | Geographical scope of application | Areas covered by the initiative | Main aims |
|---|---|---|---|---|
| World Heritage Convention Cultural Landscapes | Outstanding universal value | Global | Any appropriate area | Protect heritage values |
| Category V protected areas: Protected Landscapes/seascapes | Landscapes/ seascapes that deserve protection | National and sub-national | Areas largely unaffected by intensive development | Integrate activities and enhance natural and cultural values |

## Analysis of World Heritage Cultural Landscapes and protected areas

In order to identify the degree of overlap between protected areas (and especially Category V protected areas) and World Heritage Cultural Landscapes, all 36 of the latter were examined to see how far these areas coincided with protected areas as defined by IUCN. It has not been possible in the time available to make the detailed boundary-by-boundary analysis that is required, only to provide an initial check of the names of World Heritage Cultural Landscapes against those in the *UN List of Protected Areas*.[11]

The results are set out in full in Appendix 6 and summarised in Table 3. They must be treated with caution because the boundaries of the World Heritage site may vary considerably from those of the protected area carrying the same name. In some cases, only a part of the World Heritage Cultural Landscape is also a protected area; in other cases, the World Heritage Cultural Landscape contains several protected areas; in other cases again, the protected area will be significantly larger than the World Heritage site.

---

[10] For a fuller discussion of the relationship of Cultural Landscapes under the World Heritage Convention and Protected Landscapes/IUCN Category V, see Mitchell and Buggey, 2001.

[11] Further analytical work of this kind, to establish the details of the relationship between World Heritage Cultural Landscapes and protected areas, would be a possible task for UNEP-WCMC. Such research might also include a survey of the coincidence between protected areas and other World Heritage Cultural Properties that Prof. Fowler (Fowler, 2003) has identified as having the characteristics of Cultural Landscapes but which have not been so designated. He considers that there are at least another 70 of these, maybe as many as 100 sites.

**Table 3. World Heritage Cultural Landscapes and IUCN management categories of protected areas**

| Number of WH Cultural Landscape Sites | Protected Area Category of WH Cultural Landscape | Number which are also WH Natural Sites |
|---|---|---|
| 8 | II (includes three transboundary sites: two consist of two Category II Protected Areas, one is a Category II and a Category V site) | 3 |
| 2.5 | IV (one is partly Category V) | none |
| 8.5 | V (one is partly Category IV and one is part of a transboundary site, the other part of which is Category II) | none |
| 17 | none | none |
| **Total = 36** | **19** | **3** |

Table 3 shows that many World Heritage Cultural Landscapes coincide in whole or in part with established protected areas. Three of these, Tongariro (New Zealand), Uluru (Australia) and Mt Perdu (France/Spain), contain natural values that are so important that they have been inscribed as World Heritage properties under both natural and cultural criteria. These three areas, and another 16 of the 36 sites on the list, (see right hand column in Appendix 6) are recognised as national parks or designated as other kinds of protected area under national legislation. *In other words, more than half of all World Heritage Cultural Landscapes currently inscribed on the UN List have natural values that are considered sufficiently important to merit their designation, by national or provincial authorities, as protected areas* (in the sense defined above by IUCN).

In addition, there are also other Cultural Landscapes where the country concerned has not yet taken action to identify and protect natural values in a formal way at the site under protected area legislation, but where World Heritage measures should have the same effect. The Philippines Rice Terraces is a case in point.

Appendix 6 also relates the three categories of World Heritage Cultural Landscapes (see Appendix 4) to the six IUCN management categories of the associated protected areas (see Appendix 1). This information is summarised in Table 4 below.

Finally it is possible to combine the analyses above and in Tables 3 and 4, and Appendix 6, to attempt a typology of relationships as set out in Table 5 below. At this stage it should be regarded as a preliminary exercise only.

The following general conclusions can be drawn from Tables 4 and 5:

- The most common category of Cultural Landscape is Category 2b (Continuing Organically Evolved Cultural Landscape);
- Most of these areas coincide with a protected area, most commonly one in Category II (National Park) and V (Protected Landscape/Seascape).

It therefore follows that a fruitful partnership can be developed between those working on Category V protected areas and those engaged in work on World Heritage Cultural

Landscapes, especially those working with Continuing Organically Evolved Cultural Landscapes.

**Table 4. Cultural landscape categories and management categories of protected areas**

| Category of WH Cultural Landscape | IUCN PA management category II | IUCN PA management category IV | IUCN PA management category V | No IUCN PA management category | Total |
|---|---|---|---|---|---|
| Category 1 | nil | nil | 1.0 | 4.5 | 5.5 |
| Category 2a | nil | nil | 0.5 | 2.0 | 2.5 |
| Category 2b | 6.5 | 2.5 | 6.5 | 6.0 | 21.5 |
| Category 3 | 2.0 | nil | nil | 4.5 | 6.5 |
| **Total** | **8.5** | **2.5** | **8.0** | **17.0** | **36.0** |

Note – 0.5 indicates that the site in question is classified under two WH CL categories and/or under two IUCN protected area management categories

**Table 5. Suggested typology of relationships between World Heritage Cultural Landscapes and protected areas**

| Type of relationship | Characteristics of relationship | World Heritage Cultural Landscapes (abbreviated title) |
|---|---|---|
| Mixed site | Site is inscribed under both natural and cultural values | Uluru, Pyrénées-Mont Perdu, Tongariro |
| CL with nationally important biodiversity values | Whole site or most of site has recognition at national level primarily for biodiversity conservation (Category II and IV) | Fertö/Neusiedlersee (H), Viñales Valley, Hortobágy National Park, Rock Shelters of Bhimbetka, Curonian Spit, Mapungubwe, Matobo Hills |
| CL with nationally important landscape values | Whole or most of site has recognition at national level primarily for landscape conservation (Category V) | Wachau, Loire Valley, Upper Middle Rhine Valley, Fertö/Neusiedlersee (A), Tokaj Wine Region, Cinque Terre, Cilento and Vallo di Diano, Sintra |
| Some coincidence of interest | Part of site is designated for natural values | Hallstatt-Dachstein, Southern Öland |

Þingvellir National Park (Iceland) was inscribed in 2004 as a World Heritage Cultural Landscape of unique significance to the Icelandic people. The area has impressive natural qualities that are an integral part of its value.
*Adrian Phillips*

## Case studies

In this final section, four case studies are briefly described to show the range of interests that IUCN has in Cultural Landscapes. In each instance the nominated site is analysed with the help of an IUCN paper *IUCN's Procedures for Identifying Natural Values in Cultural Landscapes,* which is referred to in the new World Heritage Operational Guidelines (and reproduced in full in Appendix 5).

The four case studies are:

- the Rice Terraces of the Philippine Cordilleras (inscribed 1995);

- Fertö/Neusiedlersee Cultural Landscape, Hungary and Austria (inscribed 2001);

- Landscape of the Pico Island Vineyard Culture, Azores, Portugal (inscribed 2004);

- Þingvellir, Iceland (inscribed 2004).

All four of these sites were nominated as Cultural Landscapes, and two of them – Fertö/ Neusiedlersee and Pico – were also nominated as natural properties. However, in every case the field evaluation of the nomination was undertaken jointly by IUCN and ICOMOS. In the case of the Philippine Rice Terraces, the two Advisory Bodies also undertook a joint state of conservation evaluation mission.

### The Rice Terraces of the Philippine Cordilleras

The rice terraces were the first site to be included on the World Heritage Cultural Landscape list under the continuing organically evolved category, indeed they may almost be considered as a model example of this type of area (see Villalón in this volume). They are dramatically beautiful, a superb physical creation and a living example of the close links between culture and nature. But they are also an exceptional demonstration of the sustainable use of natural resources (soil, water and vegetation) and of an enduring balance between people and nature. Indeed it is astonishing that the rice terraces have existed on very steep slopes for an estimated 2,000 years in a region affected by landslips, earthquakes and typhoons. There are lessons to be

The Rice Terraces of the Philippine Cordilleras, a World Heritage Cultural Landscape, demonstrate the sustainable use of natural resources and an enduring balance between people and nature. *UNESCO /Spier-Donati*

learnt from such land management, underpinned by the cultural traditions of the Ifugao people, for wider application in the rice-growing tropics and beyond. Though the remaining conserved watershed forests are important for the plants and animal life that survive there, more significant is the area's agri-biodiversity: farmers use numerous land races of rice, each subtly adapted to local conditions in the relatively cool upland climate. The rice terraces are not recognised under national law as a protected area within the IUCN system, but in fact they manifest many of the characteristics of a Category V protected area; indeed they are given as a case study in IUCN's published advice on this topic (Phillips, 2002).

Therefore IUCN and ICOMOS together carried out the original assessment of the nomination of the site in 1995. They also undertook a joint state of conservation evaluation mission in 2001, which led to their inscription on the In Danger List at the Helsinki meeting of the World Heritage Committee (December 2001), thus becoming the first Cultural Landscape to be so listed. IUCN will continue to take a close interest in the area. Strategies for its future management should draw on experience in the management of many Category V protected areas elsewhere in the world. Examples are: integration of rice-growing with ecotourism; the development of new markets for rice and rice wine from the region; and capacity-building among the local community based on traditional values.

### Fertö/Neusiedlersee cultural landscape

The Fertö-Neusiedler Lake area, located on the Austrian-Hungarian border, is an unusual and diverse ecosystem, which has had a very long tradition of harmonious interaction between people and nature. The lake itself, which normally has no outlet, is the largest saline water body in Europe (309,000ha). The water surface and surrounding lands are subject to a variety of climatic effects, and contain unique assemblages of species from different regions, as well as a number of rare plant endemics. It is a crucial habitat for many resident and migratory bird species. Adjoining the lake proper is Seewinkel, with its 80 or so shallow saline ponds that attract thousands of geese arriving in late autumn. Other natural habitats include saline grassland and marshlands, steppe-relicts, bogs and xerotherm oak stands; many of the modified habitats are also important for nature conservation, though this depends on maintaining traditional land management practices. The area is very beautiful, with contrasts between the lake and its reed beds, forests, dry meadows, vineyards and orchards. Its cultural values are of many kinds: there are Roman stone quarries and villages of medieval origin which used the resources of the lake and adjoining lands; there is the Esterhazy palace where Joseph Haydn wrote much of his music and nearby the home of the hero of Hungarian independence, Count Istvan Szechenyi.

The lake and surrounding lands are already protected under both Hungarian and Austrian law as protected areas, as a Category II site on the Hungarian side and as a complex of Category V, IV and II protected areas in Austria. The area is also an important wetland under the Ramsar Convention and a key site in the EU's Natura 2000 system. The site was nominated both as a cultural landscape and as a natural site. In its joint evaluation with ICOMOS, IUCN recognised its great importance at the European scale but did not feel it was quite as diverse as other World Heritage sites in the region, such as the Danube Delta, nor as rich in birdlife as several other land-locked lakes in temperate latitudes. Although therefore it did not support the inscription of the site on natural grounds, it acknowledged its great regional and national importance, supported its inscription as a Cultural Landscape and indicated its continuing interest in the management of the site.

### Landscape of the Pico Island vineyard culture, Azores, Portugal

The archipelago of the Azores is situated in the mid-Atlantic: Pico is the second largest of the nine islands, dominated by Pico Mountain volcano (2,351m). Two small coastal areas on the island were nominated in 2001 as both cultural and natural properties. Both have been significantly modified for agricultural use, as one is actively farmed for viticulture, and the other was formerly used for growing vines and figs but has since been abandoned. Both areas contain numerous very small fields (of a few square metres only), each surrounded by high lava walls, producing a unique humanized landscape.

IUCN recognised the extraordinary achievement of farming in these barren areas of lava and the struggle between people and their environment that is represented by this farmed landscape. However, in terms of natural values the areas are far too small for recognition as World Heritage sites – and they exclude those parts of the island (such as the volcano) which would be of greatest interest. IUCN did not therefore recommend their inscription as natural properties and indeed would have only a limited interest in how these areas are managed, though it did indicate that there might be other parts of the archipelago which could merit inscription as a natural site. For its part, ICOMOS recognised that the area had the potential to be a cultural property but asked the State Party to consider renominating a somewhat larger area of the field system and made several other recommendations (a revised nomination was presented to the World Heritage Committee in 2004 and the site then inscribed on the World Heritage List as a Cultural Landscape).

### Þingvellir, Iceland[12]

Þingvellir National Park (IUCN Management Category II) is strikingly situated on top of the Mid-Atlantic Ridge, which arises from the splitting of the North American and European tectonic plates. The site is bounded on two sides by parallel lines of faulted fissures, and on the other two by mountains and Lake Þingvallavatn, Iceland's largest lake. Its physical setting helps to give the site its unusual and beautiful quality – as well as a distinct unity. These qualities take on an added significance, as Þingvellir has been the place where nearly all the great events in Icelandic history have taken place for well over a thousand years. Its importance was recognised when it was made Iceland's first national park as early as 1928 – one of the earliest parks in Europe. The area thus has a unique cultural significance to the Icelandic people: it is, in effect, a national shrine.

Although Þingvellir was nominated only as a cultural site, it is remarkable too because of the very strong links between natural and cultural factors. Natural values are certainly higher than in most other Cultural Landscapes on the World Heritage List, and have been well documented. IUCN therefore took a close interest in the nomination, and made a number of recommendations, jointly with ICOMOS, on the management of the site, that were considered by the World Heritage Committee in June 2004. It concluded that the area had very impressive natural qualities that are an integral part of the site's values and accordingly inscribed it as a Cultural Landscape. The site shows inter-continental rifting in a spectacular and readily understandable manner and is of great natural beauty, with an impressive variety of landforms. Also, there is a close interaction between natural and cultural/historical aspects of the site; and Lake Þingvallavatn is of great limnological interest. The site was inscribed on the World Heritage list as a Cultural Landscape in June 2004.

While Þingvellir National Park was not nominated under natural criteria, the question whether it should be was raised during the evaluation and also by some reviewers. It seems that the Icelandic authorities would like to nominate Þingvellir as a natural site in due course. Without prejudice to the evaluation of any such future nomination, the case may be made stronger if Þingvellir were part of a serial nomination that illustrated the significance of the Mid-Atlantic ridge as a whole – a global feature that occurs in several islands or island groups other than Iceland (including the Azores, see above).

### Analysis

In Table 6 below, each of these four sites has been analysed against the natural characteristics set out in Appendix 5. It shows that the natural qualities that they display are of several different kinds and that no one site is important in all respects. Indeed the natural qualities of the four sites are as varied as the cultural ones.

---

[12] 'Þingvellir' is pronounced Thingvellir.

## Table 6. Natural characteristics of the four case studies

| World Heritage Cultural Landscape | Important natural characteristics (see also Appendix 5) | | | | | | |
|---|---|---|---|---|---|---|---|
| | Biodiversity | Agri-biodiversity | Sustainable use | Scenic beauty | *Ex-situ* collection | People/nature model | Site of key findings |
| Philippines Rice Terraces | medium | high | very high | very high | no | very high | no |
| Fertö/Neusiedlersee Cultural Landscape | very high | low | medium | high | no | high | no |
| Pico Island Vineyard Culture | low | medium | medium | medium | no | high | no |
| Þingvellir, Iceland | medium | no | low | very high | no | low | yes |

## Conclusions

This paper reports a recent shift in the direction of thinking on the part of IUCN towards greater engagement in the cultural dimension of conservation. It also shows that many individual World Heritage Cultural Landscapes contain a wide range of different kinds of natural values. The analysis of existing sites already inscribed as World Heritage Cultural Landscapes in relation to nationally designated protected areas as recognised by IUCN has revealed a significant overlap. This should set the stage for increased cooperation and partnership in the management of those sites, at the national level and among international organizations.

# 3. World Heritage Cultural Landscapes: a global perspective

*Mechtild Rössler*

## Introduction

Cultural landscapes are at the interface between nature and culture, tangible and intangible heritage, biological and cultural diversity; they represent a tightly woven net of relationships that are the essence of culture and people's identity. Cultural landscapes are a centrepiece of protected areas in a larger ecosystem context, and they are a symbol of the growing recognition of the intrinsic links between communities and their past heritage, and between humankind and its natural environment.

World Heritage cultural landscapes are sites that are recognised and protected under the UNESCO World Heritage Convention for the outstanding value of the interaction between people and their environment. This paper looks at these exceptional sites in a global context and presents selected case studies from different regions of the world illustrating their value and the important role they play in a larger context of landscape linkages. These linkages include other protected areas and conservation programmes, including Biosphere Reserves, IUCN Category V protected landscapes and seascapes (see Phillips in this volume), and Category VI sites (see Maretti in this volume). Considering the rapid social and economic changes, degradation and unregulated development that affect these areas, a number of challenges need to be addressed in holistic and interdisciplinary conservation approaches.

The Convention Concerning the Protection of the World Cultural and Natural Heritage (generally referred to as the World Heritage Convention), adopted by the General Conference of UNESCO (United Nations Educational, Scientific and Cultural Organization) in 1972, establishes a unique international instrument that recognises and protects both the cultural and natural heritage of outstanding universal value. The World Heritage Convention's definition of heritage provides an innovative and powerful opportunity for the protection of cultural landscapes as "combined works of nature and man".[1] The Convention not only embodies tangible and intangible values for both natural and cultural heritage, it also acknowledges traditional management systems, customary laws and long-established customary techniques and knowledge as means for protecting heritage. Through these traditional protection systems, World Heritage sites also contribute to and illustrate sustainable local and regional development.

Today, there are 178 States Parties that are signatories to the Convention and 754 (582 cultural, 149 natural and 23 mixed) properties from a total of 129 countries included on the World Heritage List. Thus the Convention is a key international instrument and catalyst for heritage conservation and plays an important role in promoting the recognition and management of heritage in many regions of the world. The landmark decision in 1992 to encompass

---

[1] Article 1 of the Convention, which was used to introduce the cultural landscape concept into the Operational Guidelines for the Implementation of the World Heritage Convention.

landscapes as heritage has resulted in the designation of nearly 40 World Heritage Cultural Landscapes from all regions of the world and has had a considerable effect on many other programmes and constituencies, including conservation of protected areas not listed as World Heritage sites. A number of case studies in this book look at World Heritage sites designated for their natural values, such as Royal Chitwan National Park in Nepal (see Budhathoki in this volume), or the Mata Atlantica in Brazil (see Lino and Britto de Moraes in this volume), from a landscape perspective. These examples illustrate a shift in the conservation paradigm from designating exceptional natural sites without people to recognising the value of natural heritage sites in a landscape context that includes people (Phillips, 2003 and in this volume). There has also been a shift toward recognising and valuing the linkages between people and their communities and protection of World Heritage Cultural Landscapes, which are illustrated by examples from Australia[2] and the Philippines (see Villalón in this volume).

These changing concepts continue to influence the work of many States Parties around the world in identifying potential sites for World Heritage on their Tentative Lists. New Tentative Lists that have been prepared during the past ten years include numerous cultural landscapes,[3] such as those from Kenya, the United Kingdom and Canada, to name a few. The revision of the Canadian Tentative List is a model case that reviewed more than one thousand sites proposed by communities, researchers, institutions and governmental agencies. Through this consultative process across the country, those sites that meet the World Heritage criteria and are of potential outstanding universal value were identified. The new Tentative List[4] clearly illustrates the emerging interest in nominating cultural landscapes and other manifestations of diverse cultural heritage.

## Cultural landscapes on the World Heritage List: a new approach

In 1992 the World Heritage Convention became the first international legal instrument to recognise and protect cultural landscapes. This decision was based on years of intensive debates in the World Heritage Committee on how to protect sites where interactions between people and the natural environment are the key focus. The World Heritage Committee adopted three categories of cultural landscapes as qualifying for listing (see Appendix 4 for additional information):

- **clearly defined landscapes designed and created intentionally by humans**, such as many gardens and parks, for example Versailles in France, Kew Gardens in the United Kingdom, or the extended designed area of the Lednice Valtice Cultural Landscape in the Czech Republic;

---

[2]  The renomination of Uluru Kata Tjuta as cultural landscape had a world-wide effect for other indigenous communities and is a model case for change in management structures and mechanisms, (see the article by Lennon in this book).

[3]  Peter Fowler (2003) provided a complete overview on all World Heritage cultural landscapes and an analysis of all landscape categories included on official Tentative Lists submitted during the 1992–2002 period.

[4]  It is suggested that this model be used for other regions of the world – see www.parkscanada.ca

- **organically evolved landscapes** which can be either relict landscapes or continuing landscapes. This type of landscape results from an initial social, economic, administrative and/or religious imperative and has developed its present form by association with and in response to its natural environment. Such landscapes reflect that process of evolution in their form and component features. These include a number of agricultural landscapes ranging from the tobacco landscape of Viñales Valley in Cuba, the Rice Terraces of the Philippine Cordilleras or the Puszta pastoral landscape of Hortobagy National Park in Hungary; and

- **associative cultural landscapes**. The inclusion of such landscapes on the World Heritage List is justifiable by virtue of the powerful religious, artistic or cultural associations of the natural element rather than material cultural evidence, which may be insignificant or even absent. This type is exemplified by Uluru Kata Tjuta in Australia, Sukur in Nigeria and Tongariro National Park in New Zealand.

Many cultural landscapes – 36 from all regions of the world, as of 2003 – have been nominated and inscribed on the World Heritage List since the 1992 landmark decision (see Appendix 6 for a list). Cultural landscapes are inscribed on the World Heritage List on the basis

The Lednice Valtice World Heritage Site (Czech Republic) is an example of a cultural landscape designed and created intentionally by people. *Jessica Brown*

of the cultural heritage criteria, but in a number of cases the properties are also recognised for their outstanding natural values. An example is the transboundary site of Mont Perdu between France and Spain where no border exists in the ecological systems or the pastoral activities of the local communities, and which reflects an agricultural way of life once widespread in the upland regions of Europe, surviving now only in this part of the Pyrenees. This area provides exceptional insight into the past through its landscape of villages, farms, fields, upland pastures and mountain trails and is also on the World Heritage List for its natural values.

The inclusion of cultural landscapes as part of the implementation of the World Heritage Convention has had a number of significant impacts on conservation. First, the category of associative cultural landscape has contributed substantially to the recognition of intangible values and to the heritage of local communities and indigenous people. For the first time these examples of cultural heritage have received worldwide recognition alongside the Taj Mahal in India or the Pyramids of Egypt, or the natural wonders of the Victoria Falls on the border of Zambia and Zimbabwe, and the Grand Canyon in the USA. The fundamental shift was the acceptance of the value of communities and their relation to their environment, including the link between landscapes and powerful religious, artistic or cultural associations even in the absence of material cultural evidence. These landscapes are places with associative cultural values, some considered as sacred sites, which may be physical entities or mental images that are embedded in a people's spirituality, cultural tradition, and practice. The category of sacred sites has an immense potential, as many of these areas have been protected primarily because they are sacred sites of high value to society. Long before the development of categories of protected areas such as national parks, nature reserves and protected landscapes, indigenous peoples have sheltered their sacred places. Through a diverse range of mechanisms they have contributed to preserving cultural spaces and sites with biological diversity and transmitted them to future generations.

Second, recognition of cultural landscapes gave value to land-use systems that represent the continuity of people working the land over centuries and sometimes millennia to adapt the natural environment and retain or enhance biological diversity. The key world crops were developed in the spectacular agricultural systems in the High Andes (e.g., potatoes, corn), terraced rice paddies in Asia (e.g., rice, fish and vegetables) or oasis systems in the Sahara (e.g., dates). The global importance of these systems and the genetic varieties of these diverse cultural landscapes was acknowledged. At the same time, the building techniques, vernacular architecture, and ingenious schemes of these systems also received attention, as they often relate to complex social systems. Often these knowledge systems are intertwined with belief systems, rituals and ceremonials. Irrigation systems such as the mud channels in the steep terrain of the Philippine Cordilleras, the Quanat structures in Northern Africa, or the dry stone walls in the Mediterranean also show the interdependence of people in the cultural landscape. If the physical or the social structure collapses, the whole landscape and ecological system is threatened.

Third, the inscription of sites as cultural landscapes on the World Heritage List has had important impacts on the interpretation, presentation and management of the properties. The nomination process led to an increased awareness among the local communities, new pride in their own heritage, and often to the revival of traditions. In some cases new threats had to be faced with an increase in tourism and related developments. In other cases these landscapes became models for sustainable land-use and community stewardship, including the opportunities for marketing of specific agricultural products or traditional arts and crafts.

Finally, the introduction of cultural landscapes into the World Heritage arena has made people aware that sites are not isolated islands, but that they are part of larger ecological systems and have cultural linkages in time and space beyond single monuments and strict nature reserves. Thus the cultural landscape concept has contributed to the evolution in environmental thought, protected area management strategies, and heritage conservation as a whole. These impacts were recently demonstrated at the World Parks Congress in Durban in 2003 (IUCN, 2003). Cultural landscapes also reflect the extraordinary development in the interpretation of the World Heritage Convention and the diversity of approaches and experiences in preservation and stewardship worldwide.

## Diverse footprints in the global landscape: Case studies from different regions

Every cultural landscape has a unique complex of cultural and natural values, and is subject to different legal protection frameworks and diverse national management systems and institutional arrangements. The following case studies illustrate the complexity of the values and protection systems and also the diverse set of management challenges. The case studies represent diverse conservation approaches for dynamic cultural landscapes, show community-managed systems and traditional national park management, as well as illustrate a range of different systems and management structures. This set of examples also demonstrates a key aspect of the future vision for stewardship of cultural landscapes – sharing responsibilities among the stakeholders, national and international, local and regional, community-based and park authority management. This collection of examples also reflects a variety of ways to address the linkages beyond the site itself – involvement of research institutions, training and educational centres and, first and foremost, paving the way for future partnerships to transmit knowledge and stewardship practices.

### Cinque Terre (Italy)[5]

*Many of the agricultural heritage landscapes of the world are threatened both by the failure of traditional ways to maintain production in a world of changing interests and needs, and the demands of mass tourism, whose impacts threaten the very qualities that attract tourists. Cinque Terre, a World Heritage cultural landscape, exemplifies these dilemmas, but also offers hope that even in the most difficult situations, solutions may be at hand* (De Marco and Stovel, 2003).

The unique and diverse cultural land/seascape of wine-growing terraces and fishing villages has been created and maintained over centuries. Only since the 1970s have terraces been abandoned, creating adverse impacts on this complex integrated system, including the collapse of many dry stonewalls and, consequently, landslides that have been severe. The World Heritage inscription and this international recognition gave a boost to people's pride in their heritage and their territorial identity as well as to tourism and increased value of local products such as a specialty wine of the area, Sciacchetrà. The designation brought direct economic

---

[5]   The name of the World Heritage site is "Portovenere, Cinque Terre, and the Islands (Palmaria, Tino and Tinetto)" and goes beyond the National Park of Cinque Terre.

benefits to the local people and attracted international funding including support from the World Monuments Fund for terrace restoration and re-use. One of the most important pro-gramme initiatives is a system of renting out terraces to people in the city to create a fund that is used to maintain the dry stone walls that support the steep terrain above the villages. Sub-sequently, a national park was created which covers most (but not all) of the World Heritage cultural landscape. The protection of the site was enhanced and research institutions such as the University of Genoa became involved in providing assistance in management planning. With the creation of the national park, a train transport system was developed along the seaside which allows visitors to move easily between the picturesque villages, the main tourist attractions, and to hike along the seaside trail. The system provides financial support for the park as each ticket is also an entry ticket into the site. Most important for the local economy is the development of specific value-added landscape products, including wine, olives, juice, marmalade and other agricultural produce, which are proudly marketed by the locals using a Cinque Terre label that includes a World Heritage logo. Consumers of these place-specific products understand that by purchasing them they are supporting the preservation of a World Heritage cultural landscape, its communities, and their centuries-old land use traditions.

## The Rice Terraces of the Philippine Cordilleras

The Rice Terraces of the Philippine Cordilleras were included in the World Heritage List in 1995 and represent another agricultural landscape of particularly unique and dramatic scenic value of small terraces on steep mountainsides (see Villalón in this volume). This site represents an interaction between people and their natural environment over generations. In 2001 the rice terraces were included on the World Heritage In Danger list despite efforts to safeguard the property by the Banaue Rice Terraces Task Force (BRTTF) and Ifugao Terraces Commission (ITC). The BRTTF lacks full government support and, to be effective, needs more resources, greater independence and an assurance of permanence. About 25–30% of the terraces are now abandoned, which has led to damage to some of the walls. This situation has arisen because sections of the irrigation system have been neglected, due to people leaving the area. Most of the site is privately owned and traditionally managed.

## The Qadisha Valley (Lebanon)

The Qadisha Valley is a site mentioned in the Bible for its sacred cedars. It is an interesting cultural landscape example, as it was initially nominated as a natural property – The Cedar Forest of Lebanon – but was not recommended by the advisory body IUCN due to its small size and integrity issues. Subsequently the property was presented as a cultural landscape and inscribed in 1998 as a site of monastic settlements since the earliest years of Christianity, following a joint ICOMOS-IUCN evaluation mission to the site. It has currently no protected area status nationally but is located between two nature Reserves (Horsh Ehden and Tannourine Nature Reserves). A local association is working for improved protection of the site and the World Heritage Committee in June 2003 requested better legal protection, management coordination, establishment of a nature reserve and development of a manage-ment plan.

The Sukur Cultural Landscape (Nigeria), the first cultural landscape from Africa to be inscribed on the World Heritage List, is a remarkably intact physical expression of a society and its spiritual and material culture. *UNESCO*

### Sukur Cultural Landscape (Nigeria)

The first cultural landscape from Africa inscribed on the World Heritage List represents a site of traditional management and customary law. The Sukur Cultural Landscape encompasses the Hidi's stone henge palace (i.e., the dwelling place of the spiritual-political paramountcy), dominating the villages below, the terraced fields and their sacred symbols with stone paved walkways that link the low land to the graduated plateaus. The landscape also features architectural elements including stone corrals for feeding domestic stock, graveyards, stone gates and vernacular stone settlement clusters with homestead farms, all in the midst of rare species of flora and fauna. It is a remarkably intact physical expression of a society and its spiritual and material culture.

### Curonian Spit (Lithuania/Russian Federation)

This transboundary area is located at the shores of the Baltic Sea and features an unusual geomorphological phenomenon of a sandy peninsula constantly changed by waves and wind. Following a stakeholders' and planning meeting, a joint management plan was produced and the area was nominated to the World Heritage List under both natural and cultural criteria. Human habitation of this elongated sand dune peninsula dates back to prehistoric times. Even today, unique traditions such as the production of *krikstai* – wooden grave markers – and traditional fishing farmsteads are still alive. The site was inscribed in 2000 as a cultural landscape and has benefited from the international recognition and also from financial assistance for its visitor centre. However, the case illustrates that protected areas are not islands, as an oil platform was constructed in the Baltic Sea by the Russian authorities and joint preventive protection measures have been difficult to create despite international meetings and UNESCO

Curonian Spit Cultural Landscape, Lithuania and Russia, was nominated to the World Heritage List under both natural and cultural criteria. Although the World Heritage Convention is based on shared responsibilities and collaboration, addressing conservation needs in a transboundary context is challenging. *UNESCO*

missions and consultations. This case exemplifies the fragility of heritage landscapes and the need for collaborative approaches in management and risk prevention. Although the World Heritage Convention is based on shared responsibilities and international collaboration, addressing the needs in a transboundary context can be challenging. The site is also an example of the challenges associated with rapid economic development and exploitation of natural resources, while protecting the heritage assets for the benefit of present and future generations. In addition, the enlargement of the European Union in 2004 presents additional challenges, as the EU border crosses the site.[6] This situation makes the transfer from one side to the other more complicated, restricts visitor movement, and reduces the potential for collaboration.

## Protecting and managing World Heritage cultural landscapes

*Protected landscapes are cultural landscapes, ...[as they] have co-evolved with human societies. They are areas where the natural landscape has been transformed by human actions and the landscape qualities have shaped the way of life of the people. All management approaches to these areas must be based on a clear understanding of this, often complex, inter-relationship* (Beresford, 2003).

---

[6] It is not the only World Heritage site with this problem; Bialowieza Forest between Poland and Belarus is another example.

With the inclusion of the cultural landscapes category in 1992, far-reaching changes were also made to the management and legal provisions and other paragraphs of the Operational Guidelines. It became possible to nominate a site after the guidelines were modified to recognise traditional protection or management mechanisms. The site was considered eligible if there were "adequate legal and/or traditional protection and management mechanisms to ensure the conservation of the nominated cultural properties or cultural landscapes. The existence of protective legislation at the national, provincial or municipal levels and/or a well established contractual or traditional protection as well as of adequate management and/or planning control mechanisms is therefore essential.... Assurances of the effective implementation of these laws and/or contractual and/or traditional protection as well as of these management mechanisms are also expected."[7] In 1998 the Operational Guidelines were further modified to recognise traditional management mechanisms and customary law as acceptable forms of protection for natural heritage. Subsequently, for the first time in the history of the Convention, a traditionally managed natural site, East Rennell (Solomon Islands), was inscribed on the World Heritage List in 1998.

In 1992, for the first time, the involvement of local people in the nomination process was recognised as necessary and changes were introduced accordingly into the Operational Guidelines. Paragraph 14 was changed to "Participation of local people in the nomination process is essential to make them feel a shared responsibility with the State Party in the maintenance of the site". The involvement of local people was further strengthened in the new Operational Guidelines of 2004.

For the first time the word "sustainable" appeared in the text of the Operational Guidelines with "sustainable land-use". This addition was discussed at the World Heritage Committee meeting in December 1992 and the "spirit" of the Earth Summit, the Rio Conference, was evident in the debates. The conservation of World Heritage cultural landscapes can demonstrate the principles of sustainable land use and of the maintenance of local cultural and biological diversity, which should pervade the management of the surrounding environment. The management of cultural and natural World Heritage can be a standard-setter for the conservation of the environment as a whole, by establishing exemplars of what is required elsewhere. It can also help to reinforce the standing of heritage conservation at national and local levels.

## Conclusions

This review of the past thirty years of implementation of the World Heritage Convention reveals a broadened interpretation of heritage. The inclusion of cultural landscapes and, in particular, continuing and associative landscapes, has changed the perception and the practice of the Convention. This evolution in the interpretation of the World Heritage Convention represents only the beginning of recognition of the complexity and wealth of diverse values, including intangible values, in relation to protected areas, and in particular to sites of outstanding universal value. An inclusive approach is crucial for the designation and management of World Heritage sites in order to benefit people living in and around these sites, the conservation community, and humanity as a whole.

---

[7]  UNESCO 2002, paragraph 24; The new Operational Guidelines.

World Heritage sites generally are cornerstones of national and international conservation strategies. World Heritage cultural landscapes have provided a new interpretation of the "combined works of nature and man" in the World Heritage Convention. Adrian Phillips has traced the paradigm changes over the decades since the first World Parks Congress, and a parallel development has occurred in the implementation of the World Heritage Convention (Phillips, 2003a).

Although much progress has been made, new challenges lie ahead and there are several opportunities to be considered including to:

- create new institutional linkages between international instruments and also networks among protected area agencies to fully explore the relationships between the different categories and protection systems. Such complementary relationships might be formalized through close links between the World Heritage Convention and other international agreements such as the European Landscape Convention;

- enhance new partnerships, as recommended by the Venice celebration on thirty years of the World Heritage Convention (see UNESCO, 2003 and further discussion below);

- enlarge the circle to share information about protected area systems and cultural landscapes, in particular on achievements, success stories and model cases; and

- explore World Heritage best practice sites as cornerstones for sustainable local and regional development.

World Heritage can be considered a role model paralleling the development of the IUCN Category V Protected Landscape/Seascape. In cultural landscapes specifically, the local communities are acknowledged with the (co-)responsibility in managing the sites. However, as we can see from the examples there are many challenges lying ahead as cultural landscapes are dynamic systems and have to be economically and socially viable to survive. Some of the challenges, however, go beyond the means of the local communities. The effects of EU enlargement on agricultural change and economic relations, the impacts of mining and oil exploration, the rapid social changes through continued urbanization and sprawl, pollution and environmental degradation require new collaborative efforts and partnerships. Even so, the catalytic effect of landscape designations cannot be underestimated, as they can have an immediate effect on cultural identity and pride, and on potential partnerships and innovative conservation approaches.

The participants in the international workshop *Cultural Landscapes – the Challenges of Conservation* at the occasion of the 30th anniversary of the World Heritage Convention in Ferrara (Italy, November 2002), concluded that "Cultural landscape management and conservation processes bring people together in caring for their collective identity and heritage, and provide a shared local vision within a global context. Local communities need therefore to be involved in every aspect of the identification, planning and management of the areas, as they are the most effective guardians of the landscape heritage. The outstanding landscapes are selected examples, which could offer stewardship models in effective management and excellence in conservation practices" (UNESCO, 2003).

# 4. From pre-assumptions to a 'just world conserving nature': the role of Category VI in protecting landscapes[1]

*Claudio C. Maretti in collaboration with Lucia H. O. Wadt,*
*Daisy A. P. Gomes-Silva, Wanda T. P. de V. Maldonado,*
*Rosely A. Sanches, Francisco Coutinho and Severino da S. Brito*

## Introduction

This chapter discusses the role of the protected area Category VI in the conservation of landscapes. It presents perspectives on the concept of landscape and different approaches to protection of landscapes. Landscape is a concrete and a representational reality. Broader than just nature conservation with an emphasis on the cultural values of a place, the protected landscape approach must include participatory processes and integration within regional planning and management.

With a focus on Category VI, this chapter briefly reviews the evolution of protected areas – from isolated parks to systems of protected areas, and from strict protection to integration with sustainable development. Two case studies from Brazil are presented here to highlight the contribution of Category VI protected areas to landscape conservation. The Brazilian experience with extractive reserves is discussed, given their special place in the history of Category VI protected areas.

## Landscape

During the Middle Ages 'landscape' was understood to mean an area of land controlled by a lord or inhabited by a social group. Late in the nineteenth century the sense of this term was "a portion of land or territory which the eye can comprehend in a single view" (Duncan, in Johnston *et al.,* 2000). Landscapes may also be understood as 'reduced models', offering a notion of ensemble.

Although concrete, landscapes are mostly processes, defined economically and culturally by people. Landscapes are located in the social consciousness – which observes, chooses, defines, delineates, builds. Therefore, they belong to the domain of representations – where choices are made (Di Méo, 1998). Different social groups may appropriate the 'same' space in different ways (Humphrey, 1995). Landscapes represent history, and are part of on-going living processes (Cosgrove, in Johnston *et al.,* 2000; Hirsch, 1995). For a social group, the consciousness of its space is important – from that, and the exercise of power, a territory is accomplished (Claval, 1995; Santos, 1996; Maretti, 2002). Landscapes are one of the

---

[1] From the IUCN Vision Statement (2000), which notes the importance of working toward "a just world that values and conserves nature."

privileged expressions of territories – their image, live and real, sensorial, affective, symbolic and material.

Some authors may take only the natural components to comprehend the 'natural landscapes,' but 'landscape ecology' investigates relationships between its physical, ecological and cultural components, and interactions between the temporal and spatial aspects (Goudie, in Thomas and Goudie, 2000). It should not be forgotten that a landscape is, as well, a succession of cultural imprints and a representation. But, perhaps having gone sometimes too much into the semiotic qualities of landscapes, their 'substantive' aspects should not be allowed to disappear (Maretti, 2002). In fact, landscape should be expressed as a "polysemic term referring to the appearance of an area, the assemblage of objects used to produce that appearance, and the area itself" (Duncan, *op. cit.*).

## Landscape approaches

The concept of landscape is used in environmental management, through its different meanings, and in various applications – though not always in a coherent way. Landscape is an expression of understanding the earth's surface and ecological processes. There is a functioning of the landscape, a 'landscape physiology'. In the permanent work of nature conservation, we tend to make an artificial separation between the social, cultural and natural elements and processes. Landscape, as a tool and a concept, helps us to understand the relationships among them. (Examples: Cormier-Salem, 1999; Maretti, 1989.)

Landscapes and 'areas-with-natural-values-and-human-use' have been considered as important by societies all over the world. Some experts claim that these kinds of landscapes do not contribute to 'biodiversity preservation,' while others claim their importance as part of an overall nature conservation strategy. (Phillips, 2003a; IUCN, 1994. Examples: UICN and Guinea-Bissau, 1993; Szabo and Smyth, 2003.) Landscape, as an outcome of interactions between humankind and nature, reflecting relations among social groups, the heritage of social history and all the values attributed, represents an interest of conservation. (Mujica Barreda, 2002; UNESCO, 2002. Example: Britto de Moraes *et al.,* 1997).[2]

The protected landscape approach also means that planning and management of protected areas must broaden the area considered beyond the area of conservation interest to include its surroundings (CBD, 1999; Miller and Hamilton, 1999; Crofts *et al.,* 1999). The time may have come to consider nature, history, resources, culture, science, local communities' knowledge, sustainable use techniques, and social welfare as all part of the 'patrimony of humankind' – and to integrate all these values into management methodologies, with specific emphasis according to particular conservation needs.

## Protected areas and the IUCN Categories

The term 'protected area' may be commonly understood as any area protected in some way. But the *stricto sensu* definition used legally and among experts, and as it is considered here, has

---

[2]  The World Heritage Convention innovated in including cultural and natural values within the same international agreement. Natural and cultural values and sites were separated, but 'cultural landscapes' came to light as a possible common approach – unfortunately still in theory.

objectives directed to nature conservation – including related cultural values (not dissociable from, but not replacing the natural ones). International agreements do not differ much in terms of protected area definitions; all consider the nature conservation objectives, specific measures for designation, regulation and management, and spatial definition of these areas. They mention the importance of legal declaration and governmental management, but also accept other 'effective means' or 'traditional' management. (IUCN, 1994; CBD, 1992; UNESCO, 1999; Chape *et al.*, 2003.)[3]

Based on the orientation of the protected areas field over the last decades, it might appear that natural values are based only on biological diversity. Nevertheless, long before this concept was introduced, areas were protected with the intention of nature conservation, for instance in national parks or in what are now being recognised as 'community-conserved areas' (see the chapter by Barrow and Pathak in this volume). Indeed, most of the important protected areas of a certain age do not explicitly mention 'biodiversity preservation' – but today play an important role in contributing to this goal. Besides the protected areas that are explicitly designated and managed for this purpose, there are also many others that contribute and support it in important ways. Biological diversity should be taken as an important indicator of the natural values to be protected, but not as the only important value or the sole objective for protection. Attention should be directed towards ecological processes and environmental services as well. Landscapes are important not only for their biological diversity values and related values, but also for their geographic features, paleontological contents and cultural heritage, among others.[4]

Although having neither clear criteria nor a classification system, the aesthetic values of landscapes are also significant, and should remain as a window for expressing cultural impressions and desires towards nature – the very meaning of heritage. And natural heritage should be considered as cultural appreciation of different natural elements and manifestations. It should lead to a better understanding and acceptance of the diverse ways that different cultures classify and attribute value to their landscapes. The landscape is an ideal common ground for this kind of intercultural cross-reference, which is needed to overcome cultural bias and domination, and to embrace the views of diverse social groups.

Some stairs have been climbed in the evolving process of protected area systems and their management. From protection of specific and restricted sites (which has frequently led to the pitfall of these sites becoming 'islands' of conservation), protected areas have evolved to encompass new approaches. These include: declaring larger protected areas; imposing restrictions on activities on adjacent lands; extending their limits through buffer zones; diversifying objectives, and, accordingly, using distinct management categories; and managing the

---

[3] Examples of agreements, institutions or documents with international legitimacy include among others: IUCN World Commission on Protected Areas; *United Nations List of Protected Areas*; Convention on Biological Diversity; World Heritage Convention; and World Conservation Monitoring Centre.

[4] "The role of protected areas has become as much about the protection of processes – such as supply of water, prevention of erosion and maintenance of human lifestyles – as about the protection of species. [...] The full use of these six categories allows a more inclusive and flexible approach to designing protected areas systems at the national level. [...] A wider definition of protected areas has a number of advantages. [...] They are likely to lead to new management options in a wide range of situations, and open up the possibility of innovative partnerships between conservationists and other interest groups, such as indigenous peoples, the tourism industry and small-scale agriculture." (Dudley and Stolton *et al.*, 1998).

protected areas for different values, including biological diversity, natural resources, environmental services, sustainable use, and landscapes with some degree of human use. There is increasing emphasis on integration – into bioregions, mosaics of protected areas, ecological networks and conservation corridors, and individual protected areas considered as part of protected area systems.[5]

It is thus increasingly accepted that mechanisms and areas designated for landscape conservation, with some degree of human use, and the direct sustainable use of natural resources, should be included as part of an overall nature conservation strategy. Another consequence has been increasing stakeholder participation and involvement. In particular, local communities, including indigenous peoples, have been playing an increasing role in collaborative management, and have seen their rights more respected – or claimed to be respected.[6]

In retrospect, it can also be observed that nature conservation objectives have moved from the protection of hunting grounds, landscape conservation, and the protection of resources, towards the conservation of beautiful scenery and national symbols, conservation of ecological processes, and protection of biological diversity, and then back to the consideration of landscapes and direct sustainable use of natural resources. Therefore, conservation of 'areas-with-natural-values-and-human-use' – such as 'landscapes with some degree of human use' and 'areas with direct sustainable use of natural resources'– have been fitting in *stricto sensu* protected area categories for a long time. But this is also the case – and even more clearly so – in the many kinds of *lato sensu* protected areas that exist, such as community-conserved areas, and laws and mechanisms that many countries have for heritage protection.[7]

In considering the international management categories for protected areas – moving beyond what is written in manuals – it is important to understand the regional and social context in which the archetypes of these categories were developed. For instance, while Category II clearly has objectives related to nature conservation and tourism, it is important to realize that national parks were first established also as national symbols – meant to create or reinforce the identity of a 'nation' and its territory. One can best understand the need for a subdivision such

---

[5] Some definitions related to protected areas: A mosaic is a set of adjacent or close protected areas, potentially of different categories, and preferentially with common conservation goals or focus, whose management is integrated – for instance, by a sole administration or a common strategy, or through an integrated committee. An ecological network is a set of areas, not necessarily close to each other, but composing an ecologically important ensemble related to certain conservation goals – for instance, a series of nesting sites of a population of marine turtles, a series of resting sites in a route of migratory birds, or a series of sites showing the genetic diversity of a palm-tree species. The bioregional approach is regional management, considering different factors – for instance natural, social and institutional factors – but with emphasis on the conservation of biological elements. A conservation corridor (plausibly different from the traditional ecological corridor) represents a large area – usually, but not necessarily, longer in one direction then in the other – including protected areas as its core zones, but also other kind of uses and areas, and with an overall nature conservation agenda preferably with integrated management – for instance, through an integrated management committee.

[6] Phillips (2003a, among others) shows beautifully the evolution from the 'classical model' of protected areas into a 'modern paradigm,' with an emphasis on the *stricto sensu* protected areas.

[7] *Latu sensu* protected areas refer to areas outside of the official systems of *stricto sensu* protected areas. These include areas where communities have a conservation interest, as well as those areas protected in some way under official law but not part of systems of *stricto sensu* protected areas.

as Category Ib when one considers the probable demand for recognising existing 'wilderness areas' in North America. A similar kind of influence applies also in the case of Categories V and VI. The Category V (Protected Landscapes/Seascapes) can best be understood by looking at the European context, where the majority of protected areas of this category is still found. Even outside this region, the original context dominates the model, while as Phillips (2002) writes, the "principles of Category V protected areas are, in fact, universal and potentially relevant in all regions of the world." It is, therefore, important that we look beyond a European model of landscape to be protected, and consider the special characteristics of the local context – social, cultural and natural – when applying this category in other regions.

## Category VI

Originally, there were no plans to include Category VI in the most recent version of the IUCN protected area management categories (IUCN, 1994). Based on the so-called 'technical recommendations,' the system then under development included Categories I–V of the previous classification system. Category VI was not included, as it was not considered of enough importance for 'biodiversity conservation', even with the system also influenced by demands placed on IUCN – The World Conservation Union to take into account issues such as the interests of indigenous peoples, protected landscapes, and wilderness areas. What changed the situation were the events in the Amazon region, particularly in the Brazilian Amazon (see Box 1).

It should be noted that the 'hot' happenings in the Brazilian Amazon occurred not long before and not far away from some of the meetings where the IUCN protected area management categories were being reviewed, and very likely influenced the demands to include a sixth category in the evolving new system.[8] Ultimately, a new category was introduced, based on the need to consider the kind of protected area that would be managed for the "long-term protection and maintenance of biological diversity," and also the maintenance of "a sustainable flow of natural products and services to meet community needs" (IUCN, 1994) (see Appendix 1).

But, in fact, the importance of this category – at least in the case of the 'extractive reserves' of Brazil – is related not only to the "sustainable flow of products and services for the community" (IUCN, 1994). Category VI also highlights the key role played by local communities in conservation strategies, and therefore reinforces recognition of the potential to join sustainable development with nature conservation.[9]

---

[8] These meetings included the IVth International Congress on National Parks and Other Protected Areas, Caracas 1992; and the IUCN General Assembly, Buenos Aires 1994.

[9] It is interesting to note that, following the classification matrix (IUCN, 1994), Category VI is the most complete and is at the first level in terms of nature protection – defined through objectives related to the "preservation of species and genetic diversity" and "maintenance of environmental services" as well as the "sustainable use of resources from natural ecosystems." But it is curious that, although the category origins and objectives are intrinsically linked to local communities, the maintenance of cultural or 'traditional' attributes is not considered a primary objective in that matrix.

---

## Box 1.   The Phylogeny of Extractive Reserves[10]

### Peoples and the Amazon

The Amazonian region has long been the habitat of several indigenous peoples. As studies continue to show, their marks on the landscape are seen throughout the jungle and other ecosystems of the Amazon. These remote places, still very much the domain of indigenous peoples, attracted more attention – from 'official society' – for its new economic interest, with the growing exploitation of rubber over the last two centuries. Distinct waves of colonization, in the 19th and 20th centuries, increasing during the 'global wars', brought peasants to exploit rubber under the orders of concessionaires, which tended to expel the indigenous communities. But in between selling booms, these areas were abandoned by the concessionaires, leaving the previously recruited workers alone in the jungle.

The rubber-tappers, who had since arrived, were in frequent dispute with the indigenous peoples, but became companions under the same conditions, and proposed alliances as 'the forest peoples'. Besides living under the same jungle conditions, at that time the main threat to both groups came from outside the forest: the advancement of the agricultural frontier – threats from the general colonization trends and their related consequences of deforestation and land-taking. The rubber-tappers' position was to face the deforestation process head-on. Through the so-called *empates* or resistance groups, workers, often with their families, stood in front of the 'caterpillar' tractors in order to prevent deforestation – and to keep the conditions of their life and work: the exploitation of rubber within the forest.[11]

The tragic event that brought international attention to the extractive reserves was the assassination of Francisco 'Chico' Mendes in 1988. Coming from the labour movement, Chico Mendes was able to gain the attention, also, of those in the environmental movement. The evolution of this situation made possible an amalgam between the locally developed (i.e., within the jungle) 'labour union spirit', which was concerned with defending their work conditions, and 'environmentalism', at that time arising in cities, which was concerned with defending the tropical forests and trying to understand better how to build positive linkages with local communities. Born from that synergy, a new concept was proposed: the extractive reserve.

Cont.

---

[10]   Its name comes from the Brazilian term *extrativismo*, meaning activities related to the collecting, gathering, harvesting or extracting of products – generally excluding mining. 'Extractivism', therefore, expresses the activities of local communities in harvesting products associated with renewable natural resources. 'Extractivists' are those local communities or rural workers engaged in those activities.

[11]   With the declining interest in Amazon rubber (because of growing production from farms in Southeast Asia, or less demand), and the subsequent fall in price and production, during the beginning of 20th century and in between the world wars, many *seringalistas* decided to 'sell' 'their' areas (in fact, pass on their land or rubber exploitation concessions) to farmers. These farmers were interested in cattle-grazing and agriculture, without any concern for the workers who lived there, tending to deforest the area and banish the collectors. Thus, many of these workers, backed up by the labour unions of rural workers, decided not to leave the area: they stood up against deforestation and expulsion from the land through the *empates* described above – getting involved in violent confrontations, resulting in the death of many leaders. The rubber tappers were not innocent about their living context (and the violent way of doing politics or social disputes there), but the actions were intended to be more symbolic, taking the form of awareness-building and campaigns of non-violence, facing the signs of deforestation. Nevertheless, they had to face violent reactions, including several assassinations, of which those of Wilson de Souza Pinheiro and Francisco 'Chico' Mendes became the most famous and historically important ones. (If locally or nationally the confrontation of 'free rubber-tappers' was known after the death of Pinheiro in 1978, the unfortunate happening that brought international attention to the extractive reserves was the assassination of Mendes in 1988).

---

## Box 1.  The Phylogeny of Extractive Reserves (cont.)

### Reasons

The aim of extractive reserves is to combine nature conservation with sustainable development for local communities. Formal demands for the creation of such areas were first made in 1985, at the first national meeting of rubber-tappers, but within the context of agrarian reform, with the aim of recognising land rights for the people that lived and used these lands. Some years later, in 1989, as the country's rural labour union and the environmentalist movements grew closer, the Brazilian government included extractive reserves in its national policy for the environment, and subsequently enacted legislation enabling and regulating these areas.

A primary reason for the extractive reserves' existence (considered within the related legislation) was to maintain the area's vegetation in conditions for sustainable use by the local communities – i.e., the extractivism conditions. In the case of the rubber-tappers, this meant to keep the forest standing and ready for rubber extraction, as well as possible extraction of non-timber forest products (e.g., Brazil nuts) and complementary activities such as small-scale agriculture.

A second point was related to the permanence on the land of those communities that had used it for decades and wanted to keep living there and maintain their use of the natural resources. With the abandonment of the communities and rubber exploitation by the 'bosses', the conditions for their land or rubber exploitation concessions had legitimately expired. The government, for its part, preferred to have the land under its domain, in order to avoid land commercialization and the decline of the local communities, and to maintain the conditions for nature conservation.

A third point was the need to create or maintain the conditions for nature conservation and sustainable use. According to the legislation, the declaration and establishment of an extractive reserve could only be done on an area 'traditionally' used by local communities and only after they had demanded it. The local communities needed to be organized and represented through formal associations, so that management of the protected area could be done collaboratively by the government and the local communities.[12]

Cont.

---

[12] There has been a debate on how to define 'traditional' in relation to communities, to ways of living, and to uses of resources. This debate has no final formal positions or consensus, and not without problems the definitions have been considered in relation to time (some decades or generations – at least two), and in relation to the knowledge of nature, the use of natural resources, or to a non-environmentally degrading relationship between people and nature.

An interesting point would be to imagine how the region would have been evolved without the extractive reserves. Certainly, without the resistance of the local communities, led by the rubber tappers' labour union movement, there would immediately have been a significant increase in deforestation. This would have happened in connection with what one could call 'bad agriculture' for the trend was to deforest areas in order to create pastures, establish land tenure and support cattle grazing, which was not very productive and which generated little employment. As a result, the forest would be cut down, the workers would be jobless, local communities would decline, and, last but not least, the local and national economy would lose, because the value of the forest and its products is higher than the income from this kind of agriculture. As well as social degradation, valuable knowledge of nature and natural resource management would be lost, along with the cultural heritage of the area. Within a few years, assuming environmentalism were to grow, demands on Amazon conservation possibly would have increased and some strict preservation protected areas might have been declared. With those social processes underway, a continuous increase in the social stress possibly might raise important political barriers to the effective social-political support for nature conservation, or activities might be pursued that directly undermine protected areas (such as poaching, forest fire-setting, etc.). Both social development and environmental conservation would have suffered and lost.

---

**Box 1.   The Phylogeny of Extractive Reserves (cont.)**

**Characteristics**

Extractive reserves, combining nature conservation and sustainable use of natural resources by local communities, fit in with Category VI of the IUCN system of protected area management categories. They were included in the Brazilian National System of Protected Areas, established in 2000. The declaration of an extractive reserve is made following the demand of the local communities that have used the area for a long time ('traditionally'). The government is the owner of the land, but the local communities maintain collective rights of use. The respective governmental department or agency (IBAMA, or the state environmental institution, or even the municipal one) is responsible for the management of the protected area, but this must be done in a collaborative manner with local communities. Nevertheless, more than 'collaborative management', the management of extractive reserves resembles that of a 'community-conserved area'.[13]

The two first extractive reserves were declared in 1990: Alto Juruá, with around 506,000 hectares (ha); and Chico Mendes, with 971,000ha. By the beginning of 2004 there were 31 extractive reserves declared, with a total of 5,171,000ha, mostly in the Amazon. Obviously there are distinct levels of community organization, among other varying conditions – as happens with any other protected area or category. Today, governmental institutions and the rubber tappers' organizations face new challenges. These include the implementation of institutional structures and incentives for sustainable development, and the need to provide an adequate level of income to people in the forest – while maintaining the protection of tropical landscapes.

Extractive reserves are formal, people-centred protected areas. This kind of protected area is declared not despite people, but because of them. As an approach combining nature conservation and social development, extractive reserves are premised on, and legitimized by, the presence of local people and their social organizations, seeking their empowerment.

*Sources*: Wadt *et al.*, 2003; IBAMA, 2004; Pinzón Rueda, 2004; Maretti *et al.*, 2003.

# How Category VI is Protecting Landscapes: Case-studies from Brazil

Two case studies are presented here to exemplify the role of Category VI in protecting landscapes and seascapes. Because events in Brazil contributed significantly to the decision to include Category VI in the IUCN protected area classification system, and in a sense helped to define what the category is, two Brazilian cases were chosen. At the outset, the creation of extractive reserves in Brazil was related primarily to social organizations and nature in the Amazon region; the Chico Mendes Extractive Reserve was one of the first reserves to be declared. The idea then progressed towards the coastal zone, and the Mandira Extractive Reserve offers an example where more concrete work was done.[14]

---

[13]   After the *Reservas Extravistas* declaration, the local communities receive a 'real use concession' – with rights to the land and natural resources – conditioned to a 'plan of utilization', proposed by the local communities. Once the plan was also approved by IBAMA, they became co-managers of the reserve. According to Brazilian laws, any governmental level (federal, state or municipal) of the federation may declare any of the protected area categories established with the national system.

[14]   According to Brazilian law, there are other categories corresponding to the international Category VI – the 'extractive reserve' being the more interesting in terms of its origin in social movements.

## The Chico Mendes Extractive Reserve, Brazilian Amazon

As a typical example of the history that led to the creation of the category of extractive reserve, the Chico Mendes Extractive Reserve (*Reserva Extrativista Chico Mendes* – RECM), in the western part of the Brazilian Amazon, is very much a product of local communities resisting deforestation, in this case in opposition to the intentions of the forest colonizing *latifundium* farmers, as mentioned above. The resistance of the local communities in this area continued until their occupation of lands was consolidated.

The Chico Mendes Extractive Reserve is located in Acre,[15] and represents an area of 971,000ha, making it the largest extractive reserve in the country. According to Wadt *et al.* (2003), CNS (2004), and Costa (2004), among others, the dominant vegetation is tropical humid forest, which is relatively open, with areas of bamboo, palm-trees and lianas, and a small area of tropical humid dense forest. The topographical relief is gentle, with low hills predominating. During the 1990s the estimated population of the area was 9,000 inhabitants, in around 1,100 *colocações*.

A *seringal* represents a whole area of rubber exploitation, made up of *colocações*, which, in turn, compose a community. A *colocação* is a family production unit with extractive activities, defined by the rubber paths – usually from 3–7 rubber paths in each *colocação*. There are no pre-defined limits for a *colocação*, the customary rights are mostly related to traditional use and might be different depending on the uses of the land and natural resources. An *estrada de seringa* (rubber path) is made by the preparation and work on the trees for rubber exploitation. Usually this exploitation is associated with the collection of Brazil nuts. The rubber trees *Hevea brasiliensis* and Brazil nut trees *Bertolletia excelsa* define the limits to customary rights related to use of these two resources, but not necessarily those related to other natural resources.

To facilitate its management, the Chico Mendes Extractive Reserve was subdivided into three areas, under the supervision of different local community associations of which AMOPREB is one, representing about 220 associated individuals, organized into 22 smaller groups. Currently there is a participatory management structure, with smaller groups meeting for specific decisions related to activities in the extractive reserve. In the RECM the utilization plan sets an upper limit of 10% of deforested area per household, and this includes activities on lands such as residences, backyards, pastures, agricultural and abandoned fields and agro-forestry plots. The plan also includes strict regulations on the 'extraction' of rubber and Brazil nuts and the development of management plans for new forest products. Timber 'extraction' and hunting are restricted to the residents' subsistence use.

As of 1996, only 0.65% of the RECM area was deforested, representing around 606ha. Although the areas with major deforestation are not usually chosen to be protected, the data demonstrate that in the chosen areas, the communities' use, both before and after the existence of the RECM, did not damage the forest as much as happened outside of these areas – thus supporting the idea of nature conservation through a protected area "managed to provide also a sustainable flow of products and services for the community".

---

[15] Acre is a small State (152,581.39km$^2$) byAmazonian standards, in the northwest part of the country, and with a unique history, because it was obtained from Bolivia due to the occupation of the forest by the rubber tappers. After a history of social conflicts, the current state government calls itself the 'government from the forest'.

A rubber tapper in the Chico Mendes Extractive Reserve, one of the first extractive reserves to be declared in Brazil. Extractive reserves combine nature conservation and sustainable use of natural resources by local people. *Claudio Maretti*

Indeed, following Ferreira *et al.* (in press), studies have systematically shown that deforestation rates are significantly lower inside *lato sensu* protected areas (considering also indigenous lands) than outside them, even when the PAs are not well implemented in the field. In the Brazilian Amazon estimates for 2001 of the deforestation was approximately 10 times greater outside protected areas than within them – taking into account all categories. For example, in the State of Acre the deforested area outside protected areas (all categories) was 16.57% while inside these areas it was 1.26%. In the case of federally protected areas with management objectives related to sustainable use (mostly Categories V and VI), the area was only slightly higher, at 1.4%.

We might then conclude that the communities' use is not so damaging as other ones – referring mostly to activities in those areas proposed (and accepted) to become sustainable use protected areas. Those areas, even taking into account the communities' uses before and after the declaration of the extractive reserve, were able to maintain lower deforestation rates than is the case outside their boundaries. Therefore, the declaration of this kind of area clearly represents a correct choice for nature conservation in comparison with non-declaration. Not to mention the social and related benefits, the communities' use supports conservation results because it discouraged other more high-impact uses. The declaration of the extractive reserve helped to keep the local communities in place, and brought them assistance in improving their natural resources management towards better use, social benefits, and nature conservation.[16]

Social development within extractive reserves, including community facilities and services, are an essential part of meeting the extractive reserve's objectives and providing the right conditions for the local communities to remain in the area. For those harvesting forest products,

---

[16] To the possible claim that strict preservation protected areas might have been declared in such places instead of these protected areas that accommodate sustainable use, two other points may be mentioned. It is not feasible to suppose that societies could accept the establishment of enormous areas of strict preservation PAs. And the reaction when established against local peoples could result in major damages. In several cases it can be seen that land conflicts have led to setting forest fires, for instance in West Africa (UICN and Guinea-Bissau, 1993), or other kinds of pressures or 'illegal' interference. Phillips (in Borrini-Feyerabend *et al.,* 2002) was right to affirm "[…] the iron rule that no protected area can succeed for long in the teeth of local opposition."

such as rubber and nuts, a primary goal of extractive reserves has been to obtain land and resource rights to improve their forest-based lifestyle. Another goal is to improve their well-being and that of their families by, for example, increasing their income through marketing sustainable forest products and other activities, improving health care and obtaining better access to education and transportation. Nevertheless, the level of social organization within and among the reserves is extremely varied, depending on the history of each site. While in some areas local communities enthusiastically participate in the collective activities and opportunities that social organizations provide, in other areas they are still caught in the expectation that somebody will supply their needs, and retain a degree of mistrust towards organizing.[17]

In this case, as in others, the economy of the extractive reserve is not a completely resolved issue. Although extractive reserves have led to political emancipation for these communities, the economic results are still insufficient, including at the family level. In some cases, instead of diversifying their use of non-timber forest products (NTFP), rubber-tappers are gradually abandoning them in favour of other forms of land use, such as commercial agriculture, small-scale cattle-grazing and timber exploration, and are working for payment on other lands. Nevertheless, studies and management projects have been conducted on potential forest products, such as vegetal oils, palm-hearts, palm-fruit juices, forest seeds and medicinal plants, among others (e.g., *copaíba Copaifera* spp., *açaí Euterpe precatoria*, *patauá Oenocarpus bataua*, *buriti Mauritia flexuosa*, *andiroba Carapa guianensis*), which offer the potential, in the near future, to improve the income related to commercial harvest of NTFP.

As with several other extractive reserves, the Chico Mendes Extractive Reserve is the result of the rubber tappers' (*seringueiros*) claim of lands for extraction, but also of the fact that environment and land-tenure policies in Brazil have adopted new models. Along with its many social benefits, and its relevance for nature conservation, the extractive reserve is the most representative mechanism for a new development model for the Amazon. Not only does it offer tangible results in supporting labour opportunities, securing land tenure and conserving biological diversity, the model was built on the foundation of the cultural relationship between social groups and their natural space – in other words, their landscape. And, after the 'traditional' use, the declaration of the Chico Mendes Extractive Reserve, a Category VI protected area, reinforces the conditions for the area's management in a way that meets nature conservation, as well as economic, objectives.

## Mandira Extractive Reserve, South-eastern Brazil

In the rural villages of Cananéia, in south-eastern Brazil, marine-related activities are important, along with small-scale agriculture and land extractivism, in a complementary relationship linked to natural cycles, natural resource availability and market conditions (see Maldonado (2002), Sales and Moreira (1994), São Paulo and IBAMA (1996), and Maretti (1989), among others). Fishing has a long history in the region, but oyster harvesting has been of economic importance for at least 30 years, and is mostly based on familial organization. Some areas of the estuary-lagoon region are particularly important in terms of their natural productivity.

---

[17] Some analysts may consider that those could be signs of the failure of sustainable use protected areas. Astonishingly, this kind of rigour is not used when considering other models, either more liberal or free market economic activities on the one hand, or the strict preservation protected areas on the other. Partial failure in some cases does not necessarily prove that the model is not valid.

Because the area is considered to be of high environmental importance, representatives of coastal local communities have participated in several fora and other activities related to regional conservation. In fact, they have been interested in maintaining the environmental conditions and quality of marine products that support their livelihoods. In certain areas, local communities claimed the responsibility for the management of natural resources or areas that were protected.[18]

Taking into account the local communities' traditional management practices, and the initial recognition of the region's importance in the 1970s and 80s, a starting point for the history of the Mandira Extractive Reserve *(Reserva Extrativista do Mandira)* might be the period from 1984–1989, when a participatory process of coastal zone regional planning was conducted in the area. This initiative was reinforced during 1994–1997 by the collaborative planning and zoning process for the Cananéia-Iguape-Peruíbe APA. (See chapter by Britto de Moraes and Lino for more on the Cananéia-Iguape-Peruíbe Environment Protected Area, or APA – *área de proteção ambiental*). A pilot project launched in 1994, described below, led ultimately to the creation of the Mandira Extractive Reserve.

While most of the region's local fishermen have a good understanding of natural processes, those in some communities, such as Mandira, have a deeper knowledge, stronger social organization, and live in and explore areas with more ecological importance. Those were among the reasons that the Mandira community was chosen for this pilot project – under the leadership of the São Paulo State environmental institutions, but with several other important partners.[19]

The Mandiras have been established in the area since the 18th century, relying mostly on agriculture originally, but gradually shifting to seafood harvesting, due to changing economic conditions, pressures for land and environmental restrictions. Mandira is a *quilombola* community – slave-descendants – having collective rights over the land.[20]

Before the project, the market chain for oysters was dominated by brokers, who paid little regard to legislation or to hygiene and health standards for shellfish processing. There was overexploitation of some oyster stocks. Local communities felt ashamed of their work activities. Also, outside workers tended to 'invade' the region in search of natural resources (including shellfish, crabs and fish), and with little regard for local conditions.

---

[18] The State of São Paulo is the wealthiest in the country, but the Ribeira Valley is today its poorest region. Composed of mountains, wetlands, islands and coastal ecosystems, and including important remnants of Atlantic Forest and mangroves, IUCN *et al.* (1980) considered the Iguape-Cananéia-Paranaguá estuary region to be a region of high importance for nature conservation in the world (see also Maretti, 1989).

[19] The institutions and persons that collaborated are too many to list here, but some examples or among the most important are: Forest Foundation of São Paulo (FF); the Fisheries Research Institute of the State of São Paulo (IP); Mandira local community association; COOPEROSTRA – the Cooperative of Oysters Producers from Cananéia, São Paulo; NUPAUB – USP (University of São Paulo) Centre for Studies on Peoples and Wetlands; Gaia Ambiental; Secretariat for the Environment of the State of São Paulo (SMA-SP); Fisheries Pastoral Commission (CPP); Brazilian Ministry for the Environment (MMA); IBAMA-CNPT – IBAMA (the Brazilian environment federal agency) National Commission on Traditional Communities; Margaret Mee Botanical Foundation; Adolfo Lutz Institute; Ribeira Valley Inter-Municipal Development Consortium (CODIVAR); Shell; city of Cananéia; Ford Foundation; FUNBIO – the Brazilian Biodiversity Fund; World Vision; etc.

[20] This social group was officially recognised as slave-descendants *(quilombolas)* in Brazil in 2002. Therefore, following the 1988 National Constitution text, they received collective rights over their lands.

Fishermen tending nets, Brazil. For rural villages in the coastal region of Cananéia, in southeastern Brazil, maintaining environmental conditions and managing marine resources are essential for their livelihoods. *Clayton F. Lino*

In response to those problems, the local communities and environmental institutions looked for solutions. The extractive reserve model was found to be good enough to face the degrading conditions, helped by other legal definitions. But the process for the Mandira Extractive Reserve participatory proposal and the oyster regulation procedure took a long time (1994–2002), as is usual when ensuring adequate involvment of local communities – even considering that it takes much less time and leads to better results when built on the communities' knowledge and willingness. Among the necessary steps were the participatory discussion of regional problems, awareness-building within the main communities and on the part of lead people, debates on the recommended actions, and research to define appropriate solutions. Other steps included raising funds and finding other resources to put proposed actions into practice; solving legal problems, either by finding ways within the existing legal framework or elaborating new legal documents; and approaching and lobbying the authorities. It was also necessary to train local communities in new activities, search for markets, publicize the special characteristics and importance of sustainable production, and help them to begin selling the products themselves and managing these businesses.

The local project in Mandira had two main components: to implement an extractive reserve in the Mandira mangrove area; and to organize a locally controlled production chain for the harvest, processing and marketing of local oysters. The project met with some unanticipated difficulties, including the prejudice of some toward an activity viewed as 'primitive' in a so-called 'more developed' region of Brazil. On the other hand, productive partnerships developed between several institutions responsible for the process, and this unexpected response was important to the ultimate success of the project.

While the Mandira Extractive Reserve only achieved official designation in 2002, for about five years leading up that point the area was already *de facto* managed as an extractive reserve. As a coastal extractive reserve in Brazil's Southeast, it is rather small – particularly when compared with its counterparts in the Amazonian region. The extractive reserve represents some 1,175ha, mostly composed of mangroves, which are used by some 100 dwellers, basing their activity mainly on the collection of mangrove oysters *Crassostrea brasiliana.*

The project results include tangible benefits to the regional economy and the restoration of cultural values and environmental quality. Through the project, local communities that had been socially and economically oppressed and involuntarily had been provoking natural degradation, have become proud fishermen, who now take responsibility for their harvesting activities, working and environmental conditions, and the quality of their products. Also as a result, consumers have access to better and healthier products, while the harvesting and processing activities are now more environmentally sensitive. The local processing facility where the oysters are selected, cleaned and packed, now serves as the clearing-house not only for the products and for the overall production process, but for the social organization as well. The Mandiras are now widely seen as leaders in the Iguape-Cananéia estuary-lagoon region, building on their community's traditional knowledge and organizations, and as pioneers in this more interesting way of working.

A no less important result has been landscape conservation by the local communities – landscape as their own cultural reference, but also as beautiful scenery. This has not only permitted the maintenance and enhanced appreciation of their 'traditional' way of life, but also allowed mutually beneficial integration between seafood production and tourism, while maintaining the conditions for future generations to make their own choices.

The approach presented here restores extractivism to its proper place: that the knowledge and management practices of local communities are neither 'primitive' nor 'rudimentary'; they should not be despised, ignored nor idealized. The correct approach is one based on respecting, understanding and learning from them. Local communities are generally best able to improve the harvest and related production chains on which their livelihoods depend; they should be allowed to maintain control over these matters – and, consequently, over their own lives. At the same time, the need for capacity-building should not be neglected, as this can present new challenges. In fact, one of the major difficulties in the Mandira case was for the local communities to enter the market, and develop the entrepreneurial and administrative skills to create businesses and market their products.[21]

That is really what 'sustainable development' means, for it has its economic and ecological dimensions, but also its social and cultural ones – and, hopefully its political dimensions too – all integrated together and viewed from the perspective of long-term sustainability. Local communities' knowledge and social organization are at the very core of these possibilities, but appropriate nature conservation methods – including the adequate understanding, consideration and use of protected area categories V and VI and mosaics – are also extremely important.

---

[21] This process and the community management was recognised by the Equator Initiative (UNDP) in 2002 as one of the world's best and presented at the World Summit on Sustainable Development in Johannesburg 2002.

Child with bird, Brazil. *Clayton F. Lino*

The Iguapc-Cananéia-Paranaguá estuary-lagoon region – and the Ribeira Valley region as a whole – have a comprehensive approach to regional planning and management. It includes national and state parks (Category II), federal and state ecological stations (Category Ia), as well as two major environment protection areas, or APAs, (Category V), the management of which relies on transboundary cooperation between states. A portion of these protected areas is within the Southeast Atlantic Forest World Heritage site. However, the acceptance of an extractive reserve (Category VI), and the fact that it is located within an APA (Category V), was an important break-through in the process of real and effective implementation of sustainable development within this region of Brazil.

## Closing remarks

The cases discussed here show that, when appropriately addressed, local communities and their activities related to natural resources and sustainable development present an opportunity, rather than a problem, in developing an overall nature conservation strategy. When properly integrated, local communities are typically allies of nature conservation. However, simply relying on proposals to integrate local communities, zoning processes, or overly broad conservation strategies, may not be enough. Not infrequently there is a need for sharper and more specific tools with enough legal and political strength and offering practical possibilities. Provided that legitimacy is built into the process – either through autonomous control by local communities, or through their engagement in participatory processes led by respected governmental institutions – these tools can be promoted. However, the institutional existence of protected areas is also important, considering, for instance, their operational, as well as conceptual and legal, conditions. Therefore, there is a need for protected area management

---

**Box 2.  Some 'ingredients' for a 'landscape approach'; a preliminary summary**

The 'landscape approach' is a welcome concept to express a much needed overall sustainable development and nature conservation strategy, including and considering, *inter alia*:

- the concept of landscape as a concrete and a representational reality – with great importance paid to the comprehension of social and natural processes;

- an understanding of the proper place of natural and cultural elements and processes, and the interaction among them, in the building of landscapes – and an interest in their conservation and their importance in proposing visions, goals, objectives and management schemes;

- recognition of nature conservation as the major goal, always integrated within an overall sustainable development agenda – including biological diversity as one of the most important indicators of the natural values to be protected, but with conservation attention also directed towards ecological processes and environmental services, as well as landscapes, geographic features, geological and paleontological contents, and cultural heritage and related values;

- a foundation based on sound and up-to-date, but open-minded, science, the full use of the concepts and techniques from conservation biology, (physical and human) geography, social sciences (anthropology, history, sociology, etc.) along with other relevant disciplines – searching for the best understanding of ecological processes, of biodiversity (as defined by CBD) patterns and others, of processes and patterns of space appropriation and natural resource uses, among others;

- the consideration of larger areas (also called, perhaps narrowly, landscape-scale management) – including protected areas but also other kind of areas and uses, preferably all integrated within land-use zoning and planning schemes;

- the arrangement of protected areas within mosaics and networks, collaborating as the core zones of conservation corridors and within bioregional projects – including the correct consideration of buffer zones, the relationship of protected areas with surrounding areas, etc.;

- the consideration of institutional integration, and possibly of transboundary conservation agendas among countries or states;

- the full recognition of the major role of protected areas (as defined by IUCN-WCPA, CBD and UNESCO-WHC), and the complete understanding and the full use of protected area systems and categories – supposing not only a set of PAs, but also other components: the association and complementarity of different categories (i.e., diverse objectives); protected area systems governance and management, including the relationships among PAs, between PAs and their agency's central office, and among the different levels of government (national/federal, state, local/municipal); capacity-building and training schemes; and the legal framework; etc.;

- a clear understanding of the social processes that influence nature conservation – considering the society's (including stakeholders') interests, recognising rights and promoting full participation in all processes, promoting local communities' empowerment, and making room for the culturally diverse manifestations of interest in nature; and

- a complete understanding and full use of the CBD ecosystem approach with its twelve principles and five operational guidance points.

---

categories such as VI, as part of national or other levels of protected area systems, to address particular needs in specific conditions.

Along with improving the organization of local communities, support from other kinds of institutions is still needed – such as non-governmental organizations (NGOs), universities, research groups, governmental agencies responsible for environment, and international organizations. Only through partnership with local communities is it possible to seek the resources and means needed to improve the quality of life of local families.

Today it is also clear that the only economically viable option for extractive reserves, and the local communities that inhabit them, is sustainable use of the many products of the forest and the potential of its natural ecosystems – a single product is not adequate to sustain the needed economic flow. As mentioned in international statements (CBD, 2000, Ecosystem Approach; *inter alia*), perverse incentives (economic and others) block the possibilities for local communities and extractivism. A 'shared-in-common macro-economy' (a global or general economy based on solidarity) is needed to reverse the situation.[22] This would involve nothing more than respecting the real conditions of economic internalities and externalities from the perspective of the global environment, and taking into account the views of local communities living in the forests, mangroves and other landscapes. What this means, in fact, is that there is a need to pay for the environmental and social services that the whole world uses, and that these ecosystems and the communities that inhabit them provide. And the landscape approach is a wonderful concept to include these needs.

The cases presented here are examples of landscapes – socially, economically and culturally created by, and belonging to, local communities. Their ties to these landscapes became so important that, in the case of the Amazon, the communities organized themselves to oppose deforestation, even at the risk of violence and death; and in the coastal case, fishermen dared to break the dominant commercial chains. The extractive reserves were established by the communities to protect their lived-in, working landscapes. The rubber-tappers led in the creation of a concept, now accepted worldwide as part of an overall sustainable development and nature conservation strategy, and the Mandiras are demonstrating an example capable of influencing their entire region.

The cases discussed here may not be 'classical' examples of cultural landscapes (or 'European types' of landscape) – for the marks are less visible to the 'non-local' and 'untrained' eye, that may not be prepared in these settings to see the long interactions between humans and nature over time (for there are no rock-built castles, no stone walls, no completely remodelled mountains, no vegetation-transformed fields…). To the visitor's eye, and from the 'international perspective,' those areas within the Amazon and the coastal wetlands may be seen only as tropical forests, with some possible attention paid to the relationship between people and the forest and its value for nature conservation. But what then are lands that are divided by paths, shaped by use, with their limits defined by customs and respected by local communities, (as, for example, with the significance of trees) if not landscapes – cultural landscapes – and therefore ideally managed through a landscape approach?

---

[22] The term, translated from *economia solidária* refers to an economy with solidarity in the sense of respecting collective rights and production that is managed cooperatively. A 'solidary macro-economy' (translated from *macro-economia solidária*) considers also the global equilibrium of costs and prices, and takes into account related costs. It internalizes (instead of externalizing) social and environmental costs so that, for example, prices paid for goods coming from the forests or mangroves, could support proper sustainable exploitation of natural resources. It also considers the environmental (and social) values and services of natural habitats, ecosystems, protected areas and sustainable activities in order to be able to maintain them.

# Acknowledgements

This chapter was only possible with the direct or indirect collaboration of several colleagues, including Lucia H. O. Wadt, Daisy A. P. Gomes-Silva, Wanda T. P. de V. Maldonado, Rosely A. Sanches, Jessica Brown, Francisco Coutinho, Severino da S. Brito, Renato R. Sales, and Christiane Ehringhaus.

It should be mentioned, as well, that this chapter was prepared based also on the following: the work done on the establishment of Mandira Extractive Reserve and COOPEROSTRA, mostly under the leadership of Renato Sales (formerly at FF), Francisco Coutinho (president of Mandira association and COOPEROSTRA) and Wanda Maldonado (FF), with other colleagues from FF and other organizations; the description of the rise of extractive reserves and the Chico Mendes Extractive Reserve, by Lucia Wadt (EMBRAPA researcher), Christiane Ehringhaus, Daisy Gomes-Silva (associate researcher of EMBRAPA and fellow of CNPq), and Severino Brito (president of AMOPREB);[23] analysis of relationships among local communities and protected areas in Brazil, prepared for the World Parks Congress, with collaborators, mainly Rosely Sanches (ISA),[24] and in consultation with colleagues; work related to the APAs Cananéia-Iguape-Peruíbe and Ilha Comprida; the workshop on "Protecting Landscapes and Seascapes" at the WPC; and activities, on behalf of IUCN, related to the World Heritage Convention.

---

[23] EMBRAPA: the Brazilian Agency for Agricultural Research. CNPq: the [Brazilian] National Council of Scientific and Technology Development. Amopreb: the Association of Brasiléia Dwellers, Extractivists and Producers. WPC: IUCN-WCPA V[th] World Parks Congress, Durban 2003.

[24] ISA: Socio-Environmental Institute.

# 5.  Conserving "unprotected" protected areas – communities can and do conserve landscapes of all sorts

*Edmund Barrow and Neema Pathak*

## Introduction – hundreds of thousands of community-conserved areas across the globe

During the last century, state designation and protection have been the main "official" tools for the conservation of biodiversity. Formally recognised Protected Areas (PAs) have been broadly successful in conserving biodiversity but have also led to social inequity, as those who declare PAs are rarely impacted by the restrictions imposed, whereas those who are impacted have rarely been a part of the decision-making process regarding their creation or management. State-constituted PAs continue to be a dominant focus for conserving biodiversity. With over 12% of the earth's surface gazetted as PAs, one would think that a representative section of the planet's biodiversity and ecosystems had been conserved! But often these PAs are not large enough to be viable; or lack the ecological connectivity to other parts of the ecosystem or landscape; or are inefficiently managed because of limitations of staff and resources; or face serious conflicts with hostile local human populations that have been forcefully denied their 'rightful' access. In most biodiversity-rich countries, conventional PAs are ridden with internal conflicts, and are under threats from ever-expanding industry, hydro-electric projects, agricultural expansion, and growing urbanization and consumerism. Under the circumstances it seems unlikely that these "pristine islands" would survive very long. As Kolmes (1999) mentions, PAs are often set aside for protection without in any way questioning the manner in which we use our natural resources in general, or altering how people think about the use of nature in a moral sense.

In the emphasis on "official" protected areas, one aspect has been consistently overlooked, or not understood, namely that rural people conserve vast areas of land and biodiversity for their own needs, whether utilitarian, cultural or spiritual. The history of this kind of conservation, or what we will be referring to as Community-Conserved Areas (CCAs), is much older than government-managed protected areas, or even the notion of the nation-state (Pathak *et al.*, 2003). African, Asian, and Central and South American countries have a strong history of traditional systems of resource management for water, forests and rangelands. Some of these systems have existed and evolved over hundreds of years, and have their origins in traditional common property resource management regimes of pastoralists, hunter-gatherers, fishing and agricultural societies. What is also common within the communities practising conservation systems is a history of alienation from these resources by colonial rulers. Governments (pre- and post-colonial) have generally ignored CCAs until recently. Yet these CCAs have long been central to how communities all over the world have cared for the landscapes they inhabit, and should be seen as an important element in the protected landscape approach.

Estimates indicate that between 400–800 million hectares of forest are owned or administered by local communities or indigenous people (Molnar and Scherr, 2003). In 18 developing countries with the largest forest cover, over 22% of the forests are owned by or reserved for local communities and indigenous peoples (White and Martin, 2002). Not all, but a large part, of lands owned by communities are either protected as sacred or used in a regulated manner. Conservation by communities or indigenous peoples is not always restricted to lands owned by them. In most south and south-east Asian countries governments have taken over most of the land. In such situations indigenous peoples and local communities have often taken *de facto* control over the land and natural resources owned by the State to regulate management and use and protect them from external and internal threats (see for example Mendha-Lekha and Bhaonta-Kolyala).

The cultural, utilitarian and sacred associations with surrounding ecosystems have played a significant role in conserving large landscapes and other elements of biodiversity. Undoubtedly, a tremendous amount of biodiversity still survives in these CCAs, which are often outside of government-designated PAs, often forming important corridors for the long-term viability of species. For example, a large percentage of wildlife in many countries still survives today because of the efforts of local communities as they recognise the importance of conservation as a core component of their livelihood strategies, through, for example, sacred forest groves, dry season grazing areas, wetland and water sources – all examples of community-conserved areas. Yet, while a lot of attention has been paid to threats faced by formal protected areas, not enough attention or resources are being used to conserve areas outside of formal PAs. And, in instances where CCAs and sacred sites fall within a PA, their relationship with the local communities and local systems of management are rarely taken into consideration while formulating a management plan for the area.

With increasing population and land pressures, it is clear that a whole range of conservation models will be needed, ranging from those prescribing strict preservation to those supporting sustainable use, and including a range of PAs, from those governed by the State (in situations where appropriate) to PAs completely managed by indigenous and local communities. Such a wide range of conservation approaches can only be devised by taking into account the importance of cultural and spiritual values related to our landscapes and biodiversity. Fortunately, many sacred, cultural and social values and associations have survived the increasingly utilitarian cultures, the mechanistic and scientific views of nature, and adverse laws, policies and attitudes.

Many formal religions have also ignored, or at best down-played, the importance of sacred natural sites and their role in conservation of culture and biodiversity. They have tried either to substitute or subsume them and their practices into formal religion, in a manner similar to how pre-Christian sacred yew trees and groves became part of Christian churches and graveyards across Europe. Another example is the increasing trend towards construction of cemented temples in the sacred groves of India, rather than celebrating the spiritual elements of nature for which these groves were constituted.

A large number of community-conserved areas are indeed small and may not conserve critical elements of biodiversity by themselves; however they do form a critical link between people, their conserved and protected landscapes, and the wider ecosystem. This interrelationship helps in creating the ecological connectivity that also maintains local cultures and associated livelihoods. In this paper we explore how rural people view the importance of such protected or conserved areas as key components of their landscapes, and how lessons from these areas could provide significant clues for effective management of PAs in general. We argue that, because of the sheer numbers of areas that communities conserve, these CCAs need to be more responsibly recognised at all levels and should take their rightful place in achieving livelihood improvement, creating connectivity within the landscape, and conserving species, biodiversity and ecosystems.

## Community-conserved areas

In this section we discuss the efforts of indigenous, mobile or local communities towards conservation through community-conserved areas, which can be defined as "modified and natural ecosystems, whether human-influenced or not, and which contain significant bio-diversity values, ecological services, and cultural values, that are voluntarily conserved by communities, through customary laws and institutions" (Pathak *et al.*, 2003). Such areas are important culturally or for livelihood sustenance and security, and can be initiated or achieved with or without outside support. The crucial criteria include that there are efforts to maintain or enhance the habitat and species therein, and that local communities are the major players in decision-making and implementation.

The primary objectives of CCAs are not necessarily for biodiversity conservation. Some communities conserve to meet subsistence livelihood needs, or to arrest degradation of environment, or as cultural sites, for example:

- Village forests and pastures are conserved to meet livelihood requirements for fuelwood, fodder and timber. These include Joint Forest Management (JFM) and self-initiated community efforts to regenerate degraded forests or manage standing forests;

- Areas are conserved for their cultural/religious significance, such as sacred groves, sacred ponds and grasslands;

- Wetlands are conserved for drinking water or irrigation, though they may also shelter and protect important biodiversity, such as the traditionally protected heronries in India;

- Dry season grazing and forage reserved areas of the many pastoralists groups in Africa, for example the Loima and Loita forests (both over 300km$^2$ in size) in Kenya are critical dry and drought time forage refuges, as well as being important culturally;

- Traditional agricultural systems, with diverse ecological niches, conserve not only the indigenous varieties of crop but also many wild species;

- Watersheds are conserved to ensure long-term availability of water; and

- Coastal areas are protected for traditional fishing to ensure continuous supply of fish, etc. (Pathak *et al.*, 2003).

## Livelihood needs and political assertions: reasons to conserve

The examples illustrated below indicate that community conservation can be initiated because of a wide range of reasons and that it is not necessarily a traditional practice. Some efforts may be continued traditional practices, others are either the revival of broken down traditions or the evolution of completely new systems, given contemporary contexts. A wide range of objectives

*Gram sabha* (village assembly) meeting in village Mendha-Lekha, India, where all decisions are taken on consensus. This has been one of the main reasons for the success of the movement towards *adivasi* (tribal community) self-rule. *Vivek Gour-Broome*

and approaches used for conservation by the communities are illustrated by the following (Pathak *et al.*, 2003):

**Mendha-Lekha forests (India).** In the 1970s, successful mobilization by indigenous (*adivasi*) people against a dam in the thickly forested central highlands of India, united the communities into a campaign towards tribal self-rule. Villages began to be declared as small republics within the Constitution of India. Mendha-Lekha was one such village, with about 400 *adivasis* called Gonds. The move led to their re-establishing *de facto* control over about 1,800ha of forests that had been taken over by the government in the 1960s (for revenue through logging, charcoal-making and bamboo extraction). The crucial act was the establishment of the *Gram Sabha* (Village Assembly) including all adult residents, and other institutions including a Forest Protection Committee. Villagers declared that henceforth all major local initiatives required the permission of the *Gram Sabha*. Decisions in the *Gram Sabha* are taken unanimously and implemented through unwritten yet strong social rules. Informal a*bhyas gats* (study circles), where villagers gather and discuss information with or without outsiders, help make informed decisions in the *Gram Sabha*.

By adopting transparent and open decision-making processes and assuming social and ecological responsibility, Mendha-Lekha's residents have developed the capacity to deal with a range of natural resource issues. They are documenting the local biodiversity, and are handling tedious financial dealings and official procedures. All logging and other commercial exploitation of forests by outside agencies have been stopped. Non-timber forest products and bamboo are currently extracted in a strictly regulated manner (after a decade-long moratorium), jointly by the forest department and villagers. Most encroachment on forests by the villagers and forest fires have been stopped. Women, youth and economically weaker members of society have equal status in the decision-making process. Through non-violence, strong relationships have been established with government officials, who in turn have helped the villagers at many crucial points. Livelihood security is assured through access to forest resources or employment opportunities.

***Bhaonta-Kolyala village in Rajasthan and the Arvari Sansad, or Arvari River Parliament (India).*** In the drought-prone area of Rajasthan in India, Bhaonta-Kolyala twin villages have revived their traditional system of water harvesting through small earthen dams and conserved catchment areas with the help of the NGO, Tarun Bharat Sangh. The villagers' efforts have revived the river Arvari which had become seasonal. As a result of improved livelihood security, villagers no longer move out in search of employment any more (Shresth and Devidas, 2001). Bhaonta-Kolyala are not the only villages in this region to have done so. Tens of villages along the catchment of River Arvari have conserved their forests, regulating its internal use through social sanctions and protecting it from outsiders.

A few years ago about 70 such villages met and decided to form *Arvari Sansad*, or a people's parliament, to oversee matters related to the river and its catchment. The *sansad* meets every year and takes decisions related to forest conservation, prohibition on hunting, regulated use of water and so on. This is an excellent example of a river landscape and associated biodiversity being managed and conserved by the local people.

***Coron Island (Philippines).*** The Tagbanwa people of the Phillipines inhabit a stunningly beautiful limestone island called Coron Island, for which they have established strict use regulations. The forest resources are to be used for domestic purposes only. All the freshwater lakes but one are sacred and entry there is strictly restricted, except for religious and cultural purposes. The only lake accessible for tourism is Lake Kayangan, albeit with strict regulations concerning garbage disposal, resource use, etc.

Until recently, the Tagbanwas' territorial rights were not legally recognised, leading to encroachment by migrant fishers, tourism operators, politicians seeking land deals and government agencies. This caused a number of problems, in particular the impoverishment of the marine resources essential for local livelihoods. In the mid-1980s, the islanders organized themselves into the Tagbanwas Foundation of Coron Island (TFCI) and applied for a Community Forest Stewardship Agreement (CFSA). In 1990, the stewardship agreement was granted over the 7,748ha of Coron island and a neighbouring island called Delian, but not over the marine areas. In 1998 the islanders managed to get a Certificate of Ancestral Domain Claim (CADC) for 22,284ha of land and marine waters, and in 2001, with the help of a high quality map and an Ancestral Land Management Plan (ALMP), obtained a Certificate of Ancestral Domain Title (CADT), which grants collective right to land.

Despite successful community management, in 2001 the Tagnabwa CATD was put under review, as the national policies and systems were being restructured. A governmental proposal was advanced to add Coron Island to the National Integrated Protected Area System (NIPAS). The Tagbanwas resent these moves, as they fear that they will lead to the loss of control of their natural resources. From being owners and protectors of their territories, they would become only *one* of the management actors.

***Alto Fragua-Indiwasi National Park (Colombia) and el Parque de la Papa (Peru).*** The Alto Fragua-Indiwasi national park was created in February 2002, after negotiations amongst the Colombian government, the Association of Indigenous Ingano Councils and the Amazon Conservation Team, an environmental NGO. The national park is located on the piedmont of the Colombian Amazon, part of a region that has the highest biodiversity in the country and is one of the top hotspots of the world. The site protects various ecosystems of the tropical Andes including highly endangered humid sub-Andean forests, endemic species such as the spectacled bear (*Tremarctos ornatus*), and sacred sites of unique cultural value.

Under the terms of the decree that created the national park, the Ingano are the principal actors in the design and management of the park. The area, whose name means 'House of the Sun' in the Ingano language, is a sacred place for the indigenous peoples. The creation of Indiwasi National Park is a part of the Ingano Life Plan (*Plan de Vida*), or long-term vision for the entirety of their territory and the region. In addition, the creation of the park represents an historic precedent for the indigenous people of Colombia, as for the first time an indigenous community is the principal actor in the design and management of a PA fully recognised by the state. Similarly, the indigenous peoples of Australia are negotiating and constituting Indigenous PAs which would both conserve the biodiversity and indigenous cultures.

In the highlands of Peru, six communities of the Quechua peoples have established a Potato Park (*el Parque de la Papa*) in a unique initiative to conserve domesticated and wild bio-diversity. Over 8,500 hectares of titled communal land are being jointly managed to conserve about 1,200 potato varieties (cultivated and wild) as well as the natural ecosystems of the Andes. Since this region is where the potato originated, the effort is of global significance. (This case is discussed in more detail in this volume in the chapter on Andean landscapes).

The above examples indicate that livelihood needs and political assertions have been important reasons for landscape and seascape management and conservation by the local communities.

## Sacred groves: connecting the natural, social and spiritual

Another important reason that has led to the conservation and protection of landscapes, seascapes, freshwater systems and a wide range of flora and fauna across many cultures has been the spiritual association of human communities with nature. Nature engenders positive feelings toward the environment, and where they give such harmony, trees and forest groves have often been conserved as part of the landscape. For example, the placement of groves of trees with relation to wind direction or water source protection has given rise to spiritual landscapes in China. This formed one of the bases for "*Feng*" (wind) "*Shui*" (water) in China, where, in many places such *Feng Shui* groves are the only samples of the original native vegetation. There are many examples all over the world concerning the religious and spiritual importance of natural resources, which survive in spite of the dominance of mechanistic and scientific views of nature (Table 1). Trees and forests play a particularly important role, due to their relative longevity. In rural societies where natural resources play an important role, there is often a strong culture, detailed knowledge, and institutional base relating to the spiritual values of flora and fauna.

**Table 1. Indication of the scale of numbers of sacred groves**

| Country or area | Number of sacred groves | Source of information |
|---|---|---|
| Ghana | 2,000 + | (Ntiamoa-Baidu, 1995) |
| Xishunghu region of S.W. China | 400 | (Shengji, 1999) |
| Nepal | 100s | (Ingles, 1995) |
| Kenya (Kayas, sacred groves in Mt. Kenya, Loita, Loima) | 20+ | (Barrow, 1996; Brokensha and Castro, 1987; Loita Naimina Enkiyia Conservation Trust Company, 1994a; Robertson, 1987) |
| Zigna Group in Tanzania | 660 | (Mwihomeke *et al.*, 1997) |
| Coorg district of Karnatake State in India | 600+ (totalling over 4,000ha) | (Chandrakanth and Romm, 1991) |
| India | 100,000 to 150,000 | (Jeanrenaud, 2001) |

Sacred forest groves range from being completely "no use" zones to areas contributing towards local livelihoods, though such use is strictly regulated by local customs (Boxes 1 and 2). For example, in many sacred groves in the Western Ghats in India, many of which are over 200 years old, people are allowed to collect fallen dry wood, fruit from the forest floor, honey and other products. In some areas cattle grazing is allowed (Bharucha, 1999). For 15 groves which have been studied in detail, 223 species of trees and shrubs have been identified, and the species richness varied between 10 and 86 per grove. These groves represent the least disturbed

Sacred Kaya forest, Kenya. Many sacred groves contain a wide variety of biodiversity, including endemic species and relict populations of more ancient forest types.
*Grazia Borrini-Feyerabend*

71

---

## Box 1.   The Sacred Forest Groves of Ghana

Small patches of forest were set aside, as sacred lands that could not be touched, and were strictly protected by customary law. Such areas still exist in Ghana and are known as *Abosompow* or *Asoneyeso* (Shrine), *Mpanyinpow* (ancestral forests) and *Nsamanpow* (burial grounds), and are collectively known as sacred or fetish groves. Many are small, often less than one hectare, patches of forest which were protected because they supported sacred, totem or tabooed species. The Boabeng-Fiema Monkey Sanctuary is an example of a grove protected because the forest supports the black and white colobus monkeys, which are considered sacred by the people of the two villages.

Sacred groves are controlled by the traditional authority (fetish priest, chief or clan head), but the responsibility is vested in the entire community, with a select group having authority to enforce the rules. For example Nkodurom grove, of approximately 5km$^2$ has been preserved for at least 300 years, and is composed of primary forest. The final authority over this grove rests with the Ashanti king, though the functional authority is vested with the village chief. Taboos governing the grove include the prohibition of:

- all forms of use, including farming, hunting and collection of any plant material;
- access, except to traditional authorities for the performance of customary rites or other authorized persons;
- access to all persons on Thursdays (as the spirits are believed to be resting on that day); and
- access to menstruating women.

There are traditional guards patrolling the grove who will arrest intruders. The grove has not been demarcated. There are no written rules, and the grove has no legal basis. But the rules are strictly observed, and the traditional guards receive no payment. The sacred groves have survived because of the strong traditional beliefs upheld by the local people and the spiritual, religious and cultural attachments to the groves. The sacred groves in Ghana form a matrix of biotic islands with the potential for conservation of remnant communities of flora and fauna. In many areas sacred forests constitute the only remnant forest amidst severely degraded forest and farm lands. The survival of sacred groves is threatened by the erosion of traditional beliefs that have sustained the systems. The number of sacred groves has gradually shrunk in size due to encroachment by surrounding farms, and a number have been lost to development projects. As a result, a possible management strategy for the sacred groves of Ghana could include:

- a national inventory of the groves and the biological resources in them;
- legislation to reinforce the traditional regulations regarding use and access; and
- provision of resources to improve local people's capability to manage their groves.

*Source*: Ntiamoa-Baidu (1995)

---

islands of old growth in the region. The felling of trees is not allowed unless with the express permission of the deity (Jeanrenaud, 2001). In two sacred groves in Kerala, India, four threatened tree species were found (Nair and Mohanan, 1981). In Nepal, in one valley alone, sacred groves are storehouses of useful plants (up to 150 species) which are otherwise absent or rare in the rest of the valley (Mansberger, 1988). However, use may also be determined by the relative power of the deity. For example, in Nanhini village in Ghana no one is allowed to enter the sacred grove of the Goddess Numafoa, or ignore her taboos. But in the same village there is a lesser deity, and that deity's taboos are less strictly adhered to (Jeanrenaud, 2001). In Venezuela, Maria Lionza is the forest Goddess, and depicted astride a tapir. The forest home of the forest goddess Maria Lionza is a 40,000ha tropical rainforest that has not been used for

---

## Box 2.   The Holy Hills of the Dai in South West China

The Dai are an indigenous group in South West China in Xishuangbanna region in Yunnan Province with a long tradition of biodiversity conservation. This is characterized by the management of the Holy Hills, which they believe are the cradle of mankind. The holy hills or *Nong* are forested hills where the Gods reside. The spirits of great and revered chieftains go to the holy hill to live. Holy hills can be found wherever one encounters a hill of virgin forest near a Dai village, and they are a major component of traditional Dai land management.

In Xishuangbanna region there are approximately 400 hills of between 30 and 40,000ha. There are two types of Holy Hill. *Nong Man* are naturally forested hills of between 10–100ha and are worshipped by inhabitants of one village, while *Nong merg* occur where several villages form a larger community and such areas maybe many hundreds of hectares in size. The Dai keep the sanctity of these hills, and also present regular offerings to please the Gods. Near the village of Mar-yuang-kwang, the holy hill covers an area of 53ha. There are 311 plant species in this small area which makes a significant contribution to the conservation of biodiversity, and a large number of endemic or relic species of local flora have been conserved including 100 species of medicinal plants, and more than 150 economically useful plants.

Traditionally holy hills were natural conservation areas, and founded with the help of the Gods. Gathering, hunting, wood chopping and cultivation were strictly prohibited. The trees on the *Nong* mountains cannot be cut. You cannot build houses on *Nong* hills, and you must not antagonise the spirits and the Gods – Buddha. Such a large number of forested Holy Hills form hundreds of green islands, and could provide the basis for creating connectivity through improved landscape management.

*Source*: Shengji, 1999.

---

slash and burn agriculture, because of the dire misfortunes that befall any person who cuts or burns her trees. The forest was officially gazetted in 1960 as the Maria Lionza National Monument and is one of the best protected areas in Venezuela (Hamilton, 1998).

The Mbeere people of south eastern Mt. Kenya have numerous sacred groves or *matiiiri* in the forests. In the 1930s there were over 200 such groves, mainly on hill tops or along ridges, varying in size between 0.1 to 1.5ha, and comprised of large spreading trees. No cutting, clearing or cultivation was allowed, except of branches to propagate new sacred trees. The

Sacred prohibitions, Guinea Bissau. This complex construction around the trunk of a tree signals a set of sacred prohibitions, which are understood by residents of local communities.
*Grazia Borrini-Feyerabend*

73

cultural significance of these practices is being eroded by new religious practices and privatization of land tenure (Brokensha and Castro, 1987). The Loita Forest (300km$^2$) in south west Kenya is considered sacred by the Loita and Purko Maasai, as the spiritual centre for their lives. Not only is the forest important for sacred rituals, it is also a source of medicines and dry season forage, and the springs and streams which emerge from the forest symbolise enduring hope. Kipumbwi village, along the coast of Tanzania, started before the arrival of the Arabs in the 18$^{th}$ century. After a period of prolonged hardship, the village elders brought the spirits from their original home (Mombasa) to a sacred site in the mangrove forest, called *Kwakibibi*. Nobody may enter without the consent of the three elders (two men and one woman) responsible for the management of the site (Nurse and Kabamba, 1998).

**Table 2. Community-conserved areas and the IUCN Protected Area Categories – the fit**

| Category and description | CCA types | Some examples |
|---|---|---|
| Strict Nature Reserve and Wilderness area – managed for science and wilderness protection (Category I) | Sacred or "no-use" groves, lakes, springs, mountains, islands etc. Main reason for protection may be cultural or spiritual | ▪ Forole sacred mountain in northern Kenya<br>▪ Hundreds (thousands) of sacred forest groves and wetlands in India<br>▪ Sacred beaches and marine areas – Coron Island, Philippines<br>▪ Life Reserve of Awa people in Ecuador |
| National Park – managed mainly for ecosystem protection and recreation (Category II) | Watershed forests above villages, community-declared conservation areas | ▪ Safey forests, Mizoram, India<br>▪ Forest catchment in Tinangol, Sabah, Malaysia<br>▪ Isidoro-Secure National Park, Bolivia |
| National Monument – managed mainly for conservation of specific natural features (Category III) | Natural monuments which are protected by communities for spiritual, cultural and other reasons | ▪ Limestone Caves – Kanger Ghati National Park, India<br>▪ Sites of ancestor graves in Madagascar<br>▪ Mapu Lahual Network of indigenous protected areas in coastal range temperate rainforests, Chile |
| Habitat/species management area – for conservation through management (Category IV) | Areas which are protected for cultural, spiritual and other reasons | ▪ Kokkare Bellur, India (heronry) |
| Protected Landscape or Seascape managed mainly for landscape and seascape conservation and recreation (Category V) | Traditional grounds of mobile and pastoralist peoples – including rangelands, water points and forest patches, and dry and drought time forage reserves | ▪ Migration territory of Kuhi nomads (Iran), including a community-protected wetland<br>▪ Maasai, Turkana and other pastoralist territories in Kenya (including important Loima and Loita forests)<br>▪ Borana pastoral territory in Ethiopia<br>▪ Potato Park, Peru<br>▪ Coron Island, Philippines<br>▪ Island of Eigg, United Kingdom |
| Managed Resource Protected Areas – for the sustainable use of natural ecosystems (Category VI) | Resource reserves (forests, grasslands, water ways under restrict use (with rule and regulations) to assure use is sustainable | ▪ Jardhargaon, Mendha-Lekha, Arvari and hundreds of others in India (fodder, fuel, water, medicinals and other non-timber forest products)<br>▪ Community forests in Val de Fiemme, Italy<br>▪ Takieta forest, Niger<br>▪ Mangrove |

*Source*: Pathak *et al.*, 2003.

There is a great diversity of sacred forest groves, and they survive in spite of land and population pressures that would have resulted, under normal circumstances, in the conversion of these forested lands. This is testament to their resilience, and also to their cultural and spiritual importance to local villages, communities and people. At an individual sacred grove level, they may not be extensive in conservation terms, though some are quite large (Box 2). More important is the sheer number of sacred groves in many different countries, in different ecosystems and managed under different conditions (Table 2). Many of these sacred groves contain a wide variety of biodiversity, some of which may be endemic, or are relict populations of more ancient forest types. As such, they are important forest conservation assets, even though the underlying rationale is their sacrality, for the following reasons:

- The sheer age and longevity of some of the groves is important; for instance, the sacred yew groves in Europe, very old sacred trees and groves in India, and the redwood or bristle cone pine groves in the USA;

- Some groves are managed so that they conserve important biodiversity as a direct by-product of their spiritual and religious values, for example the Boabeng-Fiema sacred grove in Ghana;

- Many sacred groves are examples of remnant communities of flora and fauna, and are important in a historical ecological sense. Such remnants may only be found surrounded by large areas of converted, or worse, degraded lands, as is found outside monastic forests in Ethiopia;

- The traditional and religious management systems (institutions and organizations), while being important for the management of the sacred sites in a religious sense, are also important for the context of conservation;

- While usually not large in size, the number of sacred groves can create connectivity and could be a focus for natural forest and landscape restoration, as well as landscape management;

Bhairondev public sanctuary, declared by the villagers of Bhaonta-Kolyala in India, is not an officially recognised protected area. However, villagers protect it zealously and follow the strict rules and regulations mentioned on this wall at the entrance of the sanctuary.
*Ashish Kothari*

- The sheer number and, by implication, area of the sacred sites found across the world is important of itself. They are all protected areas, though few have formal recognition; and

- They can serve as as a key point of entry for linking rural livelihoods to conservation.

## Conserving against development threats

There are numerous examples of indigenous and local communities from Malaysia, India, Latin America, North America and Europe fighting and even laying down their lives to protect their land and seascapes from destructive logging, mining, and damming industries. These examples clearly indicate that there is a much greater threat to biodiversity from external commercial and developmental pressures than from local communities themselves, as is the common belief among policy-makers. Local communities, in effect, have often been responsible for saving such habitat from being engulfed by the ever-increasing developmental thirst of nations!

Protected area authorities are often powerless to fight strong commercial and political forces. In India, for example, such threats have resulted in the degazettement of parts of Narayan Sarovar Wildlife Sanctuary in Gujarat, Melghat Wildlife Sanctuary in Maharashtra and Darlaghat Sanctuary in Himachal Pradesh. While in Kenya and many other parts of Africa; in Malaysia and other South East Asian countries, important areas of indigenous forests have been encroached on, converted and degazetted for other forms of land use, such as logging, mining, hydro-electric power, and so on.

On the other hand a strong local people's movement against such forces has been responsible for saving areas like Sariska National Park in India from sandstone mining. In Nagarhole National Park in India the local tribal groups fought against a five star hotel being built adjacent to the National Park, and many villagers in the Kashipur district in Orissa, India have lost their lives opposing the extensive mining in their forests and lands. Fisherfolk all along the coast of India are fighting against destructive trawling and violations of coastal zone regulations all along the coast of India. Such movements have played and continue to play an important role in the conservation of areas of biodiversity significance.

Many governments in Africa and Asia are developing programmes for the participatory management of natural resources. Joint forest management in India aims at the management of resources jointly by the government and the surrounding populations and sharing of benefits. Villages in Tanzania are now allowed to formally reserve their own Village Forest Reserves (Barrow *et al.*, 2002). In Ghana people have agreements with conservation authorities to allow them to use National Parks for certain cultural and spiritual customs, while in Uganda the Government has gone a step further and allowed people access, through collaborative management agreements, to harvest certain natural resources. Coastal Zone Management Plans in Sri Lanka aim to manage coastal areas with the involvement of surrounding communities, while there is participatory management of fisheries in Bangladesh (Pathak *et al.*, 2003). However, not as much progress has been made towards participatory management of officially protected areas with the exceptions of Nepal and Uganda, where collaborative management agreements have become an important component of protected area management.

# Communities conserving – achieving the ecosystem approach and improving livelihoods

In the above sections we have tried to present evidence to support the argument that CCAs need greater attention and support as a conservation strategy and approach. However we also realize that not all communities conserve their natural resources or would be interested in doing so. Similarly, there are many successful official PA efforts that have responsibly integrated local needs. The point is, where local communities have been mobilized and responsibly involved, this has often helped save a PA, or other wildlife habitat, much more effectively than if the governments were to do it alone. Communities, in turn, have benefited from the protection offered to natural resources by PA authorities. Conservation efforts have often resulted in saving of traditional cultures and economies of sensitive communities from being swamped by external forces. For example the tribal communities inside Melghat Wildlife Sanctuary in India enjoy a better health and nutritional status than the same communities residing outside the Sanctuary or in urbanized areas. But many incidental, yet important social benefits of PAs are often masked by negative attitudes towards communities and the conflicts thus generated.

Unfortunately, little emphasis has so far been given to the importance of sacred groves and CCAs as repositories of important biodiversity that is fast being lost from the surrounding landscapes. However, it is clear that CCAs are a vital, but often hidden, component of biodiversity conservation and landscape management across the globe. The sheer number of CCAs is testament to this. Yet what makes for the success of CCAs, especially since they have received little formal recognition? There are a range of attributes required which contribute to their success. Each on its own may not be enough, but together the social, institutional and conservation basis for such CCAs becomes stronger.

This is not to say that all CCAs or sacred landscapes are perfect and can be replicated as it is in other PAs. Situations on the ground are often more complex than can be explained in this paper. However, gaining an understanding of what works and what does not work; the variety of social institutions, rules and regulations; reasons and objectives of CCAs, could provide important lessons for socially accepted, yet ecologically sound, landscape conservation strategies. Some of these lessons and emerging questions for further discussion include:

*1. Who bears the costs and why?* Whether community-based conservation is cheaper or more expensive than conventional conservation is debatable. Initially, it may be more expensive, but once the community has taken on its responsibilities, it would be cheaper as many costs are internalized by the communities. However this may not be the case for communities who border gazetted PAs, as they may bear significant costs related to wildlife and curtailed access. Experience in CCAs shows that people are ready to pay this price for conservation for the benefits that they envisage, such as long-term livelihood security; fulfilment of religious, traditional, social, cultural sentiments; and ecosystem functions. More importantly, these efforts can be expressions of their political identity and give them a sense of empowerment and belonging. True decision-making and implementing powers, social equity and wider re-cognition would help communities gain some of their objectives, thus creating a greater support for conservation.

*2. Whose rights and how secure?* An understanding of CCAs clearly indicates that a sense of belonging or stewardship is crucial for a community to feel empowered to manage an area. This sense develops through the consumptive, economic, cultural and spiritual associations and interactions people have within the wider landscape. Therefore security of tenure and access are key to ensuring responsible local management. Most successful CCAs occur where there is secure legal ownership over the area, or *de facto* control over the resources. Tenurial security will not necessarily lead to conservation, but such security makes conservation more feasible.

**3. Who manages – decentralization?** Uniform models of development and conservation are not sustainable given the increasingly complex interactions between people and nature. Community initiatives are decentralized, site-specific and vary in their objectives and approaches. Building greater flexibility into protected area management would involve more formally recognising the management categories which promote community involvement (Table 2). It is encouraging to note that, in India, two new categories, Community Reserves (managed by local communities), and Conservation Reserves (for sustainable harvesting of certain resources), have been included in the revised Indian Wild Life (Protection) Act 2003. Although here, again, the mistake is being made to bring a whole range of community conservation efforts under a single institution that has been prescribed by the Act, ignoring the diversity of already existing institutions. In Tanzania, Community Wildlife Management Areas and Village Forest Reserves are formally recognised in law.

A typology of CCAs indicates that, depending on the sites, they could fit within a wide range of IUCN categories of PAs (see Table 2), although they are neither recognised nor designated as such.

**4. Role of outsiders.** In many CCAs in India, for example, the people see a very important role being played by government or other outside agencies, but as guides and supporters rather than as their rulers. They do realize that often internal and external complexities make it difficult for them to conserve resources entirely on their own. Communities also feel the need for impartial and objective information to help them take informed decisions. They often remain physically disconnected from the larger society and feel the need to create a link. In all of the above a supportive role is needed by many communities.

**5. Whose objectives and whose decisions count?** Communities may have differing objectives for conserving an area from those of a conservation authority. These may be utilitarian, cultural or spiritual, albeit conservation may be an obvious outcome. Such objectives need to be recognised in national laws and policies, so that the responsible role that communities play in conservation is integrated into land-use, landscape and livelihood planning. If the decisions about conservation are taken by elites without consulting those who may be more dependent on the resources or affected by lost access, then such sections of society may suffer disproportionately. For example, in Kailadevi wildlife sanctuary in India, men took a decision not to cut green trees, and regulate grass cutting. The women agreed in principle, but complained about the hardships that they had to face. This was especially serious for women-headed households who had to leave small children and other family responsibilities to collect natural resources they would have otherwise harvested from the sanctuary (Pathak, 2000).

**6. How does conservation benefit?** There is a lot of biodiversity outside official PAs. If taken into account, CCAs can become an important aspect of landscape-level conservation planning, as they often form important corridors between two areas of biodiversity significance. With increased land use and population densities it is increasingly difficult to designate new official PAs; here CCAs can play a significant role. CCAs can thus provide the key link between benefits to the community and conservation of important biodiversity. By adopting collaborative management approaches, PA authorities have been able to reduce their law enforcement costs; for instance in Kibale and Mt. Elgon National Parks in Uganda (Chhetri *et al.*, 2004). The diversity of conserved area types creates improved ecological connectivity, which increases the biodiversity value of a small official or community reserve within a much larger human-used and protected landscape.

*7. CCAs face many challenges.* CCAs do still face serious challenges to their continued existence and growth. Many CCAs are disappearing because of inappropriate financial or developmental interventions, inappropriate educational models, intrusions of dominant and fundamentalist religions, and changing socio-economic and value systems. Often traditional institutions for managing CCAs have been undermined by centralized political systems, where governments or their representatives have taken over most of the relevant powers. Even decentralized policies and participatory schemes may end up sabotaging well-functioning community action by imposing new and uniform institutional structures and unfamiliar rules, rather than building on existing systems and knowledge. CCAs are often encroached on or threatened by commercial users or by community members under the influence of market forces. Because CCAs remain unrecognised in many countries, it hampers their struggle against powerful opponents and sometimes even neighbouring communities, and often they have little support from the government or the law.

## Community-conserved areas: international recognition

The conservation of biodiversity can no longer be solely the purview of governments. CCAs are increasingly being recognised at national and international levels for a number of reasons including:

- CCAs allow for multiple approaches to conservation where "official" protected or reserved areas are now seen as components of much wider human-used and protected landscapes;

- CCAs acknowledge the importance of how people manage and conserve their land, and areas of conservation value;

- CCAs help in larger landscape- and waterscape-level planning by providing corridors, ecological connectivity and linkages for animal and gene movement, and synergistic links between agricultural biodiversity and wildlife;

- CCAs ensure that rural people are central to such integrated landscape management;

- CCAs make conservation meaningful at the livelihood level – either through direct use or through other cultural values; and, ultimately,

- CCAs raise the importance of conservation to that of being a critical element in livelihood security and poverty reduction.

At the global level, this growing recognition of the importance of CCAs has led to their inclusion in:

- the key outputs of the 2003 World Parks Congress (Box 3);

- the CBD programme of work as part of the COP7 deliberations in Kuala Lumpur (Box 3); and

- the evolution of the IUCN protected area categories (Table 2).

---

**Box 3.   Community-based conservation – the international context**

Two key international events in 2003–2004 established the role of community-based approaches to protected area management and to conservation in general.

- Amongst the major outputs of the V[th] World Parks Congress (Durban, September 2003) were the Durban Accord and Action Plan, the Message to the CBD, and over 30 Recommendations on specific topics. These outputs strongly stressed the need to move towards collaborative management of government-managed PAs, with a central role for indigenous and local communities (including mobile and nomadic peoples). This includes the recognition of customary and territorial rights, and the right to a central role in decision-making. The biggest breakthrough, however, was the recognition of CCAs as a valid and important form of conservation. The Durban Action Plan and a specific recommendation on CCAs highlighted the need to incorporate and support CCAs as part of national PA systems (see www.iucn.org).

- The 7th Conference of Parties to the CBD (Kuala Lumpur, February 2004) had, as one of its main outputs, a detailed and ambitious Programme of Work on Protected Areas. A crucial element of the Programme of Work relates to "Governance, Participation, Equity, and Benefit-sharing", under which actions explicitly urge countries to move towards participatory conservation with the recognition of indigenous and local community rights. As in the case of the World Parks Congress, the Programme of Work also makes a major breakthrough in committing countries to identify, recognise and support CCAs (see www.biodiv.org).

*Source*: Ashish Kothari.

---

Models of, and approaches towards, conservation have had to adapt to contemporary local and national needs. Contemporary approaches to landscape management argue for a range of land-use types that will create the necessary balance between human use and ensuring the goods and services from the landscape, so that improved conservation connectivity can coexist with human use. Protected and conserved areas have a significant role to play in this. But managing the goods and services that conservation can supply requires a more people-based approach in order to increase the area under conservation, ensure that connectivity is maintained or improved, and that people living on such landscapes are part of the solution, not the problem.

# Part II
## Case studies from around the world

# 6. Landscape conservation initiatives in Nepal: opportunities and challenges

*Prabhu Budhathoki*

## Introduction

In Nepal, half of the country's protected areas include settlements and farmlands, and all national parks are adjacent to areas with high populations. As a result, the need for a broad landscape approach to conservation has been evident from the very beginning of protected area establishment. In fact, Nepal has been adopting a protected landscape approach to conservation in 78% of its protected areas, linking local people with resource conservation and directing the benefits of resource conservation to them. The expansion of conservation initiatives beyond protected area boundaries has received extra impetus through the 1996 enactment of Buffer Zone regulations that allow use of park revenue for community development within these zones. In addition, landscape biodiversity conservation initiatives have been envisioned that extend far beyond the periphery of parks and will create networks of protected areas, conserving the core and corridor habitats required for the long-term survival of mega fauna such as elephant, tiger and rhinos. These ambitious and complex initiatives have been adopting the principles of inclusion, partnership and linkages in order to manage large spatial coverage with varying land use practices.

This chapter reviews landscape conservation initiatives in Nepal and explores the opportunities and challenges they present for conservation, for the professionals and agencies engaged in this work, and for the general public.

## Background on Nepal and its conservation policies and practice

Nepal, on the southern slopes of the Himalayas, has a landmass (147,181km$^2$) only slightly larger than England, yet the country contains over 2% of the world's flowering plants, 8% of its birds and 4% of its mammals (Biodiversity Profiles Project, 1995). This biodiversity richness is a reflection of the country's unique geographical position as well as its altitudinal and climatic variations, ranging from lowland tropical Terai to Mt. Everest, the highest mountain in the world. The country is also rich in ethnic diversity comprising more than 102 caste/ethnic groups with about 93 spoken languages (Central Bureau of Statistics, 2002). These people have rich and diverse socio-cultural practices and possess a wealth of knowledge on the use and management of biodiversity. One study revealed that indigenous *Tharu* communities in the periphery of the Royal Chitwan National Park have been using more than 150 species of plants for various medicinal purposes (Pokhrel, 2002). This rich repository of natural and cultural diversity is a characteristic of Nepalese landscapes that has both national and international significance and is a key focus for conservation.

In 1973, the country embarked on the modern era of conservation by establishing networks of protected areas. There are now 16 protected areas of different IUCN categories covering

Nepal has been adopting a protected landscape approach in most of its protected areas, integrating conservation and traditional resource use practices.
*Elizabeth Hughes/ICPL*

about 18% of the total surface area of the country. Despite several problems and constraints, Nepal has achieved some significant successes in the protection and management of its biodiversity (HMG/MFSC, 2003). The populations of many endangered and globally significant species such as the greater one-horned rhinoceros, tiger and Indian bison have been revived. For example, government statistics suggest that the population of rhinos has increased five-fold in four years (from just over 100 in 1976, to 612 in 2000).

The protected area systems not only protect biological diversity but also contribute to the conservation of cultural and religious heritage. There are a number of centuries-old settlements and religious sites inside mountain national parks where various ethnic groups with rich and diversified cultural practices have been living in harmony with nature. For example, *Sherpa, Bhote, Rai, Tamang* and *Gurung* are the major ethnic groups in the mountain areas whereas *Tharus* – indigenous inhabitants of Terai – and hill migrants occupy the surrounding area of national parks and reserves in Terai. Annapurna Conservation Area is the home of eleven different ethnic peoples. *Sherpa* communities in Sagarmatha (Mt. Everest) National Park believe that animals, plants and even rocks have spirits, and as Buddhists, they follow traditions of non-violence that make hunting abhorrent to them (Stevens, 1997).

There are also many cultural, religious and archaeologically important sites in and around protected areas. Some of the important religious and cultural sites are Tengboche Gomba (Monastery) in Sagarmatha National Park, Shey Gomba in Shey Phoskunda National Park, Lo Monthang, a medieval walled city made of mudbrick in the trans-Himalayan region of Mustang in Annapurna Conservation Area, and Balmiki Ashram in Royal Chitwan National Park. The Balmiki Ashram, which lies on the western side of the Royal Chitwan National Park, dates back to 300–200 BC and has been mentioned in the *Ramayana* epic (Paudel, 1997). Similarly, many mountain cave systems in Mustang are believed to be prehistoric. A recent discovery of approximately 30 naturally mummified bodies in one of these cave systems is believed to be from circa 400BC to 50AD (Alt *et al.,* 2003).

While Nepal is extremely rich in natural, cultural and spiritual wealth, it is also home to many poor mountain communities. Biodiversity conservation has been a challenging task as these poor people depend on biological resources for their subsistence. For example, forests provide 81% of the total fuel and about 50% of the fodder requirements of households in Nepal (WECS, 1997). As a result, conservation in Nepal has been responsive to this social context and has sought a balance between short-term human needs and long-term ecological integrity. Conservation approaches have shifted from a species focus to an ecosystem focus and are now more participatory, rather than protective, as in the past (Table 1). Table 1 also suggests that Nepal has adopted a more holistic, inclusive and decentralized conservation paradigm than in the past. The country has been a leading innovator in the establishment of indigenously inhabited and co-managed protected areas in the mountains (Stevens, 1997).

## Table 1. Change in conservation paradigms in Nepal

| Past | Present |
|------|---------|
| ▪ Strict protection | ▪ People's participation |
| ▪ Species focus | ▪ Ecosystem focus |
| ▪ Control in resource use | ▪ Resource-and revenue-sharing |
| ▪ Island approach | ▪ Landscape approach |
| ▪ Centralized and government-controlled | ▪ Decentralized and open to NGO and private sector involvement |

Nepal has been trying to balance protective and participatory approaches to resource conservation simultaneously. At one end of this continuum, there are strictly protected Terai national parks and reserves with no, or minimal, people's participation in park protection and management. On the other hand, in the management of buffer zones (BZ) and conservation areas a participatory conservation approach with community access to the forest resources has been adopted. The Himalayan Parks, where local people are allowed to collect fuelwood, fodder and leaf-litter for domestic use, fall in the middle of this continuum (Figure 1).

## Fig. 1. Conservation continuum

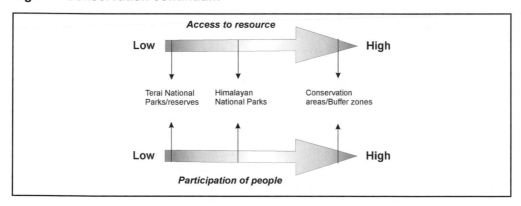

Recognising the role and importance of people and lived-in landscapes for the long-term conservation of biodiversity, Nepal has been adopting new models for conservation over the last decade and a half. Moreover, the country has been a leading innovator in the establishment of indigenously inhabited and co-managed protected areas in the mountains (Stevens 1997). The country uses a conservation area model (conservation with people) in creating new protected areas, and a buffer zone approach (conservation through people) in managing existing parks and reserves. Within three decades, Nepal's protected area management

**Fig. 2   Shifting conservation paradigms: from island to networks**

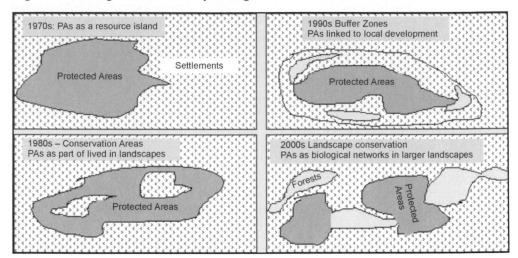

strategies have changed from 'island' to 'network' approaches, which integrate various social as well as ecological dimensions (Figure 2).

# Development of the protected landscape approach and community-based conservation

In Nepal, resource management strategies have been heavily influenced by the fact that the protection, maintenance and development of natural resources are neither possible nor practicable through government effort alone (Budhathoki, 2001). There has been a major shift in the management paradigm of protected areas from the protective to the collaborative, with the introduction of the conservation area and buffer zone concepts (Maskey, 2001). Since the mid-1980s, the approach to protected area management has recognised the existence of settlement and private farming rights within the protected area boundaries, initiated co-management of natural resources, and supported initiatives for community development.

The buffer zone concept was introduced in 1994 as a key strategy to conserve biodiversity by addressing both the impact of local people on protected areas, and the impact of protected areas on local people. In Nepal buffer zones are conceived as areas where land resources are managed and used within sustainable limits and where communities and conservation authorities work together to promote development which is not inimical to conservation (Sharma, 2001). The buffer zones include a mosaic of forests, agricultural lands, settlements, cultural heritage sites, village open spaces, and many other land-use types. The buffer zone regulations (1996) allow park authorities to invest 30–50% of the park's income in community development in the buffer zone areas. The introduction and implementation of this buffer zone approach has been a landmark in protected area management, enabling the change from conventional park management to a more collaborative approach (Maskey, 2001).

The Buffer Zone initiative also has served as a stepping stone to the empowerment of local people and has enhanced their involvement in conservation and provided for the distribution of conservation benefits to local communities (Budhathoki, 2003). Since 1997, more than US$1.2 million of park income has been recycled into the implementation of conservation and development activities in the buffer zone areas (DNPWC, 2003). To date more than 700,000 people in 185 Village Development Committees (or VDCs), which are the lowest political unit, have directly or indirectly benefited from the programme.

In Nepal, both conservation area and buffer zone management are now widely adopted and practised approaches to conservation. There are three conservation areas, which altogether cover about 42% of the total area under protected area regimes. In addition, 11 of the 16 protected areas in Nepal have been implementing a buffer zone management programme. The management of both conservation areas and buffer zones is based on a careful integration of conservation and development priorities, and incorporates all the key elements of the Category V protected landscape approach. According to Lucas (1992), the Annapurna Conservation Area, which for many years has been adopting integrated conservation concepts, is one of the best examples of protected landscape management in the developing world.

Globally, it has been accepted that protected areas cannot exist as unique islands but as places in a land-use matrix (IUCN, 2003; Phillips, 2002). In Nepal also, the landscape-based conservation approach has been adopted as an opportunity to scale up conservation initiatives for long-term biodiversity conservation. Successful experiences of conservation area and buffer zone management programmes have been instrumental in the country's effort to embark upon larger, landscape-level conservation initiatives. Nepal's National Biodiversity Strategy (NBS) has identified these as a viable strategy, linking conservation with poverty alleviation. The NBS document prescribed the lowland Terai and Eastern Himal Areas as priority landscape complexes for these initiatives. Various international conservation and development agencies such as IUCN – The World Conservation Union, the Worldwide Fund for Nature (WWF) and the United Nations Development Programme/Global Environment Facility (UNDP/GEF) have been collaborating with the government in implementing these projects.

## Fig. 3    Landscape conservation complexes

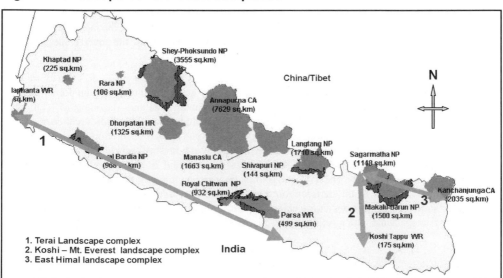

One of the recent landscape conservation initiatives is the Terai Arc Landscape (TAL) programme, a very ambitious and long-term programme being undertaken by Nepali agencies with the support of WWF-Nepal (see Box 1). The Terai Arc Landscape initiative proposes to reconnect 11 protected areas in the territory between Nepal's Parsa Wildlife Reserve and India's Rajaji-Corbett National Parks into a single functioning landscape encompassing habitat critical for the long-term conservation of tiger, rhino and elephant (WWF-Nepal, 2003). The TAL strategy plan, which was recently approved by the government, will help further in developing landscape-level conservation in Nepal. Similarly, the Himal initiative of IUCN has been proposing the Koshi River basin complex – one of the largest river basins in Nepal, which encompasses the Koshi river watershed, including the slopes of Mount Everest – as their landscape conservation complex. This indicates that conservation initiatives have been gaining momentum in both horizontal (Terai landscape), as well as vertical (Koshi watersheds) landscape complexes (Figure 3). Since Nepal has a long track record of implementation of successful participatory and co-management conservation initiatives, there are also high hopes for the successful implementation of these initiatives.

---

**Box 1.   Case study. Terai Arc Landscape conservation initiative in Nepal**

The **Terai Arc Landscape** (TAL) Programme encompasses one of the most biologically diverse habitats on the earth and is a part of the Terai Duar Savannah and Grasslands Global 2000 eco-region. The programme is envisioned to restore and maintain critical forest corridors to connect 11 protected areas in Nepal and India. The reconnection of protected areas into one secure habitat would provide the opportunity for tigers, rhinos, elephants and other species to migrate and disperse their genes, increasing the chances of long-term population survival. This programme presents an ambitious opportunity to reverse the trend of fragmentation, which, if unaddressed, will leave South Asia's rhinos, elephants and tigers in isolated habitats. The vision of the TAL programme stretches from 50 to 100 years of biodiversity conservation.

Available information suggests that in India, the TAL programme is still in a dormant stage. However, in Nepal, it is being implemented jointly by the Department of Forests (DOF), the Department of National Parks and Wildlife Conservation (DNPWC), and the WWF-Nepal Program in collaboration with local communities and NGOs. Currently TAL Nepal covers an area of over 22,288km$^2$ of protective and productive areas, including four protected areas – Parsa Wildlife Reserve, Royal Chitwan National Park, Royal Bardia National Park, and Royal Suklaphanta Wildlife Reserve. Approximately three million people, 50% of whom subsist below the poverty line, live in this landscape and depend on its resources for their livelihood.

To date, the TAL programme focuses on five critical areas in the Khata (Bardia) and Basanta (Kailali) corridors and on three "bottleneck" sites (defined as narrow but important forest areas between two large forest blocks), namely Dovan VDC, Lamahi Area and Mahadevpuri VDC in Palpa, Dang and Banke respectively. The TAL programme includes various activities related to park management and species conservation, community forestry and habitat restoration, anti-poaching, awareness-raising, income generation and capacity-building of both staff and community organiza- tions. A community-based organization has been established and is playing a key role in the programme's implementation. The TAL programme is using community forestry and buffer zone management approaches in the corridor forest areas and BZ areas respectively. It is piloting an integrated strategy that includes enforcement, incentives and education in order to balance the protection of mega fauna with meeting human needs.

Cont.

---

---

**Box 1.   Case study. Terai Arc Landscape conservation initiative in Nepal (cont.)**

Some notable outputs of the programme are the establishment of agro-forestry nurseries with the capacity of producing 330,000 seedlings; plantations in 161.5ha of land; the hand-over of five community forests to local communities; the formation of 26 community forest user groups; and the removal of encroachers from 5,500ha of land in the Basanta Forest corridor. A total of 536ha of degraded land have been restored with the participation of local people, through plantation and natural regeneration. Other activities have been the management of 250ha of grassland, construction of five waterholes, and support for the operations of 17 anti-poaching units in the four protected areas of TAL. Likewise, ten rhinos were translocated from Chitwan to Royal Bardia National Park as part of the initiative to establish a second viable population in Bardia. Other achievements include conservation awareness activities including the formation of 28 new Eco-clubs at various schools. A number of community development programmes such as biogas, community services, income-generation activities and awareness-raising programmes have been implemented in full partnership with local communities to engage them directly in conservation, enhance the income of local people, and encourage them to reduce the pressure on the forest.

Moreover, TAL's other major success has been in both community mobilization and building community institutions (termed institutionalization), which have given impetus to sustainable development and forest restoration. For the first time, community-based anti-poaching operations have been started in the forest corridors with the establishment of three community Anti-Poaching Units (APUs). It is also important to note that, despite the current insurgency problem, the local people as well as Community-Based Organizations (CBOs), Community Forest User Groups, and Community Forest Coordination Committees have endeavoured to ensure continuity in implementing TAL activities. The TAL programme has been able to gain the involvement of local people who have contributed voluntary labour and local materials valued at approximately 40% of the cost for forest conservation and management of corridors and bottlenecks. Recently, the government has approved the TAL strategic plan, which will be the main guiding document for planning and implementation of natural resource management projects and programmes in this region of Nepal.

*Sources*: EcoCircular: Vol 9 No. 7 August 2002: www.wwfnepal.org.np accessed: 18/3/04; DNPWC, 2003.

---

Scaling up conservation initiatives to a larger landscape level is not without its challenges. Biological diversity in Nepal is closely linked to the livelihoods of many people and their economic development. Among all the countries of the Himalayan region (the Himalayan part only), Nepal has the lowest percentage of forest cover and has the highest density of people and livestock per hectare of land. It also has the lowest availability of forest land per capita and grazing land per unit of livestock. Particularly in the Terai, it will be a daunting task to manage conservation initiatives at the landscape level as the human population has been growing and natural habitats have been shrinking and becoming more and more fragmented. Moreover, most of these forest frontier areas are inhabited by poor and economically marginalized communities. In this context, the issue of meeting basic survival needs is the single greatest challenge to the conservation of biological resources for the long-term survival of mega fauna such as elephants, tiger and rhinos. A study by Cracraft (1999) reveals that Nepal has the highest biodiversity-threat index and the lowest management capacity response index of all countries in South Asia. In this context, scaling up of conservation initiatives means a more complex and challenging task for conservation agencies.

Royal Chitwan National Park is one of the main sources of fodder for many villagers living in the Park's buffer zones. *Prabhu Budhathoki*

## Challenges of landscape-level conservation approaches

The challenges of landscape-level conservation initiatives in Nepal could be summarised as follows:

- **Communicating a novel approach and engaging the local communities.** There is a widespread suspicion among rural people that landscape conservation initiatives could be another way to extend protected areas and control over resource use. As described by Beresford and Phillips (2000), turning the image of protected areas from one in which they are "planned against people" to "one in which they are planned with people and, often for, and by them" requires innovative strategies and greater effort.

- **Difficulty in coordination between various stakeholders.** Due to the nature and scale of landscape conservation programmes, the challenge of co-coordinating various stakeholders and government line agencies is obvious. There exists inadequate horizontal communication between different sectors of government such as forestry, agriculture, local development as well as vertical communication between different tiers of government. The lack of co-ordination between these agencies has resulted in overlapping remits, inefficient spending of resources, and confusion among the stakeholders. A careful integration of national, regional and local interests in planning and management of landscape conservation is vital in order to fulfil the integrated objectives of landscape-level conservation.

- **Inadequate institutional capacity, human resources and necessary skills to deliver diverse responsibilities.** Landscape-level conservation is much more complex and difficult than national park management. At the landscape level, a biodiversity conservation programme requires a business-like management approach. However, protected area managers in Nepal often lack many necessary skills and knowledge to deal with the diverse and complex social and economic issues associated with resource conservation. Many protected area staff are still making the transition from an insular approach to conservation to a more inclusive and engaging approach. This change will be key to making landscape conservation initiatives successful.

- **Programmes with high conservation focus that are driven by conservation agencies and involve less engagement of local people.** Certain landscape conservation programmes focused exclusively on specific conservation goals are led by park and forestry officials in collaboration with WWF and other conservation agencies. Programmes such as forest conservation, wildlife protection and habitat restoration give high priority to the ecological dimensions, and communities often find these efforts less engaging and do not tend to participate. In contrast, the success of the protected landscape concept depends on serving both nature and people, and on cooperation and mutual commitment of people and authorities (Lucas,1992). To achieve the objective of conservation beyond boundaries, according to Beresford (2003) conservation professionals should develop new partnerships and think 'out of the box.'

- **External rather than internal funding sources.** Landscape conservation programmes currently under implementation depend heavily, if not totally, on outside funding. The sustainability of such programmes will be questionable if successful experiences have not been internalized and institutionalized within the regular government structure and programmes. Moreover, developing a "stewardship approach" that puts conservation in the hands of people most affected by it, and thereby integrates people with nature, as suggested by Brown and Mitchell (2000), could be an appropriate and sustainable landscape conservation strategy.

- **Required policy and legislation are still not in place**. For successful management of protected landscapes, a supportive legal framework is essential (Phillips, 2002). Currently, Nepal does not have comprehensive legal and institutional frameworks to coordinate diverse and complex conservation interventions at the landscape level. In the absence of an umbrella policy framework and a coordinating institution, agencies working according to different and sometimes conflicting legal mandates and priorities may compete or overlap with each other.

# Conclusion

Conservation is essential and it happens only when people understand the reasons behind it and are actively engaged. In Nepal there is a growing understanding that for biodiversity conservation to be sustainable, appropriate socio-political as well as ecological landscapes are necessary. It is important to note that 78% of the country's protected areas have been adopting a protected landscape approach to conservation and have tried to link people with resource conservation by empowering local communities to manage their resources and receive benefits from conservation.

However, at the landscape scale, successful biodiversity conservation will depend not only on productive collaboration with local people but also on coordinated, integrated planning at provincial, regional and national levels. Additionally, sustainable management of both protected and productive landscapes in collaboration with various interest groups is necessary for the successful management of protected landscapes. Amid growing population and rampant poverty, the successes of ecological linkages will largely depend on careful integration of ecological benefits with the socio-economic interests of the people. Last but not least, Nepal's landscape conservation initiatives can only be truly successful when their managers and staff adopt a sensitive and supportive attitude to people, and when local communities are enabled to become more directly engaged in conservation.

## Acknowledgement

I am grateful to Dr Liz Hughes, Executive Director, ICPL for her valuable feedback.

# 7. World Heritage inscription and challenges to the survival of community life in Philippine cultural landscapes

*Augusto Villalón*

The 21st century continues to put pressure on the traditional practices that have always maintained the delicate balance between culture and nature in many continuing cultural landscapes in the Philippines. Balancing tradition and progress is the key issue that must be answered by the two most significant Philippine cultural landscapes, the Rice Terraces of the Philippine Cordilleras and the Batanes Protected Landscape and Seascape, in order for each to determine its own path towards the sustainable preservation of its culture and the distinctive landscape that it has produced.

Continuing cultural landscapes are the result of a long and continued interaction between man and nature that persists to the present. The qualities that make each cultural landscape unique are the physical manifestations of the indelible imprint of humankind on the environment. In other World Heritage cultural landscape categories, such as associative and relict, the human factor is absent. The interaction of man and nature is completed and life has long left the site. However, the preservation of organically evolved continuing cultural landscapes involves the simultaneous preservation of both tangible and intangible heritage (see excerpt from the WHC Operational Guidelines in Appendix 4). The process links the preservation of its resident culture whose lifestyle must keep weaving tradition with the present. The challenge for continuing cultural landscapes is to avoid mummifying present human activity to a specific time in the past to protect the landscape. It requires finding a balance between the past, present and the future that assure sustainability for the site.

Little awareness of cultural landscapes exists in the Philippines. Not many citizens know that the national government passed the National Integrated Protected Areas System Act (NIPAS) in 1992 to protect areas in the following categories: (a) strict nature reserve, (b) natural parks, (c) natural monuments, (d) wildlife sanctuaries, (e) protected landscapes and seascapes, (f) resource reserve, and (g) national biotic areas. Implementation of the NIPAS Act is the responsibility of the Department of the Environment and Natural Resources. Among the sites protected by the NIPAS Act is the Batanes Protected Landscape and Seascape, which was nominated to the World Heritage List as a continuing cultural landscape in 2004 and is currently under review. The outstanding cultural landscapes in the Philippines are located in remote areas of the country that have by tradition experienced severe economic or environmental hardship due to their geographic isolation. Harsh conditions have contributed in preserving both culture and landscape, so it is understandable that, in the eyes of the residents, traditional landscape and vernacular architecture symbolise the economic deprivation that they have suffered for many generations. As soon as a rise in income occurs, their old houses are immediately replaced with new constructions of concrete walling roofed by galvanized iron sheets. Never mind that the new construction replaced a traditional house built of natural materials that was completely in tune with its environment and climate. It does not matter that the new low-pitched roofing turns houses into ovens during the summer or drives residents deaf with the sound of monsoon rain falling heavily on the iron roofing. Totally unsuited to its environment and hostile to its natural surroundings, the new house is a symbol of modernity. It is a shining symbol of progress that everyone wants. It disregards everything traditional. It shows having crossed over into the 21st century. The new house is symbolic of the principal issue at hand of finding a solution to maintaining what still remains relevant of cultural traditions while moving society towards modernity.

Residents of cultural landscapes and heritage zones deserve to enjoy the full range of 21st century benefits. The difficult issue that still goes unanswered is how to find a method to provide those benefits in a manner that sustains both traditional culture and its distinctive landscape. The local culture must determine its own path in moving towards the future as quickly as possible while maintaining one foot firmly in its past, a demanding challenge that must be handled with extreme care. There are no precedents to follow for this process. Each culture proceeds at a pace of its own that is determined by the complex issues that each individual culture must identify and settle.

The experience of two continuing cultural landscapes in the Philippines illustrates the challenges of balancing tradition and progress, and the importance of keeping local communities engaged in sustaining and protecting their landscapes. This chapter reviews two of the most outstanding continuing cultural landscapes in the Philippines: the Rice Terraces of the Philippine Cordilleras and the Batanes Protected Landscape and Seascape. The Rice Terraces of the Philippine Cordilleras was nominated to the UNESCO World Heritage List in 1994 and inscribed in 1995. The Batanes Protected Landscape and Seascape was nominated to the World Heritage List ten years later in 2004. Comparing the nomination strategies for the two sites shows the evolution of a more mature approach not only towards the preparation of the site for World Heritage nomination, but also towards eliciting community involvement in custodianship and site management that is more attuned to local traditions and expectations.

## Rice Terraces of the Philippine Cordilleras

The Rice Terraces of the Philippine Cordilleras were inscribed as the first continuing cultural landscape on the World Heritage List in 1995 with the justification that the site is "an outstanding example of living cultural landscapes. They (the terraces) illustrate traditional techniques and a remarkable harmony between humankind and the natural environment."[1] In 2001 the property was the first cultural landscape to be inscribed on the "World Heritage In Danger" list, and this has led to renewed efforts to sustain and protect this landscape.

Records show that rice has been cultivated in Asia for 7,000 years. During that long period, culture and cultivation have interwoven with each other. The rice-growing landscape interlocks agriculture, environment, and cultural practices that sustain traditional methods of site management. Instead of blending into the landscape, rice cultivation sculpts the landscape to suit the crop's needs, creating an unmistakable landscape pattern. The paddy landscape is unquestionably a cultural landscape, the unifying visual and cultural icon that ties Southeast Asian countries together in the rice culture that they share.

---

[1] UNESCO World Heritage Committee, Report of the 19th Session of the Committee, Berlin, 1955

The Rice Terraces of the Philippine Cordilleras was inscribed on the World Heritage list in 1995 as "an outstanding example of living cultural landscapes".
*Augusto Villalón*

*Augusto Villalón*

Among the Asian paddy landscapes, one stands out: the Rice Terraces of the Philippine Cordilleras. High in the remote areas of the Philippine Cordillera mountain range, mountain slopes are terraced and planted with rice. The majestic landscape shows the great length to which the Filipino, or the Asian for that matter, will go to plant rice. Terraced areas in widely varying states of conservation are spread over most of the 20,000km² land area (7% of the total land mass of the Philippines) principally centred in the provinces of Kalinga-Apayao, Abra, Benguet, and Ifugao. The improbable site is found at altitudes varying from 700–1,500m above sea level where terraces are sliced into mountainside contours that rise to a slope reaching a maximum of 70% (compared to the more gentle slopes of 40% in Bali).

In contrast to the growing conditions common to Asian lowland rice agriculture, the rice terraces of the Cordilleras grow a special high-altitude strain of rice under extremely de-manding climatic and agricultural constraints, which is found only in the rice terraces area. This particular strain germinates under freezing conditions, and grows chest-high stalks of non-shattering panicles, unlike lowland rice that grows to knee height with easily shattering panicles. Traditionally, the rice is harvested by women while they are chanting the *hud-hud*, a chant that was proclaimed by UNESCO as one of the world's 19 masterpeices of the Oral Intangible Heritage of Humanity in 2001. An example of the culture-nature connection is that the harvesters' ability to stand erect while harvesting and simultaneously chanting the *hud-hud* would not have been possible without the waist-high highland variation in the rice strain, which is different from the lowland rice variety that requires bending to harvest the stalks. A second example of the connection is that of the non-shattering panicles, which makes it possible to bundle the rice and transport the bundles manually on shoulder poles or on tops of heads for storage in granaries.

More culture-nature connections are evident. Terraces are commonly built in three ways. Walls are constructed completely of stone. The second method is by building walls of packed mud. The third variation mixes a foundation course of stone and packed mud wall above. Terraces rise in groups from valleys, climbing up the slopes stopping just below peaks continually covered with mist. Terraces normally face east, to assure a maximum of sunlight.

A ring of private forests (*muyong*) caps each terrace group. The management of the muyong are closely regimented through traditional tribal practices. The owners of the forest parcels are fully conscious that they are participating in a collective effort. Their forests are essential in maintaining ecological balance and each owner knows that any negative intervention brings disadvantage not only to him, but also to the other terrace owners.

Water, the lifeline of the terraces, is equitably shared. No single terrace is allowed to obstruct the flow of water from his downhill neighbour. A complex system of dams, sluices, canals and bamboo pipes transfers the water from the highest terrace to the lowest, draining into a stream or river at the foot of the valley. Hydraulics has been traditionally used for construction. Temporary dams constructed around rocks are flooded to allow large rocks to be manually pushed or "floated" to their desired location. Terraces are filled with earth through hydraulics. After the walls are built, the enclosed area is flooded with mud that then becomes the subsoil for the paddy.

The terraced landscape illustrates the complexity of architecture in rice. It establishes architecture as one of the many elements in the totality of agricultural, engineering, environmental and cultural traditions that come together in the growing of rice. It sets architecture in the context of a cultural and environmental system.

Of all Philippine monuments, the rice terraces are the best known throughout the country. In fact, most Filipinos regard the terraces as their greatest national symbol, an appropriate symbol because the site is not a single monument but a vast, living site that combines both the natural and cultural. It is also a significant monument because it was built voluntarily without any forced labour. What makes the symbol even more appropriate is that the rice terraces combine architecture, engineering, and environmental management in a system that is still sustainable to this day, a fitting tribute to the traditional thinkers who set the management system centuries ago. The system has been orally handed down to allow their people to continue living on the site and for them to continue to grow rice.

The cultural landscape of rice is a phenomenon that combines both natural and cultural concerns. It brings out that fact that the landscape of rice cannot be understood if its parts are studied individually. The architecture of rice, therefore, should be viewed in the context of the cultural landscape in which it exists. Although traditional knowledge orally handed down from generation to generation has guided the maintenance of the Rice Terraces of the Philippine Cordilleras, its contemporary maintenance history has always been tied into its status as a World Heritage site.

The fragile site owes its preservation to the strong spiritual values of the Ifugao culture that has been guiding all aspects of daily life for over a thousand years, as some scholars maintain. Tradition has always been the source that determined all cultural and physical actions in the site. Until this day, rituals invoke spirits to commemorate individual or communal celebrations, to seek assistance for physical afflictions, to settle disputes among villagers, and to mark planting and harvesting during the yearly agricultural cycle. The spirit world of the tribal mountain culture is deeply rooted in the highland lifestyle and environment, expressed in a wealth of artistic output and in the traditional environmental management system that remains in place today. The history of the terraces, therefore, is intertwined with that of its people, their culture and beliefs, and in their traditional environmental management and agricultural practices.

The site is one of the few living cultural landscapes that continue to exist in the contemporary world. Its UNESCO inscription has given international recognition to the site. On the national level, maintaining the traditional values, whether spiritual or physical, is under severe threat due to the pressing demands of modernization, the urgent socio-economic needs of the community, and the lack of support from national authorities who are not aware that preservation of the physical and cultural aspects of the site must go hand in hand. Most national authorities believe that it is enough to grant assistance for the physical restoration of the terraces and disregard the preservation of the cultural values that reinforce the continuation of the traditional agricultural system. Airports, highways, and tourism infrastructure are also national development priorities that will threaten the endangered site and its community even more.

The balance between tradition and progress is the key issue that the Rice Terraces of the Philippine Cordilleras must answer in order to determine the path that it must take for the future. The difficult issue is to manage the forward movement of the residents into the 21$^{st}$ century while finding a means of maintaining their culture, traditional knowledge and their landscape in a sustainable manner. How can the local culture move towards the future without being mummified into the past?

Change is difficult to manage in the Philippine Cordilleras. The terraces follow the contours of the highest peaks of the mountain range. The narrow rice fields are built in clusters from stone and mud. Privately owned forests that play an important part in maintaining the water cycle encircle terrace clusters. A traditionally designed hydraulic system with sluices and canals democratically delivers an unobstructed water supply starting from the highest terrace descending to the lowest. Change threatens the future of the terraces. Progress questions the sustainability of traditional agricultural practices; modern influences not only question the validity of traditional cultural practices but endanger the visual characteristics of the landscape.

The management history of the site has been closely linked with its World Heritage status. In preparation for site nomination, a joint effort by the UNESCO National Commission of the Philippines, the ICOMOS Philippine Committee and local citizens resulted in the organization of the Ifugao Terraces Commission. Its first task was to prepare a Master Plan for the terrace clusters proposed for World Heritage inscription (located in the municipalities of Kiangan, Banaue, Hungduan and Mayoyao) that incorporated all development and management requirements to satisfy World Heritage requirements. As soon as nomination requirements were in place, the dossier was prepared and submitted, and inscription happened in the following year. In hindsight, the process happened too quickly.

The Master Plan recognised the need to continue the existing culture-based traditional practices to assure the maintenance of the site, focusing on cultural revival as the *raison d'être* for the simultaneous educational, environmental, agricultural and reconstruction programmes being implemented by the national and local authorities. Other priorities were to: (a) set in place management units that correspond to the core management zones for terrace protection and rehabilitation as well as support zones for area-based and tourism development; (b) resolve the ownership and other policy issues impinging on the implementation of the plan; (c) set up the designs and mechanisms for resource generation and livelihood activities in support of the terraces; and (d) design and establish the monitoring and evaluation system for plan implementation. World Heritage requirements were included in the Master Plan, and the five terrace clusters became the nucleus for the World Heritage nomination.

The Ifugao Terraces Commission was the advisory and monitoring body envisioned to carry through the Master Plan. Following components identified in the plan, other government agencies were mandated to cooperate with the Commission and to fund and carry out programmes that fell within their sector. However, the reality was that the agencies felt that this was an imposition on their priorities and budgets so no projects were completed. The funds allocated to the Ifugao Terraces Commission were minimal. Not surprisingly, few projects were completed and the terraces deteriorated rapidly, due to site mismanagement.

Implementing the Master Plan was a difficult challenge. The community participated in preparing the Master Plan but did not feel any ownership towards it. Implementation was left to the Ifugao Terraces Commission staff. However, the Office of the President who had jurisdiction over the Commission did not understand that site preservation went beyond rehabilitating its tangible qualities and that much of the intangible heritage had to be revived or preserved as well. National government then concluded that the Commission's accomplishments fell short of expectations because it failed to comply with the indicators set to measure tangible rehabilitation actions. So it abolished the Ifugao Terraces Commission and organized the Banaue Rice Terraces Task Force as the replacement authority.

The short-lived Banaue Rice Terraces Task Force faced the same setback of not being able to satisfy indicators for tangible rehabilitation set by the Office of the President. As a result it suffered severe budget cuts that crippled the agency until its ultimate abolition by the President, which led to its In Danger listing in 1999.

The threats that face the Rice Terraces are complex. One threat is the apparent loss of manpower. Parents send their young to the lowlands for education. They remain there for employment opportunities not available in their traditional homes. There are a few who return to the highlands of their own choice, preferring to continue the lifestyle and agricultural activities of their parents rather than live in the lowlands. An interesting theory exists that the carrying capacity of the site is so limited that it cannot accommodate the increased population. Therefore immigration relieves potential site pressure. Nevertheless, the actual reality is that maintenance of the terraces is now left to the older generation because the younger generation has chosen to live away from the site.

Life on the terraces is extremely difficult. It is impossible to bring farm animals or machinery to the terraces because of limited access. Therefore planting, harvesting, maintenance of terrace walls and all other terrace activities must be done manually, without any mechanical aid. The freezing weather, monsoon rains and typhoons, earthquakes and tremors are some of the unpredictable natural forces that must be contended with.

The irrigation system, a fine-tuned web of natural streams, catchments, ditches, sluices and bamboo pipes that deliver water downhill, providing water evenly to each terrace, has suffered extensive damage from the cyclical earthquakes that occur in the area. The frequent slight tremors are enough to misalign the distribution system. Therefore constant repair is necessary to keep the distribution system functional. The traditional system, constructed of natural materials that possessed a pliability that allowed the irrigation network to adjust to minor earth movements due to rain or slight earthquakes, was lost with recent experiments in repairing the system with rigid concrete. The mistaken rationale is that concrete pipes are cheaper and easier to lay when compared to a tediously constructed system built of natural materials that are no longer available.

Architectural qualities are eroding as well. Clusters of villages with houses that had steep, pyramidal roofs of thatch were the most striking features of landscape. They have practically disappeared in recent years. A programme is proposed to replant thatch material as a first step towards encouraging homeowners to re-thatch rather than replace thatch with galvanized iron sheets.

Since property ownership is reckoned on traditional practices, traditional boundaries still delineate the World Heritage terrace clusters. ICOMOS-IUCN and the World Heritage Committee accepted traditional boundaries when the nomination dossier was submitted. However, to reinforce traditional knowledge with technology, a UNESCO-aided project is underway for GIS mapping of the site to generate the nonexistent baseline data needed for site management planning. The output of this project will fuse the traditional boundary system with mapping of the terraces site. It also will provide the first detailed inventory of the site.

Since the In Danger inscription, national government through the National Commission for Culture and the Arts has provided financial aid amounting to $1,000,000 for site rehabilitation programmes. Management of the site has been taken over by the Office of the Ifugao Provincial Governor, returning responsibility to the local community once again.

The Governor recognises that for the future existence of the terraces, it is essential to continue the existing culture-based traditional practices that assure site maintenance. The present focus at the Rice Terraces centres on cultural revival as the *raison d'être* for the simultaneous educational, environmental, agricultural and reconstruction programmes being implemented by national and local authorities. Furthermore, community participation has finally been seen as the most important element in assuring the conservation of the terraces. The first activity to be funded by an Emergency Assistance Grant from UNESCO was the convening of a workshop to revisit and to update the Master Plan written by the Ifugao Terraces Commission and to assure community participation in the revision of the Master Plan.

As a result of its inscription onto the In Danger list, the concerted preservation effort of the Rice Terraces of the Philippine Cordilleras is focused on community participation. The primary programme is to re-establish pride of place among the site residents and others who have migrated away from the area. There are cultural revival programmes that introduce school children to the native culture and remind older residents of the traditional knowledge of their forebears. To centralize all site information, a GIS inventory is planned, with the preparation of a land-use plan among the outputs expected. Community members are participating in preparing a revised management plan for the site that will prioritize development projects that are to be undertaken in the near future.

Given its impact on the increased awareness of national government to the needs of the site, the In Danger inscription of the Rice Terraces of the Philippine Cordilleras can be looked upon as a positive action.

## Batanes Protected Landscape and Seascape

The remote Batanes Archipelago, nominated for World Heritage inscription in 2004, is situated off the northernmost tip of the Philippines, close to the southern tip of Taiwan. Distance and unpredictable weather conditions isolate the islands most of the year. Therefore many of its cultural traditions, landscape and vernacular architecture have remained intact, safeguarded from erosion caused by outside influences. The nationally protected seascape and landscape of intense beauty is well known in the Philippines.

The Batanes archipelago is designated by the National Integrated Protected Area System law as one of 11 Protected Landscapes and Seascapes of the Philippines. It is therefore a Category V protected area, protected by national legislation enforced by the Department of the Environment and Natural Resources. Unlike the Rice Terraces, the protective legislation for Batanes was already being implemented well before the time of World Heritage nomination.

The entire area within the boundaries stipulated by the NIPAS Act as a Category V Protected Area (Batanes Protected Landscape and Seascape) was nominated as a World Heritage Cultural Landscape. The site encompasses ten islands, the sea between them reaching to the marine boundary of the archipelago. Within the boundary is a cultural landscape composed of a series of 28 natural and cultural sites that combine to illustrate the unique story of the ten islands. It is a serial nomination within the NIPAS-designated boundaries of Batanes that serves as its buffer zone.

In contrast to the nomination process for the Rice Terraces of the Philippine Cordilleras, for the Batanes Protected Landscape and Seascape the process was slow and deliberate. From the start it was agreed that community participation was essential. All preparations were done over an eight-year period, initiated by the provincial government with the complete cooperation of the community. Batanes is a site that contains a series of outstanding natural properties that have shaped the unique landscape of the archipelago. It also contains an equally outstanding series of cultural properties that are milestones in the long evolutionary process of the unique Ivatan culture in its continual process of responding to its severe natural environment. The series of natural and cultural properties interrelate to form a system of unique natural and cultural manifestations whose survival is crucial for the continuation of Batanes as a distinct whole.

The individual properties that compose this system of natural and cultural properties each represent one or more World Heritage criteria. When viewed in their entirety, the properties within the proposed World Heritage Site exhibit almost all of the natural and cultural criteria for universal value.

Due to its geographic location, waves of external influences, both natural and cultural, have funnelled through the islands. Each influence has left an indelible imprint in the unique landscape and culture of the Ivatan archipelago, which can be seen in the series of properties being nominated. Each of the 26 properties in the series represents one significant chapter in the

*Augusto Villalon*

The Batanes archipelago of islands, located in the northern Philippines, has been nominated as a World Heritage Cultural Landscape. One of 11 Category V Protected Landscapes and Seascapes in the country's protected area system, it is rich in natural values, including many endemic species, as well as cultural values, such as its architecture, which is unique to the region. *Augusto Villalón*

evolutionary story of the Batanes archipelago. When viewed in their entirety, the series of properties tells the Ivatan story.

The pre-history of Batanes begins with volcanic activity 8 million years ago that raised the islands from the sea, eventually permitting the development of endemic flora. Migratory birds, fishes and turtles followed, and finally humans, all funnelling through Batanes as the first step in their migratory journey from the Asian mainland to Southeast Asia, continuing onwards to the South Pacific. Archaeological evidence from the end of the Pleistocene documents the passing of humans through Batanes who originated from points north of the islands in their spread throughout Southeast Asia. Archaeological evidence proves that early Ivatans lived in citadel-villages carved into the highest mountain-tops for protection. Spanish colonists arrived in the 17th century, converted the Ivatans to Christianity and replaced mountain villages with coastal towns. They changed traditional grass architecture to mud and stone construction, finally introducing lime as a building material in the late 18th century. They also introduced western town planning to Batanes, the most remote location in the Philippines and the farthest flung outpost of the vast Spanish empire.

The existing landscape and culture manifest the Ivatan response to this demanding environment, as seen in outstanding natural formations, endemic species and man-made interventions such as typhoon-resistant architecture and hedgerows planted around farm plots to protect crops from wind damage. It is a landscape that continues bearing witness to a vanished culture whose response to its harsh environment has influenced the population's present existence, a phenomenon that has evolved to the existing lifestyle that links past with present.

The natural and cultural manifestations of the property demonstrate how living organisms and humans can prevail over what seem to be insurmountable environmental challenges and succeed in colonizing the most isolated areas of our planet. In Batanes that fragile but constant interaction between nature and humankind continues up to this day. Today's Ivatan culture is the outcome of human response to severe environmental demands, which developed a landscape and culture distinctly showing the long and continuing interaction between nature and man.

The Batanes landscape amazes. The rolling landscape is an emerald-green patchwork of hedgerows, a network of reeds planted in rows to form living fences that mark farm boundaries, prevent erosion, and shield root crops from windburn. It is a volcanic landscape with high cliffs that dramatically drop into the sea. Shores are covered with round rocks dating back possibly thousands of years when they were once thrown into the sea by early volcanic eruptions.

The National Museum has undertaken extensive studies on the flora of Batanes and has found that numerous indigenous species are shared with the Babuyanes Islands (south of Batanes), Lan Yu and Lu Tao Islands of southern Taiwan and the Riyuku Islands of south-western Japan (Madulid and Agoo, 2001). The Batanes Archipelago, being at the geographic centre of these islands, represents either the northern limit of the Malesian flora or the southern limit of East Asian flora, thus forming a distinct phytogeographic area.

The small islands of Batanes are a fragile habitat to numerous endemic plant species. Most of these species arrived in the islands earlier than human inhabitants and have evolved independently of human activities. The unique flora of Batanes are vulnerable to extinction because of their small population, restricted genetic diversity, narrow ranges prior to human colonization, lack of adaptability to change, or because of human disturbance such as deforestation and fire, introduction of grazing animals, cultivation, and introduction of weedy plants.

The Batanes landscape is unique, totally unlike any other in tropical Philippines, or in the rest of Asia. The Pacific Ocean and China Sea surround the islands, creating powerful and treacherous underwater currents. The surrounding water bodies, the distance from the mainland, the strong winds that blow throughout most of the year and frequent typhoons have kept the islands in isolation. Its average temperature is lower than that of the rest of the Philippines. The Batanes landscape still retains most of its original and authentic natural and cultural character.

Archaeological discoveries in Batanes have been stunning. There were ruins of pre-Spanish colonial citadels (*ijang*) on many Batanes mountaintops overlooking the sea where pottery, human and animal bones, and other artifacts were discovered. Basalt posts that once held down pre-Hispanic thatch dwellings against the strong wind that constantly battered *ijang* slopes were found. Boat-shaped stone markers in the shape of the *tatayá,* the traditional wooden boat still used today, were discovered. These marked the graves of the early Ivatan (traditional residents of Batanes). The burial grounds, always facing the sea on slopes adjacent to an *ijang,* were testimony to the seafaring culture that believed the journey to the afterlife took place in a boat. The only other place where similar grave markers are found is in Scandinavia.

Batanes was a series of astonishing discoveries, one after the other. Its archaeology speaks of an old civilization, probably one of the oldest in the Philippines, whose roots stretch back to the Austronesians who migrated from Southern Taiwan 3,500 years ago, using the Batanes islands as the first stepping-stone in their migratory wave through the Philippines that eventually reached Indonesia and Micronesia to the west and Madagascar to the east. Reinforcing the remoteness of the site, the islands were the farthest outposts of Spanish colonial rule from Manila that itself was the colonial capital city farthest from Madrid in the Spanish Empire. Within seaside towns laid out in the traditional Spanish grid of streets are still found plazas, Spanish colonial churches, parish houses, lighthouses and stone bridges.

The Batanes house is unique to the islands. Unlike any other architecture found in the Philippines, low-slung, strong and sturdy Ivatan architecture responds to its severe environment. The typical Philippine house of bamboo and thatch raised on stilts above the ground does not do for the harsh and windy Batanes environment where stone houses cluster tightly in villages, their steep thatched roofs aerodynamically deflecting the wind and resisting strong rain.

The universal significance of Batanes was obvious, but the Ivatans could not see it. They wanted to be like everyone else in the country, living in modern houses built of cement with galvanized iron roofs even if it was totally inappropriate for their climate. They allowed their traditional houses to deteriorate and let their rolling hills erode. The Ivatans took their unique cultural beautiful landscape totally for granted.

The Ivatans understandably wanted change, and the typical big city stereotype for progress was what they looked for: the old must give way to the new. Progress meant that the centre of their capital town of Basco should look exactly like other Philippine towns, to the point of even importing the urban blight and pollution that those towns suffer from. They were looking at the wrong development models and taking nature for granted. Natural formations and rocks were being mined for construction. Garbage was appearing in the once pristine landscape. Cows were grazing on archaeological sites, disturbing artifacts and kicking around stones that marked boat-shaped burial grounds.

In the year 2000, a campaign to make the Ivatans understand the unique significance of their natural and cultural heritage was established by a member of Congress and the Governor. They saw that without the preservation of Batanes heritage, the future growth of the province could not be sustainable. Since 2000, a series of consultations have been regularly held with the Batanes community. The first meetings were conducted with sceptical political authorities and with the community that refused to believe that the Batanes culture and landscape was unique in the Philippines and possibly in the world.

A team of heritage and environmental consultants, led by the Congressman and Governor, kept on with a series of meetings with community leaders that lasted for a period of three years, eventually convincing them that Batanes was indeed special and that its heritage should be protected. A programme was then developed for community training in environmental and waste management, in architectural preservation, and in preserving local heritage traditions.

Most importantly, government authorities and local residents agreed on a Management Plan that jointly empowered local government and the community to oversee the maintenance of both natural and cultural properties, guided by a provincial technical working group and the Department of Environment and Natural Resources. As part of the Management Plan, the team of consultants produced a complete set of GIS maps of the entire province that inventory and classify each individual natural, archaeological, cultural and architectural area in the province.

Provincial authorities have begun implementing very modest reconstruction programmes using strong community involvement to rebuild damaged vernacular architecture in the traditional manner rather than using modern construction materials and techniques. A provincial survey has been completed to identify recipients who qualify for a grant for repair and rehabilitation of each qualified structure that the project shall finance. Assistance is limited to the purchase of stones, lime, steel reinforcement (if necessary), *cogon* (thatch) and other materials determined as necessary. In keeping with the local tradition of *yaru* (traditional volunteerism), all beneficiaries shall supply the labour for reconstruction as their counterpart.

All the mechanisms to preserve the nature and culture of Batanes are in place, and both the provincial government and the local population are committed to the preservation of their natural and cultural heritage. What makes this case outstanding is that the Ivatan community has determined the management plan, and has pledged to implement the projects outlined in it. Because the community realizes that they are the custodians of their heritage, the system they have devised is bound to be successful.

## Conclusions

The Rice Terraces of the Philippine Cordilleras and the Batanes Archipelago are two premier locations in the Philippines where the local residents realize that their unique traditions are the special quality that assures the continuation of the site as a living cultural landscape. For both sites to continue living, they must not only struggle to find the right balance between tradition and modernization, they also must make the national government authorities and the rest of the Philippine public realize that theirs is a culture and a landscape that is unique and that requires a preservation strategy different from one of simply conserving tangible heritage.

Most importantly, the nomination process for the two sites shows that full community support is the crucial factor in assuring the maintenance of a continuing cultural landscape. Both sites show the failure of national government to understand the complexities of preserving cultural landscapes. In the Rice Terraces the failure has resulted in its inscription into the World Heritage In Danger List. In Batanes, on the other hand, local government has committed its support in the preservation of the tangible and intangible heritage of the province.

Community participation is the most important lesson to be learned from the two case studies. The management of the Rice Terraces of the Philippine Cordilleras was initially a national government initiative that failed because of the minimal participation of the local stakeholders who were not made to feel that they were the custodians of their heritage. After inscription of the site on the In Danger List, national government handed over management to the stakeholders. With local government and residents joining efforts, there is now renewed involvement in site management. Preservation of the Batanes Protected Landscape and Seascape was always a programme of the local government, which involved local residents heavily in the planning and implementation of preservation programmes. Taking full ownership of the preservation of their cultural landscape, the local community has participated in all of the planning sessions, training seminars, and in the natural and cultural preservation projects that they have decided to implement. With local residents taking custodianship of their landscape and seascape, preservation in Batanes is a community effort.

Both sites prove that tangible and intangible heritage must be preserved together to assure the sustaining of life, culture, and the physical attributes of the resident community in a cultural landscape. Without considering the nature-culture continuum, the continuing cultural landscape dies and passes into a relict cultural landscape. However, without the participation of local residents, any preservation programme is doomed to failure. The most important lesson to be learned from the two case studies is that site preservation is impossible without government and community partnership.

# 8. Pastoralists, conservation and livelihoods in East and Southern Africa: reconciling continuity and change through the protected landscape approach

*Brian T. B. Jones, Moses Makonjio Okello and Bobby E. L. Wishitemi*

## Introduction

Conservation of natural resources in Kenya and Namibia has for many years been based on the model of formal protected areas owned and managed by the state. In many cases, the establishment of these protected areas has been characterized by the government identifying an area of land based on its resource endowment, displacing local people, outlawing human settlement and proclaiming a national park or game reserve. There are 52 protected areas in Kenya covering about 8% of the total land. Namibia has 21 proclaimed parks and recreation areas covering about 13.6% of the land surface.

However, there are important limits to the extent that the protected area networks can conserve biodiversity in these two countries. In Kenya most protected areas have become increasingly isolated and fragmented conservation entities that cannot guarantee conservation for posterity (Western, 1997; Western and Ssemakula, 1981; Soulé *et al.,* 1979; Young and McClanahan, 1996). In Namibia large parts of the Namib Desert were designated as conservation areas largely because they were unsuitable for other forms of land use. Meanwhile, important biomes are not represented in the protected area network (Barnard, 1998). Further, the protected area approach in both countries has in the past focused on protection through legal means of areas in which humans are separated from nature and are only allowed to be temporary observers. Few landscapes representing unique interactions between the environment and culture and incorporating local management regimes that conserve biodiversity by means other than legal proclamation were recognised or legitimized. This bias in emphasis towards what constitutes a protected area led to parks and game reserves being synonymous with the exclusion of humans and their activities, with protection of wildlife and other natural resources and management enforced by government through legal means.

Yet in both countries pastoralist communities have for many centuries been presiding over landscapes now recognised as important for biodiversity. The land-uses of these communities and the sustainable nature of their grazing management regimes have helped to preserve landscapes that still provide important habitat for wildlife. This chapter considers the way in which pastoralists in Kenya and Namibia have sustained their landscapes in the past and are trying to cope with aspects of continuity and change in their societies. In some cases change has negative impacts on the way people are managing their land and resources. Their ability to sustain their landscapes and the natural resource base on which they have always depended is being undermined. As a result, the conservation benefits that came from their management of the land are being lost. Formal protected area approaches that separate people from their land provide few solutions for these mobile people. This chapter argues that a protected landscape approach combined with appropriate enabling frameworks can support the livelihood needs of mobile people as well as deliver positive conservation impacts.

# Maintaining wildlife dispersal areas and migration corridors in Kenya: protected landscapes and the Maasai

Most national parks and reserves in Kenya are too small to be viable and many of them must depend on intervening private lands that serve as wildlife dispersal and migratory areas. With human encroachment and different land use priorities outside on private land, biodiversity loss outside protected areas, especially in migration corridors and dispersal areas, is inevitable (Mwale, 2000; Okello and Kiringe, 2004). Parks such as Nairobi and Nakuru are now severely affected by loss of dispersal areas (Western, 1997). This case study considers how a protected landscape approach could maintain wildlife dispersal areas and migration corridors on the land of Maasai pastoralists.

## The protected landscape character of Maasai communal lands

The Maasai live in communally owned group ranches established in the early 1960s in the Olkuejado, Narok and Trans Mara districts of Kenya (Cheeseman, 2001). One of the areas inhabited by the Maasai is the Tsavo-Amboseli area, which is made up of six group ranches. This lived-in, working landscape represents one of the major remaining areas of wildlife in Kenya outside protected areas. It is rangeland of outstanding visual quality and beauty overlooked by the world famous Mount Kilimanjaro, and the scenic Chyulu Hills. The wildlife is free-ranging and abundant, moving between the protected areas of Tsavo and Amboseli

The lived-in, working landscape of the Tsavo-Amboseli Ecosystem, inhabited by the Maasai, represents one of the major areas for wildlife in Kenya outside of protected areas. The Chyulu Hills (shown here) and Mt. Kilimanjaro greatly influence the ecology of the area. *Moses M. Okello*

The Tsavo-Amboseli Ecosystem has a diversity of free-ranging large mammals, which are the main attraction to tourists visiting the area. Securing their migration corridors and dispersal areas in lands outside Tsavo West, Chyulu Hills and Amboseli National Parks is critical, but poses a greater challenge. *Moses M. Okello*

National Parks and the Maasai Group Ranches. It is still common to see herds of zebra, wildebeest and gazelles grazing harmoniously side by side with Maasai livestock. Wildlife lives and moves freely among the parks, group ranches, community wildlife sanctuaries and other dispersal areas in the ecosystem covering an area of about 6,000km$^2$ (Kimani and Picard, 1998).

An elected leadership that is mandated to regulate use of plant, water and land resources manages most group ranch affairs. They also regulate human migration and settlement patterns. Wildlife and other natural resources are unharmed and allowed to share the land. This has long been the case for most pastoral communally owned lands in Kenya, and did not change with the evolution of community group ranches in the 1960s (Cheeseman, 2001).

Most characteristics of the traditional Maasai management regime can conform to the characteristics and objectives of the protected landscape model (Aichison and Beresford, 1998). Characteristics such as lived-in, working environments; harmonious existence between nature and culture through the protection of landscape; continuation of traditional land uses (such as pastoralism); social and cultural manifestations (such as Maasai artifacts, traditional homesteads (called *bomas)*; maintaining and enhancing social lifestyle such as song, dance and dress code; land use practices that are compatible with nature (such as wildlife conservation and pastoralism); maintenance of biological diversity; provision of public enjoyment through recreation and tourism; and enhancing benefits from resources to local communities (as in *cultural bomas* where selling cultural artifacts, song and dance are presented to paying tourists). These characteristics will promote community welfare as well as conservation of natural resources.

## Continuity and change in the communal Maasai landscape

There is considerable continuity in the way in which the Maasai have managed their land since the introduction of group ranches. Movement of livestock is important to track rainfall and grazing in an area that receives less than 500mm of rain annually. Pastoralism is still integrated with the presence of wild herbivores. Leadership and age group structures are still of cultural importance and of significance in decision-making about land management. However, there are a number of changes taking place that threaten this interaction between culture and nature and which are driven by both internal and external forces (Fratkin, 1997). The Maasai population in group ranches is slightly over the national average and therefore is placing increasing pressure on plant, animal and land resources. This is leading to serious decline of ground plant cover and hence degradation of the landscape.

The collapse of the beef industry in Kenya and lack of expertise in livestock husbandry has continually eroded pastoralism as a means of economic livelihood among the Maasai. Without government incentives or a properly established beef industry to encourage efficient marketing and pricing for the Maasai livestock, alternative economic means, even though incompatible with cultural and natural resource conservation, have started to gain popularity. The impoverishment of the Maasai is obvious and their daily struggle for survival so vivid that it is not surprising to see them start embracing agriculture in marginal rangelands, or convert wetland and riverine habitats into cultivation. The rivers and their scarce water resources are frequently diverted to irrigate horticulture farms that are providing more direct and significant household income than both pastoralism and conservation combined. A study on land use changes (Okello and Nippert, 2001) showed that over 89% of the local community in the Tsavo-Amboseli area now practise both pastoralism and agriculture, with only about 9% practising only pastoralism. Further, over 96% of local community members supported agricultural expansion as an alternative land use.

Agricultural expansion not only destroys natural habitats and alters the character of the rangeland landscape, but will fuel the human-wildlife conflicts as wildlife destroys crops more frequently than it harms livestock. Over 40% of group ranch members experience crop damages annually by wildlife, compared to only about 21% who experience livestock losses (Okello and Nippert, 2001). The impacts on livelihoods are high, as over 64% of community members incur both crop and livestock losses annually. These losses as well as human deaths, insecurity and human injury have reduced support for conservation. However, despite these changes the traditional interaction over the years has created great tolerance for wildlife among the Maasai, with over 62% of the community still thinking that wildlife should roam freely on their land, and 92% stating that wildlife conservation is important.

Changes are taking place in Maasai society with regard to ownership of land. More than 80% of those surveyed demanded the subdivision of group ranches into individually owned land parcels. A number of group ranches have already been partially sub-divided, while others are in the process. More than 90% of group ranch members think that complete subdivision will soon occur, thereby permanently changing the character of Maasai landscapes as conservation and cultural entities (Okello and Nippert, 2001).

Despite the great opportunity costs to them of allowing wildlife on their lands, the Maasai continue to shoulder wildlife-related damages without compensation (banned in 1977) from the government. Meanwhile, the government continues to draw large amounts of foreign income from parks (Tsavo and Amboseli) on Maasai traditional land that was taken away without compensation or consultations. As international tourists enter and leave their backyard, all the Maasai can do is sell carvings, sing traditional songs and dance for meagre benefits while the government gains the lion's share of the benefits.

As a result of increasing human-wildlife conflicts and in the absence of greater involvement in and direct benefit from conservation, communities seem to be increasingly opting for *"separation"* rather than *"integration"* of culture and nature in the landscape. Most people (78%) support the creation of "fenced in," community-owned wildlife sanctuaries where they can benefit, yet be separated, from wildlife, so that they can practise other land uses such as pastoralism and agriculture (Okello and Nippert, 2001). Group ranches have voluntarily set aside, or are in the process of setting aside, a section of their land as exclusive wildlife sanctuaries or wildlife concession areas and are benefiting from the lucrative tourism industry in the area (Okello and Kiringe, 2004).

These changes to the landscape character where culture and natural resources were integrated in a working landscape are due to the economic impoverishment and lack of incentives within a framework of the changing socio-cultural and religious fabric of the Maasai people.

The elements of continuity in Maasai land use and culture along with enduring ecological constraints to agriculture (low and unpredictable rainfall and poor soils) suggest that the protected landscape approach may still be a viable model in the Maasai traditional lands. Through such an approach the important wildlife dispersal areas and migration corridors can

Kilimanjaro, Africa's tallest and the world's largest free-standing mountain. The diverse and spectacular landscapes of the Tsavo-Amboseli Ecosystem are important for tourism and people's livelihoods, as well as biodiversity conservation. *Moses M. Okello*

remain open through continued interaction between humans and their landscape. However, the changes that are taking place suggest that new policies and mechanisms are required that significantly alter the current approach to conservation on pastoralist land.

## Limitations of existing conservation approaches

Although Maasai communities are able to benefit from tourism in their wildlife sanctuaries, in the long-term these sanctuaries are likely to suffer from some of the same problems facing the national park system. The sanctuaries exclude human settlement and use of resources (Okello and Adams, 2002) by locals and livestock (especially when leased by tourism investors). As a result some community members are against the wildlife sanctuaries, or if they support their establishment, are against foreign investors leasing them for the tourism business (Okello and Nippert, 2001). Local residents still want to have access to wildlife sanctuaries for water, pasture, and plant resources. This confirms that even with emerging community wildlife sanctuaries, the characteristics of working protected landscapes with community members involved and benefiting economically are still strongly desired.

Furthermore, the community sanctuaries are usually too small in area to be viable conservation units. They represent a fragment of the entire ecosystem and violate good design approaches based in principles of island biogeography (Soulé *et al.*, 1979; Western and Ssemakula, 1981; Young and McClanahan, 1996). The fragmentation and isolation of wildlife populations in national parks is being replicated on the Maasai traditional land. The sanctuaries do not appear to be appropriate ways to maintain wildlife dispersal areas and wildlife corridors (Wishitemi and Okello, 2003).

Under current conservation policy in Kenya, there are no mechanisms for communities to benefit directly from wildlife through controlled user rights or for them to gain the full benefits from the wildlife-based tourism industry.

## Putting the people back into the protected landscape

The national park system in Kenya has excluded pastoral people from their former land and cut off their access to resources in the parks. National parks are becoming isolated islands and wildlife dispersal areas and migration corridors are under threat or disappearing. This situation is being replicated on Maasai land through the establishment of wildlife sanctuaries, the sub-division of group ranches and the conversion of land to agriculture. There is an increasing shift towards separation of culture and nature in the Maasai landscape. An alternative vision for conservation and rural development is needed that can meet livelihood and cultural needs as well as the maintenance of biodiversity. There is a need to put people back into the protected landscape.

The protected landscape model can provide this vision because it incorporates cultures, landscapes and biodiversity conservation. It does not involve displacement of people from their land and they do not lose access to resources important for their livelihoods. In order for this vision to be realized there needs to be formal recognition by the state of the Protected Landscape model as a framework for linking conservation and development. Then the incentives can be introduced that can keep this landscape character intact. Such incentives include the provision of controlled user rights over wildlife to local communities and the mechanisms for them to benefit fully from tourism opportunities. Unless wildlife becomes an important economic activity it is likely to be excluded in the evolving changes on the group ranches.

If the necessary incentives are in place for maintaining wildlife as a land-use, then the protected landscape approach can be achieved and maintained through appropriate land-use planning that would identify areas where agricultural potential exists. Remaining rangeland would then be left for livestock and wildlife. The existing and emerging wildlife sanctuaries could be zoned in this land-use plan as localized core wildlife areas, but within and linked to a larger multi-use and multi-species system. Land-use planning would be based on the involvement of local communities. Such a land-use plan would provide for a combination of activities (agriculture, pastoralism and ecotourism) that are likely to optimize the use of land as well as economic benefits for the Maasai, while retaining the nature and character of the Tsavo-Amboseli landscape.

# Conservation and mobile people: conflicting paradigms and agendas in Namibia's Kunene Region

## The protected landscape character of communal lands in north-west Namibia

The communal lands of the Kunene Region are inhabited by a number of different ethnic groups. In the extreme north, Himba and Herero pastoralists dominate and to the south the Damara are the main group. There are a few administrative centres where the government has provided a school and a clinic and some large settlements based around strong perennial springs, but for the most part, people are scattered in small settlements across a harsh and rugged landscape.

Many of the communal lands in Kunene Region support considerable wildlife populations, including endangered species such as black rhino and Hartmann's mountain zebra. Decimated by drought and poaching in the 1970s, wildlife numbers have increased again due to a combination of better rainfall, increased patrolling by conservation officials and NGOs and community involvement in conservation. Numbers of elephant and black rhino have also increased considerably since the early 1980s. That the last rhino poaching incident in the region was in the early 1990s is a testament to the success of community involvement. The escarpment that marks the descent from the central plateau to the desert margins in north-west Namibia is recognised as an important habitat for several endemic species. The central communal lands of the Kunene Region form a wildlife dispersal area for the Etosha National Park to the east. Because large mammals such as elephant, black rhino, giraffe and lion occur well into the Namib Desert, and the area offers spectacular desert scenery, the communal lands of Kunene are a popular tourism destination.

Community-based conservation has a long history in the region. In the mid-1980s, NGOs began working with local people in order to address the decline of wildlife. Community game guards were appointed and a pilot project was established to return some income from wildlife-based tourism to Himba pastoralists. In the mid-1990s, the Namibian Government passed legislation that gives rights over wildlife and tourism to local communities who form common property resource management institutions called conservancies. In Kunene Region there are now 16 registered conservancies. The conservancies are multiple-use areas in which residents continue with their usual land-use practices but combine them with wildlife. Some conservancies have set aside (unfenced) areas specifically for wildlife and tourism. Those conservancies with good wildlife resources and attractive scenery are able to generate considerable income and other benefits through consumptive and non-consumptive forms of tourism, live sale of game, and hunting for meat.

## Continuity and change in the communal landscape

Livestock farming forms the main economic activity of most residents of the Kunene Region communal areas. In response to the arid and uncertain climatic conditions, mobility has evolved as the pastoralists' main strategy for livestock management. The region can be divided into two main sub-areas in terms of communal livestock management. The Himba and Herero pastoralists of the northern area are still largely semi-nomadic. Despite the provision of waterpoints by government and development agencies, the pastoralists still move their livestock over large areas in search of grazing. However, according to Owen-Smith and Jacobsohn (1991) the provision of water points considerably disrupted the pastoralists' traditional rotational grazing system and led to widespread degradation of the palatable shrub and perennial grass cover in the vicinity of natural springs and artificial water points. There have also been considerable social changes among the Himba with young people looking to a formal "western" education and wage labour in the towns as the way ahead in life. Many younger men have no desire to work as herders and this also affects the ability of people to maintain appropriate grazing management regimes.

In some areas of Kunene however, pastoralist systems still appear to be working. Behnke (1997) for example reported on work carried out for a donor-funded livestock project. He concluded that grazing systems in the Etanga area were finely tuned to local environmental conditions and it was difficult to see how the project could technically improve on existing grazing management.

The southern part of the Kunene communal lands is characterized by former freehold farms that were surveyed, fenced and given to white South Africans after the Second World War. In the 1960s these farms were bought up and allocated as part of the Damaraland homeland as part of South Africa's *apartheid* plan for Namibia (then known as South West Africa and essentially a fifth province of South Africa). Typically a small group of people live on cattle posts on these farms where there are artificial water points and often the farm fences are maintained. Although people in this region are more sedentary than the Himba and Herero of further north, mobility is still important for them in times of drought, during which livestock are moved temporarily over considerable distances to find grazing.

Some important features that are important for the success of pastoralism in northern Kunene have emerged from research in the region (e.g. Owen-Smith and Jacobsohn, 1991; Bollig, 1996; Sullivan, 1996; and Behnke, 1997). One of these features is access to "emergency" pasture, in other words, grazing that is still available in times of drought. In the north-west such grazing was available because of rotational grazing being applied, but in some instances herders needed to move their livestock far west into areas of the Namib Desert where there had been rainfall, and some grass production.

Further, flexibility is a key feature of pastoralist management in north-west Namibia. It is not just necessary to be mobile, but to have the flexibility to move to different areas, and different habitats that hold key resources. Thus it might be necessary in some years to move westwards towards the desert but in others to move eastwards to the escarpment. It is important that access options are kept open for the pastoralists of this region. Another key feature is the system of negotiation and reciprocity that governs access to grazing and water. Although certain resources might be deemed to be "owned" by a certain group of people, other people can gain access in times of need through negotiation or through having helped the owners in the past.

## Pastoralists and conservation in Kunene Region

In Kunene Region a number of conservation activities have impacted on (or have the potential to impact on) pastoralist range management systems. Firstly the proclamation of a protected area, the Skeleton Coast Park, along the Atlantic seaboard and stretching some distance inland, has cut off areas that were available to pastoralists as emergency grazing. This experience made local leaders wary of later attempts in the early 1990s to establish a "contractual park" in the region. They were concerned that the proposed contractual park would lead to similar restrictions on residents' access to key grazing areas and springs. Confusion over the distinction between the word "boundary" and the word "fence" in translation during negotiations led to the failure of local leaders to agree to the park.

Despite the spread and success of community-managed areas in the form of conservancies across the Kunene Region, some conservationists have remained strong proponents of government proclamation. A move to proclaim a "Contractual Peoples' Park" was signalled in September 2002 when the Namibian Cabinet approved a proposal for a feasibility study to take place for the proclamation of an IUCN Category VI protected area. A Concept Plan was developed that included a vision statement and a number of objectives and strategies for achieving the vision. Although the concept plan paid homage to the need for community involvement and benefit, the government would have controlled decision-making, with communities being "consulted". The vision and objectives reflected the conservation objectives of the government and certain NGOs, but did not reflect the development objectives of local people who were not involved in developing the plan. At this writing these plans are somewhat in abeyance and government appears to be rethinking its approach.

The attempts to promote formal conservation in the Kunene Region of Namibia raise a number of key issues for conservation policies and strategies. Conservation approaches that are being applied rest very strongly on conventional western scientific approaches to land use planning. Units of land are identified and designated for specific purposes according to a formal written plan, based largely on conservation criteria and an assumption that land use does not need to change over time. Thus the Skeleton Coast Park was proclaimed with the assumption that the land was not owned or used by anyone. The proposals for contractual and peoples' parks are based on classic park management plan methodologies, and the objectives and strategies are largely pre-determined by wildlife officials and biologists before any community involvement. This approach represents a planning and management paradigm that conflicts strongly with the pastoralist planning and management paradigm.

The likely impact on the mobile peoples of the Kunene Region of such approaches is that the key features of their rangeland management strategies ( e.g., mobility, flexibility, reciprocity and access to emergency grazing) are likely to be restricted. Boundaries (or "fences" in the local language) that are drawn on the map according to conservation criteria will cut across the existing "mind-maps" that people in these communities have of who owns what resources and areas of key resources. Hardened boundaries, even if actually unfenced, are likely to make it more difficult to negotiate access to key resources when needed. Would people living outside the proclaimed area be able to move livestock into a zoned wilderness area, if they needed grazing there? How would the zoning of the park for different land-use practices fit with local resource management practices that view the whole area as important for different reasons at different times of the year or in different years? Much would depend upon the level of decision-making power of local communities compared to government officials.

Similar problems are posed by the community conservancies that have been, and continue to be, established in the region. Based on the self-definition of specific social units living within identified geographical boundaries, the conservancies provide rights over wildlife and tourism. Conservancies do not provide land rights, but proponents of conservancies have argued strongly that local communities should have secure group tenure over the land, which is owned by the state. The need for such tenure arrangements is justified by the argument that it is difficult under existing arrangements for communities to exclude unwanted persons from using their grazing or water. Further, it is difficult for conservancies to exclude outsiders from moving on to land being zoned specifically for wildlife and tourism. However, the conservancies are also possibly imposing a new set of boundaries over the existing network of reciprocal and negotiated relationships that govern access to resources. Following research in the southern communal lands of Kunene, Sullivan (1996) concluded that security of tenure to units of land would not ensure security of livelihood, unless options for movement between the units were retained. This means that sufficient flexibility must be retained to allow negotiated access to resources between one conservancy and another.

## Putting the people back into protected landscapes

Community conservancies in northwestern Namibia have been successful in contributing to wildlife conservation. There is no conservation crisis that requires state intervention. However, there is a need for cooperative management at a landscape/ecosystem level. Such cooperation needs to take place between the individual community conservancies, some of which could also be linked in partnerships with the Skeleton Coast Park, the Etosha National Park and informal conservation areas established by white freehold farmers bordering communal land.

A protected landscape approach in this region of Namibia could promote such cooperation and integration of conservation areas under different forms of land tenure and management regime. However, such an approach would need to put the pastoralists themselves at the forefront of decision-making concerning their own land. Planning across the greater landscape/ ecosystem would need to take into account the holistic way in which people view the land and its resources. It would also need to be based on residents' own informal, unwritten maps that record in the mind a system of tenure and access rights as well as knowledge of the location of specific resources. In this way it would ensure that the mobility, flexibility and reciprocity that have underpinned their successful range management in the past would continue into the future. At the same time people would have the opportunity to adapt to and manage some of the changes that the cash economy and links to broader Namibian society have brought to what was once a very isolated, localized society.

Maasai women. The elements of continuity in Maasai land use and culture suggest that the protected landscape approach may be a viable model in Maasai traditional lands.
*Edmund Barrow*

## Protected landscapes, pastoralist livelihoods and the bottom line

Pastoralists in both Kenya and Namibia occupy land that is important for biodiversity conservation nationally and internationally. Their land constitutes important habitat for wildlife outside of protected areas. If protected areas are not to become isolated islands in a sea of incompatible land uses these pastoralist lands need to be maintained as wildlife habitat. The characteristics of the pastoralist landscapes in both countries reflect an interaction between culture and nature that in the past helped shape a landscape in which there was a place for wildlife. However, this interaction is coming under increasing pressure in the modern world. Shifts to agriculture and the subdivision of land threaten the very fabric of pastoralism in Kenya. Increased sedentarism due to the provision of permanent water and the lure of wage labour in the town contribute to a breakdown of pastoralist grazing management systems in parts of Kunene Region in Namibia.

The experience of the pastoralist communities of formal conservation has been mixed. In the past they lost their land to national parks and game reserves and were denied access to important resources. The impacts of these losses have contributed to the pressure of change facing these societies. In more recent times, these communities have seen a different face to formal conservation. The state and national and international NGOs have been promoting various forms of community involvement in conservation. In Kenya the Maasai have formed their own wildlife sanctuaries and the residents of Kunene Region have formed their conservancies.

In each case, however the "new" conservation exhibits several of the negative characteristics of the "old". In Kenya the community wildlife sanctuaries appear to replicate the island nature of state-run protected areas. The ideology of people being separate from nature and observing it from the outside is transferred to a landscape in which people saw themselves as interacting with nature and part of an integrated system of people, land and natural resources which sustained their livelihoods. In Namibia, the new conservation has gone far in devolving rights over wildlife to local communities, but crucial aspects of the old thinking remain. Conservationists cloak the desire to impose their own control over the landscape with the language of community involvement. Formally zoned areas and conservancies based on the exclusive use of land and resources by a defined group do not necessarily fit well with pastoralist management systems.

In both contexts the protected landscape approach appears to be an appropriate mechanism for meeting livelihood needs in changing socio-economic circumstances, at the same time as conserving biodiversity. However, both case studies point to some important lessons for implementing such an approach. In the face of socio-economic changes, the right incentives are required for pastoralists to maintain land uses that support biodiversity conservation. This includes appropriate government land policies that recognise the flexible nature of the tenure and property rights that underpin pastoralist land and resource management. It means providing residents with user rights over wildlife so that wildlife can play a role in supporting local livelihoods.

It is essential that efforts to establish protected areas that aim to incorporate the needs of mobile people be based on an understanding of the strategies and key factors that underlie the resource management regimes of these mobile people. These strategies and factors include flexibility, reciprocity, negotiated access to resources and access to grazing reserves. Conventional conservation approaches to land use planning and zoning often conflict with the "mind maps" of local pastoralists. Planning should be carried out in a way that gives prominence to these "mind maps" and should recognise that pastoralists do not often work with fixed boundaries and units of land designated for specific forms of land use only.

Participatory approaches should be used that enable mobile people to map their land use and resource ownership patterns themselves and these patterns should be used as a basis for planning. Any development of formal protected areas or community conservancies that involve mobile people should be based on a full understanding by these people of the potential trade-offs brought by proclamation or zonation of community areas (e.g., loss of access to key resources or grazing reserves). Further, conservation areas need to be developed through true negotiation that enables the livelihood objectives of mobile people to be incorporated into the overall vision and objectives of the conservation area.

The bottom line is putting people back into the landscape in terms of conservation thinking so that conservation initiatives help people to stay in the landscape where they are living. In this way livelihoods and biodiversity can continue to support each other and enable pastoralists to reconcile the impacts of continuity and change in their societies.

# 9. Protected landscapes in the United Kingdom

*Adrian Phillips and Richard Partington*

## Evolving protection

Blessed by a relatively gentle climate and mostly fertile soils, the four countries of the United Kingdom (England, Wales, Scotland and Northern Ireland) have a long history of human settlement, and of the exploitation of land and natural resources. Its total population is about 60 million, and England is one of the most densely populated parts of Europe. Scotland, in contrast, has some very wild and remote landscapes, but even here almost all land and water is in some form of multiple use.

Conservation effort in the UK has therefore focused upon lived-in landscapes. The IUCN List of Protected Areas currently features only two protected area management categories in the UK: IV (Managed Nature Reserves) and V (Protected Landscape/Seascapes). The British landscape is extraordinarily varied and rich in both natural and cultural interest. It is not surprising that there has been a system designed to protect the most beautiful and vulnerable parts – from the rugged Welsh mountains of Snowdonia, to the limestone dales in the Derbyshire Peak District, to the remote, wild beauty of the Scottish Highlands, to the pastoral vales and deep country lanes that are part of "Thomas Hardy's" Dorset.

The UK has more than a half-century of experience of Category V protected areas. However, arrangements in each country have taken a rather different course. England and Wales set up a system of National Parks and Areas of Outstanding Natural Beauty (AONBs) based on legislation of 1949. This has been strengthened since: for example, each National Park is now run by a freestanding authority, most Park funding comes from central government and new AONB legislation was passed in 2000. Scotland introduced legislation for Regional Parks in 1967 and for National Scenic Areas (NSAs) in 1972. It has created its first two National Parks only in the last two years. In Northern Ireland, AONBs were first set up in 1965 and some were re-designated under 1985 legislation. In 2002, the Environment Minister commissioned research into possible National Parks in Northern Ireland, which concluded that the Mourne Mountains area would be the most appropriate starting point. The establishment of the New Forest national park in southern England was announced by the government during 2004 and work continues on the potential creration of a South Downs national park. Thus the development of the UK's Category V protected areas continues to this day and, as new challenges emerge, there is a lively debate over Protected Landscapes in the UK.

## Lived-in landscapes

The areas designated in the UK are characterised by their scenic beauty, for example, as mountain, hill, wetland and coastal scenery. They are all lived-in landscapes: 289,000 people live in the UK's National Parks according to 2001 figures (Office for National Statistics, 2001 Census) and many more in the other Category V protected areas. Most land is privately owned, mainly by farmers and landowners but also by other public and private bodies, including that managed by conservation non-governmental organisations (NGOs), like the National Trust and

## Map 1.  United Kingdom protected landscapes.

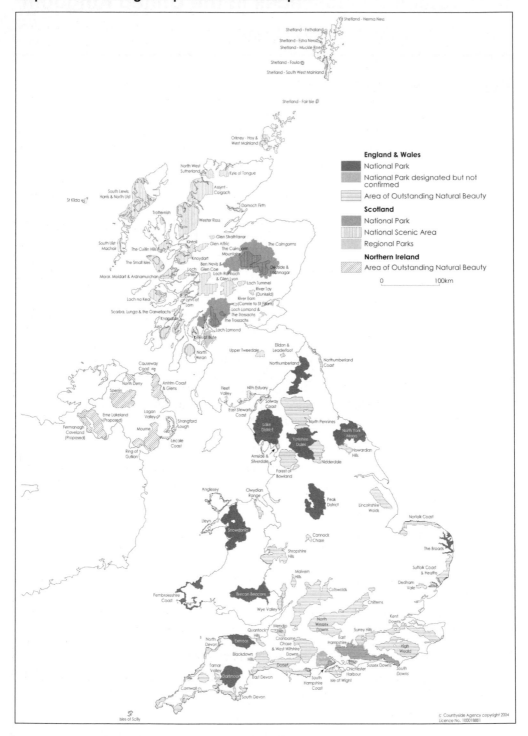

wildlife trusts. Many designated areas are important for their traditional, less intensive land use patterns, biodiversity, history and archaeology, cultural significance and recreation. Indeed, since the outset, recreation and access to the countryside for urban populations have helped shape Protected Landscape policy in the UK, and there is still a strong social bias in their planning and management.

In England and Wales, National Parks are a special kind of local authority, administered through a central/local government partnership, and subject to national guidance. In Scotland, they are non-departmental government bodies. But in all UK National Parks, the authorities are made up of (i) local government representatives, and (ii) appointees of the minister in England, of the National Assembly in Wales or of Scottish Ministers. In England, almost half the Minister's appointees represent the parishes (the lowest tier of local government). In Scotland, direct elections by local communities contribute 20% of the members. If a National Park Authority is established in Northern Ireland, its composition will be decided afer consultation. The National Parks have powers to control land use, influence the management of land and water, and promote public understanding of the area and appropriate forms of recreation. For this, they are well resourced and receive nearly all their net funding from central government (though they can 'earn' additional income through trading operations such as sales of books, maps and other merchandise in Visitor Centres; and through fees for processing planning applications as well as rentals or concessions).

AONBs and NSAs are run by local authorities (i.e., counties, districts or unitary authorities). They too are subject to national guidance but receive less public financial support than the

---

**Box 1.  Land use planning in the UK system of national parks**

All land in the UK, including the national parks, is covered by comprehensive land-use planning legislation, dating from 1947. All significant developments or changes in land-use are controlled by the local planning authority (LPA), which has to prepare a development plan for its area. In England and Wales (but not in Scotland) the national park authority (NPA) is the LPA.

At the national level, policy advice on land use planning is provided by central government through formal policy guidance. This guidance makes it clear that....*major development should not take place in the National Parks....save in exceptional circumstances...proposals must be subject to the most rigorous examination.*

Development Plans are prepared to cover all national parks in the UK, either by the NPA alone or jointly with the local authority. Plans include both strategic policies for land use and development, and much more detailed policies reflecting local needs and circumstances. Development plans, which normally have a 10-year time horizon and are reviewed every five years, are usually adopted following a public inquiry.

Once adopted, the plans guide the nature and location of development that is appropriate in the park. Implementation is mainly achieved through development control, that is the detailed system by which approval is sought for building, land use change, etc. Permission may be granted, refused or approved conditionally. There is a right of appeal against the NPA's decision.

The National Park Management Plan is not formally part of the land use system but it does provide a local framework for development plan and control policies.

*Source*: Michael Beresford.

View of Downham Hill in the Cotswolds Area of Outstanding Natural Beauty (AONB), England.
*Countryside Agency/Nick Turner*

parks. Unlike National Parks, these areas do not have land use planning powers, which remain with local authorities. Legislation now allows certain AONBs in England to set up Conservation Boards, which will be more akin to National Park authorities (though still without land-use planning powers). For more on land-use planning law in the UK National Parks refer to Box 1.

With the exception of NSAs, all Category V protected areas in the UK are run with professional office and field staff support. The National Parks are generally far better supported in this way (about 1,000 staff in England and Wales); while Regional Parks and some AONBs may employ only a handful of staff.

National agencies oversee the Protected Landscape systems of the UK: the Countryside Agency in England, the Countryside Council for Wales, and Scottish Natural Heritage. These bodies play a major role in the establishment of such areas (the New Forest and South Downs are in the process of being designated as National Parks). They also have continuing advisory, promotional and funding roles after the areas are set up, but their direct role in management is limited to a small number of National Nature Reserves. They work closely with the respective government departments in England and the devolved administrations of Wales and Scotland. In Northern Ireland, responsibility for Protected Landscapes lies with the Environment and Heritage Service, an agency within the Department of the Environment (NI).

## Diversity in approaches

The statutory purposes of the English and Welsh parks are to:

- conserve and enhance their natural beauty, wildlife and cultural heritage, and

- promote public understanding and enjoyment of their special qualities.

If these purposes cannot be reconciled, priority is given to conservation, according to a policy known as "the Sandford principle" (established by The Rt Rev. Lord Sandford, a Government Minister who undertook a review of national parks in 1974). The park authorities, in pursuing the two purposes, must foster the economic and social well being of local communities, but without incurring significant expenditure. The Norfolk and Suffolk Broads are regarded as part of the National Park family, but the enabling act gave the Broads Authority somewhat different purposes including one to protect navigation.

AONBs and NSAs have neither an explicit recreation nor a socio-economic purpose. But where a Conservation Board is established for an AONB, it is required to help increase the public understanding and enjoyment of the area's special qualities, apply the Sandford principle and pursue a socio-economic duty mirroring that of National Park Authorities.

In 1997, after many years of discussion, the Government sought advice on how National Parks for Scotland could best operate. There was an extensive programme of fact-finding and consultation, including many meetings, seminars and conferences, which drew some 450 well argued responses from individuals, communities and organisations from across the country. The outcome of the debate was the seizing of an opportunity for rural communities, land managers and businesses to create a more effective national-local contract in the running of two new national parks. Loch Lomand and the Trossachs National Park to the north-west of Glasgow was created in April 2003. The Cairngorms National Park, located in the Highlands, followed six months later in October 2003.

The four purposes of the newly established Scottish parks are to:

- conserve and enhance the natural and cultural heritage;

- promote sustainable use of the natural resources;

- promote understanding and enjoyment of the area's special qualities; and

- promote sustainable social and economic development of the area's communities.

Scottish Park Authorities are required to pursue these aims in a collective and coordinated way, and have a range of powers to achieve this. If conflict arises between these aims the legislation gives priority to conservation. Similarly, some of Scotland's Regional Parks have developed a social and economic role linked to their recreational function.

These differences between the countries of the UK illustrate a varied approach to the pursuit of social, economic and environmental aims within its Protected Landscapes. While some believe that a sustainable development agenda implies that these aims should be met in a mutually reinforcing manner within these areas, others fear this would compromise the special status of the Protected Landscapes.

The new Scottish National Parks are therefore of particular interest. Though there is an over-riding duty to protect the parks and their resources, it remains to be seen if the 'fourth aim' puts conservation objectives at risk, or if it helps secure local people's commitment to the National Park, and its protection and management.

The Scottish approach will be closely watched throughout the UK, particularly in Northern Ireland, as those tasked with moving towards designating the Mourne mountains seek a balance between protection of the natural and cultural heritage and the social and economic purposes for those living and working in the area.

## Test beds

The biggest challenge to management in Category V protected areas is to achieve conservation action that is fully integrated with all aspects of environmental, social and economic endeavour. There are many examples of such pioneer work in the UK's Protected Landscapes. The government recently announced a funding programme to support innovative sustainable development projects in the National Parks of England and Wales, and in AONBs in Wales. This, and the pioneering fourth purpose in Scotland, show that serious interest is now being taken in such a role for Category V protected areas. Thus they are being seen not only as places worthy of protection in their own right, but also as test beds from which successful experience can be rolled out to the whole countryside.

Two case studies from differing parts of the UK are presented below to illustrate innovative thinking and new ways of working. The Blackdown Hills AONB in south-west England is an example of how devolved decision-making increases local participation through community partnership, whereas the three Welsh national parks demonstrate a new paradigm of linking rural development and conservation to create sustainable futures.

## The Blackdown Hills – a model of community partnership

The activity of the Blackdown Hills Rural Partnership is focused on the Blackdown Hills Area of Outstanding Natural Beauty (AONB). The Partnership seeks to safeguard the distinctive landscape, wildlife, historical and architectural character of the AONB whilst fostering the social and economic well being of the communities and the people that live and work there. The Blackdown Hills AONB is in a relatively remote rural area based on an extensive outcrop of greensand, uplifted to form a plateau that has been dissected by rivers to create a series of farmed ridges running north-south across the Devon and Somerset county boundary.

Formed in the mid-1990s, the Partnership brings together public bodies, local organizations and voluntary groups with an active interest in the Hills. Members of the Partnership work co-operatively to an agreed five-year Management Plan and annual Business Plan, with the key funders being signatories to a six-year Memorandum of Agreement.

The structure of the Partnership is designed so that local people, businesses and organisations can share decision-making and project delivery with the public bodies and land managers. An annual Community Conference is held every March and Partnership Forums held every six months. Decisions about policy and use of resources are made by the Management Group, which consists of representatives of the seven key funders plus eight representatives drawn from the Partnership Forum. A Somerset County Councillor currently chairs the Partnership, and the small staff team is based at an office in the village of Hemyock in the heart of the Blackdowns AONB.

The Partnership is funded by seven core-funding partners and draws in other resources from a wide variety of partner organisations and the community on a project-by-project basis. Core funders are the Countryside Agency, Devon County Council, East Devon District Council, Mid

Repairing hedgerows in the Blackdown Hills Area of Outstanding Natural Beauty (AONB), in southwest England. The Blackdown Hills Rural Partnership brings together public bodies, local organizations and voluntary groups to safeguard the distinctive landscape, wildlife, and historical and architectural character of the Blackdown Hills AONB. *Countryside Agency/Pauline Rook*

Devon District Council, Taunton Deane Borough Council, South Somerset District Council and Somerset County Council.

Working in partnership is essential and there are currently over 75 member organizations of the Partnership Forum. Local people are often best placed to identify and address local concerns. The Partnership is committed to encourage and support the input of local opinion and the active participation of local people in all initiatives, and over the past year they have actively helped to shape the design of major projects such as the Local Products Strategy, as well as the more detailed delivery of smaller projects.

The special character of the Blackdown Hills landscape, its mosaic of wildlife habitats, the richness of its built environment and the distinctive history and culture of the Hills are important both for their own sake and as a means of maintaining the special identity of the area. The Blackdown Hills are not a significant tourist destination, yet there is the potential for low-impact, appropriate tourism development that will have a significant impact on the local economy. Given the decline in agricultural employment in the area and the transitional nature of rural employment, the project has a key role in providing information and supporting initiatives that will promote rural regeneration and employment diversification.

One important partner in this regard is the Blackdown Hills Hedge Association. The Association comprises an enthusiastic group of people working and living on the Blackdown Hills who are dedicated to preserving the craft of hedgelaying and other allied rural skills

Sheep grazing, East Devon Area of Outstanding Natural Beauty (AONB), England. Conservation effort in the UK has focused on lived-in landscapes. *Countryside Agency/Ian Dalgleish*

associated with hedgerows in the area. This is achieved by running the annual Hedge Event, as well as providing training events and workshops aimed at promoting and educating people about rural skills and crafts using materials from hedgerows. As a defining feature of the British countryside over centuries, hedgerows have created the characteristic structure, pattern and living record of landscape history. There are many local variations, with distinctive ecological and cultural associations, and they are an increasingly important habitat refuge for wildlife.

In addition to running classes, the Hedge Association promotes its aims by taking displays to local and national events, becoming involved with the Blackdown Woodlands Pilot, and sharing their coppicing skills with others. Also, they have assisted with the creation of the Roe Deer Sculpture located on the roadside to signify the gateway to the Blackdown Hills.

## The Welsh National Parks – models of sustainable development?

The idea that Protected Landscapes could be the places where sustainable forms of rural development are pioneered and promoted is in the IUCN guidelines on Category V protected areas: "Category V protected areas …could become pioneers in society's search for more sustainable futures" (Phillips, 2002). What can be learnt about this idea from a recent report on the Welsh national parks?

There are three national parks in Wales, Snowdonia, the Brecon Beacons and the Pembrokeshire Coast. Together they cover about 20% of the country and are home to only 2.9% of the population. The legislation that set up the parks, last updated in 1995, established them as Category V protected areas: that is as lived-in, working landscapes of great value for their natural beauty, wildlife and cultural heritage.

In 2000, many powers – including that of maintaining an oversight of the national park policy – which were previously undertaken in England, were devolved to Wales with the establishment of the Welsh Assembly. The assembly was given a specific mandate to promote sustainable development. In 2003, Welsh Ministers called for a review of the national parks, one purpose of which was to establish how these areas could contribute to the delivery and promotion of sustainable economic and social development.

The review report was published in 2004 (Land Use Consultants, 2004). It concludes that the parks could indeed be managed as models of sustainable rural development. It describes some excellent existing examples of this kind of activity; projects include small-scale renewable energy, recycling initiatives, promotion of local foods, sustainable transport and green tourism.

But if real progress is to be made – the report concludes – it will be necessary for the Welsh Assembly to give more encouragement and support to the national parks for this kind of work. But also the parks should be given a new purpose to "promote sustainable forms of economic and community development which support the conservation and enhancement of the natural beauty, wildlife and cultural heritage of the areas." While this would be subordinate to the other park purposes – conservation, and access and public understanding – it would represent an important step towards linking conservation and development.

Making sense of such words will call for partnerships between the national park authorities and other bodies in the public, private and voluntary sectors. The report says "conservation and enhancement of the special qualities of the parks has to be a shared responsibility, requiring an integrated and purposeful approach to environmental conservation and enhancement, support for the land-based and wider rural economy (including tourism) and development of the park communities together."

To reinforce partnerships for the park among bodies with responsibility for such services as roads, farming, tourism, jobs and housing, the report recommends that the law be changed so that all public bodies operating in the national parks would have a duty not only to "**have regard to** national park purposes" (as now), but to **"contribute to"** these purposes. This means that each and every scheme would have to be tested against the question – what will it do for the national park?

The report is now the subject of public debate and it is far from certain that these important proposals will be acted upon, as they will strengthen the standing of the national parks and thus may threaten some established interests. But even if the proposals are not quickly adopted, the review report on the parks in Wales offers a way forward that could have application in other Protected Landscapes.

So what can be learnt from the Welsh review that might have wider application? That there are many practical examples of linking conservation and development in sensitive environments; that it is possible to relate economic and social development to conservation purposes; and that this can be done through partnerships reinforced by a legally binding obligation on all sectors to help deliver the purposes of the protected area.

# Building local support

In the UK, as in many other countries, it is recognised that protected areas will not survive, nor achieve their aims, without local support. Since many people live in the Category V protected areas and often play an important part in the management and protection of their natural and cultural resources, such support is all the more necessary.

This means that local communities should feel that they are consulted and listened to, and have their concerns addressed. Protected Landscapes should be seen to bring social and economic benefits, or at least not unfairly disadvantage local people. There is much debate in many Category V protected areas about how to provide jobs, incomes and affordable housing in ways that are sustainable and support the protection, enhancement and enjoyment of the Protected Landscape. For example, one challenge is providing affordable housing for local people, and doing this to high design standards that complement the landscape. Many Protected Landscapes have pioneered schemes of this kind, frequently working in partnership with other bodies. Moreover, the quality of the natural environment is a key economic advantage: one in six Welsh jobs, for example, depend directly on it. Even so, some people still feel that the conservation policies of Category V protected areas can inhibit economic and social prospects, especially through restrictions imposed by land use planning.

Of course, there have to be constraints, in particular to exclude large-scale economic investment that would be out of scale with the landscape: quarrying, large infrastructure projects and mass tourism, for example, and to check cumulative trends that erode the landscape (such as poor design). On the other hand, it is widely believed that Category V protected areas can support – indeed should attract – appropriately scaled, environmentally sustainable development.

Governance is an important aspect of community involvement. As noted above, in most cases the local democratic interest is secured by the nomination of local authority members to the authorities that run the area. However these arrangements may still leave a "democratic deficit". The arrangement under which a fifth of the members of the new Scottish National Parks will be directly elected is significant therefore.

There are also less formal ways of involving local communities, e.g., through community fora, and all the Protected Landscapes authorities are required to consult widely over their plans. The governance of Protected Landscapes is likely to remain a continuing source of debate and innovation.

# Benefits for society

The early history of National Parks in England and Wales, and of Regional Parks in Scotland, was largely driven by the need to provide urban populations with recreational space and beauty to offset the drudgery of industrial life. While the advent of cheap international tourism and other social developments complicate this argument, it is as important as ever to protect relatively wild places and unspoilt countryside, and make it accessible for public use. Some 100 million visits are paid each year to UK National Parks. However, realizing their full potential for recreation and mental and physical well-being depends on greater social inclusion.

Protected Landscapes serve a far wider range of social purposes. Many Category V protected areas in the UK contain concentrations of important sites for biodiversity conservation, including prime coastal, grassland, wetland, upland and woodland habitat. Some are of international significance, and some are Category IV protected areas, set within the wider area of landscape protection.

Some Protected Landscapes are important catchment areas for water supply; while many are important for the protection of archaeology, historic buildings and vernacular architecture, and for sustaining living cultures – notably the Welsh language in much of rural Wales, and Gaelic in parts of Scotland. Their educational value is well established, with many visitor centres and other educational and interpretative facilities.

## Working landscapes

Farming and forestry of some kind are dominant land uses in most Category V protected areas in the UK, and have helped to shape much of the landscape which is now so valued nationally and by visitors. This is most notably the case in upland areas, whose scenic beauty is partly the creation of centuries of livestock rearing, as well as management for shooting and other country sports.

When undertaken in a traditional manner, farming can help conserve the landscape, wildlife and historic heritage, support essential environmental services (like soil and water conservation), and can also be compatible with access and recreation. However, intensification (or sometimes abandonment) of farming can threaten such values, leading to, for example, the ploughing up or neglect of open country, the loss of wildlife or the removal of hedgerows or other traditional field boundaries. While this conflict is not confined to Protected Landscapes –

Forest of Bowland Area of Outstanding Natural Beauty (AONB), England. Most of the land in these protected areas is privately owned by farmers and landowners, as well as other public and private bodies. *Countryside Agency/Mike Williams*

129

or even to the UK – it is particularly acute when it occurs in landscapes that are supposed to be nationally protected. But without external support, traditional farming cannot survive and its wider benefits to society will be lost.

Various programmes, often supported through European Union (EU) funding, have been developed to support traditional land management that is compatible with the protection of wildlife, landscape and heritage, and encourages public access. Increasingly, too, farming in such areas aims to secure added value to products through an emphasis on quality, marketing and branding.

Similar innovations occur in the forestry sector. Thus the planting of extensive coniferous monoculture is a thing of the past: the trend is towards support for traditional woodland practices, restoring and expanding native woodlands. Though these changes have been led by government or EU-funded agricultural and forestry programmes, the agencies responsible for the management of the Protected Landscapes have also been closely involved.

## Conclusions

The UK's Category V protected areas represent a cross-section of the country's finest land-scapes, but include, too, a cross-section of rural society. The diversity of approaches around the UK shows how adaptive the Category V approach can be in dealing with conservation aims, but also with social and economic ones – and doing so whilst also securing resources and commitment for the management of many of the UK's most important natural and cultural heritage areas.

But these areas do not stand apart and must be linked to the rest of society. So, while the historic purposes of landscape protection, recreation and access remain as relevant now as 50 years ago, the UK is especially keen to share its experience as it tries to re-design Category V protected areas to be:

- models of sustainable development, integrating economic, social and environmental aims, and contributing to global environmental protection;

- exemplars of sustainable land use practices, showing how alternative economic activity can also sustain the areas' viability and vitality; and

- relevant to society as a whole – thereby bringing wider social inclusive benefits.

## Acknowledgements

Special thanks to The Council for National Parks, a national charity that works to protect and promote the National Parks of England (www.cnp.org.uk), in allowing the use of material contained within this chapter originally prepared for the World Parks Congress, 2003.

# 10. Sustaining rural landscapes and building civil society: experience from Central Europe

*Miroslav Kundrata and Blažena Hušková*

*Cultural landscapes can be preserved only if the local public is involved, and if the implemented tools work for the economic benefit of local communities.*

## Introduction

The year 2004 marks the 15th anniversary of the fall of the Iron Curtain. During the past decade-and a-half the societies in Central and Eastern Europe have experienced for themselves how exciting and also how difficult it is to shape their own destinies. They have witnessed the many facets, paradoxes and challenges surrounding the rebirth of democracy in the region. The environment was one of the leading factors driving the political changes of 1989. Looking back, there is little question that giving people a chance to play a direct role in democracy-building and market reforms was of critical importance in Central Europe. During this period, the emerging NGO sector started to play an important role in shaping new societies, including nature conservation policies.

**Map 1. The White Carpathian and Frýdlantsko regions in the Czech Republic**

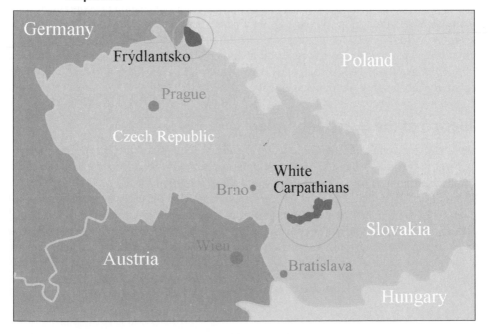

While the State continues to play a strong role in nature conservation in the Czech Republic, as evidenced by legislation enacted in the post-revolutionary period,[1] a review of history reveals a strong tradition of private conservation. For example, virgin forests in the Novohradské hory and Šumava mountains were declared nature reserves by private land-owners a full century before the State established national parks. Under the first Czechoslovak Republic (1918–1939), all protected areas were established and owned by private conservation associations, which grew and flourished during this period. A recognition of these historical roots gives our current efforts to promote and develop land stewardship in the Czech Republic a stronger position from which to build public support, as we can draw not only on experience from abroad, but also from our own country.

Today, there are 24 Protected Landscape Areas (PLA – Category V) in the Czech Republic, covering an area of 10,274km$^2$ (13% of the state territory) – all of them typical Central European cultural landscapes. The country's protected area system also includes four National Parks, as well as Nature Reserves and Biosphere Reserves, all designated on the national level. In addition, designated at the local level, are Protected Areas, Landscape Parks and Registered Landscape Features. The well known Lednice-Valtice Landscape Park was inscribed as a World Heritage Cultural Landscape in 1996. An emerging land trust movement in the Czech Republic brings new methods for preservation of significant parts of the landscape, many of them within or near formally protected areas.

Key land conservation challenges in the Czech Republic during the current post-communist period include: i) the abandonment of extensive agricultural practices, leading to loss of landscape diversity and the depopulation of rural areas; ii) uncontrolled sprawl in suburban and recreational areas and along traffic corridors; iii) lack of a pro-active nature conservation policy to respond to new development pressures, resulting in a broadening gap between public opinion and the position of nature conservation authorities; iv) insufficient economic resources for nature conservation (*e.g.*, protected area management, compensation of landowners and acquisition of new reserves); v) ongoing restitution of agricultural and forested land; vi) continuing inconsistency between agricultural and environmental governmental policies; and vii) limited capacity of NGOs for policy involvement and coordination, while they play an increasingly substantial role in management of protected areas.

## Influence of the European Union

In May 2004, ten countries from Central and Eastern Europe joined the European Union (EU), bringing new energy to what will be a new Europe – reunited for the first time since World War II. Harmonization of national legal systems was a key condition for EU accession. For most of these countries, the nature conservation legislation enacted in the early 1990s holds up well in the context of the EU, as is the case for the Czech Nature Conservation Act of 1992. The EU directive, NATURA 2000, has become an important influence on State nature conservation policies in the accession countries and, to a great extent, is shaping the management of Category V protected landscapes. In the Czech Republic, the main objectives of NATURA 2000 are:

---

[1]  For example, the 1992 Act No. 114 on Nature and Landscape Conservation in the Czech and Slovak Federal Republic.

- protection of biodiversity by maintaining the most valuable natural sites within the EU territory;

- protection of strongly endangered botanical and zoological species and natural habitats and maintaining and/or improving these habitats;

- finding consensus between nature protection and environmentally friendly economic use; and

- incorporating these valuable natural sites in the Czech Republic into the system of European Natural Heritage.

Sites to be included within the NATURA 2000 system will include Protected Landscape Areas, National Parks and Nature Reserves; development plans within these sites must have approved Environmental Impact Assessments.

## Fostering Land Stewardship in Central Europe

Land stewardship has become an increasingly important tool in tackling the challenges of managing protected landscapes in the Czech Republic. Many of the activities described here have been inspired, nurtured and developed with assistance from the Central European Landscape Stewardship programme developed by the Quebec-Labrador Foundation/Atlantic Center for the Environment (QLF), a US-Canadian NGO, and the Environmental Partnership for Central Europe (EPCE). Their integrated programme of fellowships, study-tours, work-shops and technical assistance has involved hundreds of professionals and decision-makers as well as dozens of organizations from North America and Europe (Beckmann, 2000; Brown and Mitchell, 2002).

Stewardship is a way of relating to the environment that is as old as human consciousness. It can be defined as *efforts to create, nurture and enable responsibility in landowners and resource users to manage and protect land and its natural and cultural heritage* (Brown and Mitchell, 2000). Caring for the earth is not new to Central Europe, where much of the landscape and its natural treasures have been shaped by centuries of human settlement. Only relatively recently has the long symbiosis between people and the environment in the region been strained.

Since 1989, new techniques for landscape stewardship – many of them first developed in North America – have helped people in Central Europe restore their ties to the earth. Landscape stewardship has provided powerful new tools for preserving landscape and heritage. It has also served as a valuable instrument for rural development and community revitalization. Perhaps most importantly, and somewhat unexpectedly, stewardship has proven effective in fostering a vital civil society in the post-Communist societies of the region (Beckmann, 2000; Mitchell and Brown, 2003).

## The case of two Protected Landscapes in the Czech Republic

Protected Landscapes in the Czech Republic, similar to others in Central Europe, are cultural landscapes, with many important natural and cultural values, including high secondary biodiversity that has been conditioned by centuries of human influence. The two cases presented in this chapter illustrate these characteristics. Both are landscapes in border regions.

However, while the Jizera Mountains Protected Landscape Area and Frýdlantsko region are typical of Sudetenland regions in the Czech Republic, the White Carpathians region (on the Czech-Slovak border) did not experience such a drastic population shift in modern history.[2] The clearances and resettlement of populations in Sudetenland regions such as Frýdlantsko during the middle of the twentieth century have had an impact on its landscape and social dynamics, and these pose special challenges to involving communities in stewardship.

Through two case-studies of protected landscapes in the Czech Republic we explore differences and common features of landscapes with dramatically different post-war histories. The differences include continuity of settlement, social conditions and environmental challenges. What these two cases have in common is that they are pioneering rural sustainability by testing various models of partnerships between local communities, land-owners, farmers, entrepreneurs, NGOs and state administration. In both regions, the role of NGOs has shifted significantly over the last decade from watchdog and nature conservation management to more proactive innovators and coalition-builders for sustainable development at the regional level.

## The landscape of the White Carpathians

Stretched along the Czech-Slovak border at the western edge of the Carpathian Mountain range, the White Carpathians are a patchwork landscape of rolling mountains, fields, deciduous forests, fruit orchards and flowering meadows. The area's unique cultural and natural features have gained it international recognition as a UNESCO Biosphere Reserve (1986), and designation at the national level as a Protected Landscape Area (1979–1980). Today (following the separation of the Czech and Slovak Federal Republic in 1992) the CHKO Bílé Karpaty/Biele Karpaty is a transboundary Protected Landscape Area, in keeping with a Category V designation, and encompassing 435km$^2$ of cultural landscape on the Slovak side and 715km$^2$ on the Czech side.

Centuries of human settlement and cultivation have shaped this region and its landscape, best known for its traditional hay meadows, 250 varieties of fruit trees, and over 30 rare species of orchids. The landscape and its features have, in turn, left a deep imprint on the lifestyles of the people in the area, shaping their livelihoods and their vibrant culture and traditions. Under Communism, part of the area was spared the social and ecological effects of the regime's campaign for collectivization and industrial agriculture. Since 1989, accelerated changes in the region have led to the collapse of agriculture and local industry. Unemployment in many villages is high and, drawn by new opportunities elsewhere, young people are leaving the area. The two larger cities of the region, with their relatively low unemployment rates of around 8%, attract people from the poorer villages, but even this migration does not stop the net population loss from the region as a whole. Those who remain typically are not inclined to continue

---

[2]  The social situation of of the present-day Czech Republic has been strongly influenced by developments after World War II. As a result of both international agreements and national decisions, most of the German citizens from border areas with a majority German population (the so-called Sudetenland) were forced to leave their historical homes. New settlers came to live in the area, without any relations or roots there. The centuries-long continuity of families in these mostly rural areas was severed in a year, and still, almost 60 years later, there are significant differences between the Sudetenland regions and other regions of the Czech Republic, where continuity had not been interrupted.

The orchid *Dactylorhiza majalis*, once common in the White Carpathian mountains (Czech Republic and Slovakia), is still found in upland meadows where traditional haymaking regimes are maintained.
*Veronica Archive*

traditional land management practices such as caring for fruit orchards or mowing the area's flowering meadows (Beckmann, 2000).

## The role of NGOs in nature conservation

Voluntary conservation organizations have a long history of working with natural resource preservation and with introducing land stewardship to the White Carpathians. The NGO Kosenka (a chapter of ČSOP, the Czech Union for Nature Conservation) was one of the first to respond to regional challenges by becoming involved in maintaining the region's meadow ecosystems and orchids in the 1970s. The group gained national attention for organizing brigades of volunteers each year to mow the area's flowering meadows, a management practice important to maintaining the biodiversity of the upland meadow ecosystems. The focus of Kosenka and other organizations active in the region expanded, particularly following the political changes of 1989, as they began to recognise the broader context for their conservation work. Miroslav Janík, Director of Kosenka, explained that, "We gradually realized that our efforts to save the orchids would be pointless over the long-term unless we took a more holistic approach that involved the interests of the people living in the area."

While continuing its efforts to maintain meadow ecosystems, Kosenka has begun to implement a vision that sustains local culture, cultivates a sense of regional pride and identity, and develops the community and region in a sustainable manner. For example, the traditional St Nicholas Day Fair that the group reestablished in 1994 has grown into a major annual event, attracting some 15,000 people from around the region and as far away as Prague or Vienna. In addition to providing an important focus for regional pride and identity, the fair is beginning to generate considerable economic benefits. Jobs and income-generation feature in a growing number of Kosenka's initiatives, including cooperation with local farmers to reintroduce extensive sheep- and cattle-grazing to this traditional shepherding region. The NGO raises start-up funds for establishing the herds, which help restore and maintain the meadow eco-systems while generating income for area farmers.

In 1994 Kosenka organized an international Landscape Stewardship Exchange workshop, in cooperation with the Brno-based NGO Veronica, the Czech Environmental Partnership Foundation and the US-Canadian NGO, QLF/Atlantic Center for the Environment (see Box 1). The organization has since participated in other exchanges and training programmes organized by EPCE and QLF. In the decade since the Landscape Stewardship Exchange, Kosenka has become one of the most active promoters of the land stewardship concept in the Czech Republic, and a leading land trust, joining an emerging network that now includes 35 land trusts nation-wide.

---

**Box 1.  Landscape Stewardship Exchanges in Central and Eastern Europe**

An important element in the joint programme of EPCE and QLF to foster land stewardship in Central Europe has been the Landscape Stewardship Exchange, a week-long community problem-solving exercise. Through the Exchange, an international team spends a week in a rural community or micro-region, at the invitation of local institutions, to learn about and advise on a problem identified by people in the community.  The model relies on a combination of community organizing at the local level, and the outside perspective provided by the international team, to stimulate public participation and a dialogue among diverse stake-holders.

Over the past decade, QLF and EPCE have conducted Landscape Stewardship Exchanges in ten rural sites in Central and Eastern Europe, most of which are in transboundary or border regions. The model has proven highly effective in fostering dialogue among interest groups and is frequently referred to by local leaders as having been catalytic – a watershed event in their community/regional development efforts. These sites include:

1.  Pálava Protected Landscape Area, Czech Republic (1994) – *Enlargement of the Pálava Biosphere Reserve*

2.  White Carpathian Mountains, Czech Republic and Slovakia (1995) – *Revitalization of rural communities in the Bílé/Biele Karpaty Protected Landsape Area*

3.  Kvačany Valley, Slovakia (1995) – *Alternatives to large-scale development for recreation near the High Tatra National Park*

4.  Jizera Mountains/Frýdlant, Czech Republic (1997) – *Balancing tourism and recreation with nature conservation in a fragile mountainous landscape*

5.  Morava River Floodplains, Czech Republic and Slovakia (1999) – *Development options to reduce flood risks in the lower Morava River basin, a tributary of the Danube*

6.  Zawoja/Babia Góra National Park, Poland (1999) – *Building cooperation between Babia Góra National Park and surrounding communities in Poland and Slovakia*

7.  Czech Karst Protected Landscape Area, Czech Republic (2000) – *Sustainable development and growth management in the Czech Karst Protected Landscape Area*

8.  Eastern Carpathians Greenway, Poland, Slovakia and Ukraine (2002) – *Bridging Carpathian regions and their living heritage (Bieszczady region, home of the world's only trilateral Biosphere Reserve)*

9.  The Ploučnice River, Děčín, Czech Republic (2004) – *River basin management and flood prevention*

10.  The White Carpathians Protected Landscape Area, Valašské Klobouky, Czech Republic (2004) – *Marketing local products: A tool to support rural sustainability and landscape conservation*

*Source*: Brent Mitchell, Jessica Brown and Tomáš Růžička.

---

A number of other NGOs in the region are playing an important role in sustaining the special landscape of the White Carpathian mountains. In Slavičín the Pivečka Foundation and ČSOP-Slavičín are active in nature conservation, education and renewal of local traditions (e.g., traditional local shoe production connected with revitalization of sheep-keeping). Not far from Valašské Klobouky, in the Kopanice area along the Slovak border, the Information Center for the Development of Kopanice is working to promote and develop small-scale tourism as a means of supplementing local incomes as well as organic agriculture among farmers in the White Carpathians Protected Landscape Area. Organic agriculture is becoming an important driving force in managing protected landscapes in Central Europe. Toward the south, ČSOP Bílé Karpaty has been working with the state administration of the White Carpathian Protected Landscape Area to preserve the valuable meadow ecosystems of the southern White Carpathians and has collaborated with local landowners to manage the Čertoryje reserve. This organization also initiated care of traditional varieties of fruit trees in the White Carpathians. These efforts by Czech NGOs are paralleled on the other side of the border by the work of Slovak NGOs, such as the Society for Sustainable Living-Biele Karpaty, Koza, and others.

Recognising the need for economic tools for underwriting nature conservation efforts and sustainable management of protected landscapes, the above-mentioned NGOs, producers and processors of fruit, and communities have established a joint association called "Traditions of the White Carpathians," (*Tradice Bílych Karpat*) to facilitate the renewal of small-scale processing and marketing of products as a means of preserving the natural and cultural heritage of the White Carpathians. The juice and other local products, including mutton, dried fruit and traditional crafts, are sold under the "Traditions of the White Carpathians" marketing label. The label is intended to help market high-quality products by associating them with the region and, at the same time, promote the region as a whole. In 2003 the non-profit association was transformed into a business operation with the same mission and label.

The role of nature conservation NGOs in the Czech Republic has shifted significantly from one of classical nature protection and serving a "watch dog" function during the 1980s and early 1990s to one serving as initiators and incubators of innovative approaches to regional development, respecting the principles of sustainability and local traditions. NGOs in the White Carpathians Biosphere Reserve have pioneered many new ideas in the Czech Republic and have become models for others (e.g., programmes to preserve local varieties of fruit trees by introducing fruit processing and marketing tools, reintroducing sheep and cattle to manage protected meadows, practising land stewardship and land trust concepts, and including biomass energy in the concept of sustainable landscape management). Several of these pilot projects are concentrated in the small village of Hostětín.

## The village of Hostětín – a model for rural sustainability

The small village of Hostětín (population 227), located in eastern Moravia near the Czech-Slovak border, has over the last decade been transformed into a remarkable experiment in sustainable rural development. Its location within the boundaries of the CHKO Bílé Karpaty, or the White Carpathians Protected Landscape Area (PLA), was one of the impetuses for this special development initiative. Here, the Brno-based NGO Veronica, ČSOP-Hostětín, together with the local government and the PLA administration, are cooperating to transform the village of Hostětín into a model for sustainable rural development.

Hostětín has managed to exploit for its own development what many other communities in the Czech Republic and in Central Europe more generally regard as a brake on their development. Over the past decade the community has realized a wide range of environmental projects, including a biological sewage treatment facility, solar collectors, biomass heating plant, a small juicing factory, and an educational centre, which have contributed to the environment and quality of life while producing three full-time, three part-time and eight seasonal jobs and strengthening the local economy.

The projects described here have been developed by the community of Hostětín in partnership with the civic associations noted above, along with the District Government of Uherské Hradiště and the administration of the White Carpathian Landscape Protected Area. More demanding projects have been developed in cooperation with a number of partners, both regional and foreign.

## Reed-bed wastewater treatment plant

Poor river water quality caused by insufficient treatment is considered one of the largest environmental problems for Czech communities. For smaller towns, especially in protected landscapes, a reed-bed sewage treatment plant is an optimal, low-cost solution to wastewater treatment. The reed-bed sewage treatment plant in Hostětín has been in constant use since July 1997 and was the first facility of its kind in eastern Moravia. In contrast to conventional sewage treatment facilities, the reed beds and pond also provide an attractive and valuable biotope that is home to rare species of birds, insects, reptiles or frogs, including the tree frog. Information panels explain to visitors the functioning of the natural processes as well as the features of the biotope.

## Energy and the rural landscape

Production of renewable energy and development of community self-sufficient energy policies is a must for the future of sustainable communities everywhere. In many countries of Europe, production of biomass for sustainable energy use is emerging as a viable alternative to agriculture and forest production. In most protected areas forestry together with energy crops can supply biomass for a broad range of technologies for heating or electricity generation. Biomass production and the related technologies present new options for cultivation of abandoned fields, new markets for waste wood from forestry and saw mill operations, and new employment opportunities for marginal rural landscapes. Solar technologies and new methods for energy-efficient building construction provide work opportunities for many innovative small entrepreneurs and skilled workmen.

An important milestone in energy management in Hostětín came in October 2000 when a 732kW central heating plant came into operation. The plant, which is fuelled by waste wood from nearby forests and sawmills (500–600 tons of woodchips per year), produces heat for 90% of all homes and buildings in the community connected to the grid. Savings of $CO_2$ in the Hostětín biomass heating plant are calculated as 1,500 tons per year.

Heating water with solar energy can also help rural communities to save money, create employment opportunities, and cope better with the environmental challenge of climate change. Ten of the 80 homes in Hostětín have been equipped with solar facilities for water heating since July 1997. The residents took an active part in mounting the solar panels themselves. Since 1998 a solar facilities-producing workshop has been operating in the village, as a part of the "Sun for the White Carpathians" programme developed by ČSOP Veronica.

## Preservation of traditional fruit varieties

Since 1994 Hostětín has been one of the centres of "Traditions of the White Carpathians", the initiative involving a variety of partners from throughout the region that is focused on preserving and using traditional varieties of fruit and supporting traditional extensive fruit growing through local processing and marketing of fruit products. The project connects fruit growers, small fruit processors, local governments, and consumers with the aim of reviving small-scale processing of fruit and preparing a marketing strategy for fruit products so that profit from sales can support preservation of the cultural landscape.

One of the activities of the group that has combined both cultural and natural heritage preservation has been the reconstruction in 1998 of one of the last wooden fruit drying kilns in Hostětín. For hundreds of years the small kilns were ubiquitous, with several in every village and a total of some 3,000 dotting the White Carpathians as a whole. But the practice of fruit cultivation and drying has declined over recent decades, and the traditional fruit drying kilns have fallen into disuse and disrepair. The kiln in Hostětín, which is over 200 years old, was rebuilt with financial support from the Czech Environmental Partnership Foundation and is now used by small-scale local producers from Hostětín as well as neighbouring communities to dry some 4.5 tons of fresh fruit per year.

## Juice processing plant

A more ambitious project, undertaken under the banner of the "Traditions of the White Carpathians", was the construction of a juice processing plant in Hostětín in 1999/2000. The small plant produces unfiltered fruit juice from local fruit varieties. In autumn 2000, the plant's first season of operation, it purchased and processed 200 tons of apples and produced some 140,000 litres of apple juice. A significant portion of the apples ($c$.43%) came from orchards with organic certification. Even in the first difficult year of operation, the plant endeavoured to pay local producers good prices for their apples. A premium was paid for apples produced with organic certification in order to motivate small-scale producers to introduce organic production to their orchards. During the 2001 and 2002 seasons, the production of organic juice grew to 85%, making a net profit of more than US$10,000 in 2002.

The plant, which was built by ČSOP Veronica with financial and technical support from the Luxembourg foundation Hëllef fir d'Natur, belongs to the Veronica Foundation and is operated by the "Traditions of the White Carpathians" Association. The project enjoyed strong support from the community and its citizens, without which it could not have been realized. The intention is to diversify production (mixed organic apple juice and red beet juice was introduced to the market in 2002) and to focus on organic certified production.

The juice plant has become a successful and important operation for the village. Its budget is about 10% of the total income of the local residents (including pensions and state benefits). Besides its influence on motivating local people to keep and enlarge their orchards as an important feature of a traditional landscape, it brings one permanent job, part-time employment, and about eight seasonal jobs between September and November.

During the harvest season, the juice plant in Hostětín, Czech Republic, processes about 200 tons of apples from local orchards. The fruit-processing operation, which is an important source of employment in this rural village, is part of an initiative to encourage planting of traditional fruit trees. *Petr Francán*

## Land Trust

A farm purchased by the Veronica Foundation in 1998 forms the core of a 10-hectare land trust in Hostětín that is devoted to reviving and preserving the rich cultural landscape of the region, including its rich tapestry of fruit orchards, meadows and forests. Fields and forests are managed according to traditional – in fact ecological – practices, including organic and extensive agriculture and forestry, and with special care given to cultivating traditional local varieties of plants and trees.

In 2001 the Veronica Land Trust began a pilot tree-planting project in the area of Jahodisko, formerly a traditional meadow and orchard pattern, which had been destroyed during the Communist period. In 2003 this work continued by planting a bio-corridor (a 15m wide belt of trees) dividing a large field and serving both as soil erosion control, biodiversity and land-scaping feature.

Working in close cooperation with the Hostětín community, government as well as local landowners, the Veronica Land Trust has been responsible for the planting of some 700 deciduous saplings and original large trunk varieties of apples, cherries, pears and also wild trees. This project has helped to renew the natural and cultural values that were lost especially in the 1970s due to insensitive interventions.

## Education – the Training Centre for Rural Sustainability

A long-term aim of partners in the Hostětín project – particularly of the Veronica Ecological Institute, the Czech Environmental Partnership Foundation (*Nadace Partnerství*), and the Twente Energy Institute and Biomass Technology Group (BTG) – is the establishment of a Centre for Rural Sustainability in the village. The centre will further develop the community and also provide inspiration and practical education and training for undertaking similar initiatives elsewhere. Practical educational and training courses will be organized at the centre for public authorities, representatives of local government, craftsmen, small- and medium-sized businesses, students and the broader public. In contrast to traditional educational facilities, the centre will be able to draw on the numerous model projects within the community of Hostětín and in neighbouring communities of the White Carpathians, which offer an ideal laboratory for learning by doing.

The facility, which will be located at the centre of the community next to the juice plant, will be constructed according to basic principles of ecological architecture, (concept of the passive house), with the construction phase serving as one of the training modules. The economic effect of the Centre on the village of Hostětín will be significant. While currently some 2,000 people visit the village of Hostětín each year, only a few stay for more than a day. It is anticipated that the Centre will attract visitors to the community for extended stays, during which they will spend money locally on accommodation, food and services.

## Hostětín – a model?

The aim of all of these projects has been first and foremost to support local development that responds both to the challenges, opportunities and risks of the 21$^{st}$ century. These projects provide a practical example of how reinforcing local people's relationship to nature, supporting their resources and traditions, and encouraging sensitive management of the landscape can contribute to the economic strengthening of rural areas and produce employment.

The following simplified table shows how these model ecological projects contribute to the local economy. Today, the pilot projects represent almost 16% of the estimated total income of the local population; following completion of the Centre this figure could grow to 33%, not counting the secondary effect of spending by visitors to the village.

## Table 1. Financial contribution to the local economy

| Project – income per year | FTJ | PTJ | SJ | CZK | USD | % * |
|---|---|---|---|---|---|---|
| Total net income of the village (wages, benefits, pensions) ** | 83 | | | 20,000,000 | 700,000 | 100 |
| Juicing plant (2002) | 1 | 2 | 8 | 2,260,000 | 80,000 | 11.3 |
| Biomass heating plant (2002) | 0 | 1 | 0 | 735,000 | 26,250 | 3.7 |
| Solar collectors | 0 | 1 | 0 | 120,000 | 4,250 | 0.6 |
| Reed bed sewage water treatment plant | 0 | 1 | 0 | 56,000 | 2,000 | 0.3 |
| Future Centre | 6 | 2 | 0 | 3,500,000 | 125,000 | 15.9 |
| Subtotal yearly benefit of projects today | 1 | 5 | 8 | 3,171,000 | 113,250 | 15.8 |
| After completing the Training Centre | 7 | 7 | 8 | 6,671,000 | 238,250 | 33.4 |

*Key*: FTJ – full-time job, PTJ – part-time job, SJ – seasonal job
* % of total net income of the whole village, **estimate

## Frýdlantsko and the Northern Jizerské hory Mountains

The work of the Society for the Jizera Mountains, the Frýdlantsko Association and other civic associations illustrates the important role of NGOs in encouraging sustainable economic development within a protected landscape.

The Jizera Mountains Protected Landscape (CHKO-Jizerské hory) is a protected area of $368km^2$ designated in 1967. The most valuable ecosystems preserved up until now are mixed beech forest on the steep northern slopes of the mountains, and also unique peat-bog remnants on the top plateau of the protected landscape (around 1000m above sea level). There are some 30 nature reserves, natural monuments and other designations of varying sizes within the protected landscape. The area is rich in cultural as well as natural heritage. The mountain landscape is complemented by agricultural land-use in the foothills and by the unique local architecture.

The Jizera Mountains Protected Landscape Area (PLA) is located in the Frýdlantsko region, in the northernmost tip of the Czech Republic, an area surrounded on three sides by the Polish border, with the German border not far away. The Jizerské hory Mountains act as an imposing natural barrier, which separates the region from the rest of the Czech Republic to the south. Frýdlantsko comprises the foothills of the most valuable part of Jizerské hory Mountains – the deep beech woodlands of the northern slopes – and opens out onto the Lužice (Lausitzer) Lowlands.

However, the area is threatened by environmental problems, including air pollution and acid rain due to burning brown coal in surrounding power plants in the Czech Republic, Poland and Germany. These air quality problems, which date back to the 1950s, have had a devastating impact on the region's forests, and particularly its fragile montane ecosystems. A major portion of the forest ecosystems (originally mixed forest re-planted as spruce monocultures during the 18th century) have declined due to air pollution and acid rain. Other problems include depletion of soil and water quality due to agricultural chemicals, and flooding of rivers, as upland forests are reduced. Today the quality of the region's environment is slowly improving, with the shutting down of the neighbouring power plants.

Restoration of the region's dead and dying forests is one of the major challenges facing the management of the Protected Landscape Area. Other challenges including maintaining extensive agriculture in the buffer zones of the PLA and regulating tourism pressures.

There are 24,500 permanent residents living in 18 communities in the Frýdlantsko region, the largest of which is Frýdlant with about 8,000 inhabitants. In the past Frýdlantsko had been a rich region, with successful agriculture and a textile industry, benefiting from the easy connection to the Lužice region in the north. However, most of the original German inhabitants were forced to leave after World War II in 1945 and the border became a barrier, with the result that the historical land-use patterns (e.g., agriculture and forestry) were interrupted. Today, the region faces many economic and social problems due to the closing of its textile factories, the collapse of agriculture, and a high unemployment rate (above 20% in some communities). Among much of the population, education levels, job training and employment qualifications are low, and many young people are leaving the region in search of new opportunities.

Since 1989 many NGOs have emerged in the region, several of them focused on environmental issues. The Foundation for the Jizera Mountains, probably the most important of them, was established in 1993. The Foundation has worked in close cooperation with the PLA

The fragile montane ecosystems of the Jizera Mountains Protected Landscape Area (Czech Republic) are threatened by air pollution and acid rain. Restoration of the region's forests is a major management challenge in this Protected Landscape. *Siegfried Weiss*

administration since 1993 on projects to revitalize forest ecosystems within the Jizera Mountains Protected Landscape. By combining the financial resources of the Foundation with the legislative power and expertise of the PLA, significant progress has been made. The Foundation has also been supporting the work of several local NGOs active in reforestation, nature and heritage protection.

## A rural community development initiative catalysed by international exchange

The 1997 Landscape Stewardship Exchange that the Foundation for the Jizera Mountains helped organize in Frýdlant, and a subsequent visit of New England community leaders to the region, proved to be an important turning point in the development of the foundation, and possibly of the region as well (see Box 1). The Landscape Stewardship Exchange focused on management of the Smědá River, which had caused devastating floods in the foothills, and how the protected landscape can co-exist with local communities. The expert team that spent a week in the region meeting with local leaders included participants from New England, Poland, Slovakia and the Czech Republic. As a representative of a regional development agency observed:

*People from completely different conditions came here and offered the local people a unique opportunity to talk about their problems. Our people got the chance to look at their region through the eyes of someone else.*[3]

An important turning point in the exchange came when the visiting team met with a retired forester, who recalled how when there were forests in the catchments of the Smědá River, it could rain for several days and the water level of the river would barely change. This came as a revelation to many local leaders, because, as one noted:

*Now, after two days people downstream have to watch for flooding or even evacuate their villages. I saw how people taking part in the workshop started making the connection. They suddenly realized how much a person in Višňová, twenty kilometres from the Jizera Mountains, is affected by the condition of the mountain forests.*[4]

The workshops convinced the Foundation for the Jizera Mountains to expand their activities beyond reforestation in the mountains to include a broader range of projects focusing also on economic development and social and cultural concerns in surrounding communities. In addition to establishing new grant programmes focused on community development, the foundation established a new organization, the Society for the Jizera Mountains, which has become the main motor for sustainable development initiatives in the Jizera Mountains area.

The Landscape Stewardship Exchange also led to the establishment of the Frýdlant Association by community leaders, businesspeople and NGOs, many of whom had come together at the workshop for the first time. One of their first steps was to take up the suggestion of their American visitors to use the river Smědá as a potent symbol and an axis connecting the mountains and the communities below.

## The work of the Society for the Jizera Mountains and the Frýdlant Assocation

The Frýdlant Association has since developed a rich program of concerts, educational activities and special events focused on the river and mountains, and connecting the communities along its banks. Since 1999, the projects have been implemented by the Association for the Jizera Mountains (a public benefit corporation). These projects have resulted in the development of a network of local leaders and experts, and the creation of new civic associations in the region. They have fostered cooperation between NGOs and local leaders (such as mayors), as well as State agencies, in particular the Protected Landscape administration.

Of the 18 communities in the Frýdlantsko region, several have been very active, driven by charismatic local leaders. Many are engaged in projects to strengthen local sustainability, which include:

- a reedbed waste-water treatment plant in Višňová;

- wind-power plants and a biomass heating plant in Jindřichovice;

- biking trails as part of a regional soft tourism project;

---

[3]  Katerina Lauermannová, Department for Regional Development, Liberec district.
[4]  Dušan Richter of the Foundation for the Jizera Mountains.

---

**Box 2.    Sheep-grazing and landscape stewardship in the Frýdlantsko region**

Pavel Mach, a 45 year-old farmer, lives with his wife and two children in the farmhouse that once belonged to his grandparents, who came to the Frýdlantsko region in 1945 during the resettlement of the Czech Sudetenlands. Most of his life Pavel worked in a textile factory. After the Czech Republic's "Velvet Revolution" of 1989, he began to be active in local politics, and now works as a local government official in the community of Višňová (population approximately 1,200).

In 1999 Pavel Mach participated in a study-tour to the White Carpathians region that was conducted by the NGO Stewardship Network, (a project of the Environmental Partnership for Central Europe), where he was inspired by a project to maintain the upland meadows through sheep-grazing. He pursued a new-found interest in sheep-farming with guidance from farmers and NGOs in the White Carpathians and, in 2000, started his own project, grazing 15 sheep on a five-hectare area. Now, four years later, he manages a herd of 109 sheep, maintaining 27 hectares of meadows and pastures in an extensive, environmentally friendly way. He plans to expand this grazing area to 60 hectares by 2005, much of it within the territory of the Jizera Mountains Protected Landscape Area.

As a result of his model effort, the idea of sheep-farming in the region has snow-balled, with great benefit for the rural landscape. There are now 15 sheep farmers in the Frýdlantsko region, maintaining together more than 600ha of land. They help each other and learn from each other through a civic association they have established, the "Frýdlantsko Region Sheep Farmers' Club". Through the Rural Livelihoods Program (another EPCE project in the region), Pavel Mach, in cooperation with the Society for the Jizera Mountains, has already organized four seminars attended by 300 participants.

Why is Pavel Mach so successful? Apart from his strong relationship with the place where he lives, his hard-working character, ability to plan, and openness and willingness to share, he has benefited from the support of his community and PLA administration. Importantly, he was inspired by the success of other sheep farmers, through an exchange between his protected landscape and that of the White Carpathians, enabled by the NGO Stewardship Network. His cooperation with NGOs in the region fostered his access to new ideas and resources for implementation. Today, he and the other sheep farmers of the Frýdlantsko Region are making an invaluable contribution as stewards of the Protected Landscape Area.

---

- a transboundary partnership project linking Višňová (on the Czech side) with communities on the German and Polish sides of the border; and

- sheep-farming in the Protected Landscape Area (see Box 2).

These results have been achieved thanks to close cooperation among local communities, NGOs, farmers and the PLA administration. The sustainability of the Frýdlantsko region will depend on local economic development and new job opportunities, as well as on strengthening the region's cultural and educational resources, soft tourism, agriculture and renewal energy production. The Protected Landscape Area is an important pillar in a sustainable development scenario for the region, and stewardship of the area's landscape will be key to its future.

## Conclusions

In spite of different historical and geographical conditions, the rural landscapes presented in this chapter have a lot in common. Both are Category V protected landscapes in marginal areas, they are in mountainous border regions, and they share the economic and social pressures of present-day Europe. Their future is driven by committed and competent local leaders who share a vision of sustainability, care for local heritage, are open to learning and to innovations, and are able and willing to cooperate with broader regional, national and international networks.

The case-studies from the White Carpathians and Frýdlantsko demonstrate the important role NGOs can play in bringing new vision, change and innovation to traditionally conservative rural areas while building on local roots and heritage. The land stewardship approach has emerged as a particularly powerful tool for implementing those visions locally. Its strength is that it is based on cooperation with land-owners, farmers, municipalities and small businesses. While people used to expect nature conservation to be the role only of the government, now they understand that it can be the role of other actors, too. Through land stewardship, the sophisticated concept of public-private partnership is being implemented in dozens of protected areas in Central Europe. This strengthened role for the NGO sector, and the growth in participatory and cross-sectoral approaches, contributes to developing civil society in the region.

The Environmental Partnership for Central Europe, inspired by the work of international partners – such as QLF, the Antioch New England Institute (US), the International Centre for Protected Landscapes (UK), Project for Public Spaces (US), and others – now aims to implement in the Czech Republic and in Central Europe a broader range of techniques for participatory planning in communities. They include, among others, methods for:

- **interpretation of local heritage** – an excellent tool for improving the often conflicting relations between nature conservation authorities and local people;

- **community visioning** – for use in communities where partners are ready for more sophisticated cooperation, where it can help to launch a participatory process of formulating and implementing a community's vision for its future sustainable development; and

- **planning of public spaces** – in towns and villages, as well as in protected landscapes.

Public participation is a key condition for success in reforming new democracies in Central Europe. Participatory approaches to conservation and sustainable development in protected areas, such as Protected Landscapes, are helping to foster civil society in the Czech Republic. Sharing experience in these methods through international exchange has helped to show a way forward.

# 11. Cultural landscapes of the Andes: indigenous and *colono* culture, traditional knowledge and ethno-ecological heritage

*Fausto O. Sarmiento, Guillermo Rodríguez and Alejandro Argumedo*

## Introduction

Intrinsic to the definition of culture – and, in many places, cherished as gods or demi-gods – mountainous cultural landscapes have evolved in ways that produce a symbiotic relation between nature and culture (von Droste *et al.*, 1995). In the Andes mountains, identity and ethnicity go hand-in-hand with mythical concepts of sacred hills, isolated volcanoes or specific snow-capped summits. The so-called *Apus* (or mountain deities), acting as stewards of the communities living under their protection, appear to have human-like characters. It has been said that *Apus* are superior beings that know the fate of the people leaving in nearby valleys.

Andean landscapes, hence, are the result of intellectual and spiritual constructs that are shaped by the traditional practices and the newer uses given to them by the diverse cultures that inhabit them. As components of managing the broader cultural landscape, novel approaches for the conservation of sacred sites offer insights into the importance of human influence as the driver of global change, as well as the importance of maintaining and promoting local culture, traditional knowledge and spiritual fulfilment in contemporary society (Forman, 1995). Using Andean land-use management practices as models allows us to generalize notions that unify nature and culture as an integrative whole within a protected landscape, as well as to link biodiversity and human intervention as driving forces behind the nature-culture interactions that produced the identities of Andean mountain societies at large (Brown and Mitchell, 1999; Gade, 1999; Brown, Mitchell and Sarmiento, 2000).

The three main Andean regions along the continent-long cordillera (Northern Andes, Central Andes and Southern Andes) differ according to their altitude, humidity and topographic features, being tropical evergreen in the north, dry and less vegetated in the centre, and temperate deciduous in the south. A key ecological feature in the Andes is the existence of slope and fragile lands, nested in young volcanic chains reaching several thousand metres in height. Steep slopes are prone to erosion potential, which is exacerbated when forest cover is removed by deforestation.

These mountainous lands are occupied by traditional cultures that have developed unique strategies to solve their needs for resources and survival. One of us has argued that even the name "Andes" provides a direct clue to understanding the cultural nature of Andean landscapes (Sarmiento, 2002). The built terracing system impressed the first Europeans visiting the region, who described the echelon-like construction along the sides of the mountains with Castilian shorthand as *andenes*, from which the word Andes was popularized to describe the whole cordillera.

In the Andes, culture and nature are interlocked in a closely knit fabric where the resulting mosaics of land uses have provided diversity and stability to the ecology of mountain

El Chimborazo in the western cordillera of Ecuador. In the Andes, identity and ethnicity go hand-in-hand with mythical concepts of sacred hills, isolated volcanoes or snow-capped summits, watched over by the *Apus*, or mountain deities. *Jessica Brown*

landscapes. Small isolated mountain communities grew and established specific cultural traits. New species were created by domestication of palatable varieties that were kept with pride by the local inhabitants. New agricultural systems and the use of family- and community-owned recipes led to the unique agro-ecosystem of the Andes, producing plants such as potatoes, different types of corn, ocas, mellocos and other tubers, Tarwi, Quinoa, Amaranths and other grains. As Brown and Mitchell (2000b) note, Andean landscapes are rich with examples of traditional land use that have proven sustainable over centuries, contribute to biodiversity and other natural values, and are living examples of cultural heritage.

We have discussed the cultural landscapes of the Andes, and strategies for their conservation in recent publications (Argumedo, 2001; Sarmiento *et al.,* 2000; Rodriguez, 2000; Chaurette *et al.,* 2003) and at recent regional and international workshops and conferences. In this chapter we present three case studies from Colombia, Ecuador and Peru, and we explore different criteria for stewardship of cultural landscapes. We discuss the collective effort to create the *Ruta Sagrada del Cóndor-Wiracocha* as a regional approach for conservation of cultural and natural heritage in the Andes. Finally, we argue for the need for stewardship of Andean landscapes, through the creation of Category V protected areas and other initiatives throughout South America.

# Problematique

Beresford and Phillips (2000) call for a model for conservation in the 21$^{st}$ century based on cultural landscapes. Green (1989) had already claimed the need to move into geo-ecological approaches, incorporating the lifestyle, practices and costumes particularly when dealing with rural landscapes, where the divide between the natural and the cultural has always being blurred. A few years earlier, the notion of Protected Landscapes was already instrumental within IUCN in allowing development of a new system of conservation categories, whereby the action of humans seemed to be conducive to maintaining, and as a matter of fact, creating biodiversity (Lucas, 2001). In a recent publication in the IUCN Best Practice Guidelines series, Phillips (2002) offers guidelines for the application of Category V Protected Landscapes worldwide.

However, for the Andean region, or other areas in South America, the literature is scarce. In 2002, the World Heritage Centre published a book on *Cultural Landscapes of the Andes*, followed by the 2002 publication of the *Mesoamerican Cultural Landscapes*, both publications as proceedings from regional meetings discussing the notion of world heritage and cultural landscapes.

Until quite recently, countries of the Andean region adopted the "national park model" to create and manage protected areas. The preservation of large areas of "unspoiled nature" through ownership of land has often excluded local and indigenous people from planning and implementation processes, and has ignored the importance of their traditional practices in contributing to the great diversity of cultural landscapes found in the Andes, making clear the separation of societal and natural purposes for conservation of biological resources (Sarmiento *et al.*, 2000). Typically, protected area authorities have emphasised the use of Western science and management practices and the involvement of formally trained experts. In the process, the valuable knowledge and practices of indigenous peoples and other local communities in-habiting these landscapes have largely been ignored. Paraphrasing IUCN's Programme on Protected Areas (Phillips, 2003b) a 'protectionist' mentality persists in the management of protected areas in South America, and successful work with local communities has seldom been achieved. Systematic methodologies to bring about the efficient participation of local people have not yet been developed (Sarmiento, 2003).

The *Ruta Sagrada del Cóndor-Wiracocha* initiative presents a new paradigm. It is being developed by a network of indigenous peoples from seven countries (Sarmiento *et al.*, 2000). Indigenous communities will be in charge of protected area establishment and management, within a regime that aims to conserve biological and cultural diversity through a more integrative approach. Incorporating the diverse ecosystems of the Andes, which are linked through historic and ecological attributes, the proposed route will extend from Venezuela to Chile, covering the historic pre-Hispanic Andean region, based on the ancient *Wiracocha* route. This pre-Hispanic route, which linked sacred sites, cities, areas of high biodiversity and ceremonial centres in a line spanning the Incan Empire, was devised by the wise man *Wiracocha*, according to Andean folk lore.

The proposed *Ruta Sagrada del Cóndor-Wiracocha* will follow a network of cultural landscapes where traditional agriculture predominates, and where efforts are underway to achieve protection according to the principles of the IUCN category V designation. These protected landscapes will link focal points along the route. For the purposes of this project, "focal points" have been defined as being nodal conservation areas that have already been established, as well as other bio-culturally rich areas in need of conservation. The *Ruta Sagrada del Cóndor*'s focal points will include, among others:

(a) Micro-centres of crop origin and diversity (e.g., Vavilov centres);

(b) Areas of high biological diversity (including biodiversity "hot spots," and critical and vulnerable areas);

(c) Outstanding mountain ecosystems (including high-mountain wetlands, native forests, and grasslands;

(d) Cultural areas (including sacred sites, archaeological centres, World Heritage Sites and other cultural landmarks e.g., places where there is a strong craft tradition, such as pottery and weaving); and

(e) Existing protected areas (including national parks, nature reserves, biosphere reserves).

Some of the focal points have already been established by virtue of being part of the newly created regional network of Ethnobotanical Sister Gardens, which was endorsed by the International Society of Ethnobiology during the VII International Congress of Ethnobiology in 2000. An Ethnobotanical Garden is a specialized botanical collection that allows traditional knowledge and ancestral practices to be maintained in the growing of plants used with medicinal, economical or cultural purposes. Most of the varieties selected as domesticated plants in the Andes have indeed developed as heirloom plants.

The *Ruta Sagrada del Cóndor-Wiracocha* will be implemented and managed by local communities themselves. Both the specific focal points and the larger protected landscapes making up the route will be based on the traditions and knowledge of the native peoples as well as experience from the network of Ethnobotanical Sister Gardens, the sister gardens being demonstration sites for cultural landscape conservation exercises. As some of the focal points of the route, the ethno-botanical gardens will offer examples of different conservation approaches and management goals along the route. Linkages with the already established focal points will be made in collaboration with conservation authorities in each country and arrangements will include strategies to ensure effective participation of local people in the management of such areas (Sarmiento *et al.*, 2000). The project will incorporate the goals of equity and poverty reduction of the indigenous peoples along the route. An ecotourism and indigenous tourism plan will be developed to provide economic incentives for conservation, especially by adding value to local biodiversity and landscape features.

In the current debate, indigenous and traditional people have an important locus in the political agenda of sustainable development scenarios in Latin America. Beltrán (2000) analyses the relationship between indigenous and traditional peoples and protected areas, presenting the conflict between the goals of nature conservation and the needs and wants of the human population that depends on it, living within or around the protected area. The case studies that follow demonstrate conservation of natural and cultural heritage in three distinct settings, whose characteristics exemplify the diversity of communities and landscapes in the Andean region.

In the heart of the Pisac valley (Peru), six Quechua communities are working together with the NGO ANDES to create an Andean Community-Conserved Area, *El Parque de la Papa* (Potato Park), using an integrated landscape approach that links traditional agricultural landscapes with high mountain native forests, grasslands and wetlands. *Jessica Brown*

## Empowering communities and safeguarding ethnoecological heritage in the Pisac Valley, Peru

Community self-determination and safe-guarding traditional knowledge, practices and innovation systems are central to an initiative to create a Community-Conserved Area in the Sacred Valley of the Incas in Pisac, in the southern Peruvian Andes. This effort is led by the Quechua-Aymara Association for Sustainable Livelihoods (ANDES), a Cusco-based indigenous NGO working on developing innovative landscape-based conservation models by adapting traditional management practices and indigenous knowledge systems into comprehensive and *sui generis* plans for the conservation of Andean biodiversity and ecosystems.

Since Inca times, the character of the Sacred Valley landscape has remained essentially agricultural. The area (about 45km northeast of Cuzco) is a recognised micro-centre of origin for potatoes, with more than 2,300 cultivars of potato (from a global total of 4,000) being grown (Devaux and Thiele, 2002). At the heart of this cultural landscape, ANDES and six Quechua

Community self-determination and safe-guarding of traditional knowledge, practices,and innovation systems are central to El Parque de la Papa. By maintaining the character of this landscape the local communities hope to protect the area's rich biodiversity and cultural sites, while strengthening local livelihoods and food systems. *Jessica Brown*

communities[1] are working to create an Andean Community-Conserved Area[2] (CCA) called *El Parque de la Papa*, or Potato Park, using an integrated landscape conservation approach. Bordering areas of the park link the agricultural landscape with high mountain native forests, grasslands and wetlands that play an important role by hosting a rich variety of endemic plant and animal species. By maintaining the character of this Andean landscape, the communities hope to protect the area's rich biodiversity (including native plant genetic resources, as well as wild relatives of domesticated plant and animal species), habitats and cultural sites; strengthen local livelihoods and food systems; and articulate sound poverty alleviation strategies and policies to their conservation goals.

The major problem confronting the conservation of Andean biodiversity and sustaining landscapes is the fragmentation and erosion of traditional systems of agriculture and resource management (Graves, 2000). Due to cultural erosion, migration to cities, environmental degradation and economic marginalization, Andean communities are losing their access to a

---

[1]  Under this initiative, the 8,000 villagers of the communities of Amaru, Pampallacta, Cuyo Grande, Sacaca, Paruparu and Chahuaytire have agreed to bring together the 8,661ha in their six communal land titles and manage them jointly for their collective benefit.

[2]  Proposed by TILCEPA, Community-Conserved Areas can be defined as *modified and natural ecosystems, whether human-influenced or not, and which contain significant biodiversity values, ecological services, and cultural values, that are voluntarily conserved by communities, through customary laws and institutions* (Pathak *et al.*, 2003). They are discussed in several other chapters in this volume.

diverse range of biological resources that have made high mountain agrarian societies sustainable in the past. Loss of traditional knowledge and weakening of the local institutions that can assure stewardship and sustainable management of Andean ecosystems is a major factor leading to the declining use and presence of biodiversity in the Andes (Koziell, 2001). Furthermore, national policies in food, agriculture and the environment have tended to ignore the value of indigenous institutions and the biodiversity over which they are the traditional stewards. A combination of these factors has led to the current situation where Andean crops and livestock are being replaced by other foods, crops and animals, and habitats are being converted to uses that are less sustainable and less amenable to local management. The cumulative impact is fewer livelihood choices and resources for the indigenous people of the Andes, and the erosion of a fragile habitat rich in biodiversity.

Another important feature of the traditional agricultural system under peril is exchange and connectivity across landscapes and communities. Legends as well as historical, anthropological and biological research confirm the importance that pre-Colombian Inca cultures gave to the movement and exchange of plants and other biological resources with conscious movement of materials and diversity from the northern to the southernmost extremes of the Andean zone. Especially important for domestication was the movement of plants and cultivars from tropical humid lowlands to mountain and high mountain landscapes and vice versa. This culturally managed gene flow has been much reduced; it is impeded by national borders and fragmented by different tenure regimes and monoculture production systems. The marginalization of indigenous cultures and the growth of national and global market systems have replaced traditional patterns of germplasm exchange.

Established in 1998, the Potato Park has gained extensive national and international recognition for its innovative methods of conserving native genetic diversity as well as the knowledge associated with the sustainable use and management of genetic resources. The scheme is conceived as a pilot for a larger initiative in landscape conservation in the Andes region: the *Ruta Sagrada del Cóndor-Wiracocha* (introduced in the preceding section of this chapter). The key element to this model is support to indigenous institutions for stewardship, community-based resource management and affirmation of local rights. Communities are organized into Local Learning Groups, which are local platforms for analysing and studying local phenomena. The structure of the platform is based on the format of traditional arrangements used by local people to discuss and analyse community affairs and make appropriate decisions. Traditional knowledge has been integrated into all conservation activities; this ensures that local people exercise leadership and control over the project and that any application of Western science and technology responds to cultural needs. Assessment of technological needs is based on the analysis of drivers affecting the Quechua culture and not on scientific abstractions.

Landscape conservation based on traditional knowledge, practices and innovation systems is likely to have greater success in conserving the local landscape while providing for livelihoods than those that rely solely on conventional conservation approaches. The six communities in the Potato Park have formed a park association (*Asociacion de Comunidades del Parque de la Papa*), a legal representative entity composed of the elected head of each community, which is in charge of the day-to-day governance of the park. ANDES and the Park authorities work hand-in-hand to develop alternative economic activities, based on sustainable use of the agro-ecosystem's goods and services, including agro-ecotourism, marketing of native crops as health foods, establishing local pharmacies and processing of medicinal plants. They also work jointly on capacity-building in sustainable agriculture and CCA management, and on supporting local innovations to sustain livelihoods and protect Quechua peoples' traditional resource rights. There is a strong emphasis on "learning by doing."

The experience of community participation in the establishment and management of a community-conserved area based on agro-biodiversity is providing valuable insight into the process of adapting traditional management practices and indigenous knowledge systems into a comprehensive and *sui generis* plan for the conservation of local biodiversity and the goods and services of mountain ecosystems. The Potato Park offers the elements to develop a model of sustainable agriculture that is based on the conservation and sustainable use of native crops and ecosystem goods and services in order to increase agricultural productivity and rural economy.

An example of the above assertion is the agro-ecotourism concept being developed in the Park. Agro-ecotourism activities build upon extending the existing links between the traditional Quechua agricultural system and the character of the Pisac landscape, particularly its cultural features, to non-traditional economic activities such as ecotourism in order to generate additional income for the local community while at the same time creating incentives for the conservation and sustainable use of biodiversity and the goods and services of the ecosystem. This model of ecotourism seeks to develop market niches for recreation activities based in landscape enjoyment, such as wildlife observation; gastronomic experiences based on unique native crops; and educational exchanges.

The goals of sustaining local livelihoods and ecosystems are tied to strong promotion of the local Quechua culture. By focusing attention on the conservation of native crops, particularly on the potato, the Potato Park seeks to reinforce traditional indigenous values and ensure that these coincide with today's social, economic and technological issues. This is to ensure that the community-conserved area becomes a model for indigenous self-development that projects the Quechua culture into the future. Providing the means to ensure that Quechua cultural identity evolves with dignity in the face of present economic and technological challenges is therefore of great concern.

Human wellbeing and cultural identity are central to the work of the Potato Park. Traditional Quechua values have been incorporated into all activities of the project, including the values of solidarity, equilibrium and duality, which are important to management of genetic resources and landscapes, and which are also the basis of customary laws. By linking CCA activities to Quechua values, actions acquire strong indigenous identity and therefore help to strengthen Quechua culture and achieve an authentic vision of being. The use of traditional knowledge in biodiversity and landscape management – for example in plant breeding, irrigation and weather forecasting – ensures that Quechua culture survives. Indigenous culture reproduces itself through reference frameworks packaged as knowledge, practices and innovation systems, particularly those related to agriculture and food systems; therefore the viability of the Potato Park concept is inextricably linked to projecting these reference frameworks into the future. For Quechua farmers, reality comes into being through agriculture, and therefore having potatoes as their cultural symbol converges their being into reality.

The activities and projects of the Potato Park deal with all aspects of the well-being of Andean peasants such as soil fertility, pastoral and forestry activities, materials for construction, firewood collection, and drinkable water supplies, as well as the development of social assets, such as literacy and capacity-building. By understanding and supporting strategies that enable indigenous communities to recover and strengthen their traditional institutions and social mechanisms in the face of socio-economic and ecological changes, the six communities have made tangible livelihood improvements since the implementation of the Potato Park project. In addition, the Potato Park has provided another site and a new system for conserving and restoring the rich genetic diversity of potatoes that is also of global importance.

The Potato Park model is being established along with other community-conserved areas designed around a key agro-biodiversity resource as their primary livelihood. By facilitating connectivity between these areas, which include alpaca parks, sacred parks and Andean grain parks, the revitalization and creation of material and information exchange that characterized the region before the Spanish conquest will not only strengthen indigenous identities but will improve the economic, nutritional and general social well-being of the local communities.

Peruvian authorities and institutions, such as CONAM, INRENA, INIA and the International Potato Center (CIP), recognise the potential innovative value of the scheme and its implications for agro-biodiversity conservation of heirloom species. Through a joint programme, ANDES and the International Institute for Environment and Development (IIED) have established a working group composed of governmental and non-governmental institutions to study legal options for the formal recognition of the Potato Park. The International Potato Center is working with ANDES and the communities in an ambitious project of repatriation of potato varieties to the local terraces and echelons worked out in the slopes of the Potato Park. Through this initiative, indigenous peoples are learning of their rights to biological resources and of the potential benefits derived from their use.

For the communities of the Potato Park, current legal designations, such as *Reserva Paisajística* (Landscape Reserve), are not enough. They have proposed that the current Peruvian Protected Area System be extended to include community-conserved areas with the name of Andean Community-Conserved Areas. This model would focus on the protection of Andean biodiversity and landscapes in a way that recognises the intricate role of people in the nurturing and maintenance of biological diversity, and that is in keeping with the traditions and techniques developed originally for the Andean agricultural systems and cultural needs.

## Embracing ancestral indigenous knowledge in the Sierra Nevada de Santa Marta, Colombia

The work of the *Fundación Pro-Sierra Nevada de Santa Marta* (FPSN) provides an example of how local and indigenous Colombian communities can be engaged in sustainable development and protection of mountain landscapes. Now in its 17th year, this initiative reveals the complexity of interactions between culture and nature in this region, and the importance of indigenous ancestral practices in landscape management.

In 1991 the FPSN initiated preparation of the Conservation Strategy for the Sierra Nevada de Santa Marta, inspired by *Caring for the Earth,* successor to the 1980 *World Conservation Strategy.* The development of the strategy was conceived as a participatory process that would increase the capability of stakeholders to stop the prevailing trend of environmental and social degradation. The Foundation worked with both indigenous and peasant communities, government and non-government agencies, the academic sector and representatives of private industry to identify and analyse the causes and effects of environmental degradation in the Sierra Nevada and to develop solutions.

As a result of this participatory process, the FPSN produced a Sustainable Development Plan for the Sierra Nevada (SDP), which was published with the endorsement of the National Planning Department, Ministry of Environment, Presidential Advisor for the Atlantic Coast, and three Governors of the region. The document presents a description of the physical and social characteristics and history of the region, the methodology used to prepare the strategy, the diagnosis carried out by stakeholders, and finally the plan itself.

The Sierra Nevada de Santa Marta is the highest coastal mountain in the world, reaching 5,775m elevation in a direct slope from the sea level. It is rich in biological and cultural diversity and critical to the region's water supply. It has been designated a Biosphere Reserve covering 17,000km$^2$, and contains two national parks and two indigenous reservations. Several indigenous groups, including the Kankuamos, the Wiwa, the Arhuacos and the Kogi inhabit the area (the last functioning pre-Colombian civilization), for whom the Sierra Nevada is a sacred mountain: "the heart of the world." For the tribal communities living here, the forests are vital, providing wildlife habitat and serving as sanctuaries for worship and religious ceremonies. The resources in the forests also provide shelter, fuel, clothing, household utensils, medicines, food and materials for their artistic expression.

The indigenous peoples living in the Sierra Nevada de Santa Marta believe that all native food plants have their "fathers" and "mothers" and that crop fertility has to be insured by offerings to these spiritual beings. Soil types such as clays, humus, etc. are ritually named, as are the categories of rains, winds and lagoons, along with the cardinal points to which they are associated. These offerings are real evidence of indigenous knowledge, as ritual payment for the use of a particular species of tree to build a bridge consists of clearing and feeding sacred food to saplings of the same species dispersed in the forest, favouring their survival (Rodríguez, 2003).

The intimate contact that these indigenous people have with natural phenomena gives them a clear sense of cycles that they have to maintain as environmental stewards. As a result, they have developed a unique, close connection with the mountain landscape in which they live, and have established distinct systems of knowledge. Innovation and practices relating to the uses and management of biological diversity on these lands and environments are the result of a complex system of offerings (*pagamentos*) as tributes in which each person of the community acts as steward of a sacred territory.

The national policy for the Sierra Nevada began with the declaration of a Forestry Reserve in 1959. In 1964 the government of Colombia declared part of the Sierra Nevada as a national park. In 1974 and 1982, the government declared two indigenous reservations that presently overlap the national park, returning part of the original territories to management by the traditional communities inhabiting the area. These policies have had little effect on the conservation of the Sierra Nevada, which has remained a cultural, working landscape, more in keeping with Category V characteristics; while colonization pressures continue to affect its most fragile biomes it is necessary for the government to take advice from indigenous people, in order to protect the officially declared National Park.

However, challenges remain related to public attitudes toward indigenous knowledge and the erosion of traditional cultures in the region. As the indigenous people of this region are increasingly exposed to the influences of the dominant culture, they are losing their traditional values. These factors include colonization of lands, the influence of evangelical churches on traditional religious practices, and integration into the cash economy, which is changing traditional power structures and encouraging many people to think of land as a commodity, leaving behind spiritual values.

To achieve its mission, the FPSN promotes appropriate dissemination of information to all stakeholders. Based on participation, an open dialogue and increasing awareness of the problems of the Sierra, the FPSN seeks to find social, cultural and environmentally feasible solutions to stop deterioration of this region. By focusing on water conservation as a common theme, the FPSN aims to overcome interests in conflict, limited understanding and resistance to change in the Sierra to reach required actions for its conservation with commitment and collaboration from the different sectors. In this context the FPSN promotes and stimulates the establishment of what we call the Conservation-Recuperation-Production Systems with the objective of involving small farmer communities in initiatives that include improvement of their quality of life, and environmental conservation respecting indigenous territories, customs and practices.

The indigenous communities of this region sustain a world-view and practices that naturally protect resources, regulating consumptive land use and thereby allowing natural re-vegetation to occur. Their "history" remains what the "ancient people" knew as "the sacred laws" they had established, and which continue to serve as guidelines for the communities' present-day management of resources. These cultural norms are based on the belief that every action is significant, because every action surges from a natural force that comes from those ancient beings who are present in each element of nature: the god of a particular stone, a river, a mountain, a tree, those who provide the energy necessary for life to follow its natural course. The indigenous people believe this force or motion is reflected in what they call "tradition" which, far from being static in time, moves along and reaffirms itself within the needs and opportunities that time brings. This traditional worldview selects its elements, comprehends a totality, and indicates the best paths to choose. As the indigenous community has become more open to "Western" ways, the project has opened the door for learning and exchange about the role of the indigenous communities in what we understand as conservation and sustainable use (Rodríguez, 2002).

The indigenous management offers an alternative attitude towards the environment, and although it has changed from its original one, it is still being re-created and should be shared. "Recovering a watershed, is recovering life, heart, and people and it is through history that we can first do this recovery, (following Argumedo, 2001), by recovering history, laws and norms," hopefully with plasticity to integrate the overall regulatory framework of the country.

The FPSN believes in this priority and its relevance for territorial conservation. For the local population, its history should not be forgotten by the young indigenous people and should be shared and understood by western society, or "the little brothers",[3] so that their management practices might serve as an example for other regions. In this way, a closer relationship with indigenous thinking could be established. Maybe for most of us the most important product of establishing a Protected Landscape will be the conserved and recovered forest; however, for

---

[3] The indigenous communities of this region view themselves as the *elder brothers*, since they were the area's first inhabitants.

indigenous groups, history is a more significant issue, since this strong culture includes in its essence the protection of the environment, and this guides their conduct (Rodríguez, 2000).

The *de facto* Category V management of some areas of the greater Sierra Nevada de Santa Marta conservation area should recognise the importance of becoming compliant with international guidelines for Protected Landscapes. A regulatory and statutory conservation classification inside Colombia should favour incorporating a *de jure* designation for Category V areas such as the Sierra Nevada, allowing for alternative management in the hands of indigenous people, instead of relying on a park authority that has difficulty controlling the area.

## Facing the reality of traditional *colono* landscape management

The Cumanda Ethnobotanical Reserve within the upper Quijos River valley near Baeza, Ecuador portrays a landscape that has been exposed to different management regimes, and that illustrates the impact of *colono* culture in the taming of montane wilderness in the equatorial mountains. The image of those tropical montane cloud forests has always been confused with pristine and untouched virgin mountains in the headwaters of the Amazon River. However, the so-called pristine forests hide the human imprint that people have left in many sites of the cloud forest belt and that just now are becoming known thanks to archaeological findings and new remote sensing technology that can detect built structures in the landscape. The Quijos valley

The landscapes of the Quijos River Valley (Ecuador), a "gateway to the Amazon," and surrounding valleys have been exposed to an array of management regimes. The Quijos Valley has the largest expanse of protected areas in Ecuador in three sites: Antisana Ecological Reserve, Cayambe-Coca Ecological Reserve, and Sumaco Napo-Galeras National Park and Biosphere Reserve. *Jessica Brown*

watershed constitutes one of only three main access routes into the Ecuadorian Amazon. This "gateway to the Amazon" has attracted consecutive waves of exploration and settlement: from early 16th century Spanish explorers, to the more recent incursions of *colonos,* colonists from other areas of Ecuador, particularly the provinces of Loja and Manabi, which followed the opening up of the valley in the 1970s with the construction of roads to reach oil fields lower in the Amazon forest. The most recent wave of exploration takes the form of (eco)tourism, attracted here by the region's spectacular rich biological and cultural diversity.

In Ecuador public land management regimes are perhaps the most common approach to addressing tourism and resource management issues; typically these have followed the North American model for national parks. The Quijos Valley has the largest expanse of protected areas in Ecuador, with approximately 94% of the territory of the basin under official protection in three sites: Antisana Ecological Reserve; Cayambe-Coca Ecological Reserve; and Sumaco Napo-Galeras National Park and Biosphere Reserve. The rest of the territory is located in the centre of these three conservation areas, an arrangement that resembles a reversal of the Biosphere Reserve model in which the core is pristine, a buffer zone surrounds the centre and extensive usage occurs in the periphery. In the Quijos river valley, the core pristine areas surround the valley in the upper limits of the watershed, and the valley serves as a kind of buffer zone. The Cumanda Ethnobotanical Reserve is located in this area, flanked by a colonization front that has gone from timber exploitation, to the agricultural based *naranjilla* (*Solanum quitoense*) boom, dairy production, and most recently, adventure and ecotourism, including trout fishing, whitewater rafting, trekking and bird watching.

The "reverse" Biosphere Reserve model of the Quijos river basin fits perfectly with the principles of a Category V protected landscape, because it helps consolidate a huge con-servation corridor (within what has been proposed by The Nature Conservancy as the Condor Bioreserve) and encompasses cultural features, such as the grasslands of the páramos and archaeological features of the indigenous cultures that lived in the area since before the Spanish conquest.

In the *páramo*, land is held communally. In fact, decisions regarding access to the páramo and its use, and maintenance (through controlled burning and grazing) are taken by each community as a whole during assemblies, called *Mingas,* which are held periodically. A duty roster is also maintained, assigning, on a rotational basis, a member of the community to care for the cattle grazing on the *páramo*. As a typical Andean social structure, a group of neighbours in the *comarca* or a related extended family group or *Ayllu* meet together on the property of one of them. All work there for free with the understanding that, someday in the near future, their turn will come, so that the group will come to their own parcels or *chacras* and help with their work. This is particularly important for preparing the land for planting, for removing fuelwood, for harvesting, and for other building necessities such as irrigation channel maintenance, terracing for soil erosion control, or the edification of storage rooms, or outlet stores on site. *Mingas* are frequently held to carry out various projects that benefit the whole community and also act to reinforce reciprocal relations and ties in the communities. In this way, traditional Andean beliefs and customs that have survived the hacienda rule are still very much alive in the communities of Jamanco, Oyacachi and El Tambo, and are reflected in the surrounding landscape.

All three of these communities are experimenting with tourism. Both Oyacachi and Jamanco have built rudimentary thermal bath resorts to attract visitors, while El Tambo offers guided horseback excursions around the base of the Antisana volcano. Similar to cattle-ranching on the páramo, tourism initiatives in these communities are developed communally through *mingas*, with key decisions being taken by the community as a whole during assemblies. Ideally, this mechanism should ensure that tourism develops within the limits of acceptable change set by the communities involved. Unfortunately, the communities' successes with tourism are mixed at best. Their lack of cash resources, access to markets, business and language training (few of the local inhabitants speak English) means that tourists mostly opt for the better organized and publicized Private Reserves and "eco-lodges," in other exotic Ecuadorian destinations better prepared to handle tourists, such as the downstream lowland Amazon, the coastal plains or the Galapagos islands. Moreover, the páramo on which these communities' herds depend has also come under threat from large-scale water extraction projects in the area for which the communities have not received any compensation. The unique páramo ecosystem, its critical role as a natural water reservoir for Quito, and the ways of life of the pastoral communities that depend on it and maintain it, have come to the attention of national and international groups who are seeking to find new ways to protect and conserve the area's natural and cultural heritage (Chaurette *et al.*, 2003).

Continual usage of slope-lands in the montane cloud forest belt makes this site a prime example of a living cultural landscape, which is evolving with the drives of the dominant culture, and which is already used in environmental education campaigns. Thus, the Cumanda Ethnobotanical Reserve can be seen as an organic landscape, in which colonization has left an important mark, and a site that is worth showing and protecting through stewardship. Some inaccessible areas have remained untouched and are in an excellent state of conservation, despite weak management and control, emphasising the intricate relations of nature at its best and culture at its worst.

The intricate relation of nature and cultural traits in many places of highland Ecuador, makes these areas highly appropriate for the application of the new conservation model of Category V protected areas. As of 2004, the legal designation of "Protected Landscapes and Seascapes" exists in Ecuador mainly to cover the Seascape portion of the protected Galapagos archipelago. Including the socio-economic dimension in the new theoretical frames for cultural landscapes in the Andes mountains will place people as an integral part of the evolving landscape. We have argued that the Category V designation is the best management option available for sites like the Quijos River valley or other protected areas within the páramo (Sarmiento *et al.*, 2000).

## Conclusions

The new paradigm for protected areas is taking an interesting twist in Latin America, where ancient civilization relicts and traditional communities co-exist amongst the constructs of modernity. Implications for the conservation scenario are therefore challenging. In a rather unique approach, Latin Americans are embracing the notion that cultural landscapes exist as both agent and subject of ecological and cultural traits, in many cases working towards defining new models applicable to local realities. This interesting dilemma of considering the living landscape as the continent of livelihoods and as the content of evolving cultural traits, makes it possible to use Protected Landscapes as working laboratories for ethnoecological studies in biodiversity conservation and sustainable development.

The case studies from Colombia, Ecuador and Peru presented here illustrate different options available for landscape stewardship in the Andean region, and propose new pathways for development with conservation. Andean communities are particularly sensitive to endogenous alternatives that capture their identity, empower their social and economic progress, and reassess their value in the concert of global forces affecting rural communities in the developing world.

Efforts to further the protected landscape approach in the Andes should be based on a culturally sensitive organizational and planning strategy. In contrasting and comparing experiences from the region, including the three cases studies above, we find five characteristics that are common to the new conservation paradigm:

**Communicative:** The potential of category V protected landscapes should be promoted through different media to community organizations, NGOs, local and national governments, and international agencies. The legal framework should be developed in each country to enable the use of conservation easements and demonstration sites established to provide living examples of how this conservation tool can work in the Andes.

**Inclusive and participatory:** National consultations and regional workshops should be held, bringing together grass-roots organizations, urban-based advocates, government officials, local community leaders and all other interested parties. Indigenous and traditional people become protagonists of active conservation stewardship.

**Epistemographic:** Semantics and the terminology of the highland/lowland dynamics of mountain ecosystems should be made clear within an Andean context, including notions of traditional knowledge and ethno-ecological heritage.

**Methodological:** Experience with protected landscapes in each country should be documented and shared as lessons learned, aiming to develop best practices for sustainable development scenarios in Andean landscapes.

**Transcendental:** Conservation of cultural landscapes should strive to offer lasting, sustainable options for biodiversity-based livelihoods in the Andes. Opportunities should be sought to unify and invigorate local cultures.

## Coda

The much-needed preservation and strict protection of the remnant shreds of Andean forests and local cultures is considered the highest priority in strategic scenarios for sustainable mountain development in the region. Precautionary measures should be placed in the policy-making process that affects water supply and watershed management to serve the ever-thirsty, growing Andean cities. The old approach of setting aside pristine páramos for conservation away from human interference (for example in National Parks, according to the so-called "Yellowstone model") should yield to the new approach of sustaining living landscapes for conservation in cooperation with the communities that have created and inhabit them (e.g., the approach known as the "Green Mountains model" from the mountains of Vermont (Chaurette *et al.,* 2003).

Out-dated generalizations about the pristine character of tropical ecosystems, especially about tropical mountains, should be avoided in light of new lessons for changing paradigms, modern technologies, and the increasingly sophisticated tools available to restore the degraded mountains into healthy forested ones and to keep cultural practices and beliefs alive. In dealing with National Parks and Protected Areas, we should abandon the "Yellowstone model," that is, there should be an organized effort to reforest the highlands and to recreate the neotropical forests that once were there, with the help of the people who inhabit the Andean mountains. Drawing on the traditions of indigenous and *colono* societies to meet the demands of bio-diversity conservation, the protected landscape concept of the Category V will bring practical tools for the stewardship of regional and national heritage amidst the globalization trends encroaching in the valley.

## Acknowledgements

Insights into landscape stewardship and sacred site conservation discussed here were originally catalysed at an IUCN-WCPA International Working Session on Stewardship of Protected Landscapes, which was held in Vermont, USA, by QLF/Atlantic Center for the Environment and the Conservation Study Institute of the US National Park Service. Further efforts were advanced in preparatory planning meetings held in Chivay (Peru), Guácimo (Costa Rica), Athens, Georgia (USA), Baeza (Ecuador), Abisko (Sweden), Stow-in-the-Wold (United Kingdom) and the World Parks Congress in Durban (South Africa). Meetings have been supported by the IUCN World Commission on Protected Areas, the UNESCO-World Heritage Centre, the Countryside Agency (UK), QLF/Atlantic Center for the Environment, and the Canadian International Development Agency. We thank the Andean Mountains Association for networking and the Fundación Pro-Sierra Nevada de Santa Marta, the Fundación para la Región Amazónica Ecuatoriana, the Indigenous Peoples Biodiversity Network and the Asociación Quechua-Aymara Andes for the case studies presented here. We thank Jessica Brown for substantive inputs into this chapter.

# 12. Protecting landscapes and seascapes: experience from coastal regions of Brazil

*Clayton F. Lino and Marilia Britto de Moraes*

## Introduction

In this chapter, we review Brazil's experience with protecting the landscapes and seascapes of its coastal zone, looking at two very different designations: one that is part of an international system and one that is unique to Brazil. We discuss the special conservation challenges of the coastal zone in Brazil, and introduce the national system of protected areas. We present two case-studies: the Mata Atlantica Biosphere Reserve, designated under UNESCO's Man and the Biosphere Reserve Programme, and the Cananéia-Iguape-Peruíbe Area de Proteção Ambiental (APA), a federally designated Environmental Protection Area.

These two protected area designations play an important role in protecting the landscapes and seascapes of Brazil's coastal zone. More than just compatible, these designations represent complementary approaches to protection that may work in harmony with each other and with other kinds of protected areas – such as Category II National/State Parks and Category VI extractive reserves – to manage natural resources in the coastal zone, while involving local communities and managing urban growth in densely populated areas.

The Biosphere Reserve designation and the Environmental Protection Area – *Area de Proteção Ambiental* or APA – are introduced briefly below.

## Biosphere Reserves in Brazil

Brazil today devotes nearly 15% of its national territory to Biosphere Reserves under the UNESCO Man and the Biosphere Programme, with at least one of these reserves in each of the large Brazilian biomes (Mata Atlantica, Cerrado, Pantanal, Amazon and Caatinga). UNESCO created the Man and the Biosphere (MaB) programme in 1971; one of the principal instruments involved the creation of "biosphere reserves," dedicated to sustainable development and the conservation of biodiversity, as well as the support of environmental education, research, and the monitoring of the most important natural areas of the world. While Brazil is home to only six of the 440 Biosphere Reserves created under this programme, the combined area of these reserves is equivalent to approximately 1,300,000km$^2$ – more than half of the total area of all the biosphere reserves in the world. The first of Brazil's biosphere reserves to be declared was the Mata Atlantica Biosphere Reserve, which is discussed later in this paper.

## The Area de Proteção Ambiental (APA): Brazil's Category V designation

Brazil's Environmental Protection Areas – *Areas de Proteção Ambiental* or APAs – correspond with Category V Protected Landscapes and Seascapes. This designation was created in the 1980s as part of the legislation for Brazil's Environmental Policy (Federal Law 6.902/81), and includes a strong emphasis on regional planning and management. The APAs are areas

The Praia landscape of Mata Atlantica, Brazil's first Biosphere reserve. Created in 1991 to protect the remaining fragments of threatened forest areas, the Biosphere reserve spans the Atlantic Forest biome, passing through 15 Brazilian states and incorporating hundreds of core zones. *Clayton Lino*

declared with the aim of preserving the welfare of urban populations and improving local ecological conditions, and within which restrictions may be imposed to avoid potentially polluting industries, substantial alteration of local ecological conditions, erosion processes, and any activity that threatens existing rare species of regional biota. Briefly, APAs must include zoning for ecological and economic activities; a wildlife zone; provisions to meet urban requirements (e.g., sewage systems; streets that follow the local topography; planting of native plant species); a Management Committee and a Management Plan. Federal APAs are managed by the federal government agency IBAMA,[1] attached to the Ministry for the Environment.

## The coastal zone: protecting landscapes and seascapes

The importance of the coastal zone and its resources – natural and cultural – is undeniable. People are historically linked to these areas, accustomed to using the natural resources in a sustainable way for their subsistence and livelihoods. However, the pressures of modern life and emigration of people to Brazil's coastal zones have resulted in uncontrolled urban growth and increased problems of poverty. On the other hand, the highest population densities are found precisely in this territory of Brazil, which creates special challenges for operational work in the field. These challenges include: the complexity of land uses, the involvement of three levels of government – federal, state and municipal – and the specific legislation for each

[1]  Brazilian Institute for the Environment and Sustainable Use of Natural Resources.

different kind of protected area found in the region, which ranges from strict protection to sustainable use categories, as well as protected landscape/seascapes.

Fortunately, despite several economic cycles of natural resources exploitation since the European colonists' arrival, there still remains a significant area covered with vegetation. During the 20$^{th}$ century, the concern for protecting the natural environment grew and reached more and more areas in Brazil, which resulted in the creation of national and state parks, among other protection tools, by federal and state authorities. While the latter part of the 20$^{th}$ century was a period of increasing awareness of the consequences of environmental degradation, the century ended with fishing stocks declining, and local communities being forced to move to large cities for a better quality of life, along with many other losses for the environment, culture and landscape/seascape of Brazil's coastal zone.

Protected by the Brazilian Federal Constitution, Brazil's coastal zone is a fragile ensemble of ecosystems in a transitional zone, encompassing some of the first lands occupied in the country, where nature and native cultures have faced several threats over the centuries. Sustaining multiple uses along its more than 8,000km, the Brazilian coastal zone concentrates pollution effects, at the same time that migration into urban areas has taken traditional people from lands they have occupied for centuries or more, and where they had practiced fishing, hunting and cultivating. Brazil's coastal zone is also where the greatest number of protected areas are concentrated.

The Brazilian Institute for the Environment and Sustainable Use of Natural Resources, IBAMA, is the federal agency responsible for protected areas in Brazil and is in charge of the government's environmental policies. In the Brazilian system of environmental protection, IBAMA is the executor of directives from the central government agency, the Ministry for the Environment. Generally each state has its Secretariat for the Environment and is able to keep protected areas under its responsibility; as, in turn, do municipalities. However, the basic rules are determined by federal legislation, and those imposed by state and municipal authorities may only be more restrictive.

IBAMA is also the institution responsible for implementing Brazil's National Coastal Management Plan, which dates from the 1980s, and which brought many new approaches at the outset. To date, the Coastal Management Plan, despite not achieving direct results such as zoning or the implementation of state regulations, has led to many indirect positive consequences for the planning and conserving of coastal resources. An important example is the development of coastal zoning and coastal management planning at the state level in Brazil. Moreover, concerns for the coastal zone and methods for planning have been adopted into legislation and policies by state and municipal administrations. Finally, a number of NGOs are actively working in Brazil's coastal zone on issues related to fisheries management, protection of endangered and threatened species (e.g., the golden lion tamarin), conservation of forests and other ecosystems, and the needs of local communities.

## Brazil's national system of protected areas

Since 2000 Brazil's protected areas legislation, *Sistema Nacional de Unidades de Conservação* (SNUC) has divided the country's national system of protected areas into two groups: Integral Protection and Sustainable Use. The first group of conservation units is comprised of IUCN

Categories I to IV, and the second group refers primarily to Categories V and VI; Biosphere Reserves, corridors and mosaics are also included as part of the system, recognised as special protected areas, which are complementary to the conservation units. The legislation defines a conservation unit (UC) as:

*...a territorial space and its environmental resources, including jurisdictional waters, with significant natural characteristics, legally instituted by Government, with defined purposes for conservation and limits as well, under a special regimen for its adminis-tration, on which appropriate warranties of protection are applied* (Federal Law 9985/ 2000)

The Integral Protection conservation units encompass several types of protected areas, including National Parks and State Parks. In most cases, Brazilian National Parks and State parks involve people within their limits, including traditional and rural communities and other groups that may need support in reinforcing their stewardship of the area's heritage, and meeting sustainable development objectives. In the second group, Sustainable Use, the recent legislation has created new categories with a strong emphasis on sustainable development. These include Extractive Reserves, which correspond with Category VI (refer to Maretti's chapter in this volume for more on Extractive Reserves, and Brazil's experience with this model), and the Environmental Protection Areas – *Areas de Proteção Ambiental* or APAs – which correspond with Category V. In the same law there is a separate chapter about Special Protected Areas, where the Biosphere Reserves are defined. Table 1 presents all the federal designations in Brazil's national system of conservation units.

## Table 1. Brazil's national system of protected areas – SNUC

| Integral protection | Sustainable use | Objectives | Ownership | Uses allowed |
|---|---|---|---|---|
| Ecological Station | | Nature preservation; scientific research | Public property | Scientific research; educational visits |
| Biological Reserve | | Integral preservation; no human interference | Public property | Scientific research; educational visits |
| National Park (State, Local) | | Preservation of natural ecosystems and scenic beauty | Public property | Scientific research; recreation; tourism; education |
| Natural Monument | | Preservation of rare natural sites; great scenic beauty | Public or private (expropriated) | Public access under authorization |
| Sylvan Wildlife Refuge | | Natural environment protected for species reproduction or flora/fauna communities | Public or private (expropriated) | Public access under authorization |
| | Environmental Protection Area (large, with human occupation; cultural, aesthetic and biotic attractions) | Protection of biological diversity; regulating occupation; ensuring the sustainability of natural resources; improving inhabitants' living conditions. | Public or private | Fed. law n. 6938/81 and other regulations, according to objectives |

## Table 1. Brazil's national system of protected areas – SNUC    (cont.)

| Integral protection | Sustainable use | Objectives | Ownership | Uses allowed |
|---|---|---|---|---|
| | **Relevant Ecological Interest Area** (little or no occupation; extraordinary natural characteristics; regional biota) | Maintenance of natural eco-systems of regional importance; use regulated according to nature conservation requirements | Public or private (possibility of expropriation) | Under rules for private land use, according to objectives |
| | **National Forest** (predominance of native species) | Sustainable multiple use of forest resources; scientific research into sustainable methods | Public (expropriation) | Those of the indigenous population before the creation of the PA; scientific research allowed and encouraged |
| | **Extractive Reserve** (used by indigenous people, who depend on it for subsistence) | Protection of local people's ways of life and culture; ensuring sustainable use of natural resources | Public property; use conceded to traditional people: specific regulation by contract. | Public access conducive to local interests; management plan; scientific research; sustainable exploitation of natural resources |
| | **Fauna Reserve** (natural area with native species, terrestrial or aquatic) | Technical and scientific studies about sustainable economical management of fauna resources | Public or private (expropriation) | Public access under authorization; regulated commercial activity |
| | **Sustainable Development Reserve** | Preserving nature and ensuring suitable conditions for species reproduction; to improve quality of life; permits resource use by indigenous people; supports traditional knowledge about resource management | Public private (expropriation) contract | Use by indigenous people according to specific regulations, visiting allowed and encouraged; research allowed and encouraged; limits on numbers of occupants (or resident population); cultivation according to zoning |
| | **Private Natural Heritage Reserve** | To conserve ecological diversity | Private area protected in perpetuity in the public interest | Scientific research; tourism; recreation; education |

Artisan, Mata Atlantica region. Protecting local cultural heritage and improving local people's living conditions are important goals for the Federal Environmental Protected Areas (APAs) in Brazil's coastal zone. *Clayton F. Lino*

## The Mata Atlantic Biosphere Reserve

Brazil's first biosphere reserve, the Mata Atlantic Biosphere Reserve, was created in 1991 to protect and link the remaining fragments of threatened forest areas within the Atlantic Forest biome. It consists of a large corridor passing through 15 Brazilian states and incorporating hundreds of core zones. The fact that the Mata Atlantica Biosphere Reserve was not designated until 1991, almost two decades after Brazil had first established its national committee for the MaB programme, meant that planning of the reserve was able to take advantage of many conceptual advances in conservation during the 1970s and 1980s. These include strategies such as ecological corridors, the creation of protected buffer zone areas surrounding parks, sustainable watershed management, urban green belts, private protected areas, and community participation in the management of protected areas. Moreover, in the 1980s, dozens of new parks and other protected areas were created in Brazil, many in the area of the Mata Atlantica, and these became core zones for the Biosphere Reserve.

The creation of the Mata Atlantic Biosphere Reserve followed a period of great social and political mobilization in Brazil, linked to the re-democratization of the country and intense investment in environmental protection. Public awareness of environmental issues grew during this period, and people became aware of the problems of the preservation of the rainforests of the Amazon and Mata Atlantica regions. Initially the Biosphere Reserve included only a few isolated areas in the states of Sao Paulo, Rio de Janeiro and Parana, but the involvement of environmental organizations, scientists and various communities in other states led to four enlargements of the reserve, duly presented to and approved by UNESCO, until today the

## Map 1.   Mata Atlantica Biosphere Reserve

reserve has reached the scale of the entire biome, involving 15 of the 17 Brazilian states where parts of this biome are found, and covering an area of 350,000km[2].

The Mata Atlantica, or Atlantic Forest, which is the biome in which Brazil's most urbanized and industrialized areas are located, has been reduced to nearly 7% of its original forest cover;[2] moreover, what is left is fragmented and threatened by total destruction in certain areas, although it is one of the most important tropical rainforests of the planet.

In the Mata Atlantica, one finds great biodiversity and other aspects of special scientific and social interest, as well as scenery of overwhelming beauty and numerous cultural and tourist attractions. This forest provides protection for the soil and water resources, and prevents the erosion of hillsides; it regulates the climate and contributes to the reduction of the greenhouse effect through the binding of atmospheric carbon dioxide. It also provides sustainable eco-

---

[2]   According to the most recent report from SOS Mata Atlantic, an important NGO in the region, only 7% of the Atlantic Forest remains today, which indicates that the deforestation continues.

Rich in biodiversity, Brazil's Mata Atlantica biome is one of the most important tropical rainforests on the planet. However, the region's remaining forest cover is fragmented and highly threatened in certain areas. *Clayton F. Lino*

nomic alternatives, for hundreds of local communities and many of its products have great economic importance for the country.

Since this first Brazilian Biosphere Reserve was so large, its creation presented a series of challenges. The first of these was the creation of a special autonomous system of management that would ensure institutional consolidation and the development of projects involving the conservation of biodiversity, the publicizing of relevant information, and sustainable development. In 1993, the National Council of the Mata Atlantica Biosphere was created, complete with an executive secretary and its own independent staff, located in the city of Sao Paulo, and supported by the Sao Paulo State Secretary of the Environment. Throughout the years, various state committees and sub-committees for the Mata Atlantica Biosphere Reserve have been created, the most recent being the regional colleges to integrate the various actions taken.

Special pilot areas have been defined as priority targets for the implementation of field projects, and Advanced Posts, which are institutions working as centres for the dissemination of information about principles and projects of the reserve, have been established. The whole is a single comprehensive network of institutions working for the conservation of one of the biomes in Brazil. As a consequence, the Mata Atlantica Biosphere Reserve is more than a special protected area. There are numerous protected areas in the MaB Biosphere Reserve programme, but this reserve in particular has become a very important institution.

The management of this reserve follows strict principles of participation, decentralization, transparency, and a search for consensus with no overlap in functions with already existing institutions. On the other hand, this management is characterized by administrative flexibility and a lack of bureaucracy. All of the decision-making bodies are colleagues, and the process involves simultaneous and equal participation of governmental institutions (federal, state and local) and non-governmental participants (including NGOs, and members of the scientific community, the private sector and the local population).

This first biosphere reserve coordinates a variety of technical and scientific programmes and demonstration projects in partnership with other entities, which include:

- The **core zone conservation and research programme**, which has already contributed widely to the creation and implementation of various protected areas.

- The **forestry resources programme**, which has generated the most complete inventory of the ecological, economic and social aspects involved in the use of resources from the Mata Atlantica forest. It has implemented the first programme for environmental certification based on the international standards of the Forestry Stewardship Council; this was then awarded to a native resource, the *erva mate (Ilex parguariensis)*, which is used in the preparation of *mate* tea and other products.

- The **eco-tourism programme**, which has trained more than 200 young adults to work as environmental monitors, as well as supporting the creation of various associations of tourist guides or the suppliers of tourist lodgings, and promoting exchange programmes; at present, this programme is collaborating with the elaboration of norms for certification related to sustainable tourism in Brazil.

- The **water and forest programme**, which integrates management policies with those for conservation and the recovery of water and forestry resources in the Mata Atlantica.

- The **Annual Mata Atlantica Update**, which unites and synthesizes quality information about the biome and makes it accessible to the general public.

- The **public policy programme**, which advocates the approval of laws and programmes of interest to the Mata Atlantica and other relevant areas, has had various proposals approved by the National Council for the Environment (CONAMA). Among these are the creation of a Mata Atlantica Day (May 27); the creation of regulations for the management of various native resources, including araucarias and the "palmito" (*Euterpe edulis*), which is the source of palm hearts; and the establishment of a national policy for the Mata Atlantica.

- The **international cooperation** programme, which guarantees the participation of the National Council of the Mata Atlantica Biosphere Reserve Programme in many UNESCO working groups, on themes such as agro-biodiversity, emerging ecosystem management, landscapes and linkages, the Convention on Biological Diversity, and Quality Economy economic development.

In addition, the Mata Atlantica Biosphere Reserve has had notable success in obtaining large international contributions for the protection of the Mata Atlantica from various sources (World Bank, Inter-American Development Bank, the German KfW cooperation bank, etc.), as well as in the recognition of World Heritage Sites in this biome. This biosphere reserve has also made a significant contribution to the cause of environmental education in Brazil through its publications (books, reports, and technical texts), as well as the dissemination of materials such as videos and posters.

The Mata Atlantica Biosphere Reserve has become one of the main instruments for the conservation of the Mata Atlantica biome, and its success has paved the way for the establishment of other biosphere reserves in Brazil. It has provided the experience needed to develop a "Brazilian biosphere reserve model," and to develop national policy regarding the MaB programme in Brazil. It is therefore contributing significantly to the conservation and sustainable development of critical areas in the country, as well as to an increase in international cooperation within the MaB programme.

# The Cananéia-Iguape-Peruíbe *Area de Proteção Ambiental*

The Cananéia-Iguape-Peruíbe APA is located on the southeastern coast of Brazil, in São Paulo State, and is part of the most important extension of remaining Atlantic Forest – the largest *continuum* in Brazil – including mangroves, estuaries and lagoons, rich fauna and flora. Established in 1984, it is situated within the Ribeira Valley, which is classified as part of the Mata Atlantica Biosphere Reserve and the World Heritage Site (Natural). The Mandira Extractive Reserve (see chapter in this volume by Maretti) is located within the Cananéia-Iguape-Peruíbe APA. Original communities still live in the region, maintaining many age-old traditions, an important asset in working toward sustainable management today. Table 2 presents all the federally protected APAs in Brazil's coastal zone; these represent almost half of the APAs in Brazil.

## Table 2. Federal Environmental Protection Areas (APAs) in Brazil's coastal zone[3]

| Name | Region/state | Creation | Area (ha) | Land/seascape | Protection goals |
|---|---|---|---|---|---|
| **Anhatomirim** | South/Santa Catarina | 1992 | 3,000 | Land, sea | *Sotalia fluviatis,* Atlantic Forest, water resources for traditional fishermen |
| **Bacia do rio S.João/ Mico-Leão -Dourado** | Southeast/ Rio de Janeiro | 2002 | 150,700 | Land, rivers | Spring-water resources, Atlantic forest remnants, environmental and cultural heritage, *Leontophitecus rosalia* |
| **Baleia Franc** | South/Santa Catarina | 2000 | 156,100 | Land, sea, islands | *Eubalena australis,* rational use of resources, occupation of water and land, tourist and recreational uses, research and traffic |
| **Barra do Rio Mamanguape** | Northeast/ Paraíba | 1993 | 14,640 | Land, marine and river waters | *Trichechus manatus* (peixe-boi marinho)and other endangered species, mangrove, Atlantic Forest and water resources, improvement of local peoples' living conditions; promoting environmental education and ecological tourism |
| **Cairuçu** | Southeast/ Rio de Janeiro | 1983 | 32,688 | Continental lands, water, islands | Remarkable landscapes and seascapes, hydrological systems, traditional communities, natural environment and rare species |
| **Costa dos Corais** | Northeast/ Alagoas, Pernambuco | 1997 | 413,563 | Land/sea | Coral and sandstone reefs, *Trichechus manatus*, mangroves in estuaries, support existence of the local cultures and contribute to the revival of regional cultural diversity |

---

[3] Especially in some states, there is also a significant area of land contained within State Environmental Protection Areas; for example, in Bahia, where 28 state-level APAs cover more than 5% of the state territory totalling 3,069,787ha. Also, Sao Paulo State and Minas Gerais have important portions of territory protected by APAs, among others.

**Table 2. Federal Environmental Protection Areas (APAs) in Brazil's coastal zone (cont.)**

| Name | Region/state | Creation | Area (ha) | Land/seascape | Protection goals |
|------|------|------|------|------|------|
| Cananéia-Iguape-Peruíbe | Southeast/ São Paolo | 1984 | 234,000 | Continental lands, waters, islands | Ecosystems – mangroves to mountains, bird nesting areas, archeological sites, water quality, Atlantic forest, maintenance of traditional communities' standards |
| Delta do Parnaiba | North/Piauí Ceará, MA | 1996 | 313,800 | Continental lands, water, islands | River mouths and dunes, typical vegetation and threatened animal species: *Trichechus manatus*, fishes, shrimps and crabs; improvement of local people's living conditions; preservation of local cultural traditions |
| Fernando de Noronha, Rocas, S. Pedro-S. Paulo | Northeast/ Pernambuco | 1986 | 93,000 | Sea, islands | Environmental quality and necessary conditions for survival of fauna and flora; searocks, atoll |
| Guapi-Mirim | Southeast/ Rio de Janeiro | 1984 | 13,961 | Land, water | Mangrove in Guanabara Bay, mouths of rivers |
| Guaraqueçaba | South/Paraná | 1985 | 283,014 | Continental areas, islands | Atlantic Forest, mangrove, traditional communities, archeological sites |
| Jericoacoara | Northeast/ Ceará | 1984 | 6,443 | Continental lands | Dunes, beaches, mangrove, marine turtles, birds, maintenance of traditional communities' activities |
| Piacabuçu | Northeast/ Alagoas | 1983 | 9,143 | Continental lands | Dunes, beaches, birds, turtles, surroundings of Ecological station Praia do Peba |

This region was (and still is) very productive in terms of aquatic life, thanks to a barrier island, *Ilha Comprida* (Long Island), which measures 70km by 3km and protects the estuaries of several rivers, forming an estuary-lagoon system. The *Ilha Comprida* island is also important for its genetic material and as a stopping point for migratory birds. The ecosystems of the region, including naturally flooded areas, sandbanks and dunes are naturally dynamic, but also fragile and vulnerable to urban pressures.

There was, and still is, amazing evidence of prehistoric man, with several *sambaquis*[4] which provided whitewash for painting buildings along the coast in older times. The area was one of the principal Brazilian targets for settlement by the Portuguese in the 16th century, and Cananéia village dates from 1531; along with Iguape, it is one of the oldest towns in Brazil. In the 18th and 19th centuries Ribeira Valley was important for rice production, with the advantage of a harbour allowing export and trade. However, canalization of the rivers led to silting up of the harbour and, as rice production moved to the interior of Brazil, economic development declined and the region was abandoned. This marginalization continued through the 19th

---

[4] Archeological protected heritage. *Sambaquis* look like small hills, covered with rich vegetation. They are basically middens (domestic refuse heaps) and date from 10,000BP–5,000BP.

century, resulting in emigration to other parts of the state where economic development was flourishing.

However, a local people named *caiçaras* – a blend of indigenous, African and European people – remained in the area, fishing, hunting and gathering products both from the forest and the mangrove, and practising subsistence agriculture. They lived according to communal rules and natural cycles – expressing their culture through dance, music and religion. This picture was unchanged until the 1950s, when roads (and later highways) expanded in Brazil. Other communities – such as the *quilombolas*, descended from settlements of escaped slaves – also survived and lived in the area until today. At the same time, an antiquated political structure, based on a few family oligarchies, has also been preserved.

The Cananéia-Iguape-Peruíbe APA was created during a wave of protected area establishment in Brazil in the 1980s, reflecting growing concern about environmental protection. The Serro do Mar APA (also in the state of São Paulo) was established during the same period. An important aim for both APAs was conservation of the Atlantic Forest; their designation provided a way to create not only a vegetation corridor, but also to promote the linkage between the coastal and mountain eco-systems. In addition to the exceptional environmental resources and wildlife in the area, an important attribute to be protected by the Cananéia-Iguape-Peruíbe APA was the *caiçara* people's way of life, which emerged as a strong motivating factor for participatory involvement in management.

The Cananéia-Iguape-Peruíbe APA encompasses seven municipalities in the Ribeira Valley, with a total area of about 234,000ha. The objectives of this APA are: a) to allow the local original people (*caiçaras*) to maintain their traditional activities according to historical patterns and techniques; b) to control erosion; c) to protect and preserve ecosystems ranging from mangroves to high-altitude vegetation, as well as to protect threatened species, nesting areas for marine and migratory birds, archeological sites, Atlantic Forest remnants and the quality of hydrological resources.

A participatory process was undertaken in 1996 to develop a management plan for the Cananéia-Iguape-Peruíbe APA. Because the local context and people are fundamental to stewardship, during the stakeholder identification phase secondary data was used to provide basic information about the local communities: who is who, individuals' roles in the community, and what people were thinking about key issues. Following this phase, stakeholders were contacted and asked to become involved in the process. Based on two sub-regional meetings of stakeholders, it was possible to select those who should represent the different sectors in a five-day workshop.

Meanwhile, other activities were underway, aimed at defining zones for Management Units within the Landscape Units, which overlaid the pre-existing coastal zoning in the region. Zoning of these Management Units also had to take into account the administrative and management factors, as well as the existing legal restrictions[5] and range of restricted protected areas in the region. The analysis determined that what the region really needed, instead of more restrictive rules, was the adequate use of its resources, based on efficient management and careful monitoring. The important goal, it was decided, was to promote sustainable development.

---

[5] An Atlantic Forest Decree prohibits the cutting of this kind of vegetation.

With this in mind, the workshop designed a Management Plan, which proposed programmes and projects aimed at improving local citizens' standard of living, by using natural resources according to principles and techniques of sustainability. In addition, health and education initiatives were developed, and the plan included strong emphasis on local/regional economy, through the implementation of a framework for ecotourism. In addition to programmes on health, education and eco-tourism, were those focusing on heritage conservation, environmental conservation, sustainable management of natural resources and agriculture.

A Management Committee was established to steer and implement the programme, an approach that was very advanced at the time, although it has since become mandatory. Speakers from each of the 20 communities that had been visited were chosen for a second five-day workshop, which resulted in a new format for the Management Committee. This new governance structure included community members from each Management Unit, allowing decision-making processes to be closer to local problems, perceptions and wishes.

A management system is important for raising funds to implement decisions, and may facilitate involving people in achieving the mission of development and conservation. The inclusion of local people in a real development process, with clear opportunities to contribute to and participate in this process, can make a difference in fostering a stewardship approach to conserving the landscape and seascape.

## Final considerations

These case-studies demonstrate the important and complementary roles played by the Biosphere Reserve and the Environmental Protection Area (APA) designations in Brazil's coastal zone.

The Mata Atlantica Biosphere Reserve is playing an important role both in conservation of the Mata Atlantica biome and, as noted earlier, in the development of Brazil's biosphere reserve programme. The Brazilian experience with Biosphere Reserves is a recent one, and the programme still faces constant challenges, including the consolidation of biosphere reserves to make them an effective instrument in the various biomes. In these areas it is necessary to create systems for permanent monitoring, reverse the degradation of the natural and cultural patrimony, and promote territorial organization and the sustainable use of natural resources, while fostering an improvement in the quality of life of the people. It is obvious that the creation of Biosphere Reserves alone cannot do all this, but they have certainly helped consolidate some of these objectives.

The special characteristics of APAs – for example, their emphasis on participatory and democratic approaches to management, their reliance on stewardship by local communities, and their ability to be flexible and adapt to different contexts – make that protected area category a useful tool for the management of working landscapes and, more generally, rural lands. In a vast country such as Brazil, where planning and management are so often absent, the APA designation may be considered not only a protected area, but also an instrument for environmental planning and management. The APA designation can be developed with a view toward accommodating another approach: the conservation of private lands through the promotion of stewardship and participatory processes.

Brazil's coastal zone is traditionally an occupied area, with various and often contradictory typical uses, ranging from strict preservation to high-technology activities. Particularly needed in a region such as the Brazilian coastal zone are tools allowing landscapes and seascapes to be worked in a healthy and sustainable fashion, rather than those that rely on the land to be totally empty of people. Issues such as industrial-scale mariculture, overexploitation of fisheries, the impact of tourism on local cultures, loss of self-esteem by traditional peoples when forced to leave their lands – all demand treatment by a coordinated management system that allows all sectors to be heard and respected.

There is still insufficient protected area coverage in the coastal zone and marine biome of Brazil; this is especially true for marine protected areas. Following the creation of a protected area, zoning is not enough to ensure its implementation; there must also be in place a management system, including a management committee and plan. These should rely on participatory and inclusive approaches to management.

While financial support is still a problem, it is not the only reason that protected areas are not successful. There must be more emphasis on exemplifying through actions that will demonstrate the potential of protected areas and their ability to link elements in the landscape and seascape, both products and processes.

Innovative legal tools are now available in Brazil, such as easements, shared management with NGOs,[6] and other possibilities currently available through the Brazilian System for Protected Areas, including financial sponsorship and creating partnerships. These innovative tools give real encouragement to conservation in a way that supports making linkages within the landscape, and between the landscape and people. They require a new approach: learning by doing.

The current challenge is to work with different protected area designations and tools, such as the two discussed in this chapter, and to link them through a land/seascape approach in a way that takes advantage of their strengths, linking people and nature for conservation. Brazil has great potential to demonstrate an alternative for development that supports quality of life. Coastal and marine protected areas are important elements that can contribute to this kind of sustainable development through eco-tourism, cultural and historical heritage, local handicrafts, fishing and aquaculture.

The ideal approach is one in which these activities are conducted with a view toward maintaining a healthy and sustainable use of land and its resources. Protected areas contribute to this goal by conserving and managing cultural and natural heritage – in other words, our landscapes and seascapes.

---

[6] Social Organization for Public Interest (OSCIP) Fed.Law 9790/99.

The terraced landscape of Cinque Terre (Italy) has been created and maintained over centuries. Marketing of value-added landscape products, such as olives, juice and wine, under a Cinque Terre label featuring the World Heritage logo is helping to support centuries-old land use traditions. *UNESCO*

The Rice Terraces of the Philippine Cordilleras are the work of the Ifugao culture, and are believed to be 2,000 years old. This continuing cultural landscape, which was inscribed on the World Heritage List in 1995, illustrates the challenges of balancing tradition and progress, and the importance of keeping local communities engaged in sustaining their landscapes. *Adrian Phillips*

Plate 1

Maasai women, Kenya. In Eastern and Southern Africa pastoralist communities have been presiding for generations over landscapes now recognised as important for biodiversity. Their land uses and growing management regimes have helped to preserve important habitat for wildlife; however, this relationship is coming under increasing pressure. *Moses M. Okello*

Kilimanjaro, Africa's tallest and the world's largest free-standing mountain. The diverse and spectacular landscapes of the Tsavo-Amboseli Ecosystem in Kenya are important for tourism and people's livelihoods, as well as biodiversity conservation. *Edmund Barrow*

Plate 2

Sagarmatha National Park. In Nepal, new landscape-scale conservation initiatives extend beyond the boundaries of parks to create networks of protected areas, and are adopting principles of inclusion, partnership, and linkages.
*Elizabeth Hughes/ICPL*

Conservation at the landscape level is key to long-term conservation of mega fauna, such as the greater one-horned rhinoceros (*Rhinoceros unicornis*). While the population of rhinos has increased substantially in recent years, poaching and loss of natural habitat continue to threaten this species.
*Henk Ruseler*

Fishing in the Park's river is the main source of livelihood for the communities living in the buffer zone of Royal Chitwan National Park, Nepal.
*Prabhu Budhathoki*

Plate 3

A public meeting with communities in the Mata Atlantica Biosphere Reserve (Brazil). The protected landscape approach is inclusive, relying on participatory processes and partnerships with diverse stakeholders. *Clayton F. Lino*

Regeneration of catchment forests by a few villages in the catchment of River Arvari in the drought-prone state of Rajasthan has turned this once seasonal river into a perennial river. Now nearly 90 villages have resolved to form a River Parliament and protect the catchment of the river. Shown here are a traditional water-harvesting structure, the regenerating thorn forest in the background, and some of the villagers involved with the River Parliament. *Ashish Kothari*

Plate 4

Ebey's Landing National Historical Reserve en-compasses 17,400 acres in the central part of Washington State's Puget Sound. The Reserve is managed through a partnership among the U.S. National Park Service, local and state government and the private sector. *Rob Harbour*

Marsh-Billings-Rockefeller National Historical Park (Vermont, USA) protects a working landscape that includes a forest and farm. The 550-acre forest is a living exhibit of more than a century of forest stewardship activities, from historical techniques to current best practices. *Barbara Slaiby*

Sahtu Dene continue traditional land use and lifestyle activities at Sahyoue/Edacho National Historic Site, Northwest Territories (NWT), Canada. Sahyoue/Edacho was the first protected area moved forward under the NWT Protected Areas Strategy, developed collectively by First Nations organizations, governments, industry, and environmental groups. *John McCormick*

Plate 5

Kosciuszko National Park was the largest national park in Australia at the time of its establishment (1944). A new management plan, being developed in cooperation with neighbouring communities, will recognise the rich cultural heritage of the park's landscape, including Aboriginal and non-Aboriginal values. *New South Wales National Parks and Wildlife Service*

Uluru-Kata Tjuta National Park, re-inscribed as a Cultural Landscape on the World Heritage List in 1994, is managed jointly by traditional owners and the Australian government. For example, the traditional practice of selective vegetation burning (foreground), part of Anungu "caring for country", has been adapted as a management tool in the park. *Jane Lennon*

Plate 6

Artisan, Mata Atlantica region of Brazil. The UNESCO Biosphere Reserve designation is dedicated to sustainable development and the conservation of biodiversity, as well as environmental education, research and monitoring. *Clayton F. Lino*

The Mata Atlantica Biosphere Reserve is rich in biodiversity, including species such as the Golden lion tamarin (*Leontopithecus rosalia*). *Clayton F. Lino*

The Mata Atlantica Biosphere Reserve, covering an area of 350,000km$^2$, encompasses core and buffer zones, ecological corridors, urban greenbelts, and many federal, state and private protected areas. *Clayton F. Lino*

Plate 7

Fishing boat, Brazil. In coastal zones, sustainable management of fisheries and other marine resources is important for conservation and local livelihoods. *Clayton F. Lino*

The Pitons World Heritage Site (St. Lucia) overlooks the Soufriere Marine Management Area (SMMA). Planning and management of the SMMA is undertaken by a multi-stakeholder group. *Saint Lucia National Trust*

Plate 8

Forest of Bowland Area of Outstanding Natural Beauty (AONB), England. The UK has more than a half-century of experience with Category V Protected Areas. *Countryside Agency/Charlie Hedley*

Sea kale growing on Cogden beach, Dorset AONB (England). In England and Wales the protected area system includes National Parks and Areas of Outstanding Natural Beauty. These are lived-in landscapes, characterized by their scenic beauty. *Countryside Agency/ Ian Dalgleish*

Tin Mine engine house remains, Cornwall AONB. Many protected landscapes in the UK contain sites important for biodiversity conservation, as well as for protection of archaeology, historic buildings and other cultural heritage values. *Countryside Agency/ Paul Glendell*

Plate 9

Indigenous village in the Sierra Nevada de Santa Marta (Colombia), a Biosphere Reserve. For the indigenous communities living in the area, the Sierra Nevada is a sacred mountain, "the heart of the world", and their ancestral practices are key to managing the area's landscape. *Ricardo Rey-Cervantes/Fundacion Pro Sierra Nevada de Santa Marta*

The Sacred Valley of the Incas in southern Peru is a micro-centre of origin for potatoes, where more than 2,300 cultivars of potatoes are grown. *El Parque de la Papa* (Potato Park) has been created by Quechua communities seeking to maintain their cultural landscape. *Jessica Brown*

Video technology helps Quechua residents of this community-conserved area to record the diversity of cultivars. The project is adapting traditional knowledge and management practices into comprehensive and *sui generis* plans for the conservation of Andean biodiversity and ecosystems. *Alejandro Argumedo*

Plate 10

Fruit orchards are a traditional feature of the White Carpathian cultural landscape. A project to restore these orchards and encourage extensive agriculture includes planting of heritage cultivars of apples and other fruits. *Veronica archive*

In the White Carpathians Protected Landscape Area (Czech Republic and Slovakia), an autumn festival celebrates the cultural traditions associated with the apple harvest. *Veronica archive*

In Hostětín, Czech Republic, local residents use traditional methods for drying apples and pears, and operate a processing plant that produces organic apple juice. These dried fruit and juices are marketed under the logo of Tradice Bílých Karpat (Traditions of the White Carpathians) (see right). Regional branding and certification programmes are an important tool in marketing value-added landscape products. *Petr Francan*

Plate 11

The Jizera Mountains Protected Landscape Area (PLA) is one of 24 PLAs in the Czech Republic, and protects mixed beech forest and peat bogs in the upland areas. Local NGOs and civic associations are playing an important role in encouraging sustainable development in this protected landscape. *Siegfried Weiss*

Meadows in the White Carpathian mountains (Czech and Slovak Republics) support rich biodiversity, particularly orchids such as *Orchis mascula* (see right). To maintain meadow ecosystems in the Protected Landscape Area, NGOs are working with local farmers to continue traditional haymaking practices and reintroduce sheep grazing. *Brent Mitchell*

Plate 12

# 13. Protected landscapes and seascapes and their relevance to Small Island Developing States in the Caribbean: the case of Saint Lucia

*Giles Romulus*

## Introduction

For many years since their emergence from colonialism into independence, the small islands of the Caribbean have been searching for a development paradigm that responds to their strengths and vulnerabilities. Located in the Western Atlantic within the penumbra or immediate geopolitical and cultural sphere of influence of a "Hyper Power" (Tisdell, 1994), these islands were at one time the centres of the international economic system, providing raw materials to the factories of Europe at minimal rates and being sold manufactured products at high rates. Today, these islands exhibit all the characteristics of Small Islands Developing States (SIDS), including small economic space, monocultural economies, large and growing populations, high poverty and indigence rates, growing international debts, high debt service ratios, high illiteracy rates, and, by virtue of their location, vulnerability to natural disasters. These islands are not only vulnerable to natural disasters but also to slight variations in the global economic system because of the openness of their economies. The reality of existence in the Caribbean is usually distorted by the television and movies, which portray the area as a tropical paradise for exotic vacations.

Tourism and its related services are, in the minds of many, the only comparative advantage the islands possess in an era of globalization and trade liberalization. It is within this context that Caribbean people are rediscovering their natural and cultural heritage as a means for sustainable development. The *St. George's Declaration of Principles for Environmental Sustainability in the OECS*[1] captures in its preamble the new consensus for development in the Caribbean. The Declaration states that:

> ... *the effective management of environmental resources at local, national and international levels is an essential component of sustainable social and economic development, including the creation of jobs, a stable society, a buoyant economy and the sustaining of viable natural systems on which all life depends.* (OECS, 2000)

This integrated approach to sustainable development as summarised in the St. George's Declaration also means effective management of natural and cultural resources based on the principles of *equity* (access to natural and cultural resources and land); *participation* (in decision-making and in management of resources); and *sustainability* (optimal use of natural

---

[1] The OECS are a group of islands in the Caribbean which include Antigua and Barbuda, Dominica, Grenada, Montserrat, St. Kitts and Nevis, St. Lucia, St. Vincent and the Grenadines, Anguilla and the British Virgin Islands. These islands share a common currency and are slowly moving towards a single economic space and political union. The St. George's Declaration was ratified by all the governments of the OECS.

and cultural resources without compromising the ability of future generations to do the same). It is therefore within this context that the Small Island Developing States of the Caribbean will closely examine any protected area category – i.e., will it take into consideration the needs, vulnerabilities and strengths of the islands and will lands be acquired from citizens?

The purpose of this paper is to illustrate how two protected areas in the Caribbean country of St. Lucia have used varying approaches to *in situ* management of natural ecosystems while still meeting the needs of people. Both sites offer examples of how the Protected Landscape/ Seascape approach can work in the Caribbean, and both are, in effect, actualizing the spirit of the St. George's Declaration.

## The proposed Praslin Protected Landscape

The Praslin Protected Landscape (PPL) is 874ha of coastline and sea on the east coast of St. Lucia. The area is comprised of mangroves, coral reefs, sea-grass beds, a delta, xerophytic vegetation, 17 archaeological sites, and natural beauty. A rapid inventory of flora and fauna in the area discovered 116 plant species, 38 bird species (of which three are endemics), eight species of reptiles (of which four are endemics), and two species of amphibians (Andrew and Anthony, 1997).

The Praslin Protected Landscape is one of 27 management areas in St. Lucia's protected area system. The St. Lucia National Trust is the country's largest conservation, membership and non-profit organization charged with the responsibility to conserve St. Lucia's natural and cultural heritage. Established by an Act of Parliament in 1975, the Trust is a statutory body that receives some support from government. In 1992 the Trust developed St. Lucia's protected area plan following a four-year participatory planning process. The plan advocates conservation as an indispensable basis for a form of development that is "equitable, sustainable and harmonious." It regards natural and cultural resources as the capital on which St. Lucia's development strategy can be built, and defines protected areas as:

> *Portions of the national territory ... which are placed under special management status to ensure that the resources they contained are maintained and made accessible for sustainable uses compatible with conservation requirements* (Hudson *et al.,* 1992).

Living on the periphery of the Praslin Protected Landscape are the coastal communities of Praslin and Mamiku with a combined population of approximately 400. Historically, the communities have depended on fishing and small-scale farming, with bananas being the main cash crop prior to the 1990s. Over the last decade, St. Lucia, like many other SIDS and developing countries, has lost preferential markets in the United Kingdom, which has brought about a creeping economic depression in rural communities. This depression has caused the marginal survivors in these communities to become poor, and the poor in certain cases to become indigent.

In 1989 when the St. Lucia National Trust (SLNT) began work in the area it was to preserve the biodiversity and the potential of the area as a Heritage Tourism Site. Before establishing the Frégate Islands Nature Reserve, which is one component of the Praslin Protected Landscape, the SLNT realized that the communities could not be ignored. Most of the land was in private ownership and the community depended on the area for fishing, cutting poles for their gardens, charcoal production, medicinal herbs, and some grazing. The environmental problems at the time included pollution caused by disposal of solid waste in small ravines and the presence of human waste in the fringing mangroves. A village census undertaken by the people of Praslin and Mamiku in 1994 discovered a total of 41 households with no toilets, which explained the pollution in the mangrove. There was also a great need for improving the supply of potable water to the communities. In short, in the early 1990s there was little happening in the communities in terms of self-help, as people typically waited for the Government to make something happen, which never did.

In 1994 the St. Lucia National Trust launched its efforts to create the Praslin Protected Landscape through a participatory planning process, which produced a Strategic Plan for the Community. Within four to six years the SLNT and the local communities, with funding from the Global Environment Facility/Small Grants Programme, the Government of St. Lucia, the Caribbean Natural Resources Institute, the St. Lucia Rural Enterprise Project, the German GTZ and other donors, had made substantial progress. An important step was the establishment of the Praslin-Mamiku Development Committee (PMDC) as a coordinating group. The many achievements included: providing basic amenities like toilets to 37 households; establishing a garbage disposal system; improving the communities' water supply through a US$30,000 project; the construction of a jetty for marine tours with trained guides; and the engineering of the longest coastal nature trail in St. Lucia. Another important achievement was the re-establishment of a sea moss micro-industry that also included the construction of the first sea moss factory processing plant in St. Lucia. Training was also an integral part of the project and community members were trained in conservation and resource management, facilitation, managing meetings, conflict resolution, basic record-keeping and accounting, and under-standing the tourism industry.

The majestic Pitons of St. Lucia. The Pitons Management Area, which includes terrestrial and marine components, was declared a World Heritage Site in 2004. *Saint Lucia National Trust*

While these benefits were tangible and obvious, there were other intangible benefits which were a result of the many interventions. They included a greater awareness of impacts on the environment, increased knowledge of the natural and cultural heritage of the area, a growing sense of community pride, the discovery of community power in negotiating with Government, and the realization that with the appropriate mechanisms they could have a greater say in designing their future.

In addition to all these achievements, the SLNT entered into an agreement with the PMDC and one of the landowners to transfer EC$1 (US$ 37 cents) for each adult tourist who visited the area and walked the trails and EC$ .50 (US$ 19 cents) for each child. This arrangement flourished for over four years until problems surfaced, caused primarily by the dominance of the PMDC by one individual and the reversion to a non-participatory mode of operations. This occurred in the aftermath of the withdrawal of the SLNT from the area, which was precipitated by a sudden and drastic reduction of its budget by 27%.

Today, the Praslin Protected Landscape still exists in name but not in law. However, there is voluntary compliance and the managed area is still supported, even as the communities continue to struggle to survive, their situation exacerbated by an economic recession in St. Lucia and the Caribbean. What is critical to note here is that the establishment of the Praslin Protected Landscape focused attention on the socio-economic plight of the people of Praslin and Mamiku, which was alleviated to a significant extent (Romulus and Ernest, 2003) while addressing environmental problems.

A sea moss farmer in Praslin Bay, Saint Lucia. For the communities of Praslin and Mamiku in the Praslin Protected Landscape, the re-introduction of sea moss cultivation and processing has made an important contribution to sustainable livelihoods. *Saint Lucia National Trust*

## The case of the Soufriere Marine Management Area

The Soufriere Marine Management Area (SMMA) remains St. Lucia's most successful marine protected area, though it was born out of serious resource-use conflicts.

Located on the south-west coast of the island of St. Lucia is one of the Caribbean's and the world's most outstanding areas of natural beauty. The area is part of the *Soufriere Volcanic Centre*, which experienced major volcanic activity 5–6 million years ago, with the most recent being a phreatic blast in the Sulphur Springs Area in AD1766. Offshore are St. Lucia's best coral reefs, which attract many divers every year and two of the world's most scenic volcanic mountains in Gros Piton (777m) and Petit Piton (743m). Many researchers and visitors consider these natural monuments among the best and most unique in the world and worthy of World Heritage designation.[2]

The area is inhabited by over 7,000 people who live in the Administrative Quarter of Soufriere and in the town of the same name. In the past they depended on agriculture, fishing, and coconut oil production for survival, all of which have been in a depression for some time. In more recent times, tourism has emerged as the saviour of the area, as Soufriere has become the most visited part of the island. The area is known not only for its scenic coastline but also for its very high unemployment, underemployment and poverty.

In the early 1990s the use of offshore resources came under increasing pressure between different resource users. According to Wulf (1999), the Manager of the Soufriere Marine Management Area, there were many environmental problems which included the:

- "degradation of coastal water quality, with direct implications for human health and for the protection of the reef system;

- depletion of the near-shore fisheries resources;

- loss of the economic, scientific and recreational potential of coral reefs, particularly in the context of diving tourism;

- degradation of landscapes and general environment quality, notably on or near beaches; and

- pollution generated by solid waste disposal in ravines or directly in the sea."

In addition to these environmental problems, the specific problems of resource management according to Wulf (ibid) manifested themselves in the form of:

- "conflicts between commercial dive operators and fishermen over the use of, and the perception of impact on, the coral reefs;

- conflicts between yachts and fishermen because of anchoring in fishing areas;

- conflicts between the local community and hoteliers over the access to beaches;

- conflicts between fishermen and authorities at both the local and national levels over the location of a jetty in a fishing priority area; and

---

[2] The Pitons Management Area, which includes a terrestrial and marine component, was declared a World Heritage Site at the 28th session of UNESCO's World Heritage Committee in Suzhov, China, June–July, 2004.

- conflicts between fishermen and hoteliers over the use of the beaches for commercial fishing or recreational and tourism-oriented activities".

To address these issues, a planning process was facilitated which brought all the stakeholders to the table, and in boats, to undertake a participatory conflict resolution and planning exercise. The stakeholders took part in participatory mapping and zoning exercises and helped to design the institutional and legal arrangements. All stakeholders are now party to an agreement to manage the Soufriere Marine Management Area. Notwithstanding such an agreement, at various periods in the last five years there have been problems stemming from breaches of the agreement for various reasons. However, the adaptive and flexible nature of the planning and management process resulted in acceptable solutions to all stakeholders on each occasion. Such success has been recognised and crowned by various international awards.

In a case study of the Soufriere Marine Management Area, Pierre-Nathoniel (2003) identified several achievements of the planning process and the SMMA which include:

- a significant improvement in communications among all stakeholders which has reduced conflict;

- establishment of an institutional arrangement that enhances communications and allows conflicts to be addressed quickly;

- agreement on the management zones by all stakeholders (Map 1);

- improvement in the health of coral reefs and in fish stock in the marine reserves and the fishing priority areas;

- the approval of the site as a management area by the Cabinet of Ministers of St. Lucia and the legal establishment of the site under the Fisheries Act of 1984 as a Local Fisheries Management Area. The management authority was also designated a Local Fisheries Management Authority under the Fisheries Act, which resulted in the devolution of some authority to the newly named Soufriere Marine Management Association;

- increased awareness of environmental issues among stakeholders and the community;

- a better planned and implemented environmental monitoring and research programme;

- support to community projects;

- capacity-building of poorly organized stakeholders such as water and land taxi operators;

- generation of user fees;

- greater surveillance;

- the establishment of customs services to assist with the processing of visiting yachts; and

- international awards such as the 1997 British Airways Tourism for Tomorrow IUCN Special Award for National Parks and Protected Areas and a position in the top five marine management areas along with Algeria, USA, Spain and Canada for the 1997 World Underwater Confederation (CMAS) International Marine Environmental Award.

## Map 1.  Management zones of the SMMA.

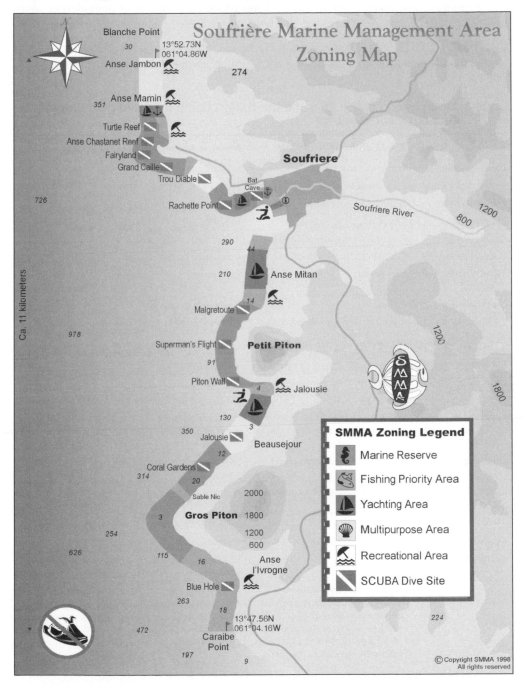

Soufrière Marine Management Area Zoning Map

SMMA Zoning Legend

- Marine Reserve
- Fishing Priority Area
- Yachting Area
- Multipurpose Area
- Recreational Area
- SCUBA Dive Site

183

The Soufriere Marine Management Area remains one of the best-known dive sites in the Caribbean and, though there are problems, it has proven the success of multiple-use zoned areas where people can live with nature and where sustainable livelihoods can be generated.

**THE PPL AND THE SMMA:** Comparing the Praslin Protected Landscape and the Soufriere Marine Management Area reveals a number of similarities and differences as summarised in Table 1.

**Table 1. Comparison of the PPL and the SMMA using selected planning and management variables**

| VARIABLES | Praslin Protected Landscape | Soufriere Marine Management Area |
|---|---|---|
| Land ownership | Private and crown lands | Crown (the sea) |
| History and culture | Studied and known | Studied and known |
| Planning process | Participatory but hurried | Participatory; evolving; adaptive and flexible |
| Planning time | Truncated | Extended |
| Decision making | Participatory but later top-down | Top-down but later participatory |
| Political power | Shared but later centralized | Centralized but later shared |
| Environmental education | High priority | High priority |
| Communications | *Ad hoc* | A plan was developed |
| Conflict resolution mechanism | A structure and systems existed but are now dormant | A structure and systems evolved |
| Zoning | Did not get to this stage | Participatory mapping and demarcation of management zones |
| Capacity building | Limited | Ongoing |
| Legal | Voluntary compliance | Voluntary compliance and laws |
| Institutional | Established a new structure with community support as there was none | Initially built on the existing structure but later developed a new structure which was twice modified |
| Financing | NGO; tours; grants; government | NGO; tours; landing fees; mooring fees; grants and government |
| Economic opportunities | Sea moss cultivation; tour guiding; craft; and fishing | Marine and land taxi operators; tour guiding; yacht services; fishing; and craft |
| Marketing | Intermittent | Consistent by government and private sector |
| Evaluation | Summative evaluation | Formative and summative evaluation |
| Monitoring | Inadequate | Periodic and considered an integral part of the decision-making process |
| RESULT | A management area, which is recognised by the community, protects biodiversity and has brought some form of community pride along with a modest impact on sustainable livelihoods. *Insufficient time for large-scale community learning.* | An effectively managed protected area with a legal and institutional mechanism for resolving conflicts, protecting biodiversity, building pride and creating sustainable livelihoods<br>*Community learning is an ongoing process.* |

**Box 1. The Maya Mountain Marine Corridor and the Port Honduras Marine Reserve (Belize)**

The people of Monkey River Village, Punta Negra and Punta Gorda with a combined population of over 5,300 people are working closely with the Toledo Institute for Environment and Development (TIDE), founded in 1997, to conserve the rich biodiversity of the Toledo District of Belize. The mission of TIDE *is to assist in protected areas planning and management, and to lead the development of responsible tourism and other environmentally sustainable economic alternatives by providing training and support to local residents*.

The Toledo district is an area rich in tropical ecosystems ranging from mountain forest to lowland tropical rainforest and marine ecosystems comprising coral reefs, sea grass beds and mangroves. Among the many species found in the area are the jaguar, the West Indian Manatee, the American saltwater crocodile and the scarlet macaw. Prior to 1997 the Toledo Region was subjected to various environmental impacts including manatee poaching, illegal fishing, illegal logging and destructive farming practices.

To address these problems TIDE, working closely with local communities, has created the Maya Mountain Marine Corridor, which comprises 1 million acres of land and approximately 1,000 square miles of sea. The Port Honduras Marine Reserve, which makes up the marine and coastal segment of the Corridor, comprises just over 50% of its sea area. Declared in 2000, the Port Honduras Marine Reserve encompasses six watersheds that empty directly into it, delivering freshwater, sediments and nutrients washed from the uplands into the rivers and carried to the coastal areas. These drive the production of mangrove forest and sea grass beds, which in turn support the coastal fisheries. The area is a rich nursery and recruitment ground for many of the commercial finfish and shellfish species caught in Belize; therefore protecting these functions has become an important part of its management.

The primary management goals as stated in the management plan for the Maya Mountain Marine Corridor are to:

- protect the physical and biological resources of the reserve by creating a zoning plan for preservation;
- provide educational and interpretive programmes and develop appropriate protocols for researching and monitoring the resources;
- preserve the value of the area for fisheries and genetic resources by protecting habitat through patrolling and surveillance;
- develop recreational and tourism services that are sustainable; and
- strive for sustainable financing through user fees and other strategies.

Recent achievements of this programme demonstrate the value of sustainable resource management in the Toledo District. There is a vibrant environmental education programme, which uses meetings, workshops and even public radio to reach the resource-users. A community ranger programme has been introduced and is destined to integrate the resource-users into the resource management programme by building a sense of stewardship among them. Surveillance through patrolling is also ensuring that illegal activities in the management area are on the decline. To create options for survival, TIDE is working with The Nature Conservancy to introduce sport fishing, as well as fly fishing and tour-guiding.

Elements in the success of the programme include:

- the involvement of a committed and vibrant NGO;
- community participation;

Cont.

---

**Box 1.   The Maya Mountain Marine Corridor and the Port Honduras Marine Reserve (Belize) (cont.)**

- environmental education;

- a management plan for the area with clear objectives;

- an integrated ecosystem approach with a conservation corridor linking the sources of major rivers to the marine environment;

- activities that help support sustainable livelihoods; and

- linkages with other organizations.

The Maya Mountain Marine Corridor is an example of how developing countries and SIDS are working to find a new development paradigm, that ensures sustainability, includes people's participation, and protects the natural resource base, while generating sustainable economic activity.

*Source*: Wil Maheia.

---

A careful examination of both case studies will illustrate the reasons why both examples met with so much support from inception. These reasons include the:

- participation of local people and other stakeholders in the planning process;

- concerted effort that was made to generate sustainable livelihoods;

- facilitation role of various agencies and the attracting of co-financing;

- contribution of these protected areas to other developmental needs;

- use of a multiplicity of planning techniques;

- emergence of appropriate management structures; and

- integration of flexibility into the planning process, particularly in the case of the Soufriere Marine Management Area.

Whereas both the Praslin Protected Landscape and the Soufriere Marine Management Area can be categorized as Protected Landscapes, they also fit Category VI of the IUCN classification, i.e., Managed Resource Reserves (MRR). MRRs are mainly managed for the sustainable use of ecosystems. In both the Praslin Protected Landscape and the Soufriere Marine Management Area the goal has been to protect the natural resources while simultaneously generating sustainable livelihoods. Within both sites can be found strict protection areas such as marine reserves and wildlife reserves, as well as areas where humans and nature can co-exist. Also in both cases there was no deprivation of people's right to own land; rather there was a consensus to manage. Outside forest reserves, marine reserves, and wildlife reserves where strict preservation principles are applied, Protected Landscapes and Managed Resource Reserves are the most relevant protected areas categories for Small Island Developing States like St. Lucia.

# Conclusion

The thirst for land and the scarcity of such an essential asset in SIDS makes it impossible to adopt the traditional models of protected areas where public ownership of all land is considered a prerequisite. Caribbean people are aware of the need to conserve the natural and cultural heritage of their islands, for that is all they have in a hostile global environment, which is less friendly to their vulnerabilities. Their unique historical circumstances also make land owner-ship a precondition to progress, and a form of negation of an exploitive mode of production that relegated Caribbean people to "hewers of wood and drawers of water." Land ownership is an affirmation of self and as Cesaire (1996) has told us:

> *... and now we know that our land too is within the orbit of the sun, which shines on this little plot we have willed for ourselves, that without constraint we are free to move heaven, earth and the stars.*

A protected area category that deprives Caribbean people from owning land will never be acceptable, as it goes against their aspirations and realities. The Protected Landscape/Seascape and Managed Resource Reserve categories are therefore most relevant as they take into consideration the needs of Small Island Developing States.

# 14. Collaborative management of protected landscapes: experience in Canada and the United States of America

*Nora Mitchell, Jacquelyn Tuxill, Guy Swinnerton, Susan Buggey and Jessica Brown*

## Introduction

This chapter explores some of the recent collaborative management experience with conservation of protected landscapes in the United States and Canada. In both countries, national park systems – including natural areas, historical sites and culturally significant places – were created in the mid-nineteenth century. Both park systems began with a strategy of federal ownership and management of nationally important places in remote western areas and for many years this government-based approach dominated the conservation agenda (for Canada see McNamee, 1994; MacEachern, 2001; for USA see Runte, 1979; Rettie, 1995; Sellars, 1997). However, recent innovations have extended this approach to create more diverse protected area systems as well as a wide array of diverse management partnerships.

In both countries conservation strategies now recognise multiple values, are more inclusive, encompass the interests of local communities and indigenous peoples, and craft collaborative management approaches that involve all key stakeholders. These changes reflect a number of broader trends around the world, including an expanded understanding of the values of protected areas, both tangible and intangible (Harmon and Putney, 2003). In particular, recognition of the cultural value of landscapes has redefined the relationship of nature and culture, enhanced the conservation value of lived-in landscapes and broadened the potential stakeholder base for conservation efforts (Rössler, 2000; UNESCO, 2003). The concept of protected landscapes, IUCN Category V, and the concurrent evolution of a new paradigm for conservation represent changes to protected areas thinking and practice (Beresford and Phillips, 2000; Phillips, 2002; Phillips, 2003a; Beresford, 2003).

There has also been a growing recognition of the importance of partnerships and community engagement – even in the oldest and most traditional parks (Tuxill, Mitchell, and Brown 2004; Tuxill and Mitchell 2001; Sonoran Institute, 1997). The idea of stewardship – engaging people in taking care of places they value – puts communities in a leadership role in conservation, often referred to as community-based conservation (Brown and Mitchell, 2000a). Concurrently, the stewards of conservation areas have become more diverse – ranging from different levels of government and non-governmental organizations (such as land trusts), to private landowners and communities. In some cases, community-centred conservation efforts include innovative place-based education initiatives that lead to involving youth and cultivating the next generation of stewards. These shifts represent fundamental changes in both the conceptual framework and conservation practice in the United States and Canada.

The John H. Chafee Blackstone River Valley National Heritage Corridor (Rhode Island and Massachusetts) is one of 24 national heritage areas in the United States. The Valley's distinctive character was shaped by the American Industrial Revolution. *U.S. National Park Service*

Industrial Revolution, which transformed the Blackstone Valley's landscape. Linked by the Blackstone Canal, many historic features from this era still exist, including mill villages, roads, trails, dams and millponds. The Industrial Revolution also left behind distinctive living landscapes of neighbourhoods where ethnic traditions, languages and foods are still important parts of the culture. The Blackstone River Valley Corridor's natural areas – hilltop vistas, glacial outcroppings, verdant valleys and fields, and abundant water bodies – provide habitat for indigenous and migrating wildlife species and recreational opportunities for residents and visitors (Blackstone River Valley National Heritage Corridor Commission, 1998).

The heritage corridor designation has three broad purposes: to enhance and protect cultural landscapes and natural resource values, to improve public understanding and heritage appreciation, and to stimulate community and economic development. In the legislation establishing the heritage area, Congress established a Corridor Commission to provide a management framework to engage the National Park Service, the state governments of Massachusetts and Rhode Island, dozens of local municipalities, businesses, nonprofit historical and environmental organizations, educational institutions, and many private citizens in working together to protect the Valley's special identity, develop and implement management programmes, and prepare for its future (Creasey, 2001).

Operating within a working landscape of strongly independent New England communities, the Commission leverages limited human and financial resources to carry out an extensive and geographically broad mission. Without authority to own land or powers to regulate land use, the Commission has had to be diligent and entrepreneurial in its outreach and ability to be responsive to opportunities. To this end it relies on a combination of public education, public-private partnerships and "targeted" investments. The Commission has been able to integrate issues related to the environment, community development and preservation, land-use planning, and economic development.

The Commission has reached out to other institutions and built cooperative linkages to address management issues within the Blackstone River Heritage Corridor including partnerships with local institutions such as Chambers of Commerce, tourism councils, and conservation NGOs. A good example is the creative approaches used to bring public attention to water quality problems along the river. According to the Corridor's Superintendent, Michael Creasey, "We knew that a typical 'Save our Watershed' approach wouldn't work here... so instead we brought people to the river to show them the potential benefits of the river to their communities and the local economy." It takes local people out in canoes for tours and involves them in voluntary clean-up projects. It has built a 49-passenger boat to serve as a "river classroom," is building a series of river landings along the historic canal, and is establishing a bicycle path. These and other projects help to create connections among the many environmental, historical, and economic and community values of the landscape. As Creasey notes, "the success of the Heritage Corridor is based on creating a vision and engaging people so they place value on their region and on something that others might not readily see" (Creasey, 2001).

## Beaver Hills Ecosystem, Alberta

The Beaver Hills ecosystem constitutes part of the last remaining natural habitat in east-central Alberta. Covering a large area, approximately 1,500 km$^2$, the knob and kettle topography of the Cooking Lake Moraine rises 60m above the surrounding plains. The area, with abundant tree cover and numerous water bodies, is highly productive for wildlife – in particular, ungulates, waterfowl and migratory birds. Beaver Hills lies 45km east of Edmonton, one of the fastest growing metropolitan regions in Canada. The amenity value of the Beaver Hills landscape provides highly sought-after living and recreation space. Residential development, infrastructure expansion, agricultural improvement, oil and gas development, and demands for outdoor recreation have fragmented the region's traditional land-use mosaic.

Protection of the Beaver Hills has a long history and over 25% is now in designated conservation areas. Elk Island National Park (194km$^2$) is the largest of these, but other significant protected areas include the Cooking Lake-Blackfoot Grazing, Wildlife and Provincial Recreation Area; the Ministik Bird Sanctuary; Miquelon Lake Provincial Park; the Strathcona Wilderness Centre; and a number of provincially designated natural areas. Some of the government-managed areas have integrated sophisticated community engagement into their management planning (see Box 2 on Cooking Lake-Blackfoot Grazing, Wildlife and Provincial Recreation Area). In addition, conservation initiatives involving private landowners have become increasingly important in recent years (Burak and Swinnerton, 1998; Kwasniak, 1997).

One recent partnership project, the Beaver Hills Initiative, has evolved to safeguard the area's natural capital and the local quality of life. The need for a bioregional approach to protect

---

**Box 2. Beaver Hills Ecosystem: Cooking Lake-Blackfoot Grazing, Wildlife and Provincial Recreation Area**

Cooking Lake-Blackfoot Grazing, Wildlife and Provincial Recreation Area (hereafter referred to as Blackfoot Recreation Area) covers 97km² of the Beaver Hills ecosystem and is listed as a Category V area on the UN List of Protected Areas. Integrated management of the area accommodates cattle grazing on 2,875ha, as well as wildlife management, trapping, hunting, industrial activity associated with natural gas wells, and a wide range of summer and winter recreation. Aboriginal hunting also occurs within the area.

Although the Parks and Protected Areas Division of Alberta Community Development has overall management responsibility, cooperation with partners and stakeholders is extremely important. Many of the concerns arising from conflicts between the various interests were successfully addressed during the development of the current management plan (Alberta Environmental Protection, 1997). A committee representing a cross section of community groups and stakeholders (referred to as CORE) identified issues and made recommendations for resolving concerns. Friends of Blackfoot, a not-for-profit society that was established as a direct outcome of the CORE process, has been instrumental in delivering the management plan and providing an important mechanism for two-way communication between user groups and Provincial Recreation Area staff.

The Blackfoot Recreation Area provides an innovative example of integrated-use management within the Alberta Parks and Protected Areas system. This experience demonstrates the applicability of the Category V approach to protecting representative biodiversity within a region that is experiencing significant land-use pressures and escalating demands for outdoor recreation. At the same time, the Blackfoot Area makes an important contribution to the local ranching economy. The overall success of this Category V area is largely dependent on approval of the management plan that resulted from a transparent, multi-stakeholder planning process and its commitment to sustainable land-use practices (Swinnerton and Buggey, 2004).

---

the Beaver Hills ecosystem has been advocated for a number of years (Burak and Swinnerton, 1998; Kwasniak, 1997), with Parks Canada staff at Elk Island National Park taking the initial lead because of their concern over external threats to the park's ecological integrity. Of parallel importance was a commitment to cooperate across management boundaries, partnering with local people and other stakeholders in seeking joint action to ensure the socio-economic viability and quality of life of local communities within the natural capacity of the Beaver Hills landscape (Swinnerton and Otway, 2003).

The Beaver Hills Initiative, formalized in September 2002, was precipitated by the recent rapid growth and associated land use change within the Edmonton region. This initiative, created a coordinating committee with representatives from the five local municipal governments, both federal and provincial governments, and non-government associations that represent industry and environmental interests. Their stated mission is to work for a sustainable region through shared initiatives and coordinated action. The Beaver Hills Initiative's vision statement values the region's natural beauty and quality of life, and supports cooperative efforts to sustain water, land, air, natural resources, and community development.

Although the region is not formally recognised as a Protected Landscape by IUCN, the Beaver Hills Initiative exhibits a number of the principles and concepts inherent in the management of Category V areas (Swinnerton, 2003; Swinnerton and Otway, 2003). The process used to date is inclusive and characterized by collaboration and partnership. This

## Box 3.   The National Capital Greenbelt, Ottawa, Ontario

Urbanization is invariably seen as being in marked contrast to nature conservation and the establishment of protected areas. However, within the diversified land-use mosaic of the urban fabric a variety of green spaces frequently exists that provides opportunities for nature conservation and outdoor recreation. One category of urban protected area is the urban greenbelt (see McNeely, 2001). Greenbelts, with their planning role of curtailing urban sprawl often involve both semi-natural areas and the lived-in landscape of a rural economy. The experience of the National Capital Greenbelt around Ottawa affords one such example where protection of a lived-in landscape is achieved through collaboration and partnership.

Surrounding Canada's capital to the south of the Ottawa River, the National Capital Greenbelt is a 20,000ha green space and rural landscape that varies between two and eight kilometres wide. Recorded as a Category V area in the UN List of Protected Areas, it is a rural landscape of farmland, forests, wetlands, recreational open space, small rural communities, and land used by public and private institutions.

The National Capital Commission (NCC, a Federal Crown corporation) owns approximately 16,000ha of the Greenbelt and the remainder is owned by Federal Government agencies. Lands owned by the NCC comprise approximately equal proportions of farmland, forestry and conservation areas. The Greenbelt serves as a significant setting for public activities that require a rural or natural environment. These include a variety of nodal and linear sites for outdoor recreation, and educational and interpretive opportunities associated with the diverse biological and cultural heritage of the area. Specific sites are recognised through a Ramsar designation as well as class 1 provincial wetlands and a provincial historic site.

Protection of the essential character of the Greenbelt is attained through the implementation of the Greenbelt Master Plan (National Capital Commission, 1996). This Plan represents a commitment by the NCC to serve as the custodian of the Greenbelt on behalf of the Canadian public. Two of the Greenbelt roles and their associated land designations are specifically relevant to its recognition as a Category V area. These are: (1) the "Continuous Natural Environment," which includes: "core natural area", "natural buffer" and "natural area link" land designations; and (2) the "Vibrant Rural Community" role, which includes both "cultivated land" and "rural landscape" land designations. A Greenbelt Management Plan supports the implementation of the Greenbelt Master Plan.

The success of the National Capital Greenbelt in protecting a rural landscape adjacent to a metropolitan area is largely due to collaborative partnerships that are evident in several ways (see Swinnerton in Phillips, 2002):

1. The development and implementation of a Greenbelt Master Plan (1996) has been achieved through an open process involving all levels of government, the general public, and specific interest groups.

2. Although the NCC is not subject to the laws and requirements of lower levels of government, the NCC complies from a policy perspective. The planning and management of the Greenbelt is a partnership involving federal, provincial and municipal levels of government. Land-use planning provisions mirror the NCC policy for the Greenbelt.

3. The NCC, as the dominant landowner within the Greenbelt, encourages its tenant farmers to follow best management practices and promotes sustainable forestry.

4. Protection of significant natural and cultural heritage resources within the Greenbelt depends on a variety of partnership arrangements.

The National Capital Commission Greenbelt (shown here with the Ottawa skyline in the background), in Ontario, Canada, encompasses farmland, forests, wetlands, recreational open space, and small rural communities. The success of the Greenbelt in protecting a rural landscape adjacent to a metropolitan area is due to collaborative partnerships. *Guy Swinnerton*

process also approaches planning as a social learning process, using participatory techniques to focus on task-oriented action.

An evident strength of the Initiative is the commitment by municipal governments in the five counties in the Beaver Hills to play a central role in determining the patterns of growth and land use change across the broader landscape, and their elected officials provide a touchstone for local opinion, concerns, and attitudes. One potentially important outcome of the Beaver Hills Initiative will be development of a regional plan that retains or enhances the connectivity between the region's designated protected areas, and buffers these areas from inappropriate land uses and management practice. The Initiative views good stewardship as crucial to improving and restoring the ecological integrity of the Beaver Hills.

Shorter-term targets with measurable outcomes (e.g., invasive alien species and weed management, fire protection, information and data sharing, and watershed and landscape planning) complement the long-term goals for landscape protection and a sustainable quality of life for local residents. Short-term outcomes help to ensure ongoing commitment by the partners by providing important indicators of the benefits to be realized through the Initiative. The Beaver Hills Initiative demonstrates the applicability of the Category V approach to landscape management, environmental stewardship, and community development within the challenging environment of an urban-centred region.

# Ebey's Landing National Historical Reserve, Whidbey Island, Washington State

Established by Congress in 1978, Ebey's Landing National Historical Reserve encompasses 17,400 acres in the central portion of Whidbey Island in Washington State's Puget Sound. The Reserve contains a landscape rich in cultural history and natural variety. The scenic views are spectacular, whether looking west across Admiralty Inlet to the Olympic Mountains or toward the eastern horizon of the Cascade Mountains. Unlike the more traditional units of the US National Park System, this is a Category V landscape in which people live and work. In addition, the Reserve is managed through a partnership among the National Park Service, local and state government, and the private sector.

Whidbey Island's old glacial lakebeds contain some of the richest soils in the state, and have attracted people as far back as 1300, when Native Americans[2] cultivated these "prairies" for growing favoured root crops. After the Donation Land Law of 1850 offered free land in the new Oregon Territory to any citizen who would homestead for four years, Colonel Isaac Ebey and other European-Americans filed claims on the prairies and shorelines of central Whidbey Island. Today, the old-field patterns, fence lines and farm buildings of the early homesteaders are still visible in the landscape. While there has been some loss of farmland to development within the Reserve (indeed, it was such development that led to Reserve designation), some of

---

## Box 4. Stewardship begins with people: an atlas of places, people, and hand-made products

**A Cooperative Project of the National Park Service's Northeast Region, Marsh-Billings-Rockefeller National Historical Park, NPS Conservation Study Institute and Shelburne Farms National Historic Landmark (CSI, 2004)**

Stewardship begins with people. This atlas celebrates the personal stories of stewardship, while illustrating its broad, rich geography. Its inspiration comes from people taking care of special places. Dave Evans, a fifth-generation Pierce Point rancher at Point Reyes Seashore, California is developing innovative, sustainable approaches to keeping agriculture alive on the peninsula. Judy and Bill Carson and Kit Trubey, owners of Alta Pass Orchard in Spruce Pine, North Carolina, along the Blue Ridge Parkway, encourage local theatre and music, while growing heirloom apples. For more than 30 years, Mary Lee Begay has woven traditional Navajo rugs for Hubbell Trading Post National Historic Site in Ganado, Arizona.  These are faces of stewardship – friends, neighbours and communities in and around our national parks, heritage areas and national historic landmarks. They preserve authentic traditional cultures and landscapes, demonstrating for local residents and visitors alike an enduring stewardship ethic and a commitment to sustainability.

This is the beginning of an exploration of the connections between places, people and special products. The project has started with three initial case studies illustrating good stewardship, and highlighting traditions and innovations that advance conservation and sustainability. The *Atlas of Places, People & Hand-Made Products* will include more stories from more places. Ultimately, we plan to produce a series of regional travel guides for landscapes and special products, and build a network of park people and producers eager to share their knowledge and experiences.

The project objectives are to:

1. Recognise people practicing stewardship that sustains important landscapes and living cultures;

Cont.

---

[2]  "Native American" is the generally preferred term used in the United States.

---

**Box 4. Stewardship begins with people: an atlas of places, people, and hand-made products (cont.)**

2. Demonstrate the relationship between people, special products, and landscapes;
3. Highlight the biodiversity value of cultural landscapes;
4. Model sustainable behaviours to visitors and neighbors, demonstrating a commitment to community stewardship of landscapes;
5. Enhance relationships between parks and neighboring communities; and
6. Build a network of people and organizations involved in this work.

The concept for this atlas also draws inspiration from a series of exchanges between the U.S. National Park Service and the Italian Nature Conservation Service and Lazio Regional Park Agency under an international agreement to promote innovation and cooperation in the protection and management of national parks and protected areas. Through these exchanges park managers on both sides of the Atlantic shared ideas and experiences and discussed ways to "promote and market local products that enhance park operations, community relations, local traditions and culture, and sustainable practices." The Italian parks, in cooperation with Slow Food Italia, produced an atlas that highlights an extraordinary array of authentic traditional food products identified with the park areas in which they are grown or made.

Diné (Navajo) weaver, Hubbell Trading Post National Historic Site, Arizona, USA. *Jeff Roberts*

---

the land is still farmed today by descendant families of the early homesteaders. Many long-time residents feel deep ties to the land.

But the story is much more than just farming history. Penn Cove, on Whidbey Island's protected eastern shore, and the nearby abundance of tall timber in Whidbey's forests attracted sea captains and shipbuilders. Captain Thomas Coupe claimed the shoreline acres that eventually became the town of Coupeville, the main town within the reserve. Maritime trade along Penn Cove, combined with farming, made Coupeville a thriving commercial centre. Once water-borne transportation gave way to land-based transportation, Coupeville was no longer a hub of Puget Sound commerce. Coupeville's prosperous past is reflected in the wide array of historic buildings that in 1972 were officially listed as the Central Whidbey Island Historic District. In addition, Whidbey's strategic placement at the entrance to Puget Sound brought a military presence to the island in the late 1800s, which remains today. Aspects of this military past are also preserved and interpreted through the Reserve (Gilbert *et al.*, 1984).

The designation of Ebey's Landing as a national reserve grew from a decade-long controversy sparked by the question of whether to allow development of Ebey's Prairie, the most spectacular of the three major prairies and the heart of today's Reserve. The end result, after many twists and turns over the ten-year period, was unusual for the USNPS at that time. Ebey's Landing was the first unit of the National Park System intentionally set up to be managed collaboratively by a trust board of individuals representing the USNPS and state, county and local government. The Reserve is a "partnership park" in which the federal government's role is not as landowner, but as a partner with local residents and communities. This partnership works to protect a valued cultural landscape that visually documents the region's history, while also ensuring the public right to recreational access and enjoyment of scenic views (McKinley, 1993).

From its establishment the Reserve has remained largely in private ownership. To fulfil the management goal of preserving the historic landscape of open space, farmland, and historic settlements has meant – and continues to mean – close cooperation with private landowners. To this end, partners have relied on the tools of private land conservation, including purchase or exchange of development rights, purchase of scenic easements, land donations, tax incentives, zoning, and local design review. In addition, to successfully sustain the working agricultural landscape, the partners are seeking ways to support the local economy and are evaluating the most effective strategies for this (Harbour, 2003; Rottle, 2004). In other similar areas, special traditional products associated with the cultural landscape are being branded with the place name and marketed so that consumers are aware that with their purchase they are supporting a landscape and a community that stewards it (see Box 4).

Although today visitors to the reserve can hike trails and seaside bluffs, stroll beaches, walk through Coupeville's historic district, and follow a driving tour outlined in an USNPS brochure, there is no large "park presence". In the reserve, farms are still farmed, forests are still logged, historic buildings are still used as homes and places of business. The work and the challenge of this partnership lie in guiding and managing change in a way that respects the cultural values and historic landscape. Ebey's Landing will always represent a balancing act between the needs of the people and communities within the Reserve and the goal of preserving a historically important working rural landscape.

## Sahyoue/Edacho – Protected Landscapes and First Nations, Northwest Territories

Protection of landscapes in Canada's north begins with respect for the values, uses and behaviours of people associated with the landscape so that enduring relationships with the land continue. Integrating management of the landscape into the lifestyle of the community and using community traditions and practices for protection and presentation are essential to the long-term "health" of the landscape. To the Sahtu Dene people, the two peninsulas Sahyoue/Edacho on the western shores of Great Bear Lake in Canada's Northwest Territories are sacred sites, used since time immemorial. This area of 5,587km$^2$, also known as Grizzly Bear Mountain and Scented Grass Hills, "blend[s] the natural and cultural worlds of the Sahtu Dene

Old fishing boats along part of the interpretive trail in the village of Hecla, located on the western shoreline of Lake Winnipeg in Hecla/Grindstone Provincial Park, Manitoba, Canada. *Guy Swinnerton*

and helps define them as a people." The open boreal forest leading up from raised beach ridges is also an important wildlife area, including woodland caribou winter habitat, staging areas for wildfowl, and a fish migration route. High landscape integrity and biodiversity have enabled the Sahtu Dene to continue their traditional land use and lifestyle activities of hunting, trapping, fishing, camping, gathering medicinal plants, and knowing the land.

The fundamental relationship of the Sahtu Dene with the Sahyoue/Edacho peninsulas is expressed in the continuing cultural meaning, ecological integrity and biological diversity of the landscape. Landscape features and archaeological resources mark places significant in the history, cosmology, spiritual law, language, land use, and traditional lifestyles of the Sahtu Dene. Ancient tribal narratives related to Sahyoue/Edacho tell of giant animals whose bodies comprise specific features of the landscape as well as ancestral spirit beings and shamans whose heroic actions made the earth safer and sustaining for those who continue to practise behaviour respectful of the spirits (Hanks, 1996). Such traditional stories and associated place names, passed by Elders to youth from generation to generation, provide verbal maps by which people know the landscape. The association of place and story contained in the narratives sustain Sahtu Dene culture by transmitting language, prescribing behaviour, and identifying sacred sites (Buggey, 1999). Protection of these sacred sites and the associated story-telling are therefore essential to the continuity of Sahtu Dene culture and livelihood.

First Nations[3] land claim agreements in Canada incorporate the values of the respective First Nations, their equitable involvement in decision-making, and First Nations ownership as key components in managing lands, waters, natural resources, and places related to culture and history. Under the Sahtu Dene and Metis Comprehensive Land Claim Agreement (1993), the Sahtu Heritage Places and Sites Joint Working Group was established to consider and make recommendations to appropriate governments and the Sahtu Tribal Council on Sahtu heritage places. As its report *Rakekée Gok'é Godi: Places We Take Care Of* states: "[o]ne of the most important themes in understanding Sahtu Dene and Metis history is the relationship between culture and landscape. Virtually all of Sahtu Dene and Metis history is written on the land. As such, places and sites that commemorate this relationship are an integral part of Sahtu Dene and Metis identity" (Sahtu, 2000).

Two recent actions recognise the importance of this cultural landscape – designation of Sahyoue/Edacho as a national historic site (1996) and a Commemorative Integrity Statement, developed by the Deline Dene community and Elders with Parks Canada, that articulates the commemorative values, significant resources and considerations for management. Neither action, however, carries any legal or protective measures for the designated place.

To afford further protection to Sahyoue/Edacho, the Sahtu Dene community drew upon the powers and processes of the Northwest Territories Protected Areas Strategy (NWT PAS). Sahyoue/Edacho was the first protected area moved forward under the NWT PAS (NWT, 1999). Developed collectively by First Nations organizations, governments, industry and environmental groups, the NWT PAS responds to intensifying threats to territorial lands from mining development and proposed pipelines with a framework for identifying and establishing protected areas. Guided by a set of principles, the PAS has an eight-step community-driven planning process that provides for analysis of options for identification, protection, designation and management of a proposed protected area.

---

[3] "First Nations" is the generally preferred term used in Canada.

In 2000, strongly focused community action (with coordinated environmental group activity) pushed the federal Ministers of Canadian Heritage and Indian and Northern Affairs to withdraw land at Sahyoue/Edacho from development. The resulting five-year interim land withdrawal provides protection for Sahyoue/Edacho while stakeholders work towards an effective mechanism for long-term safeguard and management consistent with its ecological and cultural values (CPAWS, 2001; Canada Department of Justice, 2001). Evaluations of ecological, cultural and economic values are now being completed toward formal establishment of Sahyoue/Edacho as a protected area. The process should result in a plan for how the two peninsulas will be managed for long-term protection.

Implementation of the NWT Protected Areas Strategy at Sahyoue/Edacho reflects the trend in Canada's north to identify new protected areas which will protect cultural values, harvesting areas and traditional travel routes rather than focusing selection only on natural region representation, and recreation and tourism values (Stadel *et al.*, 2002). In this region, landscape protection needs to be integrated – by means of a participatory process – with community priorities, local planning, economic development, tourism initiatives and their associated funding sources. Sahyoue/Edacho illustrates how many parties working from the community base may provide a model for cooperative action among First Nations peoples, NGOs, and levels of government in protecting such areas.

## Concluding remarks

This diverse set of case studies demonstrates the wide applicability of the protected landscape concept throughout the US and Canada. The case studies range from bioregional planning in urban-centred regions, to the protection of cultural landscapes associated with indigenous peoples and rural working landscapes of European settlement, and the conservation of areas with high natural resource value. These large-scale landscapes are cohesive units due to a regional identity, a shared history or culture, a watershed or other ecosystem boundary. These are complex landscapes with multiple values where nature and culture live alongside human communities, often for many generations. In many cases, the value of the landscape is due to the interaction with people over time, and the protection of the landscape requires sustaining that relationship and the communities' stewardship. The ownership of the land is mostly private with some limited public holdings. The threats facing these places are many and challenging and include changing economies and land uses, suburban growth from development and recreation, and extractive industries.

It is within these complex and challenging settings that innovative approaches to conservation are being crafted. Although there is great diversity among the case studies presented, there are also similarities in approach. In each case, there is a management framework and an entity that serves as the forum for collaboration and as a venue for creating a collective vision of the future. Many of these large landscapes cross political boundaries, so some type of new entity is created to facilitate exchange and cooperation, overcoming the barriers of boundaries. Existing legal tools are employed in many instances, such as the national designation of parks or other protected areas, but there is innovation in the type of relationship between responsible government agencies and the communities within the area. Government agencies become catalysts and facilitators, working as partners with local communities and local people to develop strategies for effective conservation. Through a variety of participatory methods, the communities and local organizations are involved in identifying the values, developing a vision, and often become the co-managers or managers of the designated area that is part of a larger conservation strategy. Importantly, this larger strategy encompasses socio-economic dimensions of community and regional vitality, as well as quality of life and access to resources. Education is an integral part of many of the strategies, engaging all sectors of the community as well as involving the younger generation to develop their leadership skills. The key investment in the role of local communities is important both to successful conservation, but also to the sustainable future of conservation.

These case studies confirm that the term "protected landscapes" refers not only to particular large-scale landscapes with a human history and natural resource values, but also to a landscape management process that accommodates and guides change. This represents a fundamental shift in thought and practice in the USA and Canada and extends conservation into new areas. While the work of conservation becomes more challenging, these case studies demonstrate the effectiveness of a "protected landscape approach" for building a broad-based commitment to stewardship.

# 15. The evolution of landscape conservation in Australia: reflections on the relationship of nature and culture

*Jane L. Lennon*

## Introduction

Australian landscapes represent wild nature, are the product of Indigenous[1] peoples, and have been extensively shaped by Europeans. This landscape heritage is complex, woven by the interaction of people and their environment over time. The development of Australia's landscape conservation has been influenced by changing perceptions of the relationship between nature and culture and has, for many years, placed a higher value on natural heritage. The development of heritage protection has been dramatically altered by the World Heritage Convention, which ushered in many nominations of natural sites of global significance. Recognition of cultural landscapes in the guidelines for the implementation of the World Heritage Convention in 1992 enhanced the value placed on cultural sites, including those with intangible values and on the importance of recognising management by Indigenous people. This chapter examines the history of landscape protection and changing attitudes in three case studies – Uluru-Kata Tjuta, Kosciuszko National Park, Castlemaine Diggings National Heritage Park – and contributions from urban parks and the Landcare movement. These examples illustrate an evolution of environmental thought and development of conservation strategies at the local, state and national level.

## National characteristics and their influence on shaping Australia's landscape heritage

Australian landscapes are the product of 80 million years of evolution of the land and its flora and fauna since separation of the current land mass from Gondwana, and of at least 60,000 years of Indigenous occupation and more than 200 years of European occupation (Lennon *et al.*, 2001). Australia, the only nation to occupy a whole continent, is biologically diverse and the undisputed world centre for marsupials and *Eucalyptus* vegetation.

The first Australians, the Aboriginal and Torres Strait Islander peoples, modified the environment through the use of fire and hunting, changing the species composition of flora and fauna, and may have driven the Pleistocene megafauna to extinction as well (ASEC, 2001). They also gave the landscape its creation stories and peopled it with heroic ancestors; and they created non-architectural but spectacular evidence of their culture in rock art, occupation sites and sacred landscapes. They made the whole of Australia a cultural landscape, a fact not well recognised in heritage management practice in Australia.

---

[1]   The term "indigenous" is capitalized in this chapter to reflect conventional usage in Australia where it applies to Aboriginal and Torres Strait islander people.

The impact on the indigenous landscape of the waves of European migration since the 1788 settlement of Sydney has been dramatic. Within a few generations, large tracts of the country were irreversibly modified by the introduction of sheep and cattle. Today, Australia's population of 20 million is highly urbanized, with 62% living in the five largest cities and 85% living within 50km of the coastline.

The Commonwealth of Australia was formed through the federation of the six separate British colonies in 1901. Under the constitution, the States and Territories are responsible for management of the environment including national parks and heritage places while the Commonwealth is responsible for other national matters like defence, quarantine, taxation and matters associated with international treaties and conventions.

## History of protected area management

From the 1860s, public lands were reserved from sale to protect scenic wonders such as waterfalls, volcanic features and lakes. In 1915, the Scenery Preservation Board was established in Tasmania, the first authority in Australia created specifically for the management of parks and reserves (Lennon, 2003a). For most of the last century landscape conservation was linked to the English 'garden city' movement or to the national parks and wildlife protection movements.

Natural heritage was long considered separate from cultural heritage. This dichotomy has its origins in European philosophy imported with the settler society of the nineteenth century (Griffiths, 1996). Cultural heritage legislation was introduced in the 1960s, and the concept of heritage was broadened to recognise Indigenous places and sites significant to non-British Australians. There were efforts to protect certain landscape types such as coastal scenery through State government and municipal planning scheme controls.

Protection of natural resources was part of a much wider global movement. Following the adoption in 1972 by UNESCO of the *Convention Concerning the Protection of the World Cultural and Natural Heritage*, identifying landscapes with outstanding universal values and inscribing them on the World Heritage List became a priority for Australian nature conservation agencies.

In 1976, the Australian Heritage Commission was established to identify and conserve the National Estate, which was defined as:

*...those places, being components of the natural environment of Australia, or the cultural environment of Australia that have aesthetic, historic, scientific or social significance or other special value for future generations as well as for the present community* (section 4 (1), Australian Heritage Commission Act, 1975).

Soon after, Australia ICOMOS developed its Charter for the Conservation of Places of Cultural Significance, the Burra Charter, to assist in assessing the significance of cultural heritage values present at a place (www.icomos.org/australia/charters). Creating the Register of the National Estate has kept Australians aware of heritage landscapes due to the many controversies about listing these places. Some places such as Uluru-Kata Tjuta have iconic status, but listing others has been very contested. Where States had inadequate land-use protection, conservation advocates used the listing process to draw attention to threatened places ranging from potential World Heritage sites to local landscapes with remnant natural vegetation.

In 1981, the Great Barrier Reef, the world's largest living organism, was entered on the World Heritage List, as was Kakadu with its expansive wetlands and Aboriginal art, and Willandra Lakes, a series of former lakes and dunes containing the oldest documented human remains in Australia. This reinforced the view that Australia's large-scale landscapes had international value. In 1982 the Tasmanian Wilderness, occupying one quarter of the State, was added to the World Heritage List, despite complete opposition from the State government. A new Federal government had won the election on this issue of protection of wilderness using the external treaties power in the constitution and passed the *World Heritage Properties Conservation Act* in 1983, making Australia the only nation then to have legislation protecting World Heritage properties. World Heritage listing was used as an instrument to protect key Australian landscapes, especially in those States that had previously ignored conservation.

This set the scene for some of the key elements of World Heritage management in Australia: the emphasis on universal as opposed to local values, the emphasis on natural as opposed to European heritage values, and the imposition of a centralist model of decision-making versus local involvement, a trend which is now being reversed. The problem of relying solely on external treaty power to prevent destructive land-uses is one of the reasons for the invention of the National List of Australian heritage places. The Council of Australian Governments reviewed the roles and responsibilities for heritage identification and environment protection, including the major gap between World Heritage and National Estate sites in their protection regimes. This review resulted in the Commonwealth's new *Environment Protection and Biodiversity Conservation Act 1999* (EPBC), which defines environment to include Australia's natural and cultural heritage (see www.environment.gov.au/epbc). Amendments to the EPBC Act, enacted in January 2004, enable creation of a National Heritage List of natural, Indigenous and historic places with outstanding national heritage value. Under the new system, National Heritage will become "a matter of national environmental significance" protected by the EPBC Act. (www.deh.gov.au/heritage/law/heritageact/distictively/index.html).

In 1968, only 1.2% of Australia's land was devoted to parks and reserves (Warboys *et al.*, 2001) but by 2002 this figure had risen to over 10% or 77,462,000ha managed for nature conservation in over 6,755 protected area reserves. However, only 172 (less than 3%) of these terrestrial reserves totalling 788,779ha are specifically classified as IUCN Category V, that is, protected landscapes (www.deh.gov.au/parks/nrs/capad/index.html). In 2000, a new category of Indigenous Protected Areas was established and 13 areas have been declared covering almost 13,500,000 million hectares ranging from Ngaanyatjarra (Western Australia) covering 9,812,900ha to Chappell and Badger Islands (Tasmania) covering 1,270ha (www.deh.gov.au/indigenous/fact-sheets/ipa.html). Many of the 13,000 places currently entered in the Register of the National Estate are now covered by State, Territory and local government heritage legislation. National parks and other protected areas have become an integral part of the 'political landscape,' as the result of the popular movement in urbanized Australia to save wild places.

# Evolution of landscape concepts

Changing perceptions of the Australian landscape are recorded in the work of painters, poets and writers, and in political rhetoric. The initial Register of the National Estate concentrated on archaeological sites, historic buildings and natural areas. The Commission registered modified landscapes such as historic precincts, townships and mining areas. However, the term *cultural landscape* was not used by the Commission until 1980 when the Tasman Peninsula was promoted as a cultural landscape as a means of linking all the historic convict sites and their surrounding landscapes. The cultural landscape concept has now become accepted in heritage agencies and represents a shift from valuing Eurocentric monumental heritage and areas of predominantly visual value, to also appreciating the expression of values relating to practices of cultures (AHC, 2000). The concept of 'place', linking natural heritage and cultural values, was applied by Australia ICOMOS in the Burra Charter (Australia ICOMOS, 2000). This concept enabled the idea of conserving extensive landscapes with cultural significance.

In 1992, the World Heritage Committee of UNESCO revised the cultural heritage criteria for nominations to include cultural landscapes (see Rössler and Phillips in this volume). This change recognised the role of hunter-gatherer societies in managing landscapes and acknowledged the intangible values of these landscapes to Indigenous peoples. In 1993 Tongariro National Park in New Zealand, already inscribed on the World Heritage List for its natural values, was included as a universally outstanding example of a landscape strongly associated with Maori beliefs (Titchen, 1994). This listing set a precedent for recognising cultural values in natural areas and living cultural values expressed in the landscape.

Australians have traditionally perceived 'nature' and Aboriginal culture as the key types of heritage, which partly explains the absence of any historic place in the representation of Australia's heritage of outstanding universal significance.[2] Initially the World Heritage Convention was used in Australia to protect large expanses of undisturbed natural environment. This has delayed recognition of landscapes with cultural values, especially those with historic values. Despite extended research into the range of historic values in some natural areas like the Tasmanian Wilderness World Heritage Area, these values have not been officially recognised even though they form the basis of popular tourist itineraries (Lennon, 2003b). This is repeated in other World Heritage areas such as the Wet Tropics and Fraser Island.

World Heritage methodology has played a significant role in Australia in drawing attention to the obvious heritage evidence in the landscape especially following the 1992 amendments to the World Heritage criteria (see Rössler in this volume). These amendments provided for the following cultural landscape categories: intentionally designed – as in gardens; relict – as in archaeological sites; organically evolving or continuing use with material evidence of its evolution; and associative landscapes with powerful religious, artistic or cultural associations of the natural element rather than material cultural evidence. These categories have been applied by some managers at national park level and at local level in municipal planning schemes as a means of protecting diverse heritage values in their landscapes.

The rest of this chapter discusses adoption of the cultural landscapes concept over the last ten years in three designated protected areas in many parts of Australia. The role of urban parks and the Landcare movement are also examined for their role in involving different constituencies in conservation of human-modified landscapes (see Boxes 1 and 2).

---

[2]   The Royal Exhibition was added to the World Heritage List in June, 2004.

---

**Box 1. Landscape conservation in urban parks: innovative financing scheme**

Large areas of public land set aside from sale have been a feature of Australian cities since the earliest days of colonial administration. Both Sydney and Melbourne have large Domains in the centre of their downtown areas providing open space, botanic gardens and cultural facilities like art galleries. They are treasured places and protected through heritage legislation.

Brisbane, the fast-growing capital of Queensland, supports more plants and animal species than any other Australian capital. There are more than 1,900 parks within the city limits. Karawatha Forest of 840ha of bushland and coastal lowlands on the southern edge of Brisbane has over 200 species of native wildlife. Boondall Wetlands, Brisbane's largest wetlands on the edge of Moreton Bay between Nudgee Beach and Shorncliffe, include more than 100ha of tidal flats, mangroves, salt marshes, melaleuca wetlands, grasslands, open forest and woodlands. Moreton Bay is a Ramsar site and the birdlife at the wetlands is prolific; boardwalks provide access through these to hides on the bayside from where flocks of birds on their migratory journeys to and from the northern hemisphere may be observed.

Brisbane supports these urban parks – purchasing and developing bushland areas throughout the city – with an innovative bushland levy of $30 per household on the annual rates paid by home-owners. Over the last decade, the levy totalling $60 million has helped to preserve almost 1700ha. This has included forests, a green corridor linking new residential developments, koala habitat, scenic forested ridge tops and bayside wetlands. There are approximately 78,000ha of bushland throughout Brisbane, representing a little more than 30% of the city area.

---

# Uluru-Kata Tjuta National Park

This case study describes the evolution of attitudes to landscape management through a series of four management plans, a name change from Ayers Rock-Mt Olga to Uluru-Kata Tjuta, and recognition of intangible Indigenous values and their protection through a joint management strategy with Indigenous values being paramount. The national publicity following the 1994 re-inscription of Uluru-Kata Tjuta as a cultural landscape on the World Heritage List changed the popular view of Uluru as the 'big rock in the Centre'. The park, covering about 1,325km$^2$, contains outstanding examples of rare desert flora and fauna as well as the major geological features of Uluru (a sandstone monolith some 9.4km in circumference and rising 314m above the plain) and Kata Tjuta (36 rock domes rising about 500m above the plain). It was designated an international biosphere reserve in 1977 and listed as World Heritage for its natural heritage values in 1987. But for the Anangu, the traditional owners of the park, there was a time when ancestral beings in the form of humans, animals and plants travelled widely across the land performing remarkable feats of creation and destruction. The journeys of these beings are celebrated and the record of their activities exists today in the landscape. The Anangu have primary responsibility for maintaining these values by caring for the land using traditional methods.

In 1982, the first management plan promulgated for the park gave priority to biodiversity and environmental protection. While cultural heritage was recognised, this management plan was a 'classical' Australian protected area plan based on bio-centric international models. This phase of park management protected cultural heritage as a few relatively small sites containing artefacts (such as rock paintings) dotted within a 'sea' of traditional national park management concerns.

After the park was handed back to the traditional owners and the Uluru-Kata Tjuta Board of Management was established, the priority given to cultural heritage increased substantially. The second management plan, which was prepared in 1986 after the park had been nominated for World Heritage listing for its natural values, clearly articulated the enormous cultural importance to Aboriginal peoples of the landscapes within the park, as well as identifying more traditional national park values and programmes.

The third management plan, completed in 1991, contains an even more overt manifesto regarding the importance of cultural concerns (Uluru-Kata Tjuta Board of Management, 1991). It seems that the previous, subtle statements on cultural heritage had not resulted in appropriate adjustment in either management practice, or perhaps more importantly, behaviour of other stakeholders such as tour operators or visitors in general. The 1991 plan, while superficially structured like any other protected area management plan, contained a major new section [2: Tjukurpa (law) as a guide to management (pp.11–26)]. This new section provided a renewed explicit priority for cultural heritage that was expressly designed to underpin all other management. At about the same time, the park was also re-nominated for World Heritage listing under the cultural landscape criteria in addition to its already recognised natural values.

In 1994, Uluru-Kata Tjuta became the second cultural landscape on the World Heritage List. This honour provided international recognition of Tjukurpa as a major religious philosophy linking the Anangu traditional owners to their environment and as a tool for caring for country. The listing represented years of work by Anangu to assert their role as custodians of their traditional lands. In addition, at the request of the Anangu, the lands of the Park were referred to by their traditional names Uluru and Kata Tjuta, rather than the non-Anangu names given by nineteenth century European explorers.

The expansion of values by the World Heritage listing enabled a change in priorities at park level. This is reflected in the current management plan, which states that acknowledgement of the place as a cultural landscape is fundamental to the success of the joint management arrangement. This 2000 plan details how traditional owners and the Australian government work as partners by combining Anangu natural and cultural management skills with conventional park practices (Uluru-Kata Tjuta Board of Management and Parks Australia, 2000). For example, Aboriginal people learned how to patch burn the country from the Tjukurpa of lungkata, the blue tongue lizard. Although modern methods are now used, the practice of lighting small fires close together during the cool season continues to leave a mosaic of burnt and unburnt areas. This traditional knowledge and practice have been adopted as a major ecological management tool in the park. Tjukurpa also teaches about the care of rock holes and other water sources (Environment Australia, 1999). This 2000 plan is the first to recognise the primacy of cultural practice in land management by the traditional owners, and the bilingual presentation of the plan highlights the fundamental concern of ensuring joint management. It integrates cultural heritage concerns with natural heritage management. Monitoring will demonstrate whether this aim is achieved (Lennon, 2000).

The 2001 Cultural Heritage Action Plan and Cultural Landscape Conservation Plan, which operates under the 2000 Plan of Management, provides a more detailed operational guide for the implementation of cultural site and landscape management programmes. It was compiled through a series of community workshops in the park. This plan provides for the conservation of the cultural values of specific sites, storylines and story places, including sacred sites, birthplaces, rock art, camping places, rockholes and places important in the recent Anangu and Piranpa ("white fella") history of the area. Equally importantly, this plan also provides for the conservation of the cultural landscape in which these places exist and from which they are inseparable. It requires both physical conservation actions and attention to the maintenance of cultural heritage values that enliven it. This will be achieved through training of young Anangu, involvement of traditional owners who live outside the park, keeping the stories about places strong, providing privacy for ceremonies, explaining cultural restrictions to visitors, and recording oral history connected to people's early experiences in the park including the struggle to win back their land. In addition to this park-wide cultural landscape plan, there are plans for specific sites, such as Mutitjulu Kapi (Mutitjulu waterhole), associated rock art sites and the physical features of the Kuniya and Liru stories, which require actions for managing visitor use as well as vegetation, fire, rock art, and restoration of trampled areas and the waterhole.

The evolution and current practice of planning and management at Uluru-Kata Tjuta illustrates how cultural heritage has gained primacy in land management. It is an exciting example of traditional owners reclaiming their ways of living in the land, referred to as 'keeping country straight.' It also represents reconciliation between Europeans whose practices often damaged the land and the Anangu whose traditional methods can restore the land to a new ecological balance. It is symbolic of what needs to be done throughout much of rangeland Australia.

## Kosciuszko National Park

Kosciuszko National Park was the largest national park in Australia in the 1940s, and regarded by some as the 'Yellowstone of Australia'. It illustrates the important role of acknowledging cultural values and involving neighbours in park planning. The Kosciuszko region in south-eastern New South Wales has the highest altitude in Australia (2,228m), a large percentage of

Alpine view in Kosciuszko National Park, Australia. Development of its new management plan illustrates the important role of acknowledging cultural values and involving neighbours in park planning. *New South Wales National Parks and Wildlife Service*

land above the snow line, rugged terrain, and a severe and unpredictable climate. Aboriginal people came to the region at least 21,000 years ago and to the area that is now national park 4,000–5,000 years ago (Mulvaney and Kamminga, 1999). By the 1820s, pastoralists were taking cattle and sheep into the higher alps. Payable gold was discovered at Kiandra in November 1859, creating the first alpine gold rush. Mining became more highly capitalized during the 1880s with the introduction of hydraulic sluicing and dredging, which remained in operation until the 1930s. The area was also used for logging of native timber, harvesting of eucalyptus oil, and establishing forestry plantations. Skiing, introduced by miners at Kiandra in the 1860s, has developed into a major industry, along with other types of outdoor recreation, especially bushwalking.

Recognition of the unique qualities of Kosciuszko inspired research in many fields almost from the beginning of European exploitation of the area (Scougall, 1992). Two developments occurred in the 1940s – the creation of Kosciusko State Park (later expanded into Kosciusko National Park) and the initiation of the Snowy Mountains Hydro Electric Scheme – that brought great physical and social change to the area. Recent evidence indicating higher levels of Aboriginal use of the alpine country provides important information about human adaptation to this ancient landscape. The traditional European emphasis on scientific (archaeological) research and on the role of men in Aboriginal society has left a legacy of biased recording and analysis of Aboriginal cultural heritage which has yet to be redressed. This bias led to misunderstanding and downplaying some aspects of Aboriginal culture in the park, and an emphasis on archaeological sites at the expense of broader landscapes (Lennon, 2002).

Pastoralists used prior Aboriginal land use patterns and every explorer and squatter of note in the alpine district was assisted by at least one Aboriginal guide. By the early 1850s, most of the Australian Alps had been nominally occupied by pastoralists though the severe winters of the high country checked permanent occupation and grazing there (Sullivan and Lennon, 2002). The sub-alpine landscape has been affected by this pastoral phase in national development and presents continuing evidence of this era in impressive cultural landscapes, vegetation change, a changed fire regime, the presence of wild horses and other introduced species, and distinctive erosion patterns. Much of this evidence constitutes damage to the pre-European environment, but it also has significant historic and scientific value. This is true also for evidence of mining, timber-getting, water-harvesting and recreation.

Concentration on nature conservation has also had its costs. Removal of stock from the high country has been demonstrated as an ecological necessity, but there was initially insufficient recognition of the loss of way of life and treasured traditions and the impact of severing strong emotional ties to the land, which resulted from the cessation of grazing in the high country excluding both pastoralists and Aborigines (Read, 1996). The zeal to restore a 'pristine' environment initially ignored the long Aboriginal heritage of the park, and also led to the destruction or damaging neglect of valuable historic heritage fabric, most notoriously at Kiandra, the goldfields village. This in turn has led to protest, lobbying, and research by heritage conservationists, and a gradual revision of policies to better protect cultural heritage.

Cultural landscape zones have not been formally delineated even though management guidelines have been prepared for obvious areas such as Currango and Kiandra (Lennon and Mathews, 1996). Currango is of national historic significance, being the largest and most intact pastoral settlement above the snowline in Australia with 25 remaining buildings and ruins spanning 150 years of European occupancy (Sullivan and Lennon, 2000). The physical setting of pastoralism is of national aesthetic significance, having been used for over a century by

Former pastoralist settlements in Kosciuszko National Park (Australia) span 150 years of history of European occupancy. Today, huts remaining from this area are managed for recreational uses, such as bushwalking and ski touring.
*New South Wales National Parks and Wildlife Service*

Australian artists to create works of literature and art now nationally celebrated and forming part of the national psyche. The pastoral theme has strong social value, demonstrated in the active continuation of its traditions and respect for its physical remains including its landscapes, wild horses and stock routes. *The Man from Snowy River* is an Australian cultural icon. The huts remaining from this era have been managed by agreement with the Kosciusko Huts Association (KHA) for bushwalking and ski touring (www.kosciuskohuts.org.au/the huts. html).

As the largest and highest profile park in Australia at the time of its establishment in 1944, Kosciuszko has also played an important role in the evolution and development of the profession of park management. Like Uluru, it was designated an international biosphere reserve in 1977. Despite the extensive identification and assessment of cultural values in Australian alpine areas and official recognition of some on heritage registers, park managers still need to better weave the evidence of long-term historical processes into their management planning and to consider climate change, fire histories, and impacts of previous occupation. Importantly, the knowledge of this history can provide baseline data from which to measure change and provide frameworks for assessing the impacts of current landscape interventions (Lennon, 2002).

The New South Wales National Parks and Wildlife Service (NPWS) is currently preparing a new management plan for Kosciuszko National Park which addresses many of these issues in the first major revision since 1982. In managing cultural heritage in the park, the Service has only recently fully recognised the importance of heritage artefacts to both the Aboriginal and non-Aboriginal people who generated them and the living nature of many cultural connections. Partnerships with local communities, families and individuals with strong connections to places not only acknowledge the legitimacy and authenticity of their histories, they also provide the best means of ensuring that the diversity of cultural values associated with the park survive. The new plan, developed with input from a community forum, an independent scientific committee and an Aboriginal working group, acknowledges that park management

---

## Box 2. The Landcare movement: landscape conservation by private owners

Landcare, a voluntary community group movement, began in Victoria in the late 1980s in response to land degradation from over-clearing. It is a locally based approach to addressing environmental problems and protecting the future of natural resources. There are now more than 4,500 Landcare groups across Australia, and about one in every three farmers is a member of a Landcare group. Government-funded coordinators assist groups to plan work and obtain funding on a matching formula. Work ranges from stock exclosures, fencing riparian vegetation, pest plant eradication to tree replanting. Landcare has been extremely successful and has heightened awareness of long-term conservation requirements. By changing public attitudes to land, water, vegetation and biodiversity management over the last decade, Landcare has cultivated a growing acceptance of constraints on resource use. There has also been transfer of information and knowledge to farmers, building capacity and social cohesion in the face of global changes economically and technologically. A review of the programme in 2003 showed that 91% of Landcare participants had been influenced to change farming practices by introducing no-till cropping to minimize soil erosion, stubble retention, alley and phase farming, cell grazing and controlled track cropping (www.affa.gov.au/corporate_ docs/publications/pdf/nrm/landcare/nlp_review_report_final.pdf).

The Natural Heritage Trust was set up by the Australian Government in 1997 to help restore and conserve Australia's environment and natural resources. As the largest environmental rescue plan ever undertaken in Australia, the Australian Government recognised the importance of this on-ground work inspired by Landcare and the need to continue to support it. The $2.7 billion Natural Heritage Trust is the largest financial commitment to environmental action in Australia's history. The Trust has invested much needed funds to help local communities deliver cleaner beaches, healthier waterways, less air pollution, and more productive agricultural land and to save threatened species through Landcare, Bushcare, Coastcare, and Rivercare programmes (www.nht.gov.au/ overview.html). To date, $1.4 billion has been invested in the Trust and related programmes for more than 11,900 projects around Australia. More importantly, an estimated 400,000 Australians have been involved in these projects.

Over the last decade, much practical conservation effort identifying and protecting remnant vege-tation has occurred at whole-farm and water catchment levels through the federally funded National Heritage Trust. Even so, there has been little effort at regional landscape protection or managing delineated cultural landscapes either on private property or in public land reserves. The historic components of the cultural landscape such as historic roads and fences, place names, gardens and plantations, and structures require identification as part of a whole landscape as well as funding for conservation treatments. In the implementation of these major funding programmes, the natural heritage view has proven to dominant the cultural values in the landscape, with the exception of some scenic areas. The extension of funding for the National Heritage Trust to 2007 has resulted in a transition to a regional delivery model. The focus is on implementing the National Action Plan for salinity reduction and improved water quality and this will tackle natural resource management issues at a landscape scale. Hopefully, the historical trends will also be assessed and cultural resources in those landscapes conserved as part of the overall strategy.

---

will be based upon recognition that all elements of the landscape have been influenced by human activities to varying degrees. As part of its work programme, the cultural values of entire landscapes and natural elements of the landscape will be identified and assessed through:

- A systematic programme of Cultural Landscape Mapping exercises with appropriate Aboriginal and non-Aboriginal communities and individuals;

- Examination of the available documentary evidence; and

- Information collected through oral histories through the Memories Project.

Management of heritage places with shared histories across different phases of human land use and between different communities will ensure that:

- All aspects of the history of a place are identified, recorded and assessed;

- Both Aboriginal and non-Aboriginal cultural values are acknowledged at places where they co-exist;

- Management of the remaining physical evidence of one historical theme or story is not at the expense of that of another; and

- Visitor interpretation covers all aspects of the layered histories of such places.

Those parts of the Park containing concentrations of material cultural heritage will be managed as discrete Heritage Precincts in which protection of historic features and landscapes will receive high priority (www.nationalparks.nsw.gov.au). These new directions, in accord with National Parks and Wildlife Service policies, suggest that cultural heritage assessment work should use the following principles:

- An integrated, or whole-of-landscape, approach with regard to the identification and assessment of all cultural (both historic and pre-contact Aboriginal) and natural values; and

- A cultural landscape approach to understanding the values of the item within its wider environmental/biogeographic, historic and social setting (NPWS, 2002).

This case study illustrates the current response of a management agency to the need for more cooperation with its neighbours by acknowledging their prior use of and associations with this large national park and its treasured landscapes.

## Castlemaine Diggings National Heritage Park

The applicability of the World Heritage cultural landscape categories to the Central Victorian goldfields, a historic mining landscape, was tested as part of the 1996 State of Environment reporting process and found to be applicable to a range of landscapes (Lennon, 1997). There is increasing interest in understanding heritage landscapes as a means of linking communities with these places (Cotter *et al.*, 2001). In Victoria there is a heritage overlay in all local government planning schemes. State heritage agencies incorporated cultural landscapes into their categories of heritage places which cover private lands protected through planning scheme controls similar to those for English national parks. The expansion of Victoria's *Heritage Act 1995* allowed listing of landscapes (http://heritage.vic.gov.au/Heritage_Landscapes/).

In 2003, the Castlemaine Diggings National Heritage Park of 7,442ha was listed. It had been gazetted in the 1970s as the Castlemaine-Chewton Historic Area (Regional Park) which contained historic mining relics and archaeological evidence of the original (1852) rush to the diggings. This area was re-examined as part of the Environment Conservation Council's Box-Ironbark Forests and Woodlands Investigation. The Council recommended creating a new category of public land principally to protect and recognise outstanding cultural landscapes (ECC, 2001). This designation is a first for Australia. The Castlemaine Diggings are significant

An 1850s house site and grave in Castlemaine Diggings National Heritage Park, Australia. The National Heritage Park designation brings high levels of recognition to cultural values, especially landscapes of exceptional value. *D. Bannear*

at an Australian scale, in the extent to which their goldfields landscapes have been preserved. The importance of the Castlemaine Diggings is not just in the considerable significance of the individual relics and sites themselves but in the cultural landscapes formed where large numbers of sites and relics persist in their original settings and demonstrate a range of cultural themes over several phases of human occupation.

Existing historic parks are characterized by aggregations of cultural sites and relics, as opposed to cultural landscapes. In addition, recognition and protection of natural and other values is generally peripheral in historic parks. At the other end of the scale, the primary purpose of national and state parks is the recognition and protection of natural values and, as significant as they are, the natural values of the Castlemaine area are not of the order, nor does the area cover the range, which these categories warrant. What was essentially required was a category, similar to national park, for cultural values, and with the scope for appropriate recognition and protection of natural and other values of moderate to high significance.

Accordingly, the Environment Conservation Council (ECC) envisaged a 'national heritage park' as a category that primarily brings high levels of recognition to cultural values, especially landscapes of exceptional quality. Protection will also be provided for other environmental values, especially natural values. As a result, harvesting of forest products and grazing by domestic stock will not generally be permitted. New surface mining and exploration will require approval under section 40 of the *National Parks Act 1975* and the park would only be reserved to a depth of 100m. One of the most important requirements of national heritage park status is heightened recognition, including promotion (where appropriate) of the cultural heritage it protects (ECC, 2001).

This case study illustrates how a range of government agencies have redesignated a well-loved historic landscape to recognise the primacy of its heritage values which have been an inspiration for artists, tourists and field naturalists alike. The designation has also led to better protection of related heritage values on surrounding private lands. This cultural landscape has been nominated for the new National List of Australian Heritage Places.

## Conclusion

Australians are proud of their protected landscapes – in national parks and reserves and in farmlands with sustainable new production techniques. Australian cultural landscapes such as Uluru and Kakadu are recognised as having universal associative cultural values through inclusion on the World Heritage List. These sites are icons of Indigenous landscape management over millennia with intangible heritage as the driving force for current management by 'keeping country straight'. The case studies in this chapter demonstrate the importance of involving people living in or having connections to the place to incorporate their beliefs and practices into management of the landscape. Even so, the diffusion of this concept to other protected areas has been slow, at least in part due to the dominance of the natural heritage paradigm.

The introduction of the new national heritage regime will create a National List which may assist Australians to appreciate all the values present in a place, as the debate about what constitutes national significance will lead to a greater realization of all the values present. Conflicting values and levels of significance will be exposed and whether those values are considered to meet the threshold for national listing will depend on public knowledge of history and ecology. Urban parks and Landcare schemes also play a role in cultivating conservation experiences among an urbanized population and among rural communities.

The three levels of government in Australia have traditional roles in land management, which have evolved and changed as Australia's constitution has been tested and interpreted through the courts over the last 30 years. Today Australia is at a new threshold, as individual owners and the State and Commonwealth governments realize the need to manage landscapes at local and regional scales for sustainable outcomes conserving all heritage values.

# Part III
## The way forward

# 16. Building leadership and professionalism: approaches to training for protected landscape management

*Elizabeth Hughes*

## The nature and complexity of protected landscapes

Protected Landscapes aim to conserve tangible and intangible landscape values that are the outcome of the interaction of people and nature. These are lived-in, working landscapes, represented by Category V of IUCN's category system of protected areas (IUCN, 1994). They are constantly evolving through a combination of natural processes and human activities that are inextricably interwoven. The key feature of protected landscapes, therefore, is that by their very definition their conservation objectives are framed not only within the context of their biodiversity status, but also within a social, cultural and economic context. They represent an holistic approach to conservation, and the management styles and skills that they require reflect this. It follows that they also offer test-beds for sustainability, the policies and practices of which can be transferred to the management of the wider landscape.

Historically, protected landscapes have been regarded as a European model with limited application elsewhere, yet over the last decade a sea change has occurred such that this model is now recognised as widely applicable. This shift in perception has been both ethical and pragmatic, but has arisen largely from a new awareness and understanding that has come from the growing body of experience around the world, including:

- Recognition of a number of examples of protected areas around the world that have traditionally been managed according to more 'exclusionary' models – for example Categories I and II (IUCN, 1994) – where it is now clear that the landscape has been moulded by human activity and where this activity is an essential component of a healthy ecosystem (Keoladeo National Park and World Heritage Site in Rajasthan, India is a case in point (WWF, 1996)). Increasingly, management styles that characterize the protected landscape approach are being adopted to enhance the conservation of these areas.

- Strict protection measures alone are now recognised as being inadequate to secure the biodiversity values of protected areas. While strictly protected areas are of unequivocal importance to global conservation, there is a need to adopt alternative approaches to management, which re-engage with local communities and other stakeholders, thereby generating much greater support for conservation. It is evident that many of the professional skills and practices that characterize the management of protected landscapes can also be applied in these situations.

- In the wider landscapes surrounding or linking strictly protected areas, human activity is often dependent upon the natural resources or environmental services they provide. The protected landscape approach is also appropriate here and is being widely adopted in this context. The Buffer Zone Programme of Nepal (see Budhathoki, 2003 and in this volume) and the integrated conservation and development programmes of the African 'Heartlands' (Muruthe, 2000) are good illustrations of this.

Thus the protected landscape model has a very wide application, and is now recognised as reflecting the attributes of what has become known as the "new paradigm for protected areas in the twenty-first century" (Beresford and Phillips, 2000, and see Phillips in this volume). However, the management approach it represents has yet to be universally acknowledged and professional development for this complex approach is still in its infancy.

## Protected landscape management

Protected landscape management represents a strategic and integrated "package" of management activities, which aims to link local development needs to the sustainable use of resources and the conservation of cultural heritage and biological diversity. As argued by Beresford and Phillips (2000), the management objectives of protected landscapes can only be achieved through an inclusive approach "where local communities are treated as central to the future of the area" and where its management "is directed at enabling them to share in both the responsibility and benefits of designation." Furthermore, working at the individual level, building and supporting a sense of landscape stewardship among land-users may be as important in some cases as working at the community level. Multi-sectoral and multi-level partnerships are by implication essential to this inclusive approach.

Thus, while necessarily visionary and strategic in its approach, protected landscape management is extremely complex and has also to be highly adaptive, and sufficiently flexible to meet the needs and priorities of each and every area to which it is applied.

In the IUCN publication *Management Guidelines for IUCN Category V Protected Areas: Protected Landscapes/Seascapes,* Phillips (2002) has developed practical guidance for protected landscape managers to help them in the application of this intricate web of concepts and principles. Certainly, never before has protected area management been so complex, embracing a wide range of disciplines, requiring multiple skills, involving many interest groups and often demanding a highly sensitive approach.

It is clear, therefore, that one of the most critical issues for protected landscapes is building the new professionalism required for the effective implementation of this challenging conservation approach. Given that our landscapes are now under enormous pressure from the seemingly immutable pace of modern development, it is only by providing conservation professionals with the appropriate conceptual framework, tools and techniques, that we can hope to manage change and conserve the best of what we have, for generations to come.

As long ago as 1993, *Parks for Life: Action for Protected Areas in Europe* (IUCN, 1993) highlighted the critical need for professional development of protected area staff in general. It argued that "staff are vital to the effective management of protected areas and their training should be a top priority" (IUCN, 1993). It recommended that "each country should prepare and implement a training programme to provide regular training to staff of protected areas" …and that "the programme should ensure that staff at every level (including volunteers) are well trained initially and that their skills are continually developed and updated." More than a decade on, there has been relatively little progress in this regard and it is certainly true to say (as

Conservation management training in the Pacific Island States. The management of Protected Landscapes today requires an array of management and specialist skills.
*Shaun Russell, ICPL*

in any sector), that when economies are stretched and budget constraints are introduced, staff training provision is often the first activity to be curtailed.

The Durban Accord, an output of IUCN's World Parks Congress 2003, again highlighted concerns about the "lack of access to technology, knowledge, lessons learned and best practice models for effective and adaptive management" experienced by many protected area practitioners around the world and urged a greater commitment to "building the capacity of protected arca managers."

## Training needs for protected landscape managers

Protected area professionals, including protected landscape managers, have traditionally come from the natural science disciplines – they are likely to be, for example, foresters, ecologists, biologists or zoologists. They are specialists in their own fields and clearly have a great deal to offer in terms of technical expertise. However, as described above, the management of protected landscapes today requires a much broader perspective, coupled with a range of new management skills, which were not formerly considered the realm of conservationists. An understanding of the conceptual framework of the protected landscapes approach and a wide range of both specialist and generic skills are important for managers to be effective. Specialist skills include, for example: policy development, management planning; biodiversity conservation; development control; heritage conservation; sustainable economic/social development; agricultural liaison; visitor/tourism management; information, education and interpretation; landscape assessment; information management; and financial management. The specialist skills embrace both natural and social sciences and, importantly, their practical and technical application within the philosophical framework of the protected landscape approach. They are both scientific and technical; they concern economics, planning, multiple land-use, social processes, education and information dissemination, and participatory planning and management.

Generic skills – necessary for the implementation of the specialist activities identified above – include, for example: partnership-building; participatory approaches; collaborative leadership; team skills; inter-personal skills; communication; presentation; facilitation; consensus-building; conflict resolution; monitoring and evaluation; networking; and business and accounting. These generic skills are just as essential to protected landscape management as the scientific/technical skills, as they provide the foundation for working with people in defining and accomplishing conservation goals. It is these skills that are critical to generating the political will and community support that are now regarded as essential for effective conservation.

In protected landscape management, the director's role, in particular, is one of leadership and co-ordination of a very broad compass of management and planning functions that embrace many disciplines and involve a number of people from diverse levels and sections of society. He/she thus has to be a "specialist generalist", with sufficient knowledge of each of the specialist functions to understand why, when, how and by whom, particular activities need to take place, and how they fit into the overall scheme of things. He/she also needs excellent leadership, team-building and organizational skills; negotiation skills; communication skills, conflict resolution and consensus-building skills. Critically, he/she also needs to build and to lead a highly skilled and committed team.

# Identifying training needs

At both regional and international levels, a number of useful efforts have been, and continue to be made to identify training needs in protected area management. Significantly, these initiatives all identify as a priority those skills associated with the protected landscape approach. For example, in 1993, a Protected Area Conservation Strategy (PARCS) survey assessed and evaluated the training needs and opportunities of 200 protected area managers in 16 countries throughout Eastern, Central and Southern Africa. This assessment concluded that the greatest need expressed by protected area managers across the region was for organizational training in policy development techniques and procedures, business management skills, and programme/project evaluation skills and techniques (AWF, 1993). In 1997, the South Pacific Regional Environment Programme (SPREP) also made an assessment of skill and knowledge requirements within its region, for the purpose of capacity-building. Here again, a number of generic skills were identified as those of highest priority in terms of organizational training needs. They include, for example, project design and proposal writing, personal planning and work programming, communication, facilitation, presentation, budgeting, financial management, marketing, monitoring and evaluation.

In South-East Asia, the ASEAN Centre for Biodiversity Conservation (ARCBC) adopted an alternative approach to addressing concerns regarding the training needs and management capacities of protected areas in the region. In order to capture the diversity of experiences in the region, the Centre devised a system of occupational competencies (Appleton, 2002), based on a framework of 24 typical (for the region) protected area jobs. Within this framework, 16 categories of protected area activities were identified (Figure 1), calling for a total of 291 skills (variously required in a range of contexts) and their associated knowledge-base. According to the skills and knowledge requirement, occupational standards were agreed for up to five staffing levels within each category.

**Fig. 1.  Categories of protected area activities for which skills and knowledge were identified, for the purpose of setting occupational standards**

| | |
|---|---|
| Universal "soft" skills | Socio-economic and cultural assessment |
| Financial and resources management | Sustainable development and communities |
| Staff development and training | Protected area planning and management |
| Communications | Site management |
| Technology and information | Enforcement |
| Project development and management | Recreation and tourism |
| Field craft | Awareness, education and public relations |
| Natural resources assessment | |
| Conservation management of habitats and species | |

*Source*: Appleton, 2002.

The potential use of such standards is wide-ranging but, in the context of this discussion, this system has a major role both as a tool for identifying the gaps in professional skills and expertise, and by implication the individual and organizational training needs in the region, and as a framework for curriculum/course development for training providers. Indeed, the World Parks Congress 2003 recommended that the World Commission on Protected Areas (WCPA) "agree generic global competency standards for protected area staff, which can be adapted at local, regional and national levels, and encourage and enable the use of standards and self-assessments to support improved effectiveness of protected area staff and training" (IUCN, 2003).

Interestingly, the skills and competencies listed in Figure 1 and the findings of the ASEAN study, both drawn from experience with the wider family of IUCN protected areas, reflect the inclusive and integrative approaches that are the key feature of protected landscape management.

# Developing a training strategy: case studies from the field

Strategic provision of staff training (at all levels) can be a highly effective approach for building capacity and improving organizational performance. Critically, however, the challenge in organizational training is to ensure that the knowledge and skills gained by individuals are "captured" by the organization, so that once something is learned it also becomes part of the institutional knowledge. Investment in training and staff development is futile (for the organization) if staff members leave and take the knowledge and skills with them. Indeed, "there are too many cases in which organisations know less than their members. There are even cases in which the organisation cannot seem to learn what every member knows" (Salafsky *et al.*, 2001).

Training therefore should be based on a clear strategy, so that members of the organization are aware of its direction and progression (McGahan and Bassett, 1999). It should also be subject to regular review and evaluation to ensure that it remains appropriate and responsive within what must necessarily be flexible and adaptive management systems.

Box 1 provides an example of the provision of academic and professional training programmes for Protected Landscape Management that aims to deliver both the knowledge base and the range of professional skills and techniques required to effectively implement the approach. The International Centre for Protected Landscapes is an NGO based in Wales, UK. Established in 1990, the Centre advocates integrated approaches to the management of protected areas around the world, highlighting the inextricable linkage between the conservation of natural and cultural resources, good governance, poverty alleviation and sustainable development. The Centre promotes the "protected landscape approach" as a strategic management approach that can accommodate these complex and multi-dimensional relationships.

---

**Box 1. The International Centre for Protected Landscapes**

**Status:** Non-profit NGO

**Mission:** To promote an international awareness of the protected landscape concept, recognising the crucial role that protected landscapes can play in achieving cultural and biological conservation within a development context.

**Programmes:** ICPL focuses particularly on strategic approaches in academic and professional training for protected landscape management. Its global Master of Science programme in "Protected Landscape Management: integrating conservation and development programmes" is structured to provide training in the planning and management of protected landscapes, built on a strong theoretical and conceptual foundation. Offered by distance learning, the programme is designed for in-post practitioners at middle/senior management level. Many participants (most of whom are from developing countries) are managers of protected areas – not only Category V areas – where there is increasing recognition that principles and practices of the protected landscape model can be adapted and incorporated into management to enhance its effectiveness.

The Centre is now working in partnership with regional institutions in order to build local training capacity and to offer more focused curricula. Current partners include, for example, Moi University in Kenya, the University of the South Pacific in Fiji, and La Molina Agricultural University in Peru. A new partnership with the Centre for Environment and Development at the University of Natal is under negotiation. In all these cases, vocational academic training in protected landscape management is part of a package which also aims to establish facilities for continuing professional development, supported by resource centres and offering short-course professional training programmes. The emphasis, however, is always on enabling national or regional institutions to offer a strategic and comprehensive approach to vocational education and training in this complex field.

ICPL also works with protected areas and other conservation agencies to undertake training needs analyses and deliver organizational training programmes based on identified needs, with participant follow-up an integral part of the programme. An example of this approach is a recently completed programme in partnership with the South Pacific Regional Environment Programme (SPREP). In order to ensure the sustainability of this particular programme, ICPL focused on training trainers and produced a comprehensive 'training manual' for the benefit of local trainers and facilitators (Falzon, 2002).

The training 'themes' offered by ICPL reflect the breadth and complexity of the protected landscape approach. These include:

- Protected Areas: IUCN designations; purposes; systems and networks;
- Land-use planning: the principles; formulation of planning policy;

Cont.

---

---

**Box 1.  The International Centre for Protected Landscapes (cont.)**

- Environmental management: designing environmental strategies and action plans; appraising and evaluating policy; environmental and social impact assessment; strategic environmental assessment; running Integrated Conservation and Development Projects;
- Management planning: from areas to sites; the preparation and presentation of plans;
- Business planning for protected area managers: financial planning; management systems and structures;
- Management skills: organisation; team, time and change management; assessing performance;
- Generic skills training: interpersonal skills; communication, presentation and negotiation;
- Consensus-building and conflict resolution; building partnerships with communities;
- Collaborative management and participatory approaches;
- Education, information and interpretation: the principles and purposes; planning interpretation programmes;
- Sustainable tourism: principles and application;
- Marketing for recreation and tourism: analysing visitor needs; strategic marketing;
- Visitor management: planning for recreation and tourism; evaluation of impacts; integrating the needs of conservation and recreation; and
- Training for trainers; planning and managing training programmes; skills and techniques; evaluation.

---

## Alternative approaches to professional development

A variety of approaches to continuing professional development are currently being used in addition to in-service training, short courses and formal education. The role of activities such as international exchanges, seminars and workshops should not be underestimated – all have a major part to play in this process. As noted by Jessica Brown and Brent Mitchell of the QLF/Atlantic Center for the Environment,

> *...protected areas managers world-wide face new and increasingly complex challenges, [and thus] there is a growing need to learn from the experience of counterparts working in other regions of the world. Focused exchanges and partnerships, built on the principle of mutual learning, can make an important contribution to fostering innovative conservation strategies, building effective partnerships and coalitions, and strengthening the capacity of participating institutions* (Brown and Mitchell, 2002).

Box 2 illustrates an initiative by QLF/Atlantic Center for the Environment that has been highly successful in promoting landscape stewardship, using international exchange in particular as a means of professional development and organizational capacity-building.

While historically the emphasis of protected area management in the USA has been on IUCN Category II national parks, including areas of 'wilderness,' with which its national park system is most closely associated, an increasing trend demonstrated by new designations is towards conserving privately owned or public/private partnership landscapes for their natural and cultural heritage value. These are lived-in landscapes, and their conservation requires a protected landscape or "stewardship" approach to management.

---

**Box 2.   The Quebec-Labrador Foundation/Atlantic Center for the Environment (QLF)**

**Status:** private, non-profit organization, incorporated in the United States and Canada.

**Mission:** to support the rural communities and environment of eastern Canada and New England (United States), and to create models for stewardship of natural resources and cultural heritage that can be applied worldwide.

**Programme:** International Program on Land Conservation and Stewardship.

**Purpose:** through this programme, QLF works with conservation practitioners and community leaders to develop leadership skills and new strategies for conservation of natural and cultural heritage.

**Activities:** QLF works in partnership with local institutions; the programme links the organization's domestic region of north-eastern North America with four target regions: Central Europe, Latin America, the Caribbean and, more recently, the Middle East. The programme relies on an array of methods for training, technical assistance, research and exchange, which are designed to reinforce each other, and which are united under the broad theme of Stewardship. These include: an annual fellowship programme in north-eastern North America; on-site workshops on stewardship topics; retreat meetings for fellowship alumni; partnership assignments with alumni; community problem-solving workshops; and study-tours for local leaders. Each of these projects is founded on the principle of true exchange – one in which learning can take place on both sides.

Since the programme's inception, several hundred conservation and community development practitioners from their four target regions have participated in fellowships, workshops and peer exchanges. QLF's growing cadre of alumni includes protected area managers, as well as leaders of NGOs, local and regional government agencies, and community organizations. The programme has evolved differently in each region, responding to the particular conditions affecting stewardship and the needs identified by our partners, and also reflecting geographic factors. Although distinct, QLF's projects in each target region build on each other through the gathering of information about common challenges and strategies.

Now in its eleventh year, QLF's Central European Stewardship Program encompasses an array of training, technical assistance, professional exchange and community-based planning projects. Its geographic focus to date has been the Czech Republic, Hungary, Poland and the Slovak Republic, with occasional participation from other countries in the region; there are now plans to extend the program to several Balkan countries. In conducting this programme over the past decade, QLF has worked in partnership with local NGOs and with the Environmental Partnership for Central Europe Consortium-EPCE (which is operating in Bulgaria, the Czech Republic, Hungary, Poland, Romania and Slovakia). A core element of QLF's work in Central Europe is the annual fellowship, which brings 6–10 conservation practitioners to the New England region for an intensive month-long programme incorporating seminars, a study- tour, individual placements with host organizations and a group case-study project. Another key element is the Landscape Stewardship Exchange, a week-long community problem-solving exercise; many of these have been conducted within Category V Protected Landscapes in Central Europe. (QLF's and EPCE's joint work to promote landscape stewardship in Central Europe is described further in the chapter by Hušková and Kundrata).

*Source*: Jessica Brown and Brent Mitchell.

---

The emergence of this new conservation model is reflected in the work of the Conservation Study Institute (CSI), established by the US National Parks Service to develop leadership and create a forum for discussing new directions in the field. A major role for CSI is that of raising

At a recent workshop in Mexico, QLF Fellowship alumni discussed a regional strategy for land conservation. *Brent Mitchell*

---

**Box 3.   Conservation Study Institute (CSI)**

**Status**: Government sector – US National Park Service – operated in partnership with other organizations.

**Mission**: The Conservation Study Institute serves the US National Park Service and the conservation community by creating opportunities for dialogue, inquiry, and lifelong learning to enhance the stewardship of parks, landscapes, and communities. The Institute was established by the US National Park Service to enhance leadership and to stay informed of new developments in the field of conservation. Although a national program, the Institute is based at Marsh-Billings-Rockefeller National Historical Park in Woodstock, Vermont – a national park that tells the story of conservation and the evolving nature of land stewardship in America.

**Activities**: Through a variety of programs, CSI assesses new directions in conservation, identifies best practices, and shares this information through a publications series and website as well as seminars and workshops. For example, the experience of 50 national and international conservation practitioners is described in *The Landscape of Conservation Stewardship* (2000). The analysis of these case studies identifies three common threads of successful conservation stewardship: 1) a sense of place that is complex and multi-faceted; 2) community-based conservation that is comprehensive, collaborative, respectful, and self-sustaining; and 3) a foundation of commitment and passion that works in concert with a sound scientific understanding to provide enduring inspiration. More recently, CSI was a co-sponsor of a national symposium on the future of conservation. *Reconstructing Conservation: Finding Common Ground* (2003), a book synthesising the findings of this symposium, describes conservation as encompassing a broad range of values, linking nature and culture, working at a larger scale across disciplines and political boundaries, and collaborating with a wide range of stakeholders.

The Institute also works with partners to explore contemporary practice and examine key strategies such as partnerships and collaboration. For example, CSI and QLF/Atlantic Center for the Environment convened two workshops on partnerships to create the opportunity for practitioners to reflect on what they have learned and have a focused dialogue with their peers. Two CSI reports (*Collaboration and Conservation*, 2001 and 2004) document their insights and lessons learned. CSI and QLF have also cooperated on international exchange as a means to foster innovation and develop leadership. Through this program, colleagues from the US and other countries exchange experience, explore common challenges, and develop creative strategies for conservation. In 1999, CSI and QLF co-sponsored an International Working Session on the Stewardship of Protected Landscapes and one of the important outcomes was creation of the IUCN/World Commission on Protected Areas's Protected Landscapes Task Force. This group provides a network for ongoing communication and, in particular, exchange of successful models for conservation of lived-in landscapes.

*Source*: Nora Mitchell

All references cited above can be found on the CSI web site: www/nps.gov/csi

---

A Conservation Study Institute workshop for educators in Vermont, USA.
*Kathleen Diehl/U.S. Forest Service*

awareness of the new approach and providing professional development for the National Park Service and other conservation organizations through a variety of means, as described in Box 3.

## Protected landscape partnerships

Box 4 draws our attention to partnerships as an emerging feature of the management of protected areas that is also of value in professional development and organizational capacity-building. Partnerships can take many forms and be established for a variety of purposes. The

---

**Box 4. EUROPARC Federation**

**Status:** Federated membership NGO

**Programme:** Partnership and Exchange Programme

   This programme (conducted between 1994 and 1998) facilitated partnerships for technical co-operation between protected areas in Europe, Asia and Latin America. The programme had financial support from the European Commission and helped to establish 15 long-term partnerships, which led to the sharing of information and expertise, staff exchanges, joint workshops and seminars, and joint problem-solving. In an Expertise Exchange Programme (conducted from 2000–2001), the Federation used partnership-building as one tool to facilitate expertise exchange for sustainable nature protection. Through this programme, eight partnerships were established, including that between Snowdonia National Park in the UK (a protected landscape) and the Krkonoše (Czech Republic) and Karkonosze (Poland) National Parks, which together comprise a transfrontier Biosphere Reserve. In this example, the partnership "has already secured a strong and secure base for the continuation of co-operation long into the future." Activities have included staff exchanges, and joint situation analysis and problem-solving.

*Source*: EUROPARC, 2001, 2004.

---

role of multi-sectoral partnerships in enhancing management – particularly those between protected area agencies and NGOs – is now recognised and well documented. Indeed, in many instances, NGOs now play a fundamental role in management capacity – particularly so in protected landscapes, where the nature and compass of management necessarily demands the sharing of responsibility through partnership agreements.

This example describes an initiative by the EUROPARC Federation to encourage and facilitate partnerships *between* protected areas as a means of facilitating professional development.

The role of partnership brokers, such as that played by the EUROPARC Federation in this instance, is to facilitate partnerships that are purposeful, pro-active and mutually beneficial to all partners. Only then can partnerships be of value as frameworks for mutual learning, exchanging information and expertise, broadening experience and perspectives, addressing common issues, and resolving common problems.

## The Durban Action Plan

Recognising the importance of professional development in building the capacity of protected area management (particularly in relation to the demands of the 'new paradigm') and also the paucity of training opportunities to achieve this, the V[th] World Parks Congress proposed a number of actions to improve on the current situation. According to the Durban Action Plan (IUCN, 2003) these include:

- to encourage partnerships between training institutions;

- to establish regional networks of trainers and training institutions;

- to create a pool of learning sites as best practice models for training;

- to improve opportunities for non-conventional learning (for example, distance education, learning networks and practical on-the-job-training);

- to ensure that each protected area has recruitment, training and continuing professional development plans and programmes for managers and staff; and

- to develop the Protected Areas Learning Network (PALnet), an interactive, web-based knowledge management tool, through which stakeholders at all levels can acquire and share best practice.

The actions (to be led by the IUCN WCPA Capacity Development Task Force) are challenging and inevitably subject to many external influences, not least of which is funding. However, while little progress was made between 1993 and 2003 as alluded to earlier in this paper, it is to be hoped that the commitment to professional development is now greater and that more will be achieved in the coming decade.

## Conclusions

Professional development for protected landscape managers is about building leadership qualities and the skills required to create management systems that are effective in conserving the natural and cultural heritage of the landscape within viable economic frameworks and supportive social structures. It is about learning from "test beds" of sustainable development that can serve as models for the wider environment. It is also about a management paradigm that recognises people are at the heart of every conservation effort and its sustainability. It is clear, however, that professional development cannot be disassociated from the wider process of capacity-building and, as suggested by Beckmann (2000), "for training to be effective it has to be linked to other strategies that can support the capacity-building process."

The "ideal" protected landscape management team's members have a keen awareness and appreciation of the theoretical and philosophical basis for their work. They have a clear understanding of the natural and cultural resources of the landscape in which they work and are able to work with others to identify and analyse the range of tangible and intangible landscape values within their own context. They work with others to craft and regularly review a management plan, based on a collective vision and a strategy for the area. Critically, the management plan highlights the need for multi-disciplinary and multi-sectoral co-operation and for collaboration between professionals and communities. The team works with a wide range of partners and is able to implement a variety of integrated participatory planning and management approaches. There is a good working relationship with local communities and other stakeholders. The agency seeks feedback on its approaches and priorities; monitoring and evaluation of effectiveness are ongoing and management is responsive and adaptive. The structure of the agency is based on this strategy, ensuring that staff expertise is comprehensive and complementary. The strategy is supported by specific policies, objectives and work programmes. All levels of staff are appraised on their performance, and staff training and development are a regular and integral part of the agency's functions. The agency is part of a national and international network that exchanges information and expertise.

The demands of this protected landscape approach are clearly considerable and effective-ness can only be achieved with the support of rigorous training and professional skills development, focussed on improving the performance both of the individual and of the organization, within a strategic framework. The foregoing discussion reveals that while there are various tools for achieving this, there is a shortage of institutions for delivery. While some excellent initiatives have been illustrated, there is undoubtedly a need for further opportunities and these need to be made more accessible to staff at all levels. Fundamentally, building a high level of professionalism is critical if we are to achieve conservation of natural and cultural resources within a framework of sustainable development.

# 17. Conclusions – the protected landscape approach: conservation for a sustainable future

*Nora Mitchell, Jessica Brown and Michael Beresford*

"*...we must ensure that national parks are transformed – we need to break with traditional thinking, to catalyze a new vision, and to join hands in new partnerships.*"

Nelson Mandela, opening plenary at the World Parks Congress
Durban, South Africa – September 2003

This collection of case studies from many regions of the world illustrates the successful application of a *protected landscape approach* in a wide range of situations and circumstances. This approach has a diversity of expression since it is adaptable and is interpreted and defined by each place and its people – relying on their traditions as well as innovation and creativity – listening to the voices of elders and to those of the next generation. These case studies demonstrate how the protected landscape approach has been crafted from experimentation and innovation over many years and in many places.

This approach does not focus solely on the protection of nature and biodiversity but rather recognises the critical links between nature, culture, and community for long-term sustainability of conservation. As described in the introduction, a fundamental aspect of this approach is the complex meaning of the term "landscape". In this context, landscape encompasses a mosaic of land uses from cultivated to wild lands over a large geographic area that has been shaped and influenced by human interaction over time. This multi-dimensional and dynamic definition of landscape is a foundation for the protected landscape approach. This approach confirms that stewardship depends on people and recognises the importance of an inclusive, participatory, and democratic process for accomplishing conservation.

At the opening of the V[th] World Parks Congress in South Africa, Former President Nelson Mandela (as quoted above) challenged participants from around the globe to break with traditional thinking, embrace a new vision for protected areas, and create new partnerships. The protected landscape approach meets this challenge. While remaining intimately tied to

---

**Box 1.  The Durban Accord – a new paradigm for protected areas**

In this changing world, we need a fresh and innovative approach to protected areas and their role in broader conservation and development agendas. This approach demands maintenance and enhancement of our core conservation goals, equitably integrating them with the interests of all affected people. In this way the synergy between conservation, the maintenance of life support systems and sustainable development is forged. We see protected areas as vital means to achieve this synergy efficiently and cost-effectively. We see protected areas as providers of benefits beyond boundaries – beyond their boundaries on a map, beyond the boundaries of nation-states, across societies, genders and generations.

*Source*: www.iucn.org/wpc2003

---

protecting nature and biodiversity, the protected landscape approach incorporates cultural heritage, respects the relationship between people and place, and creates a link with sustainable strategies that together represent the new conservation paradigm endorsed at the World Parks Congress in Durban (see Box 1).

# Key characteristics of the protected landscape approach

There is wide diversity in the application of the protected landscape approach evidenced in this volume as it represents a strategy for conservation of biological and cultural diversity linked to sustainable community development that is tailored to a particular place. Elizabeth Hughes has remarked on the diversity and complexity of this approach resulting from the need to be "highly adaptive, and sufficiently flexible to meet the needs and priorities of each and every area to which it is applied." Similarly, Mechtild Rössler in her work with the World Heritage Convention has noted the "extraordinary development in the interpretation of the ... Convention and the diversity of approaches and experiences in preservation and stewardship worldwide."

In spite of the adaptability and the diversity inherent in this approach, collectively these case studies offer seven key characteristics distilled from this breadth of experience. This synthesis draws on the point made by many contributors to this volume that it is important to include both the characteristics of *place* as well as characteristics of *process*. Together these two dimensions provide an operational framework for the protected landscape approach that is further explored in the sections below.

# Characteristics of place

The focus of this conservation approach is, in general, on large-scale bioregional landscapes with interwoven natural and cultural resource values held by associated cultural groups who have interacted with the place over time.

## 1. The protected landscape approach is bioregional in scale and represents a mosaic of designations and land uses.

The scale of conservation, as many of the case studies in this book demonstrate, is large for a number of reasons. As discussed in the introduction, the field of conservation biology has highlighted the pressing need to work on the scale of ecosystems and the wider landscape to conserve biological diversity. Co-authors Brian Jones, Moses Okello and Bobby Wishitemi agree, and observe that many designated protected areas "are too small to be viable and depend on intervening private lands that serve as wildlife dispersal and migratory areas". Edmund Barrow and Neema Pathak point out that "protected areas also lack the ecological connectivity to other parts of the ecosystem or landscape". Consequently, the humanized, lived-in landscapes have become an integral part of conservation for their contributions to biodiversity and also since, as Adrian Phillips has pointed out, "nature conservation ...cannot be achieved sustainably within 'islands' of strict protection surrounded by areas of environmental neglect."

The recognition of cultural landscapes has added impetus to the efforts to increase the scale of conservation and pay more attention to lived-in landscapes. Rössler noted "the introduction of cultural landscapes into the World Heritage arena has made people aware that sites are not isolated islands, but that they are part of larger ecological systems and have cultural linkages in time and space beyond single monuments and strict nature reserves." In this way, "the cultural landscape concept has contributed to the evolution in environmental thought, protected area management strategies, and heritage conservation as a whole."

The large scale for conservation requires consideration of a complex mosaic of designations and land use, and a diversity of landownership and management goals. Consequently, the geographic focus for conservation has shifted from isolated protected areas to networks and interconnected systems of protected areas, inclusive of rural settlements and urban areas. These areas include a mixture of private and public land as well as designated protected areas and stewardship by owners and communities without formal designations. Claudio Maretti reports an "...increasing emphasis on integration – into bioregions, mosaics of protected areas, ecological networks and conservation corridors, and individual protected areas considered as part of systems of protected areas." In Nepal's protected area system the designation of buffer zones and conservation areas, which are managed in cooperation with local communities, serves to reconnect the strictly protected areas into a network. Jones, Okello and Wishitemi note that the protected landscape approach can sustain wildlife dispersal areas and migration corridors on the land of Maasai pastoralists.

## 2.    The protected landscape approach embraces the interrelationship of nature and culture.

Many authors discussed the critical recognition of social and cultural values in accomplishing natural resource conservation, the value of cultural heritage, and the connection between natural and cultural diversity. Rössler, in writing about cultural landscapes, observes that each is "a unique complex of cultural and natural values." That biological diversity often coincides with cultural diversity has been widely documented (e.g., Harmon, 2002) and is illustrated by many of the case studies in this volume. Hughes describes landscapes as "constantly evolving through a combination of natural processes and human activities that are inextricably inter-woven." The Philippine Rice Terraces, as Augusto Villalón writes, provide many examples of culture-nature connections, such as the management of *muyong*, private forests that cap each terrace group and are managed as a collective effort through traditional tribal practices. This interrelationship is illustrated in Australia where "landscapes represent wild nature, are the product of Indigenous peoples, and have been extensively shaped by Europeans" as Jane Lennon writes. In both the US and Canada, recognition of the value of lived-in landscapes has increased, along with a growing appreciation for community engagement.

There are many areas around the world, including previously identified natural areas " ... where it is now clear that the landscape has been moulded by human activity and where this activity is an essential component of a healthy ecosystem", according to Hughes. Phillips cites well documented evidence that some areas thought of previously as wilderness have, in fact, been modified by people over long periods of time (Phillips 1998). Rössler writes of the importance of recognising cultural land-use systems that represent continuity of people work-ing the land over centuries and sometimes millennia to adapt the natural environment and retain or enhance biological diversity. Miroslav Kundrata and Blažena Hušková use the term "secondary biodiversity" to describe species richness in areas that have been conditioned by centuries of human influence and where intervention now sustains many species. The sacred forest groves in Western Ghats in India and in Nepal have been recognised as islands of natural biodiversity yet many are managed to accommodate some use for local livelihoods.

Fausto Sarmiento, Guillermo Rodriguez and Alejandro Argumedo describe Andean landscapes as " … the result of intellectual and spiritual constructs that are shaped by traditional practices ... and the newer uses given to them by the diverse cultures that inhabit them". They note that this has led to the unique agro-ecosystems of the Andes, for example, a Potato Park with 2300 cultivars of potato. This biodiversity includes native plant genetic resources, such as wild relatives of domesticated plants and animal species. Other important world crops have been developed and this agro-biodiversity conserved in traditional agricultural systems such as the terraced rice paddies in Asia (with rice, fish and vegetables), oasis systems in the Sahara (with dates), or livestock. The global importance of these systems and the genetic varieties supported by these diverse cultural landscapes have not always been recognised and included in conservation strategies.

Michael Beresford has written of the importance of developing a management approach "based on an understanding of this inter-relationship [between nature and culture]…[since] the landscape we see is the tip of the iceberg, underpinned by these unseen complex interactions, based on a series of past and on-going decisions." Maretti concurs on the importance of understanding the relationships among social, cultural, and natural elements and processes since "landscapes are mostly process, defined economically and culturally by people." Taghi Farvar, chair of IUCN's Commission on Environmental, Economic and Social Policy, makes a cogent point when he observes that "…cultural and biological diversity are natural, powerful allies and it is this alliance that may eventually succeed in saving both" (in Borrini-Feyerabend, 2002).

## 3. The protected landscape approach recognises the relationship between tangible and intangible values and the value of both.

Tangible values – as described above – are usually the primary focus of conservation. Many authors in this volume, however, make a compelling case for more consideration of the intangible values of landscapes, and also explore the relationship with tangible values, challenging the concept that one can be conserved without the other. Rössler describes a fundamental shift in environmental thought and practice with the acceptance of the "value of communities and their relation to their environment, including the link between landscapes and powerful religious, artistic or cultural associations even in the absence of material cultural evidence… sacred sites, which may be physical entities or mental images that are embedded in a people's spirituality, cultural tradition, and practice."

The IUCN World Commission on Protected Areas has a Task Force on Cultural and Spiritual Values that defines intangible heritage as "the intrinsic value of nature as well as that which enriches the intellectual, psychological, emotional, spiritual, cultural and/or creative aspects of human existence and well-being" (Harmon, 2004). David Harmon, Executive Director of the George Wright Society, an NGO, notes that while the focus of conservation is usually on biodiversity, it is these intangible values that motivate many people since "they lie at the heart of the protective impulse that drives the modern conservation movement." Harmon and his co-author Allen D. Putney create a typology of eleven intangible values that include cultural and identity, spiritual, and aesthetic and artistic values among others (Harmon and

Putney, 2003). This typology of intangible values complements a selected list of those identified by authors in this book (see Table 1).

## Table 1.  Selected tangible and intangible values recognised in the protected landscape approach

| | |
|---|---|
| **Environmental values** | ▪ safeguard and enhance biological diversity.<br>▪ safeguard vital environmental services, for example, clear water, clean air, soil fertility.<br>▪ attract and encourage beneficial developments.<br>▪ reduce or eliminate harmful developments.<br>▪ maintain the diversity and value of the visual landscape.<br>▪ provide sustainable development models for wider rural areas. |
| **Cultural values** | ▪ raise awareness of the cultural heritage and identity.<br>▪ safeguard and enhance traditional cultural resources and practices.<br>▪ protect unique landscapes and artifacts.<br>▪ inspire artists and writers.<br>▪ develop a heightened sense of place and promote appropriate recreational developments.<br>▪ maintain the interaction between nature and culture. |
| **Spiritual values** | ▪ safeguard places/areas of spiritual and sacred significance to local and national communities.<br>▪ secure and improve access and facilities for appropriate enjoyment of such places. |
| **Educational values** | ▪ provide information and interpretation facilities to raise awareness and understanding.<br>▪ promote a greater understanding of the human/nature relationship.<br>▪ provide study and research facilities to increase understanding of the area.<br>▪ build wider support for sustainable use of the environment. |
| **Scientific values** | ▪ encourage scientific research.<br>▪ develop indicators to measure and evaluate change caused by human activity. |
| **Recreational values** | ▪ provide a wide range of opportunities for public enjoyment through recreation and tourism appropriate in type and scale to the essential qualities of the area. |

The list in this table is not intended to be comprehensive, but rather to draw examples from the case studies in this text to illustrate the wide range of values considered in the protected landscape approach. The tangible environmental and cultural values have been discussed previously, so included here are a few descriptions of intangible values. In the Andes, there is an important spiritual connection to landscapes where mountains are revered as *apus*, or mountain deities, and sacred sites are important landscapes based on spiritual constructs. Sarmiento, Rodriguez and Argumedo explain the spirtitual associations that indigenous peoples of the region have with the landscape, and the associated ritual naming of plants, soil types, water bodies, even types of weather.

Villalón describes the importance of spiritual values in the *Ifugao* culture, such as the role of rice in rituals. Conservation of a landscape such as the rice terraces requires continuing the culture-based traditional practices that have created and maintained them. For this reason, he argues "tangible and intangible heritage must be preserved together". Similarly, Barrow and Pathak note that conservation is "intimately tied to social mores and ethics, and that the erosion of culture often leads to loss of natural systems". They cite the threat to the survival of sacred forest groves in Ghana posed by the erosion of traditional beliefs that have sustained the bio-rich systems for generations. Traditional knowledge systems are often intertwined with belief systems, rituals and ceremonials.

Nora Mitchell, Jacquelyn Tuxill, Guy Swinnerton, Susan Buggey and Jessica Brown observe that the protected landscape approach recognises multiple values and encompasses the interests of local communities and indigenous peoples. From this foundation it crafts collaborative management approaches that involve all key stakeholders. The next section describes the importance and some of the characteristics of this type of process in conservation.

# Characteristics of process

In describing the importance of the process of conservation, Hughes writes that conservation objectives are framed within a social, cultural and economic context. Working within this complex context requires an approach that integrates a number of key characteristics of process described in the sections below.

## 4. The protected landscape approach is community-based, inclusive and participatory.

The direct engagement of key stakeholders with an emphasis on local and indigenous people and communities is a theme that is present in all of the case studies. Many papers cite the involvement of local people and communities to enhance understanding and support for conservation, to shape conservation that it is relevant, and to retain and build commitment and engagement in stewardship. Rössler notes that "...conservation processes bring people together in caring for their collective identity and heritage, and provide a shared local vision within a global context [and] local communities need therefore to be involved in every aspect of

Sherpa children in Nepal. Involving local communities in conservation of their landscapes is critical to sustaining their natural and cultural heritage for future generations. *Paul Rogers/ICPL*

the identification, planning and management of the areas, as they are the most effective guardians of the landscape heritage" (UNESCO, 2003).

Adrian Phillips and Richard Partington report an increase in local participation through community partnerships when the decision-making was devolved in the Blackdown Hills Area of Outstanding Natural Beauty in southwest England. Prabhu Budhathoki describes the enhanced empowerment of local people through their involvement in conservation and the distribution of conservation benefits to local communities. In Nepal's innovative buffer zone and conservation area designations, the role and importance of people in lived-in landscapes are recognised as integral to the long-term conservation of biodiversity.

In the Philippine Rice Terraces, the importance of self-determination by communities is critical to "balancing tradition and progress ...for each [community or region] to determine its own path towards sustainable preservation of its culture and distinctive landscape." In the Andes, community self-determination and safeguarding traditional knowledge and practices are central aspects of conservation strategies. In Australia, Lennon writes of the importance of involving the people living in, or having connections to, a place so that their beliefs and practices are incorporated into the management of the landscape. As noted in the introduction, fostering stewardship by those closest to the resource taps their wealth of knowledge, traditional management systems, innovation and love of place. For protected areas to continue to be important for biodiversity conservation, they must forge linkages with people based on equity, linked rights, and responsibilities.

## 5. The protected landscape approach is based on cross-sectoral partnerships.

The key stakeholders and stewards of conservation areas are diverse – ranging from different levels of government, non-governmental organizations, to private landowners and communities and, of course, youth, the next generation of stewards. Consequently, as Hughes observes, multi-sectoral and multi-level partnerships are essential to an inclusive and participatory approach to conservation.

As described above (in the previous section), the involvement of local communities is key. Barrow and Pathak note that "where local communities have been mobilized and responsibly involved, this has often helped save a protected area, or other wildlife habitat, much more effectively than if the governments were to do it alone." Lennon also points out the importance of involving people living in or having connections to the place in order to incorporate their beliefs and practices into management of the landscape.

In many parts of the world, the NGO sector is growing and providing another level of capacity for conservation. Several excellent examples from Central Europe illustrate the role of NGOs, as "proactive innovators and coalition-builders for sustainable development at the regional level." Kundrata and Hušková describe models of partnerships among local communities, NGOs and state administration that are pioneering projects of rural sustainability.

In many countries, it is not possible nor practical nor preferable to accomplish resource management through government effort alone. Based on experience in the US and Canada, Mitchell, Tuxill, Swinnerton, Buggey and Brown note that the traditional role of governments is changing from land-owner and manager to one of partner, facilitator and catalyst, providing

Stage Cove in Conche, Newfoundland (Canada). Benefits of the protected landscape approach include those related to cultural traditions, community-building and economic improvement.
*Candace Cochrane*

the legal framework and often financial and technical support for others to develop strategies and implement effective conservation.

## 6. The protected landscape approach is founded on planning and legal frameworks that create an environment of engagement through equity and governance for a diverse set of stake-holders.

"[I]t is clear that a whole range of conservation models will be needed, ranging from those prescribing strict preservation to those supporting sustainable use, and including a range of PAs, from those governed by the State (in situations where appropriate) to PAs completely managed by indigenous and local communities", according to Barrow and Pathak. It is often through the process of planning that agreements between key stakeholders can be crafted. In the Philippines, it was the management plan that served to jointly empower government and the communities in the conservation of the rice terraces. Budhathoki, in reflecting on his experience in Nepal, noted that successful biodiversity conservation depends not only on "productive collaboration with local people but also on coordinated, integrated planning at provincial, regional and national levels". In many cases, a legal and management framework creates a forum for collaboration and a venue for creating a collective vision of the future. In the US and Canada, and in England and Wales, partnership fora were created to bring together public bodies, local organizations, and volunteer groups for conservation of regional landscapes. A legal framework can shape the form of governance and can provide recognition of traditional management systems and customary law.

Several authors in this volume develop principles for planning and management that create an inclusive, participatory approach. Based on successful experience with the Mata Atlantica Biosphere Reserve serving as a coordinating institution, Clayton Lino and Marilia Britto de Moraes offer lessons for "strict principles of participation, decentralization, transparency, and a search for consensus…" combined with "administrative flexibility and a lack of bureaucracy…[and a process that] involves simultaneous and equal participation of governmental institutions (federal, state, and local) and non-governmental participants (including NGOs, and members of the scientific community, the private sector and the local population)". Other authors note that this proactive participatory management process proved effective in guiding landscape change.

Some form of national or international designation of protected areas can serve as an important tool and catalyst for conservation. Experience with World Heritage Site designation has illustrated the catalytic effect "on cultural identity and pride, and on potential partnerships and innovative conservation approaches". Villalón reports the positive impact on conservation action when the rice terraces were listed as a World Heritage Site "In Danger".

Overlapping designations can serve to create linkages among conservation areas across a landscape. In Brazil's coastal zone, an international biosphere reserve by UNESCO and a national APA, are used as complementary designations with each other and with other kinds of PAs. Uluru-Kata Tjuta National Park in Australia is designated as an IUCN Category II and a Biosphere Reserve and is also listed as a World Heritage cultural landscape. This layering of designations has assisted in the recognition of the diverse set of values of this place.

However, it is also noted by several authors that the emphasis on "official" protected areas tends to overlook that rural people conserve vast areas of land and biodiversity informally, and that conservation of these areas by community (CCAs) pre-dates government-managed protected areas. Community-Conserved Areas and co-management systems illustrate the variety of ways communities are engaged in conservation from management systems, land tenure, and legal instruments to the recognition and adaptation of traditional systems and traditional knowledge of conservation. An IUCN inter-Commission Working Group, the Theme on Indigenous/Local Communities, Equity and Protected Areas (TILCEPA), has been instrumental in the recognition and continuing role of these communities in conservation.

## 7. The protected landscape approach contributes to a sustainable society.

A synthesis of environmental and social goals is fundamental to the protected landscape approach. Many authors stressed the importance of perceiving conservation as part of a "dynamic system" that needs to be "economically and socially viable to survive", and stressed the importance of "innovative economies". Budhathoki summarised these points as a "growing understanding that for biodiversity conservation to be sustainable, appropriate socio-political as well as ecological landscapes are necessary". Giles Romulus demonstrates the importance of addressing community development and quality of life improvements alongside conservation in small island nations in the Caribbean. Successful experience in Kenya and Namibia also focused on "community welfare as well as conservation of natural resources". In Nepal, the buffer zones and conservation areas proved to be effective by linking conservation with poverty alleviation. Maretti notes that IUCN's Category VI "highlights the key role played by

The Liptov region in the High Tatra mountains of northern Slovakia. Protected landscapes can serve as models and test beds for sustainable development.
*Brent Mitchell*

local communities in conservation strategies and reinforces recognition of the potential to join sustainable development with nature conservation".

Many authors note the importance of the protected landscape approach as models and test beds for sustainable development. Phillips writes that these landscapes are "an environmental resource, also a *medium* through which to pursue sustainable development." Rössler concurs that they can "illustrate sustainable local and regional development" and serve as "models of sustainable development – drawing on traditional practices of sustainable use of resources." Phillips and Partington report on recent innovative policies in Wales using protected areas as places where sustainable forms of rural development are pioneered and promoted, giving national parks a new purpose. These conservation areas become "test beds from which successful experience can be rolled out into the whole countryside".

## Benefits of the protected landscape approach

A review of the case studies presented in this book reveals a range of benefits derived from using the protected landscape approach to safeguard and enhance special areas within viable programmes of social and economic development (see Table 2).

This table is not meant to be all-inclusive but serves to illustrate the wide range of benefits experienced from this approach. The protection of ecological services and cultural heritage has already been discussed. It is, however, important to note the important civic engagement and educational benefits observed by several authors. In many cases, people and organizations not traditionally involved in conservation became engaged. Jones, Okello and Wishitemi credit the long history of community-based conservation in Kenya and Namibia and the level of community involvement with reducing wildlife poaching. Rössler emphasises the educational benefits of community engagement in the nomination of sites as cultural landscapes to the World Heritage List, which has increased awareness and instilled new pride among the local communities for their heritage and has often led to revival of their traditions.

## Table 2. Benefits from the protected landscape approach

| | |
|---|---|
| **Ecological services** | ▪ retain biological diversity, both wild and cultivated;<br>▪ for example, protect soil and water resources, prevent erosion, regulate climate. |
| **Cultural traditions** | ▪ sustain and/or revive cultural traditions;<br>▪ support traditional management and governance;<br>▪ support community lifestyles which are in harmony with nature;<br>▪ encourage traditional products as part of an economic strategy;<br>▪ promote the continuation of traditional land uses and seeking new uses through innovative development. |
| **Civic engagement** | ▪ generates involvement and support of communities;<br>▪ engages new constituencies;<br>▪ promotes participation and inclusion;<br>▪ increases awareness of heritage;<br>▪ builds community pride;<br>▪ creates inclusive governance structures;<br>▪ fosters civil society. |
| **Community-building** | ▪ provides livelihood improvements and increased welfare through the development of natural products for example agriculture, horticulture, forestry, fisheries and through the provision of services;<br>▪ promotes community partnerships and benefit-sharing;<br>▪ generates opportunities for public agency and private sector partnerships;<br>▪ promotes a collaborative management approach, based on community welfare. |
| **Economic improvement** | ▪ alleviates poverty and improve quality of life;<br>▪ improves economic vitality and viability;<br>▪ promotes sustainable development initiatives;<br>▪ promotes diversification of local economies;<br>▪ identifies opportunities to develop new products and services and create new employment opportunities;<br>▪ promotes responsible tourism and leisure activities. |

Many authors also note the pursuit of innovative sustainable economies that market the place and its traditions and also support conservation (see also Phillips, 2002). Sarmiento, Rodriguez and Argumedo describe a model of ecotourism that develops market niches for recreation activites based on landscape enjoyment and education, such as wildlife observation, and also on gastromonic experiences using unique native crops. In Brazil's coastal zone, Lino and Britto de Moraes cite examples of sustainable development through ecotourism, cultural and historical heritage, fishing and aquaculture and marketing local handicrafts. Similarly, countries in Central Europe are pioneering rural sustainability by building on traditions of the region and experimenting with partnerships among landowners, NGOs and government to create business opportunities with the aim of supporting local economic development. The village of Hostětín in the White Carpathian Protected Landscape Area, for example, has become a model of rural sustainable development. Over the past decade this village has used innovative technologies such as biomass in a heating plant, solar collectors, and biological sewage treatment facility. Hostětín is also one of the centres of "Traditions of the White Carpathians", an association focused on preserving traditional varieties of fruit, creating the infrastructure for traditional local processing, and marketing of fruit products. The products are marketed under the "Traditions of the White Carpathians" label that helps market high-quality products by associating them with the region and, at the same time, promotes the region as a whole. In the USA, an *Atlas of People, Places and Hand-made Products* is being produced to celebrate stories of stewardship and explores the idea of consumer awareness through marketing products associated with place to support sustainable economies.

Romulus cites intangible benefits from the participatory planning process that include "greater awareness of impacts on the environment, increased knowledge of natural and cultural heritage of the area, a growing sense of community pride, the discovery of community power in negotiating with the government, and the realization that with the appropriate mechanisms they could have a greater say in designing their future." Kundrata and Hušková conclude that participatory approaches to conservation have been critical in fostering civil society and reforming new democracies in Central Europe. Collectively, this range of benefits is compelling evidence of the effectiveness of the protected landscape approach as a positive force for protection of natural and cultural heritage but also for community-building, social change and democracy.

## Challenges remaining

Although this set of case studies demonstrates much success, challenges remain. Threats facing these places and their stewards are many, and highlight their vulnerability and a sense of urgency. In many parts of the world, changing economies and land uses, poverty as well as rapid growth from development and recreation, put these places and the interrelationships between the environment and people at risk. According to Phillips and Partington, one of the largest challenges ahead is to integrate conservation fully with all aspects of social and economic endeavours.

The need to change perceptions of conservation also presents a challenge. Beresford writes that "the main challenges lie with creating or reinforcing a positive social perception of protected areas as positive assets for communities and building a broad constituency which includes local people, politicians, land owners and the business community." Budhathoki agrees and cites the challenge of engaging local communities in Nepal, given the widespread suspicion among rural people towards conservation which appears to be another way to control their resource use.

These observations are mirrored in perceptions and in many cases, misperceptions of conservationists toward local communities and their stewardship. Many conservation professionals resist the idea of community-based management and are distrustful of the possibility of creating sustainable economies compatible with conservation objectives. Maretti notes how important it is, in developing an overall nature conservation strategy, to view local communities and their activities related to natural resources and sustainable development as an opportunity rather than a problem. In the past, this suspicion of local stewardship has sometimes resulted in overlooking the conservation value of existing cultural traditions and undermining the social systems that were providing biodiversity protection. Clearly there is a need for a new image of conservation among diverse constituencies for the protected landscape approach to succeed.

The effectiveness of the protected landscape approach is directly linked to its complexity. According to Hughes, "never before has protected area management been so complex, embracing a wide range of disciplines, requiring multiple skills, involving many different interest groups and often demanding a highly sensitive approach." This approach involves unprecedented cooperation and partnerships across many sectors on a landscape and among many organizations at the local, regional, national and international levels. Working on large-scale landscapes relies on coordination among key stakeholders, across a diversity of land uses and land ownership, and often involving multiple types of designation and corresponding legislation.

This approach to conservation also rests on managing – even embracing – change, since landscapes and associated societies are dynamic systems that rely on social and economic viability for survival. For many cultures, they are finding the balance between the past, present and future, between continuity and change, or as Villalón describes it "weaving tradition with the present." The concept of adaptive management is applicable as the lessons learned can provide feedback for constant improvement based on experience (Phillips, 2002).

The threats and challenges facing conservation are indeed myriad, yet the will of many who strive for a vision of a sustainable society is powerful. Ultimately, to meet these challenges, new approaches and new leadership are needed. It is through the type of innovation demonstrated by these case studies and the hope of these new directions that a way forward for conservation can be crafted.

## A way forward

The protected landscape approach is a "new face" for conservation. Most fundamentally, the goals for conservation are dramatically expanded from protection of nature and biodiversity to include a broader cultural context and social agenda. For it is within this broader context that a wide diversity of people can find their connection to biological and cultural heritage, and commit to stewardship. The protected landscape approach is a process that accommodates and guides change. This approach creates networks across the landscape and respects the relationships between people and place. These large-scale landscapes are cohesive venues for conservation due to their regional identity, shared history or culture, and shared ecosystem boundaries. These are complex landscapes with multiple values where nature and culture exist alongside human communities, often for many generations. In many cases, the value of the landscape is intimately influenced by the interaction with people over time, and the protection of the landscape requires sustaining this relationship and associated stewardship.

Langshaw field barn, North Pennines Area of Outstanding Natural Beauty, England. The protected landscape approach creates networks across the landscape, sustains cultural and natural values, and helps to guide change. *Countryside Agency/Charlie Hedley*

The characteristics of this approach are described in an earlier section of this chapter. These together constitute a framework of principles and best practices for the protected landscape approach (Table 3). This framework, while drawn directly from this set of international case studies, has much in common with findings of other recent discussions on new directions in conservation (Minteer and Manning, 2003; Mitchell, Hudson and Jones, 2003; UNESCO, 2003; WPC outputs such as the Durban Accord; Phillips, 2002; Stolton and Dudley, 1999). This contemporary body of work further reinforces and validates this set of best practices and principles for the future of conservation.

### Table 3. Framework for the protected landscape approach

| Characteristics of place | Characteristics of process |
|---|---|
| 1. Bioregional with a mosaic of designations and land uses | |
| 2. Interrelationship of nature and culture | |
| 3. Relationship between tangible and intangible values | |
| | 4. Community-based, inclusive and participatory |
| | 5. Cross-sectoral partnerships |
| | 6. Planning and legal frameworks for engagement through equity and governance |
| | 7. Contributes to sustainable society |

Cultivating new leadership among key stakeholders is essential to implementing this approach more broadly. There is a need for committed and competent leaders who share a vision of sustainability, are open to learning, and seek cooperation with regional, national and international networks. Hughes explores various models for leadership development and emphasises the role of exchange for learning and fostering new ideas. Kundrata and Huskova note the success of both regional and international exchange in inspiring inventiveness and conservation action. Both Phillips and Rössler describe the opportunities for creating new institutional linkages among international organizations and building networks among protected area stewards as a means of sharing and advancing this protected landscape approach.

Collectively, the experiences described in this volume show how the protected landscape approach can transform places through innovation and creativity. By using experimentation to meet new challenges and learning through adaptive management, these landscapes can serve as "seed beds" for developing new models of sustainability and strengthening civil society. IUCN President Yolanda Kakabadse, quoted in the chapter by Phillips, has written that the protected landscape approach "is not a soft option [since] managing the interface between people and nature is just about the toughest challenge facing society," and is "an idea whose time has come". It is an idea that people are at the heart of conservation and it is their commitment to stewardship that makes the stories presented here stories of hope. With a protected landscape approach, conservation has meaning in people's lives, becomes more relevant to a larger constituency, and contributes to a sustainable future.

# References

African Wildlife Foundation (AWF). 1993. *Protected Area Conservation Strategy: Assessing the Training Needs of Protected Area Managers in Africa.* In cooperation with World Wide Fund for Nature (WWF) and the Wildlife Conservation Society.

Aichison, J. and Beresford, M. 1998. *Protected Area Systems and the Protected Landscape Concept.* Module Two. International Centre for Protected Landscapes, Aberystwyth, Wales, UK.

Alberta Environmental Protection. 1997. *Cooking Lake-Blackfoot Provincial Recreation, Wildlife and Grazing Area: Management plan.* Alberta Environmental Protection, Natural Resources Service, Edmonton, Alberta, Canada.

Alt, K.W., Burger, J., Simons, A., Schon, W., Grupe, G., Hummel, S., Grosskopf, B., Vach, W., Tellez, C.B., Fischer, C.H., Moller-Wiering, S., Shrestha, S.S., Pichler, S.L. and von den Driesch, A. 2003. Climbing into the past – first Himalayan mummies discovered in Nepal. *Journal of Archaeological Science* **30(11)**: 1529–1535.

Andrew, M. and Anthony, D. 1997. *A Survey of the Flora and Fauna in the Terrestrial Section of the Praslin Protected Landscape.* Report prepared for the Saint Lucia National Trust, Saint Lucia.

Appleton, M.R. 2002. Raising the Standard: The development of competence standards for protected areas occupations in South East Asia. Unpublished MSc thesis. International Centre for Protected Landscapes, Aberystwyth, UK and University of Greenwich, UK.

Argumedo, A. 2001. Agriculture and Working Landscapes in the Andes. In Conservation Study Institute, 2001. (qv).

Australia ICOMOS. 2000. *The Burra Charter: the Australia ICOMOS Charter for Places of Cultural Significance 1999*, with associated Guidelines and Code on Ethics of Co-existence. Australia ICOMOS, Canberra, Australia.

Australian Heritage Commission (AHC). 2000. *Overview of the Identification, Assessment and Management of Cultural Landscapes.* Prepared for the Australian Heritage Commission meeting 148, 13 June 2000.

Australian State of Environment Committee (ASEC). 2001. *Australia State of the Environment, 2001.* CSIRO Publishing on behalf of the Department of Environment and Heritage, Canberra, Australia.

Barnard, P. (Ed.) 1998. *Biological Diversity in Namibia: a country study.* Namibian National Biodiversity Task Force, Windhoek, Namibia.

Barrett, B. and Mitchell, N. (Eds). 2003. Stewardship in Heritage Areas. *George Wright Forum* **20(2)**: 5–7.

Barrow, E., Clarke, J., Grundy, I., Kamugisha, J.R. and Tessema, Y. 2002. *Analysis of Stakeholder Power and Responsibilities in Community Involvement in Forest Management in Eastern and Southern Africa.* IUCN Regional Office for Eastern Africa, Nairobi, Kenya.

Barrow, E.G.C. 1996. *The Drylands of Africa: Local Participation in Tree Management.* Initiatives Publishers, Nairobi, Kenya.

Beckmann, A. 2000. *Caring for the Land: A decade of promoting landscape stewardship in Central Europe.* Commissioned by the Environmental Partnership for Central Europe

Consortium and the QLF/Atlantic Center for the Environment. NP Agentura, Stare Mesto, Czech Republic.

Behnke, R. 1997. *Range and Livestock Management in the Etanga Development Area, Kunene Region*. Progress Report for the NOLIDEP Project. Ministry of Agriculture, Water and Rural Development, Windhoek, Namibia.

Beltrán, J. (Ed.) 2000. *Indigenous and Traditional Peoples and Protected Areas: Principles, Guidelines and Case Studies*. IUCN, Gland, Switzerland and Cambridge, UK.

Beresford, M. and Phillips, A. 2000. Protected Landscapes: A Conservation Model for the 21st Century. *The George Wright Forum* **17(1)**: 15–26.

Beresford, M. (Ed.) 2003. Category V Protected Landscapes/Seascapes – thematic issue of *PARKS* **13(2)**:1–2. IUCN, Gland, Switzerland.

Bharuca, E. 1999. Cultural and spiritual values related to the conservation of biodiversity in the sacred groves of the Western Ghats in Maharashtra. In Posey, D.A. (Ed.), *Cultural and Spiritual Values of Biodiversity – A Complementary Contribution to the Global Biodiversity Assessment*. Intermediate Technology Publications and UNEP, London, UK and Nairobi, Kenya.

Biodiversity Profiles Project. 1995. *Biodiversity profiles of the Terai and Siwalik physiographic zone*. Biodiversity Profiles Project publication No. 12. Department of National Parks and Wildlife Conservation, Kathmandu, Nepal.

Bishop, K. and Phillips, A. 2004. *Countryside Planning*. Earthscan Publications, London, UK.

Blackdown Hills Rural Partnership. Website: www.blackdown-hills.net

Blackstone River Valley National Heritage Corridor Commission. 1998. *"The Next Ten Years" An Amendment to the Cultural Heritage and Land Management Plan*. Blackstone River Valley National Heritage Corridor Commission, Woonsocket, Rhode Island, USA.

Bollig, M. 1996. *Resource Management and Pastoral Production in the Epupa Project Area*. Report for the Epupa Hydropower Feasibility Study. NAMANG, Windhoek, Namibia.

Borrini-Feyerabend, G. (with Banuri, T., Farvar, T., Miller, K. and Phillips, A.) 2002. Indigenous and local communities and protected areas: rethinking the relationship. *PARKS* **12(2)**: 5–15. IUCN, Gland, Switzerland.

Borrini-Feyerabend, G., Kothari, A. and Oviedo, G. 2004. *Indigenous and Local Communities and Protected Areas: Towards Equity and Enhanced Conservation. Guidance on policy and practice for Co-managed Protected Areas and Community Conserved Areas*. IUCN, Gland, Switzerland and Cambridge, UK.

BRASIL, República Federativa, 2000. *Lei 9985, de 18 de julho de 2000: Sistema Nacional de Unidades de Conservação*. Câmara Federal, Brasília, DF, Brazil.

Britto de Moraes, M. 2000. *Área de proteção Ambiental como Instrumento de Planejamento e Gestão: APA Cananéia-Iguape-Peruíbe, SP*. Master Thesis. São Paulo University, São Paulo, Brazil.

Britto de Moraes, M. 2003. Protecting Seascapes: Brazil's Experience with the APA Designation in Coastal Areas. Paper presented at the Vth World Parks Congress, Durban, South Africa.

Britto de Moraes, M. 2003. Linkages between protected areas and surrounding land uses. Report by IUCN WCPA-Brazil for Stream 1: Linkages in the landscape/seascape, Vth World Parks Congress, Durban, South Africa, September 2003. Maretti C.C. (coord.), IUCN WCPA-Brazil.

Britto de Moraes, M. Maretti, C.C., Lima, W. and Arruda, M. 1997. APA Cananéia-Iguape-Peruíbe: proposta de regulamentação-convênio IBAMA/SMA. In *Anais do Congresso Brasileiro de Unidades de Conservação*. Volume II. IAP and Unilivre/ RNPUC, Curitiba, Brazil.

Brokensha, D. and Castro, A.H.P. 1987. Common Property Resources. Background paper presented February 1988, Bangalore, for the Expert Consultation on Forestry and Food Production/Security. FAO, Rome, Italy.

Brown, J. and Kothari, A. (Eds.) 2002. Local Communities and Protected Areas – thematic issue of *PARKS* **12 (2)**.

Brown, J. and Mitchell, B. 1999. Private initiatives for private protected areas in South America. In Stolton, S. and Dudley, N. (Eds), 1999.

Brown, J. and Mitchell, B. 2000a. The stewardship approach and its relevance for protected landscapes. *The George Wright Forum* **17(1)**: 70–79.

Brown, J. and Mitchell, B. 2002. Crossing boundaries to promote stewardship through international partnerships and exchange. In Harmon, D. (Ed.) *Proceedings of the 11th Conference on Research and Resource Management in Parks and on Public Lands*. George Wright Society, Hancock, Michigan, USA.

Brown, J. and Mitchell, N. 2000b. Culture and nature in the protection of Andean landscapes. *Mountain Research and Development* **20(3)**: 212–217.

Brown, J., Mitchell, N. and Sarmiento, F.O. (Eds). 2000. Landscape stewardship: new directions in conservation of nature and culture. *The George Wright Forum* **17(1)**: 12–14.

Brown, J., Mitchell, N. and Tuxill, J. 2003. Partnerships and lived-in landscapes: an evolving US system of parks and protected areas. *PARKS* **13(2)**: 31–41.

Budhathoki, P. 2001. Participatory biodiversity conservation initiatives in Nepal. Paper presented at the Seminar on Regional Networking for Natural Resource Management, Forum of Natural Resource Managers (FONAREM). Kathmandu, Nepal, February 2001.

Budhathoki, P. 2003. A Category V Protected Landscape approach to buffer zone management. *PARKS* **13(2)**: 22–30. IUCN, Gland, Switzerland.

Buggey, S. 1999. *An Approach to Aboriginal Cultural Landscapes*. Parks Canada, Ottawa, Canada.

Burak, P. and Swinnerton, G.S. 1998. An exploratory application of the biosphere reserve concept in the Aspen Parkland of Alberta. In Munro, N.W.P. and Willison, J.H.M. (Eds).

Canada, Department of Justice. 2001. Order respecting the withdrawal from disposal of certain lands in the Northwest Territories (Sahyoue/Edacho (Grizzly Bear Mountain and Scented Grass Hills), N.W.T.), SI/2001-26. See: laws.justice.gc.ca/en/T-7/SI-2001-26 (accessed 22 February 2004).

Canadian Parks and Wilderness Society (CPAWS). 2001. *Celebrating with people of Deline as Sahyoue/Edacho National Historic Site gets interim protection*. Published electronically at www.cpaws.org/news/sahyoue-edacho-2001-0323.html (accessed 22 February 2004).

Central Bureau of Statistics (CBS). 2002. *Statistical pocket book – Nepal*. HMG/NPCS/CSS, Kathmandu, Nepal.

Chandrakanth, M.G. and Romm, J. 1991. Sacred forests, secular forest policies and people's actions. *Natural Resources Journal* **31**: 741–755.

Chape, S., Blyth, S., Fish, L., Fox, P. and Spalding, M. (compilers). 2003. *2003 United Nations List of Protected Areas*. IUCN, Gland, Switzerland and Cambridge, UK and UNEP-WCMC, Cambridge, UK.

Chaurette, E., Sarmiento, F.O. and Rodríguez, J. 2003. A Protected Landscape candidate in the tropical Andes of Ecuador. *PARKS* **13(2)**: 42–51.

Cheeseman, T. 2001. *Conservation and the Maasai in Kenya: Tradeoff or Mutualism?* Published electronically by Cheesemans' Ecology Safaris at www.environmentalaction. net/kenya/kenya_policy_failure.html

Chhetri, P. B., Barrow, E.G.C. and Muhweezi, A. (Eds). 2004. *Securing Protected Area Integrity and Rural People's Livelihoods: Lessons from Twelve Years of the Kibale Semliki Conservation and Development Project*. IUCN Regional Office for Eastern Africa, Nairobi, Kenya.

Claval, P. 1995. *La géographie culturelle*. Nathan Université, Paris, France.

Conklin, H.C. 1980. *Ethnographic Atlas of Ifugao: A Study of Environment, Culture, and Society in Northern Luzon*. Yale University Press, New Haven, USA.

Conselho Nacional dos Seringueiros (CNS). 2004. *Reserva Chico Mendes*; in: Memorial Chico Mendes. Conselho Nacional dos Seringueiros. Published electronically at www.chicomendes. com.br/cmendes/cmendes.htm (accessed April 2004).

Conservation Study Institute (CSI). 2004. *Stewardship Begins with People: An Atlas of Places, People & Hand-made Products*. Project update. See www.nps.gov/csi/pdf/Atlas.pdf

Conservation Study Institute (CSI). 2001. *Landscape Conservation: An International Working Session on the Stewardship of Protected Landscapes*. Conservation and Stewardship Publication No. 1. Conservation Study Institute, IUCN – The World Conservation Union, and QLF/Atlantic Center for the Environment, Woodstock, Vermont, USA.

CBD. 1992. *Convention on Biological Diversity, convention text*. Secretariat of the Convention on Biological Diversity (CBD), United Nations Environment Programme (UNEP).

CBD (SBSTTA). 1999. *Ecosystem approach: further conceptual elaboration; note by the Executive Secretary*. Fifth Meeting of the CBD Subsidiary Body on Scientific, Technical and Technological Advice, 31 January–4 February 2000, Montreal, Canada. UNEP/CBD/SBSTTA/5/11.

CBD. 2000. *Annex III: Decisions adopted* […]. Fifth Meeting of the Conference of the Parties to the Convention on Biological Diversity, 15–26 May 2000, Nairobi, Kenya. UNEP/CBD/COP/5/23.

Cormier-Salem, M.C. (Ed.) 1999. *Rivières du Sud; sociétés et mangroves ouest-africaines*. Two volumes. IRD, Paris, France.

Costa, S.S.M. 2004. Reserva Extrativista Chico Mendes (Acre). UFSCar-Lapa. Published electronically at www.lapa.ufscar.br/portugues/index.html (accessed April 2004).

Cotter, M., Boyd, W.E. and Gardiner, J. (Eds). 2001. *Heritage Landscapes: Understanding Place and Communities*. Southern Cross University Press, Lismore, Australia.

Council of Europe (COE). 2002. European Landscape Convention, www: conventions.coe.int/ Treaty/EN/cadreprincipal.htm

Cracraft, J. 1999. Regional and global patterns of biodiversity loss and conservation capacity: predicting future trends and identifying needs. In Cracraft, J. and Grifo, F.T. (Eds). *The Living Planet: Biodiversity Science and Policy in Crisis*. Colombia University Press, New York, USA.

Creasey, M. 2001. Case Study on the John H. Chafee Blackstone River Valley National Heritage Corridor. Submitted to the WPCA Protected Landscapes Task Force meeting, November 2001.

Crofts, R., Maltby, E., Smith, R. and Maclean, L. (Eds). 1999. *Integrated Planning: International Perspectives*. Workshop on Integration Planning, April 1999, Battleby, Scotland, UK. IUCN UK National Committee and Scottish Natural Heritage.

Das, P. 1997. Kailadevi Wildlife Sanctuary: Prospects for Joint Forest Management. In Kothari, A., Vania, F., Das, P., Christopher, K. and Jha, S. (Eds). *Building Bridges for Conservation: Towards Joint Management of India's Protected Areas*. Indian Institute of Public Administration, New Delhi, India.

DNPWC. 2003. *Annual report (2002–2003)*. Department of National Parks and Wildlife Conservation, Kathmandu, Nepal.

De Marco, L. and Stovel, H. 2003. Cinque Terre: a landscape carved from stone. *World Heritage Review* **33**: 54–65. UNESCO Publishing, Paris, France.

Devaux, A. and Thiele, G. (Eds.) 2002. *Compendio de Papa Andina. Logros y Experiencias de la Primera Fase. 1998–2002*. Centro Internacional de la Papa (CIP), Lima, Peru.

Di Méo, G. 1998. *Géographie sociale et territoires*. Nathan Université, Paris, France.

Drost, A. 2001a. Establishing an International Heritage Corridor in the Champlain-Richelieu Valley. In *International Concepts in Protected Landscapes: Exploring Their Value for Communities in the Northeast*. Conservation and Stewardship Publication No. 2, Conservation Study Institute, Woodstock, Vermont, USA.

Drost, A. 2001b. Case study on the proposed Champlain-Richelieu Heritage Corridor. Submitted to the WCPA Protected Landscape Task Force meeting, November 2001.

Drost, A., Horn, T. and Huffman, P. 2002. *Developing a Heritage Strategy for the Champlain-Richelieu-Upper Hudson Region*. Report to the Lake Champlain Basin Program. Published electronically at www.lcbp.org/reports.htm

Dudley, N. and Stolton, S. 1998. *Protected areas for a new millennium; the implications of IUCN's protected area categories for forest conservation*. Joint IUCN/WWF discussion paper. WWF IUCN Forest Innovations Project, Gland, Switzerland.

Environment Australia. 1999. *Australia's World Heritage*. Department of Environment and Heritage, Canberra, Australia.

Environment Conservation Council (ECC). 2001. *Box-Ironbark Forests & Woodlands Investigation, Final Report*. East Melbourne, Victoria, Australia.

EUROPARC Federation. 2001. *EUROPARC Expertise Exchange – Sustainable Nature Protection, Final Report 2000–2001*. EUROPARC/Phare, Grafenau, Germany.

EUROPARC Federation. 2004. Published electronically at www.europarc.org (accessed March 2004).

Falzon, C. 2002. *Community-Based Conservation Training for the Pacific Island States: A Manual for Trainers and Facilitators*. Volumes I and II. International Centre for Protected Landscapes and University of Wales, Aberystwyth, UK.

Ferreira, L.V., Venticinque, E.M., Lemos de Sá, R. and Pinagé, L.C. [In press]. *Protected areas or paper parks: The importance of protected areas in reducing deforestation in Rondônia, Brazil*. WWF-Brasil and INPA-PDBFF.

Forman, R.T. 1995. *Land Mosaics: The Ecology of Landscapes and Regions*. Cambridge University Press, Cambridge, UK.

Foster, J. 1988. *Protected Landscapes – Summary Proceedings of an International Symposium.* Countryside Commission, Cheltenham, UK.

Fowler, P. 2003. World Heritage Cultural Landscapes 1992–2002. In UNESCO, 2003. (qv).

Fratkin, E. 1997. Pastoralism: Governance and Development Issues. *Annual Review of Anthropology* **26**: 235–261.

Gade, D. 1999. *Nature and Culture in the Andes.* University of Wisconsin Press, Madison, Wisconsin, USA.

Gilbert, C.A. with Luxenberg, G. and Comp, T.A. 1984. *The Land, the People, the Place: An Introduction to the Inventory.* National Park Service, Washington DC, USA. Published electronically at www.nps.gov/ebla/lpp/lpp.htm

Gratz, R.B. 2001. *A Frog, a Wooden House, a Stream and a Trail: Ten Years of Community Revitalization in Central Europe.* A report for Rockefeller Brothers Fund in cooperation with the Conservation Fund, New York, USA.

Graves, C. (Ed.) 2000. *The Potato: Treasure of the Andes.* Centro Internacional de la Papa (CIP), Lima, Peru.

Green, B. 1989. Conservation in Cultural Landscapes. In Western, D. and Pearl, M. (Eds). *Conservation in the Twenty-first Century.* Oxford University Press, New York, USA.

Griffiths, J., Beckmann, A., Serafin, R., Vesely, M. and Kundrata, M. 2004. *Rural Livelihoods for Sustainability: Stories of rural regeneration from Central Europe.* Nadace Partnerství, Brno, Czech Republic.

Griffiths, T. 1996. *Hunters and Collectors: The Antiquarian Imagination in Australia.* Cambridge University Press, Melbourne, Australia.

Hamilton, L.S. 1998. Forest and Tree Conservation through Metaphysical Constraints. In *Natural Sacred Sites: Cultural Diversity and Biological Diversity, Proceedings of the International Symposium.* UNESCO, Paris, France, September 1998.

Hanks, C. 1996. Narrative and landscape: Grizzly Bear Mountain and Scented Grass Hills as repositories of Sahtu Dene Culture. Unpublished report for Parks Canada, Ottawa, Canada.

Harbour, R. Personal communication March 4, 2003. See also Ebey's Landing National Historical Reserve website: www.nps.gov/ebla

Harmon, D. 2002. *In Light of Our Differences: How Diversity of Nature and Culture Makes Us Human.*: Smithsonian Institution Press, Washington, DC.

Harmon, D. (Ed.) 2004. Intangible Values of Protected Areas – thematic issue of the *George Wright Forum* **21(2)**: 9–22.

Harmon, D. and Putney, A.D. (Eds). 2003. *The Full Value of Parks: From Economics to the Intangible.* Rowman and Littlefield Publishers, Lanham, Maryland, USA.

Hirsch, E. 1995. Landscape: between place and space; introduction. In Hirsch, E. and O'Hanlon, M. (Eds). *The anthropology of landscape: perspectives on place and space.* Clarendon, Oxford, UK.

His Majesty Government/Ministry of Forests and Soil Conservation (HMG/MFSC). 2002. *Nepal biodiversity strategy.* MFSC/GEF/UNDP, Kathmandu, Nepal.

Hornedo, F. 2000. *Taming the Wind*: *Ethnocultural History on the Ivatan of the Batanes Isles.* University of Santo Tomas Publishing House, Manila, Philippines.

Hudson, L., Renard, Y. and Romulus, G. 1992. *A System of Protected Areas for Saint Lucia.* Saint Lucia National Trust, Saint Lucia.

Humphrey, C. 1995. Chiefly and shamanist landscapes in Mongolia. In Hirsch, E. and O'Hanlon, M. (Eds). *The anthropology of landscape: perspectives on place and space.* Clarendon, Oxford, UK.

IBAMA. 2004. *Reservas extrativistas.* In IBAMA web site. [Brasília], IBAMA, MMA. Published electronically at www2.ibama.gov.br/resex/resex.htm (accessed April 2004).

IBAMA.www.ibama.gov.br

Ifugao Terraces Commission. 1994. *The Six-year Master Plan for the Restoration of the Ifugao Rice Terraces.* Ifugao Terraces Commission, Baguio City, Philippines.

Ingles, A.W. 1995. Religious Beliefs and Rituals in Nepal — Their Influence on Forest Conservation. In Halladay, P. and Gilmour, D. (Eds). *Conserving Biodiversity Outside Protected Areas: The Role of Traditional Agro-Ecosystems.* IUCN, Gland, Switzerland and Cambridge, UK.

Instituto Socioambiental (ISA). 2002. Unidades de Conservação Federais e Estaduais no Brasil. Unpublished paper. Instituto Socioambiental, São Paulo, Brazil.

IUCN. 1993. *Parks for Life: Action for Protected Areas in Europe.* IUCN, Gland, Switzerland and Cambridge, UK.

IUCN. 1994. *Guidelines for Protected Area Management Categories.* IUCN, Gland, Switzerland and Cambridge, UK.

IUCN. 2003. *Recommendations, Message to the Convention on Biological Diversity, Durban Action Plan*, and the *Durban Accord.* V[th] World Parks Congress, Durban, South Africa, September 2003. Published electronically at www.iucn.org/themes/wcpa/wpc2003

IUCN, WWF and UNEP. 1980. *World Conservation Strategy.* IUCN, WWF and UNEP, Gland, Switzerland and Nairobi, Kenya.

Jeanrenaud, S. 2001. An international initiative for the protection of Sacred Natural Sites and other places of indigenous and traditional peoples with importance for biodiversity conservation. Concept paper. WWF International – People and Conservation, Gland, Switzerland.

Johnston, R.J., Gregory, D., Pratt, G. and Watts, M. (Eds). 2000. *The Dictionary of Human Geography.* Blackwell Publishing, Oxford, UK.

Kimani, K. and Picard, J. 1998. Recent Trends and Implications of Group Ranch Sub-division and Fragmentation in Kajiado District, Kenya. *The Geographical Journal* **164(2)**: 202–219.

Kolmes, S.A. 1999. Mental Cartography in a Time of Environmental Crisis. In Dempsey, C.J. and Butkus, R.A. (Eds). *All Creation is Groaning: An Interdisciplinary Vision for Life in a Sacred Universe.* Liturgical Press, Minnesota, USA.

Koziell, I. 2001. *Diversity not Adversity; Sustaining Livelihoods with Biodiversity.* International Institute for Environment and Development, London, UK.

Kwasniak, A.J. 1997. *Reconciling ecosystem and political borders: A legal map.* Environmental Law Centre Society, Edmonton, Alberta.

Land Use Consultants. 2004. *Review of the Welsh National Parks Authorities.* Available from the Welsh Assembly Government, Cardiff, Wales, UK.

Laughlin, I. 1996. The Outline of a Human Settlements Approach to Land Stewardship. In *Proceedings of a Caribbean Land Stewardship Workshop, Gros Islet, 26th to 30th March, 1996.* Saint Lucia National Trust, Castries, St. Lucia.

Lennon, J. 1997. *Case Study of the Cultural Landscapes of the Central Victorian Goldfields*. Australia: State of the Environment Technical paper Series (Natural and Cultural Heritage), Commonwealth of Australia.

Lennon, J. 2000. Cultural Landscapes: Conserving Cultural Heritage Values in Natural Areas. *Historic Environment* **14(5)**: 44–52.

Lennon, J. 2002. The Cultural Significance of Australian Alpine Areas. In *Celebrating Mountains – An International Year of Mountains Conference proceedings*. Jindabyne, NSW, Australia. Edited version (2003) in *Historic Environment* **17(2)**: 14–18.

Lennon, J. 2003a. Re-engaging with the Land, Designed Cultural Landscapes. *Australian Garden History* **15(5)**: 9–20.

Lennon, J. 2003b. Values as the Basis for Management of World Heritage Cultural Landscapes. In UNESCO, 2003. (qv).

Lennon, J. and Mathews, S. 1996. *Cultural Landscape Management: Guidelines for identifying, assessing and managing cultural landscapes in the Australian Alps national parks*. Report for the Cultural Heritage Working Group, Australian Alps Liaison Committee, Canberra, Australia.

Lennon, J., Pearson, M., Marshall, D., Sullivan, S., McConvell, P., Nicholls, W. and Johnson, D. 2001. *Natural and Cultural Heritage: Australia State of the Environment Report 2001*. Theme Report. CSIRO Publishing on behalf of the Department of Environment and Heritage, Canberra, Australia. Also available electronically at www.ea.gov.au/soe/heritage

Lino, C.F. 2003. Protecting our future: the Mata Atlantica Biosphere Reserve and the MaB Programme Experience in Brazil. Paper presented at the V[th] World Parks Congress, Durban, South Africa, September 2003.

Loita Naimina Enkiyia Conservation Trust Company. 1994a. *Forest of the Lost Child – Entim e Naimina Enkiyio – A Maasai Conservation Success Threatened by Greed*. Nairobi, Kenya.

Loita Naimina Enkiyia Conservation Trust Company. 1994b. Statement by the Loita Naimina Enkiyia Conservation Trust to the Second Session of the Intergovernmental Committee on the Convention on Biological Diversity. *Forest, Trees and People Newsletter* **25**: 45.

Lucas, P.H.C. 1992. *Protected Landscapes: A guide for policy-makers and planners*. IUCN and Chapman and Hall, London, UK.

Lucas, P.H.C. 2001. New Ways with Special Places. In Conservation Study Institute, 2001. (qv).

MacEachern, A. 2001. *Natural Selections: National Parks in Atlantic Canada, 1935–1970*. McGill-Queen's University Press, Montreal and Kingston, Canada.

Machlis, G.E. and Field, D.R. 2000. *National Parks and Rural Development: Practice and Policy in the United States*. Island Press, Washington DC, USA.

Madulid, D. and Agoo, E. 2001. The Flora of Batanes: Its Conservation Significance and Potential. Paper presented at the Stakeholders Consultative Workshop on the Conservation and Management of the Batanes Archipelago and Ivatan Archaeological Landscape. Organized by the Provincial Government of the Batanes Islands and the Office of the UNESCO Regional Advisor for Culture in Asia, June 2001.

Maldonado, W.T.P.V. 2002. *Ordenamento da exploração de ostra do mangue no estuário de Cananéia, SP*. Fundação Florestal, São Paulo, Brazil.

Mansberger, J.R. 1988. In Search of the Tree Spirit: Evolution of the Sacred Tree *Ficus religiosa*. In Daragavel, J., Dixon, K.E. and Semple, N. (Eds). *Changing Tropical Forests*. CRES, Australian National University, Canberra, Australia.

Maretti, C.C. 1989. *Exemplos de geologia aplicada ao planejamento ambiental costeiro: cartografia geológico-geotécnica da região estuarino-lagunar de Iguape e Cananéia e da ilha Comprida*. MSc. dissertation. Depto. Geotecnia, EESC-USP, São Carlos, Brazil.

Maretti, C.C. 2001. Comentários sobre a Situação das Unidades de Conservação no Brasil. São Paulo, *Revista de Direitos Difusos*, ano I, vol. 5, (Florestas e Unidades de Conservação), pp. 633–52, fev. 2001.

Maretti, C.C. 2002. *Comunidade, natureza e espaço: Gestão territorial comunitária? Arquipélago dos Bijagós, África Ocidental*. PhD. thesis. Department of Geography, FFLCH-USP, São Paulo, Brazil.

Maretti, C.C. [in press]. Conservação e valores: relações entre áreas protegidas e indígenas, possíveis conflitos e soluções. In *Desafios socioambientais: sobreposições entre terras indígenas e unidades de conservação no Brasil*. Instituto Socioambiental, São Paulo, Brazil.

Maretti, C.C., Sanches, R.A. *et al.* 2003. Protected areas and indigenous and local communities in Brazil: lessons learned in the establishment and management of protected areas by indigenous and local communities. Paper presented at the V[th] World Parks Congress, Durban, South Africa, September 2003.

Maskey, T.M. 2001. Biodiversity conservation in Nepal with reference to protected areas. In *Proceedings of WCPA South Asia Regional Workshop on Protected Area Management*, 22 February 2 March, 2001, Kathmandu, Nepal.

McGahan, P.G. and Bassett, J.A. 1999. *Training Needs Analysis of Site Managers on the Participation of Local Communities in Natural World Heritage Site Management in South-East Asia, West Pacific, Australia and New Zealand*. UNESCO World Heritage Centre, Paris, France.

McKinley, L. 1993. *An Unbroken Historical Record: An Administrative History of Ebey's Landing National Historical Reserve*. U.S. National Park Service, published electronically at www.nps.gov/ebla/adhi/adhi.htm

McNamee, K. 1994. *The National Parks of Canada*. Key Porter Books, Toronto, Canada.

McNamee, K. 2002. From wild places to endangered spaces. In Dearden, P. and Rollins, R. (Eds). *Parks and protected areas in Canada: Planning and management*. Second Edition. Oxford University Press, Don Mills, Ontario, Canada.

McNeely, J.A. (Ed.) 2001. Cities and protected areas: An oxymoron or a partnership? *PARKS* **11(3)**: 1–3. IUCN, Gland, Switzerland.

Miller, K.R. and Hamilton, L.S. (Eds). 1999. Bioregional approach to protected areas. *PARKS* **9(3)**:1–6. IUCN, Gland, Switzerland.

Minteer, B.A. and Manning, R.E. (Eds). 2003 *Reconstructing Conservation: Finding Common Ground*. Island Press, Washington, DC, USA.

Mitchell, B. and Brown, J. 2003. Stewardship and Protected Areas in a Global Context: Coping with Change and Fostering Civil Society. In Minteer, B.A. and Manning, R.E. (Eds). 2003.

Mitchell, N. and Buggey, S. 2001. Category V Protected Landscapes in Relation to World Heritage Cultural Landscapes: Taking Advantage of Diverse Approaches. In Conservation Study Institute, 2001. (qv).

Mitchell, N. J., Hudson L. and Jones, D. (Eds). 2003. S*peaking of the Future: A Dialogue on Conservation*, Conservation Study Institute, Woodstock, Vermont, USA.

Molnar, A. and Scherr, S. 2003. *Who Conserves the World's Forests? Community Driven Strategies that Protect Forests and Respect Rights.* Forest Trends, Washington DC, USA.

Mujica Barreda, E. (Ed.) 2002. *Paisajes culturales en los Andes.* Report of the Expert Meeting, Arequipa y Chivay, Perú, May 1998. UNESCO, Lima, Perú.

Mulvaney, D.J. and Kamminga, J. 1999. *Prehistory of Australia.* Allen and Unwin, Sydney, Australia.

Munro, N.W.P. and Willison, J.H.M. (Eds). 1998. *Linking protected areas with working landscapes conserving biodiversity.* Science and Management of Protected Areas Association, Wolfville, Nova Scotia, Canada.

Muruthe, P. 2000. African Heartlands: Recent Experience Integrating Landscape Conservation and Rural Livelihood Approaches in Africa. Paper presented to the Conference on African Wildlife Management in the New Millennium. Mweka, Tanzania, December 2000.

Mwale, S. 2000. Changing Relationships: The history and future of wildlife conservation in Kenya. *Swara* **22(4)**: 11–17.

Mwihomeke, S.T., Msangi, T.H. and Yihaisi, J. 1997. Quantity, distribution and current status of sacred forests in the Ziqua Ethnic group, Handeni District. *The Arc Journal* (Tanzania) **6**.

Nair, N.C. and Mohanan, C.N. 1981. On the rediscovery of four threatened species from sacred groves in Kerala. *Economic Taxonomy and Botany* **2**: 233–234.

National Capital Commission. 1996. *The National Capital Commission: Greenbelt Master Plan.* National Capital Commission, Ottawa, Canada.

National Park Service Heritage Area web site, published electronically at www.cr.nps.gov/heritageareas/

New South Wales National Parks and Wildlife Service (NPWS). 2002. *Cultural Heritage Conservation Policy.* NSW National Parks and Wildlife Service, Hurstville, Australia.

Northwest Territories Protected Areas Strategy Advisory Committee (NWT). 1999. *NWT Protected Areas Strategy: A balanced approach to establishing protected areas in the Northwest Territories,* 1999. Published electronically at www.gov.nt.ca/RWED/pas/pdf/ strat&supp.pdf (accessed 20 February 2004).

Ntiamoa-Baidu, Y. 1995. *Indigenous vs. Introduced Biodiversity Conservation Strategies: the Case of Protected Area Systems in Ghana.* WWF-Biodiversity Support Program, Washington DC, USA.

Nurse, M. and Kabamba, J. 1998. *Defining Institutions for Collaborative Mangrove Management: A Case Study from Tanga, Tanzania.* Workshop on Participatory Resource Management in Developing Countries. Mansfield College, Oxford, UK.

Organisation of Eastern Caribbean States (OECS). 2000. *The St. George's Declaration of Principles for Environmental Sustainability in the OECS.* OECS/Natural Resources Management Unit, Castries, Saint Lucia.

Okello, M.M. and Adams, K.E. 2002. *Criteria for Establishment of Kuku Community Conservation Area (KCCA), Kenya: Biological Endowment, Tourism Potential, and Stakeholder.* SFS Centre for Wildlife Management Studies, Kenya.

Okello, M.M. and Kiringe, J.W. 2004. Threats to biodiversity and the implications in protected and adjacent dispersal areas of Kenya. *Journal for Sustainable Tourism* **12(1)**.

Okello, M.M. and Nippert, H. 2001. *The ecological and socio-economic potential of Kuku Community Conservation Area, Kenya.* SFS Centre for Wildlife Management Studies, Kenya.

Oviedo, G. and Brown, J. 1999. Building Alliances with Indigenous Peoples to Establish and Manage Protected Areas. In Stolton, S. and Dudley, N. (Eds), 1999. (qv).

Owen-Smith, G. and Jacobsohn, M. 1991. Pastoralism in Arid and Semi-arid North-West Namibia. Paper presented at the Nordic Man and Biosphere meeting.

Pathak, N. 2000. *Joint Forest Management and Gender: Women's Participation and Benefit Sharing in Joint Forest Management in India.* Report prepared for ADITHI, Patna, India.

Pathak, N., Hufeza, T. and Kothari, A. 2003. *Community Conserved Areas: A Bold Frontier for Conservation.* CENESTA, Iran.

Pathak, N., Islam, A., Ekaratne, S.U.K. and Hussain, A. 2002. Lessons learnt in the establishment and management of protected areas by indigenous and local communities in South Asia. Unpublished report. (South Asia regional report for the global synthesis on *Lessons Learnt in the Establishment and Management of Protected Areas by Indigenous and Local Communities* by Grazia Borrini-Feyerabend.)

Paudel, B.H. 1997. Paryatan ka dristreele Chitwan: eak chinari (Chitwan in relation to tourism: an introduction). *Sirjana* **6**. Chitwan, Nepal.

Phillips, A. 1998. The nature of cultural landscapes – A nature conservation perspective. *Landscape Research* **23(1)**: 21–38.

Phillips, A. 2002. *Management Guidelines for IUCN Category V Protected Areas: Protected Landscapes/Seascapes.* IUCN, Gland, Switzerland and Cambridge, UK.

Phillips, A. 2003a. Turning Ideas on Their Head: The New Paradigm of Protected Areas. *The George Wright Forum* **20(2)**: 8–32. (Republished in Jaireth, H. and Smyth, D. (Eds). *Innovative governance: indigenous peoples, local communities and protected areas.* Ane Books, New Delhi, India.)

Phillips, A. 2003b. Cultural Landscapes: IUCN's changing vision of protected areas. In UNESCO, 2003. (qv).

Phillips, A. and Clarke, R. 2004. Our Landscape from a Wider Perspective. In Bishop, K. and Phillips, A. (Eds). (qv.)

Pierre-Nathoniel, D. 2003. Towards the Strengthening of the Association: The Case of the Soufriere Marine Management Area (SMMA), Saint Lucia. Paper presented at the Second International Tropical Marine Ecosystem Management Symposium (ITMEME II). Passy City, Metro Manila, Philippines, March 2003.

Pinzón Rueda, R. 2004. Evolução histórica do extrativismo. In IBAMA, *Reservas extrativistas.* IBAMA web site: www2.ibama.gov.br/resex/historia.htm (accessed April 2004).

Pokhrel, D.R. 2002. *Nikunja ra janatak bichko dwanda ra ekata* (Park-people conflict and cooperation). Environmental Service Centre, Chitwan, Nepal.

Read, P. 1996. *Returning to Nothing: the meaning of lost places.* Cambridge University Press, Melbourne, Australia.

Rettie, D.F. 1995. *Our National Park System, Caring for America's Greatest Natural and Historic Treasures.* University of Illinois Press, Urbana and Chicago, USA.

Robertson, S.A. 1987. *Preliminary Floristic Survey of Kaya Forests of Coastal Kenya.* Report to the Director of Museums of Kenya. National Museums of Kenya, Nairobi, Kenya.

Rodríguez, G. 2000. Indigenous knowledge as an innovative contribution to the sustainable development of the Sierra Nevada de Santa Marta, Colombia. *Ambio* **29(7)**: 455–458.

Rodríguez, G. 2002. Spiritual significance and environmental effects of offerings amongst the indigenous people of the Sierra Nevada de Santa Marta. In Mountain Agenda (Ed.) *Community development: between subsidy, subsidiarity and sustainability.* Symposium proceedings. Interlaken, Switzerland.

Rodríguez, G. 2003. Los indígenas de la Sierra Nevada de Santa Marta. In Sarmiento, F.O. (Ed.) *Las Montañas del Mundo: Una Prioridad Global con Perspectives Latinoamericanas.* Editorial Abya-Yala, Quito, Ecuador.

Romulus, G. and Ernest, P. 2003. *Towards Environmental Action and Community Learning – A Case Study of the Praslin and Mamiku Communities on the Island of Saint Lucia.* Saint Lucia National Trust, Saint Lucia.

Rössler, M. 2000. World Heritage Cultural Landscapes. *The George Wright Forum*, **17(1)**: 27–34.

Rottle, N. 2004. Ebey's Landing National Historic Reserve: An Analysis of Land Use Change and Cultural Landscape Integrity, report for the National Park Service, Columbia Cascades Region. Jones and Jones Architects and Landscape Architects, Seattle, Washington, USA.

Runte, A. 1979. *National Parks: The American Experience.* University of Nebraska Press, Lincoln, USA.

Sahtu Heritage Places and Sites Working Group. 2000. *Rakekée Gok'é Godi: Places we take care of.* Report of the Sahtu Heritage Places and Sites Working Group, Yellowknife, Northwest Territories, Canada. Available electronically at: pwnhc.learnnet.nt.ca/research/Places/execsum.html (accessed 20 February 2004).

Salafsky, N., Margolius, R. and Redford, K. 2001. *Adaptive Management: A Tool for Conservation Practitioners.* Publication No. 112. The Biodiversity Support Program, Washington DC, USA.

Sales, R.R. de and Moreira, A. de C.C. 1994. *Estudo de viabilidade de implantação de reservas extrativistas no domínio da Mata Atlântica, município de Cananéia.* Nupaub-USP, CNPT-IBAMA, FF and CPLA-SMA-SP, São Paulo, Brazil.

Santos, M. 1996. *A natureza do espaço; técnica e tempo, razão e emoção.* HUCITEC, São Paulo, Brazil.

São Paulo (Estado, SMA). 2001. *Atlas de Unidades de Conservação No Estado de São Paulo.* São Paulo, Brazil.

São Paulo (Estado, SMA) and IBAMA. 1996. *Regulamentação da APA Cananéia-Iguape-Peruíbe.* Plano de gestão: Unidades de gestão. IBAMA and SMA, São Paulo, Brazil.

Sarmiento, F.O. 2002. Anthropogenic landscape change in highland Ecuador. *The Geographical Review* **92(2)**: 213–234.

Sarmiento, F.O. 2003. Protected landscapes in the Andean context: worshiping the sacred in nature and culture. In Harmon, D. and Putney, A.D. (Eds). 2003. (qv).

Sarmiento, F.O., Rodríguez, G., Torres, M., Argumedo, A., Munoz, M. and Rodríguez, J. 2000. Andean Stewardship: Tradition linking nature and culture in protected landscapes of the Andes. *The George Wright Forum* **17(1)**: 55–69.

Schama, S. 1995. *Landscape and Memory.* Harper Collins, London, UK.

Scougall, B. (Ed.) 1992. *Cultural Heritage of the Australia Alps*. Proceedings of the symposium held at Jindabyne, New South Wales, 16–18 October 1991, Australia Alps Liaison Committee.

Sellars, R.W. 1997. *Preserving Nature in the National Parks: A History*. Yale University Press, New Haven, USA.

Sharma, U.R. 2001. Cooperative management and revenue sharing in communities adjacent to Royal Chitwan National Park. *Bano Janakari* **11(1)**: 3–8.

Shengji, P. 1999. The Holy Hills of the Dai. In Posey, D.A. (Ed.) *Cultural and Spiritual Values of Biodiversity: A Complementary Contribution to the Global Biodiversity Assessment*. Intermediate Technology and UNEP, London, UK and Nairobi, Kenya.

Shresth, S. and Devidas, S. 2001. *Forest Revival and Water Harvesting: Community Based Conservation at Bhaonta-Kolyala, Rajasthan, India*. Kalpavriksh and Indian Institute of Environment and Development, Pune, India.

Sonoran Institute. 1997. *National Parks and Their Neighbors, Lessons from the Field on Building Partnerships with Local Communities*. Sonoran Institute, Tucson, Arizona, USA.

Soulé, M.E., Wilcox, B.A. and Holtby, C. 1979. Benign neglect: a model of faunal collapse in game reserves of East Africa. *Biological Conservation* **15**: 259–272.

Stadel, A., Taniton, R. and Heder, H. 2002. The Northwest Territories Protected Areas Strategy: How community values are shaping protection of wild spaces and heritage places. In Watson, A.E. *et al.* (Compilers). *Wilderness in the circumpolar north: Searching for compatibility in ecological, traditional, and ecotourism values*. USDA Forest Service Proceedings RMRS-P-26.2002. Published electronically at: leopold.wilderness.net/pubs/466.pdf (accessed 19 February 2004).

Stevens, S. 1997. Lessons and directions. In Stevens, S. (Ed.) *Conservation through Cultural Survival: Indigenous Peoples and Protected Areas*. Island Press, Washington DC, USA.

Stolton, S. and Dudley, N. (Eds). 1999. *Partnerships for Protection, New Strategies for Planning and Management for Protected Areas*. Earthscan Publications, London, UK.

Sullivan, S. 1996. *The 'Communalisation' of Former Commercial Farmland: Perspectives from Damaraland and Implications for Land Reform*. SSD Research Report No. 25. Social Sciences Division, Multi-Disciplinary Research Centre, University of Namibia, Windhoek, Namibia.

Sullivan, S. and Lennon, J. 2002. Cultural Values. In Independent Scientific Committee, *An Assessment of the Values of Kosciuszko National Park*. Interim report. NSW National Parks and Wildlife Service, Australia.

Swinnerton, G.S. 2001. Protected Landscapes in Canada: An examination of the use of IUCN Management Category V. Poster session presented at the George Wright Society Biennial Conference, Crossing boundaries in park management: On the ground, in the mind, among disciplines. Denver, Colorado, April 2001.

Swinnerton, G.S. 2003. Protected areas and quality of life: Planning for sustainability at the regional level: Elk Island National Park and the Beaver Hills Partnership. Poster session presented at the George Wright Society Biennial Conference, Protecting our diverse heritage: The role of parks, protected areas, and cultural sites. San Diego, California, April 2003.

Swinnerton, G.S. and Buggey, S. 2004. Protected Landscapes in Canada: Current practice and future significance. *The George Wright Forum* 21(2): 78–92.

Swinnerton, G.S. and Otway, S.G. 2003. Collaboration across boundaries – Research and practice: Elk Island National Park and the Beaver Hills, Alberta. Paper presented at the Fifth International Science and Management of Protected Areas Association Conference, Making ecosystem based management work: Connecting researchers and managers. Victoria, BC, Canada, May 2003.

Szabo, S. and Smyth, D. 2003. Indigenous protected areas in Australia. In Jaireth, H. and Smyth, D. (Eds). *Innovative governance: indigenous peoples, local communities and protected areas.* Ane Books, New Delhi, India.

Thomas, D.S.G. and Goudie, A. 2000. *The Dictionary of Physical Geography.* Blackwell Publishing, Oxford, UK.

Tisdell, C. 1994. Conservation, Protected Areas, and the Global Economic System: How Debt, Trade, Exchange Rates, Inflation, and Macroeconomic Policy Affect Biological Diversity. In Munasinghe, M. and McNeely, J. (Eds). *Protected Areas Economics and Policy: Linking Conservation and Sustainable Development.* World Bank and IUCN, Washington DC, USA and Gland, Switzerland.

Titchen, S. 1994. Towards the inclusion of Cultural Landscapes of Outstanding Universal Value on the World Heritage List. *ICOMOS Landscapes Working Group Newsletter* **7(March)**: 20–24.

Tolles, R. and Beckmann, A. 2000. *A Decade of Nurturing the Grassroots: The Environmental Partnership for Central Europe, 1991-2000.* NP Agentura, Stare Mesto, Czech Republic.

Turner, T. and Wiken, E. 2002. CCEA workshop 2001: IUCN classification of protected areas. *Eco* **14**: 2–5.

Tuxill, J.L. (Ed.) 2000. *The Landscape of Conservation Stewardship: The Report of the Stewardship Initiative Feasibility Study.* Marsh-Billings-Rockefeller National Historical Park, Conservation Study Institute, and The Woodstock Foundation, Inc., Woodstock, Vermont, USA. Published electronically at www.nps.gov/csi/pdf/feasibility.pdf

Tuxill, J.L. and Mitchell, N.J. (Eds). 2001. *Collaboration and Conservation: Lessons Learned in Areas Managed through National Park Service Partnerships.* Conservation and Stewardship Publication No. 3. Conservation Study Institute, Woodstock, Vermont, USA.

Tuxill, J.L., Mitchell, N.J. and Brown, J. 2004. *Collaboration and Conservation: Lessons Learned from National Park Service Partnerships in the Western U.S.* Conservation and Stewardship Publication No. 5. Conservation Study Institute, Woodstock, Vermont, USA.

UICN and Guinea-Bissau (MDRA-DGFC). 1993. *Planificação Costeira da Guiné-Bissau: relatório técnico.* UICN and MDRA-DGFC, Gland, Switzerland and Bissau, Guinea-Bissau.

Uluru-Kata Tjuta Board of Management. 1991. *Uluru (Ayers Rock-Mount Olga) National Park plan of management.* Australian National Parks & Wildlife Service, Canberra, Australia.

Uluru-Kata Tjuta Board of Management and Parks Australia. 2000. *Uluru-Kata Tjuta National Park Plan of Management.* Commonwealth of Australia.

UNESCO. 1995. *Report of the 19ᵗʰ Session of the Committee.* UNESCO World Heritage Committee, Berlin, Germany.

UNESCO. 1999. *Directrices prácticas sobre la aplicación de la Convención para la Protección del Patrimonio Mundial.* UNESCO World Heritage Centre (CPM-Centro del Patrimonial Mundial), Paris, France.

# Appendix 2

---

**Guidelines for Category V Protected Areas – (Extract from the IUCN**
**Guidelines for Protected Area Management Categories)**

**Category V: Protected Landscape/Seascape: protected area managed mainly for landscape/seascape conservation and recreation**

*Definition*: Area of land, with coast and sea as appropriate, where the interaction of people and nature over time has produced an area of distinct character with significant aesthetic, ecological and/or cultural value, and often with high biological diversity. Safeguarding the integrity of this traditional interaction is vital to the protection, maintenance and evolution of such an area.

*Objectives of Management*

- to maintain the harmonious interaction of nature and culture through the protection of landscape and/or seascape and the continuation of traditional land uses, building practices and social and cultural manifestations;
- to support lifestyles and economic activities which are in harmony with nature and the preservation of the social and cultural fabric of the communities concerned;
- to maintain the diversity of landscape and habitat, and of associated species and ecosystems;
- to eliminate where necessary, and thereafter prevent, land uses and activities which are inappropriate in scale and/or character;
- to provide opportunities for public enjoyment through recreation and tourism appropriate in type and scale to the essential qualities of the areas;
- to encourage scientific and educational activities which will contribute to the long term well-being of resident populations and to the development of public support for the environmental protection of such areas; and
- to bring benefits to, and to contribute to the welfare of, the local community through the provision of natural products (such as forest and fisheries products) and services (such as clean water or income derived from sustainable forms of tourism).

*Guidance for Selection*

- The area should possess a landscape and/or coastal and island seascape of high scenic quality, with diverse associated habitats, flora and fauna along with manifestations of unique or traditional land-use patterns and social organisations as evidenced in human settlements and local customs, livelihoods, and beliefs.
- The area should provide opportunities for public enjoyment through recreation and tourism within its normal lifestyle and economic activities.

*Organisational Responsibility*

The area may be owned by a public authority, but is more likely to comprise a mosaic of private and public ownerships operating a variety of management regimes. These regimes should be subject to a degree of planning or other control and supported, where appropriate, by public funding and other incentives, to ensure that the quality of the landscape/seascape and the relevant local customs and beliefs are maintained in the long term.

*Equivalent Category in 1978 System*

Protected Landscape

*Source*: IUCN, 1994:22.

UNESCO. 2002. *Operational Guidelines for the Implementation of the World Heritage Convention.* UNESCO, Paris, France.

UNESCO. 2003. Cultural Landscapes: the Challenges of Conservation. (Proceedings of an international workshop, Ferrara, Italy, November 2002.) *World Heritage Papers*, No. 7. UNESCO World Heritage Centre, Paris, France.

UNESCO. 2004. *Operational Guidelines for the World Heritage Convention.* UNESCO, Paris, France.

UNESCO, Provincial Government of Batanes, and the Batanes Heritage Foundation. 2001. *Stakeholders Consultative Workshop on the Conservation and Management of the Batanes Archipelago and Ivatan Archaeological Landscape.* Report by UNESCO, Provincial Government of Batanes, and the Batanes Heritage Foundation.

Villalón, A.F. 1994. The Rice Terraces of the Philippine Cordilleras. World Heritage Nomination Dossier.

Villalón, A.F. 2002. *Lugar: Essays on Philippine Heritage and Architecture.* Bookmark Publishing, Manila, Philippines.

Villalón, A.F. 2003. The Batanes Archipelago and Ivatan Archaeological Landscape. World Heritage Nomination Dossier.

Von Droste, B., Plachter, H. and Rössler, M. (Eds). 1995. *Cultural Landscapes of Universal Value. Components of a Global Strategy.* Gustav Fischer, Jena, Germany, in cooperation with UNESCO.

Wadt, L.H.O., Ehringhaus, C., Gomes-Silva, D.A.P. and Brito, S. da S. 2003. Category VI protected areas: Brazil's experience with extractive reserves, Acre, Brazil. Paper presented at the V[th] World Parks Congress, Durban, South Africa, September 2003.

Warboys, G., Lockwood, M. and De Lacy, T. 2001. *Protected Area Management: Principles and Practice.* Oxford University Press, Melbourne, Australia.

Water and Energy Commission Secretariat (WECS). 1997. *WECS Bulletin* **8(2)**.

WPC Durban Accord, www.iucn.org/wpc2003

WWF. 1996. *Conservation with a Human Face.* Documentary film directed by P.V. Satheesh and produced by Development Perspectives for WWF.

WWF-Nepal. 2003. *Terai Arc Landscape programme.* Published electronically at www.wwfnepal.org.np (accessed 18 March 2004).

Western, D. 1997. Nairobi National Park is slowly being strangled by development. *Swara* **19(6)** and **20(1)**: 19–20.

Western, D. and Ssemakula, J. 1981. The future of savanna ecosystems: ecological islands or faunal enclaves? *African Journal of Ecology* **19**: 7–19.

White, A. and Martin, A. 2002. *Who Owns The World's Forests? Forest Tenure and Public Forests in Transition.* Forest Trends, Washington DC, USA.

Wishitemi, B.E.L. and Okello, M.M. 2003. Application of the Protected Landscape model in southern Kenya. *PARKS* **13(2)**: 12–21.

Wulf, K. 1999. Conflict Resolution and Participatory Planning: The Case of the Soufriere Marine Management Area. Unpublished paper. Soufriere Marine Management Area, Soufriere, Saint Lucia.

Young, T.P. and McClanahan, T.R. 1996. Island Biogeography and Species Extinction. In Young, T.P. and McClanahan, T.R. (Eds). *East African Ecosystems and Their Conservation.* Oxford University Press, New York, USA.

# Appendix 1

---

## IUCN Protected Area Management Categories

**Category Ia: Strict Nature Reserve:** protected area managed mainly for science – area of land and/or sea possessing some outstanding or representative ecosystems, geological or physiological features and/or species, available primarily for scientific research and/or environmental monitoring.

**Category Ib: Wilderness Area:** protected area managed mainly for wilderness protection – large area of unmodified or slightly modified land and/or sea, retaining its natural character and influence, without permanent or significant habitation, which is protected and managed so as to preserve its natural condition.

**Category II: National Park:** protected area managed mainly for ecosystem protection and recreation – natural area of land and/or sea designated to (a) protect the ecological integrity of one or more ecosystems for present and future generations, (b) exclude exploitation or occupation inimical to the purposes of designation of the area and (c) provide a foundation for spiritual, scientific, educational, recreational and visitor opportunities, all of which must be environmentally and culturally compatible.

**Category III: Natural Monument:** protected area managed mainly for conservation of specific natural features – area containing one or more specific natural or natural/cultural feature of outstanding or unique value because of its inherent rarity, representative or aesthetic qualities or cultural significance.

**Category IV: Habitat/Species Management Area:** protected area managed mainly for conservation through management intervention – area of land and/or sea subject to active intervention for management purposes so as to ensure the maintenance of habitats nd/or to meet the requirements of specific species.

**Category V: Protected Landscape/Seascape:** protected area managed mainly for landscape/seascape conservation and recreation – area of land, with coast and sea as appropriate, where the interaction of people and nature over time has produced an area of distinct character with significant aesthetic, ecological and/or cultural value, and often with high biological diversity. Safeguarding the integrity of this traditional interaction is vital to the protection, maintenance and evolution of such an area.

**Category VI: Managed Resource Protected Area:** protected area managed mainly for the sustainable use of natural ecosystems – area containing predominantly unmodified natural systems, managed to ensure long-term protection and maintenance of biological diversity, while providing at the same time a sustainable flow of natural products and services to meet community needs.

*Source*: IUCN, 1994.

# Appendix 3

**Guidelines for Category VI Protected Areas – (Extract from the IUCN *Guidelines for Protected Area Management Categories*)**

**Category VI: Managed Resource Protected Area: protected area managed mainly for the sustainable use of natural ecosystems**

*Definition*

Area containing predominantly unmodified natural systems, managed to ensure long term protection and maintenance of biological diversity, while providing at the same time a sustainable flow of natural products and services to meet community needs.

*Objectives of Management*

- to protect and maintain the biological diversity and other natural values of the area in the long term;
- to promote sound management practices for sustainable production purposes;
- to protect the natural resource base from being alienated for other land-use purposes that would be detrimental to the area's biological diversity; and
- to contribute to regional and national development.

*Guidance for Selection*

- The area should be at least two-thirds in a natural condition, although it may also contain limited areas of modified ecosystems; large commercial plantations would *not* be appropriate for inclusion,
- The area should be large enough to absorb sustainable resource uses without detriment to its overall long-term natural values.

*Organizational Responsibility*

Management should be undertaken by public bodies with an unambiguous remit for conservation, and carried out in partnership with the local community; or management may be provided through local custom supported and advised by governmental or non-governmental agencies. Ownership may be by the national or other level of government, the community, private individuals, or a combination of these.

*Source*: IUCN, 1994:23.

# Appendix 4

## Cultural Landscapes under the World Heritage Convention

**(Extract from the World Heritage Convention Operational Guidelines)**

*The following are excerpts on Cultural Landscapes from Annex 3 of the Operational Guidelines to the World Heritage Convention, which govern the implementation of the convention*

"3.    Cultural landscapes represent the "combined works of nature and of man" designated in Article 1 of the Convention. They are illustrative of the evolution of human society and settlement over time, under the influence of the physical constraints and/or opportunities presented by their natural environment and of successive social, economic and cultural forces, both external and internal. They should be selected on the basis both of their outstanding universal value and of their representativity in terms of a clearly defined geo-cultural region and also for their capacity to illustrate the essential and distinct cultural elements of such regions.

4.    The term "cultural landscape" embraces a diversity of manifestations of the interaction between humankind and its natural environment.

9.    Cultural landscapes often reflect specific techniques of sustainable land-use, considering the characteristics and limits of the natural environment they are established in, and a specific spiritual relation to nature. Protection of cultural landscapes can contribute to modern techniques of sustainable land-use and can maintain or enhance natural values in the landscape. The continued existence of traditional forms of land-use supports biological diversity in many regions of the world. The protection of traditional cultural landscapes is therefore helpful in maintaining biological diversity".

Three kinds of Cultural Landscape are recognised:

(1)    **Landscapes designed and created intentionally by people:** examples are gardens and parklands constructed for aesthetic reasons.

(2)    **Organically evolved landscapes:** these result from an interaction between a social, economic, administrative and or religious imperative and the natural environment. Two forms exist:

a)    A relict or fossil landscape where the evolutionary process has ceased;

b)    A continuing landscape where the evolutionary processes continue to this day, with an active social role in contemporary society closely linked with the traditional way of life, at the same time exhibiting significant material evidence of its evolution over time.

(3)    **Associative cultural landscapes:** these are landscapes that are important by virtue of the powerful religious, artistic or cultural associations of the natural elements, rather than material cultural evidence.

*Source*: UNESCO, 2004.

UNESCO. 2002. *Operational Guidelines for the Implementation of the World Heritage Convention.* UNESCO, Paris, France.

UNESCO. 2003. Cultural Landscapes: the Challenges of Conservation. (Proceedings of an international workshop, Ferrara, Italy, November 2002.) *World Heritage Papers*, No. 7. UNESCO World Heritage Centre, Paris, France.

UNESCO. 2004. *Operational Guidelines for the World Heritage Convention.* UNESCO, Paris, France.

UNESCO, Provincial Government of Batanes, and the Batanes Heritage Foundation. 2001. *Stakeholders Consultative Workshop on the Conservation and Management of the Batanes Archipelago and Ivatan Archaeological Landscape.* Report by UNESCO, Provincial Government of Batanes, and the Batanes Heritage Foundation.

Villalón, A.F. 1994. The Rice Terraces of the Philippine Cordilleras. World Heritage Nomination Dossier.

Villalón, A.F. 2002. *Lugar: Essays on Philippine Heritage and Architecture.* Bookmark Publishing, Manila, Philippines.

Villalón, A.F. 2003. The Batanes Archipelago and Ivatan Archaeological Landscape. World Heritage Nomination Dossier.

Von Droste, B., Plachter, H. and Rössler, M. (Eds). 1995. *Cultural Landscapes of Universal Value. Components of a Global Strategy.* Gustav Fischer, Jena, Germany, in cooperation with UNESCO.

Wadt, L.H.O., Ehringhaus, C., Gomes-Silva, D.A.P. and Brito, S. da S. 2003. Category VI protected areas: Brazil's experience with extractive reserves, Acre, Brazil. Paper presented at the V[th] World Parks Congress, Durban, South Africa, September 2003.

Warboys, G., Lockwood, M. and De Lacy, T. 2001. *Protected Area Management: Principles and Practice.* Oxford University Press, Melbourne, Australia.

Water and Energy Commission Secretariat (WECS). 1997. *WECS Bulletin* **8(2)**.

WPC Durban Accord, www.iucn.org/wpc2003

WWF. 1996. *Conservation with a Human Face.* Documentary film directed by P.V. Satheesh and produced by Development Perspectives for WWF.

WWF-Nepal. 2003. *Terai Arc Landscape programme.* Published electronically at www.wwfnepal.org.np (accessed 18 March 2004).

Western, D. 1997. Nairobi National Park is slowly being strangled by development. *Swara* **19(6)** and **20(1)**: 19–20.

Western, D. and Ssemakula, J. 1981. The future of savanna ecosystems: ecological islands or faunal enclaves? *African Journal of Ecology* **19**: 7–19.

White, A. and Martin, A. 2002. *Who Owns The World's Forests? Forest Tenure and Public Forests in Transition.* Forest Trends, Washington DC, USA.

Wishitemi, B.E.L. and Okello, M.M. 2003. Application of the Protected Landscape model in southern Kenya. *PARKS* **13(2)**: 12–21.

Wulf, K. 1999. Conflict Resolution and Participatory Planning: The Case of the Soufriere Marine Management Area. Unpublished paper. Soufriere Marine Management Area, Soufriere, Saint Lucia.

Young, T.P. and McClanahan, T.R. 1996. Island Biogeography and Species Extinction. In Young, T.P. and McClanahan, T.R. (Eds). *East African Ecosystems and Their Conservation.* Oxford University Press, New York, USA.

# Appendix 1

---

## IUCN Protected Area Management Categories

**Category Ia: Strict Nature Reserve:** protected area managed mainly for science – area of land and/or sea possessing some outstanding or representative ecosystems, geological or physiological features and/or species, available primarily for scientific research and/or environmental monitoring.

**Category Ib: Wilderness Area:** protected area managed mainly for wilderness protection – large area of unmodified or slightly modified land and/or sea, retaining its natural character and influence, without permanent or significant habitation, which is protected and managed so as to preserve its natural condition.

**Category II: National Park:** protected area managed mainly for ecosystem protection and recreation – natural area of land and/or sea designated to (a) protect the ecological integrity of one or more ecosystems for present and future generations, (b) exclude exploitation or occupation inimical to the purposes of designation of the area and (c) provide a foundation for spiritual, scientific, educational, recreational and visitor opportunities, all of which must be environmentally and culturally compatible.

**Category III: Natural Monument:** protected area managed mainly for conservation of specific natural features – area containing one or more specific natural or natural/cultural feature of outstanding or unique value because of its inherent rarity, representative or aesthetic qualities or cultural significance.

**Category IV: Habitat/Species Management Area:** protected area managed mainly for conservation through management intervention – area of land and/or sea subject to active intervention for management purposes so as to ensure the maintenance of habitats nd/or to meet the requirements of specific species.

**Category V: Protected Landscape/Seascape:** protected area managed mainly for landscape/ seascape conservation and recreation – area of land, with coast and sea as appropriate, where the interaction of people and nature over time has produced an area of distinct character with significant aesthetic, ecological and/or cultural value, and often with high biological diversity. Safeguarding the integrity of this traditional interaction is vital to the protection, maintenance and evolution of such an area.

**Category VI: Managed Resource Protected Area:** protected area managed mainly for the sustainable use of natural ecosystems – area containing predominantly unmodified natural systems, managed to ensure long-term protection and maintenance of biological diversity, while providing at the same time a sustainable flow of natural products and services to meet community needs.

*Source*: IUCN, 1994.

# Appendix 2

---

**Guidelines for Category V Protected Areas – (Extract from the IUCN**
*Guidelines for Protected Area Management Categories***)**

Category V: Protected Landscape/Seascape: protected area managed mainly for landscape/ seascape conservation and recreation

*Definition:* Area of land, with coast and sea as appropriate, where the interaction of people and nature over time has produced an area of distinct character with significant aesthetic, ecological and/or cultural value, and often with high biological diversity. Safeguarding the integrity of this traditional interaction is vital to the protection, maintenance and evolution of such an area.

*Objectives of Management*

- to maintain the harmonious interaction of nature and culture through the protection of landscape and/or seascape and the continuation of traditional land uses, building practices and social and cultural manifestations;

- to support lifestyles and economic activities which are in harmony with nature and the preservation of the social and cultural fabric of the communities concerned;

- to maintain the diversity of landscape and habitat, and of associated species and ecosystems;

- to eliminate where necessary, and thereafter prevent, land uses and activities which are inappropriate in scale and/or character;

- to provide opportunities for public enjoyment through recreation and tourism appropriate in type and scale to the essential qualities of the areas;

- to encourage scientific and educational activities which will contribute to the long term well-being of resident populations and to the development of public support for the environmental protection of such areas; and

- to bring benefits to, and to contribute to the welfare of, the local community through the provision of natural products (such as forest and fisheries products) and services (such as clean water or income derived from sustainable forms of tourism).

*Guidance for Selection*

- The area should possess a landscape and/or coastal and island seascape of high scenic quality, with diverse associated habitats, flora and fauna along with manifestations of unique or traditional land-use patterns and social organisations as evidenced in human settlements and local customs, livelihoods, and beliefs.

- The area should provide opportunities for public enjoyment through recreation and tourism within its normal lifestyle and economic activities.

*Organisational Responsibility*

The area may be owned by a public authority, but is more likely to comprise a mosaic of private and public ownerships operating a variety of management regimes. These regimes should be subject to a degree of planning or other control and supported, where appropriate, by public funding and other incentives, to ensure that the quality of the landscape/seascape and the relevant local customs and beliefs are maintained in the long term.

*Equivalent Category in 1978 System*

Protected Landscape

*Source:* IUCN, 1994:22.

# Appendix 3

---

**Guidelines for Category VI Protected Areas – (Extract from the IUCN**
*Guidelines for Protected Area Management Categories*)

**Category VI: Managed Resource Protected Area: protected area managed mainly for the sustainable use of natural ecosystems**

*Definition*

Area containing predominantly unmodified natural systems, managed to ensure long term protection and maintenance of biological diversity, while providing at the same time a sustainable flow of natural products and services to meet community needs.

*Objectives of Management*

- to protect and maintain the biological diversity and other natural values of the area in the long term;
- to promote sound management practices for sustainable production purposes;
- to protect the natural resource base from being alienated for other land-use purposes that would be detrimental to the area's biological diversity; and
- to contribute to regional and national development.

*Guidance for Selection*

- The area should be at least two-thirds in a natural condition, although it may also contain limited areas of modified ecosystems; large commercial plantations would *not* be appropriate for inclusion,
- The area should be large enough to absorb sustainable resource uses without detriment to its overall long-term natural values.

*Organizational Responsibility*

Management should be undertaken by public bodies with an unambiguous remit for conservation, and carried out in partnership with the local community; or management may be provided through local custom supported and advised by governmental or non-governmental agencies. Ownership may be by the national or other level of government, the community, private individuals, or a combination of these.

*Source*: IUCN, 1994:23.

# Appendix 4

**Cultural Landscapes under the World Heritage Convention**

**(Extract from the World Heritage Convention Operational Guidelines)**

*The following are excerpts on Cultural Landscapes from Annex 3 of the Operational Guidelines to the World Heritage Convention, which govern the implementation of the convention*

"3.    Cultural landscapes represent the "combined works of nature and of man" designated in Article 1 of the Convention. They are illustrative of the evolution of human society and settlement over time, under the influence of the physical constraints and/or opportunities presented by their natural environment and of successive social, economic and cultural forces, both external and internal. They should be selected on the basis both of their outstanding universal value and of their representativity in terms of a clearly defined geo-cultural region and also for their capacity to illustrate the essential and distinct cultural elements of such regions.

4.    The term "cultural landscape" embraces a diversity of manifestations of the interaction between humankind and its natural environment.

9.    Cultural landscapes often reflect specific techniques of sustainable land-use, considering the characteristics and limits of the natural environment they are established in, and a specific spiritual relation to nature. Protection of cultural landscapes can contribute to modern techniques of sustainable land-use and can maintain or enhance natural values in the landscape. The continued existence of traditional forms of land-use supports biological diversity in many regions of the world. The protection of traditional cultural landscapes is therefore helpful in maintaining biological diversity".

Three kinds of Cultural Landscape are recognised:

(1)    **Landscapes designed and created intentionally by people:** examples are gardens and parklands constructed for aesthetic reasons.

(2)    **Organically evolved landscapes:** these result from an interaction between a social, economic, administrative and or religious imperative and the natural environment. Two forms exist:

   a)    A relict or fossil landscape where the evolutionary process has ceased;

   b)    A continuing landscape where the evolutionary processes continue to this day, with an active social role in contemporary society closely linked with the traditional way of life, at the same time exhibiting significant material evidence of its evolution over time.

(3)    **Associative cultural landscapes:** these are landscapes that are important by virtue of the powerful religious, artistic or cultural associations of the natural elements, rather than material cultural evidence.

*Source*: UNESCO, 2004.

# Appendix 5

## Evaluation of Cultural Landscapes by IUCN

**(Extract from the draft revised Operational Guidelines to the World Heritage Convention that are expected to come into force by 2005)**

IUCN has an interest in many properties of cultural value, especially those nominated as cultural landscapes. For that reason, it will on occasion participate in joint field inspections to nominated cultural landscapes with ICOMOS (see Part C below). IUCN's evaluation of such nominations is guided by an internal paper, "The Assessment of Natural Values in cultural landscapes", available on the IUCN web site at www.iucn.org/themes/wcpa/wheritage/culturallandscape.htm

17. In accordance with the natural qualities of certain cultural landscapes identified in Annex 3, paragraph 9, IUCN's evaluation is concerned with the following factors:

   (i) Conservation of natural and semi-natural systems, and of wild species of fauna and flora

   (ii) Conservation of biodiversity within farming systems;

   (iii) Sustainable land use;

   (iv) Enhancement of scenic beauty;

   (v) Ex-situ collections;

   (vi) Outstanding examples of humanity's inter-relationship with nature;

   (vii) Historically significant discoveries

The following table sets each of the above list in the context of the categories of cultural landscapes in Appendix 4, thereby indicating where each consideration is most likely to occur (the absence of a consideration does not mean that it will never occur, only that this is unlikely):

| Cultural Landscape type (see also Annex 3) | Natural considerations most likely to be relevant (see paragraph 16 above) | | | | | | |
|---|---|---|---|---|---|---|---|
| Designed landscape | | | | | (v) | | |
| Organically evolving landscape – continuous | (i) | (ii) | (iii) | (iv) | | | |
| Organically evolving landscape – fossil | (i) | | | | | (vi) | |
| Associative landscape | | | | | | | (vii) |

*Source:* UNESCO, 2004.

# Appendix 6

**Preliminary Analysis of World Heritage Cultural Landscapes and IUCN Protected Areas; Categories of Cultural Landscapes and Management Categories of Associated Protected Areas**

| Country | Title of World Heritage Cultural Landscape | Date inscribed | Category of Cultural Landscape | Associated protected area | Management category of associated PA (see Appendix 1) |
|---|---|---|---|---|---|
| Afghanistan | Cultural Landscape and Archaeological Remains of the Bamiyan Valley | 2003 | 2a | None | |
| Australia | Uluru-Kata Tjuta National Park | 1987–1994 | 3 | Uluru-Kata Tjuta National Park | II (*also inscribed as a natural WH site*) |
| Austria | Hallstatt-Dachstein Salzkammergut Cultural Landscape | 1997 | 2b | Dachsteingebiet | IV |
| | Wachau Cultural Landscape | 2000 | 2b | Wachau und Umgebung | V |
| Austria/ Hungary | Fertö/Neusiedlersee Cultural Landscape | 2001 | 2b | Ferto-tavi (H) Neusiedlersee und Umgebung (A) | II<br><br>V (also areas of II + IV) |
| Cuba | Viñales Valley | 1999 | 2b | Viñales National Park | II |
| | Archaeological Landscape of the First Coffee Plantations in the Southeast of Cuba | 2000 | 2b | None | |
| Czech Republic | Lednice-Valtice Cultural Landscape | 1996 | 1 | None | |
| France | Jurisdiction of Saint-Emilion | 1999 | 2b | None | |
| | The Loire Valley between Sully-sur-Loire and Chalonnes | 2000 | 2b | Loire Anjou Touraine Regional Nature Park | V |
| France/Spain | Pyrénées – Mont Perdu | 1997–1999 | 2b | Pyrénées Occidentales (F) Ordesa y Monte Perdido (S) | II<br><br>II (*also inscribed as a natural WH site*) |
| Germany | Garden Kingdom of Dessau-Wörlitz | 2000 | 1 | None | |
| | Upper Middle Rhine Valley | 2002 | 2b | Several Nature Parks | V |
| Hungary | Hortobágy National Park – the Puszta | 1999 | 2b | Hortobágy National Park | II |
| | Tokaj Wine Region Historic Cultural Landscape | 2002 | 2b | Tokaj-Bodrogzu g Landscape Protection Area | V |

| Country | Title of World Heritage Cultural Landscape | Date inscribed | Category of Cultural Landscape | Associated protected area | Management category of associated PA (see Appendix 1) |
|---|---|---|---|---|---|
| India | Rock Shelters of Bhimbetka | 2003 | 2b | Ratapani Wildlife Reserve | IV |
| Italy | Portovenere, Cinque Terre, and the Islands (Palmaria, Tino and Tinetto) | 1997 | 2b | Bracco-Mesco Cinque Terre Montemarcello Regional Nature Park | V |
| | Costiera Amalfitana | 1997 | 2b | None | |
| | Cilento and Vallo di Diano National Park with the Archeological sites of Paestum and Velia, and the Certosa di Padula | 1998 | 2a/2b | Cilento and Vallo di Diano National Park | V |
| | Sacri Monti of Piedmont and Lombardy | 2003 | 3 | None | |
| Lao People's Democratic Republic | Vat Phou and Associated Ancient Settlements within the Champasak Cultural Landscape | 2001 | 3 | None | |
| Lebanon | Ouadi Qadisha (the Holy Valley) and the Forest of the Cedars of God (Horsh Arz el-Rab) | 1998 | 3 | None | |
| Lithuania/ Russian Federation | Curonian Spit | 2000 | 2b | Kursiu Nerija National Park (L) Kurshskaja Kosa National Park (R) | II |
| Madagascar | Royal Hill of Ambohimanga | 2001 | 3 | None | |
| New Zealand | Tongariro National Park | 1990–1993 | 3 | Tongariro National Park | II *(also inscribed as a natural WH site)* |
| Nigeria | Sukur Cultural Landscape | 1999 | 2b | None | |
| Philippines | Rice Terraces of the Philippine Cordilleras | 1995 | 2b | None | |
| Poland | Kalwaria Zebrzydowska: the Mannerist Architectural Park and Landscape Complex | 1999 | 1 | None | |
| Portugal | Cultural Landscape of Sintra | 1995 | 1 | Sintra-Cascais Nature Park | V |
| | Alto Douro Wine Region | 2001 | 2b | None | |
| South Africa | Mapungubwe Cultural Landscape | 2003 | 2b | Mapungubwe National Park (proposed) | II |
| Spain | Aranjuez Cultural Landscape | 2001 | 1 | None | |

| Country | Title of World Heritage Cultural Landscape | Date inscribed | Category of Cultural Landscape | Associated protected area | Management category of associated PA (see Appendix 1) |
|---------|---------|---------|---------|---------|---------|
| Sweden | Agricultural Landscape of Southern Öland | 2000 | 2b | Several areas | IV and V |
| United Kingdom | Blaenavon Industrial Landscape | 2000 | 2a | None | |
| | Kew Gardens[1] | 2003 | 1/3 | None | |
| Zimbabwe | Matobo Hills | 2003 | 2b | Matobo Hills National Park | II |

---

[1] Kew Gardens is a special case: though inscribed as a Designed Cultural Landscape, it has (in the rather understated words of the World Heritage Committee record) "contributed to advances in many scientific disciplines, particularly botany and ecology". In that sense it may be said to be associative landscape as well. IUCN's close and long standing interest in Kew Gardens arises from its central place in plant conservation, its world wide scientific standing, and the outstanding quality of its *ex situ* plant collection, even though the site is not a protected area in the strict IUCN meaning.